Federalism, the Supreme Court, and the Seventeenth Amendment

Federalism, the Supreme Court, and the Seventeenth Amendment: The Irony of Constitutional Democracy

Ralph A. Rossum

LEXINGTON BOOKS

Published in the United States of America
by Lexington Books
4720 Boston Way, Lanham, Maryland 20706

12 Hid's Copse Road
Cumnor Hill, Oxford OX2 9JJ, England

British Library Cataloguing in Publication Information Available

Library of Congress Cataloging-in-Publication Data

Rossum, Ralph A., 1946–
    Federalism, the Supreme Court, and the Seventeenth Amendment : the irony of
constitutional democracy / Ralph A. Rossum.
        p. cm.
    Includes bibliographical references and index.
    ISBN 0-7391-0285-0 (cloth : alk. paper) — ISBN 0-7391-0286-9 (pbk. : alk. paper)
        1. Federal government—United States. 2. United States. Supreme Court. 3. United
States. Congress. Senate—Elections. 4. United States. Constitution. 17th Amendment.
5. State rights.

KF4600 .R67 2001
320.473'049—dc21

                                                                                    2001038133

Printed in the United States of America

⊛™ The paper used in this publication meets the minimum requirements of American
National Standard for Information Sciences—Permanence of Paper for Printed Library
Materials, ANSI/NISO Z39.48–1992.

To my wife, Constance,
and our children, Kristin, Brent, and Pierce

Contents

Preface

This book had its origins in a course on the American founding that Professor John Baker of the Louisiana State University Law Center and I team-taught with Justice Antonin Scalia at the University of Aix-Marseille Law School in Aix-en-Provence in the summer of 1987. One day Justice Scalia commented that the people of the United States demonstrated that they no longer believed in federalism when they ratified the Seventeenth Amendment, providing for direct election of the United States Senate. By ending the Constitution's original mode of electing senators by state legislatures, he argued that the Seventeenth Amendment eliminated the most important structural feature of the Constitution for protecting the interests of states as states. His comment came as he reflected on the Supreme Court's then-recent decision in *South Dakota v. Dole*, 483 U.S. 203 (1987), in which it upheld the constitutionality of a congressional enactment that withheld 5 percent of federal highway funds from those states that permitted the sale of alcoholic beverages to persons under twenty-one years of age. He said that, while he saw no constitutional problem with what Congress had done, he could not imagine that a pre-Seventeenth Amendment Senate would have approved such a measure, for the senators would have known that, to be reelected, they would eventually have to appear before their state legislators and explain to those who had power over their reelection why they had so little confidence in their state legislature to address the issue of drunken driving by young people and why they felt justified in voting to impose this burdensome regulation on their state.

Justice Scalia's commentary was provocative; I had not heard that argument before. I soon made it my own and used it through the years to respond to my undergraduate students at Claremont McKenna College and my graduate students at Claremont Graduate University who defended the Supreme Court's invalidation of New Deal economic legislation on the grounds that it was protecting the original federal design. I would point out that (1) a Senate elected by state legislatures would not have agreed to these measures that gave so much power to the federal government at the expense of the states, (2) the Seventeenth Amendment changed not only how senators were elected but also the principal structural protection of federalism and, therefore, the very nature of federalism itself, and (3) it is not the proper job of the Court to fill the gap in the structural wall protecting federalism introduced by the Seventeenth Amendment.

While my argument worked well in class, I did not have the opportunity to undertake the detailed research sufficient for me to know if what Justice Scalia had announced and I had subsequently asserted could be sustained in print. That opportunity presented itself when I was asked by Gary L. Glenn of the Department of Political Science at Northern Illinois University to prepare a paper for delivery at a panel he had organized for the 1998 American Political Science Association annual meeting. The very positive response to that paper encouraged me to expand it initially into a law review article and eventually into this book.

I wish to acknowledge my gratitude to the many organizations and individuals who have assisted me in bringing this project to completion. The appointment as a visiting scholar at the Liberty Fund, Inc., Indianapolis, Indiana, provided me the time and resources to undertake the first phases of this study. A subsequent year-long sabbatical granted by Claremont McKenna College provided a break from teaching to complete "The Irony of Constitutional Democracy: Federalism, the Supreme Court, and the Seventeenth Amendment," *San Diego Law Review* 36 (summer 1999): 671-741. It also allowed me to complete the research on the congressional history of what was an eighty-six-year campaign to secure direct election of the Senate. Charles R. Kesler, director of the Salvatori Center for the Study of Individual Freedom in the Modern World at Claremont McKenna College, and Ken Masugi, director of the Center for Local Government at the Claremont Institute for the Study of Statesmanship and Political Philosophy, invited me to deliver papers at conferences they were organizing, thereby providing me the occasion to undertake additional research and the opportunity to incorporate the helpful comments of discussants. At the invitation of Gary L. McDowell, director of the Institute of United States Studies at the University of London, I presented a version of what became chapter 4 at the Institute's Seminar on American Politics and Law. Bradley C. S. Watson, conference director at the Center for Economic and Policy Education at St. Vincent College, asked me to deliver the center's 1999 Constitution Day lecture, which allowed me to receive valuable reactions to what became chapters 2 and 3. Judge Susan A. Ehrlich of the Arizona Court of Appeals, George W. Carey of Georgetown University, Charles A. Lofgren of Claremont McKenna College, and James McClellan of the Institute of United States Studies at the University of London provided valuable and much appreciated comments on various drafts. Melanie Marlowe, my graduate assistant at Claremont Graduate University, provided able research assistance; without her help, this book would have been much more difficult to complete. To all of them, I am most grateful. I also wish to express my appreciation to the *San Diego Law Review* for allowing me to incorporate major portions of my article into this book.

Ralph A. Rossum
Claremont, California
March 23, 2001

Introduction

This book is a critical commentary on the spate of controversial federalism decisions recently handed down by an activist United States Supreme Court. Twelve times since 1976 (and, with much greater frequency, eleven times since 1992), the Court has invalidated federal laws—many of them passing both houses of Congress by wide margins—in order to preserve what it has described as "the original federal design."[1] This book challenges the Court's fundamental jurisprudential assumptions about federalism and argues that (1) the framers did not expect federalism to be protected by an activist Court but rather by constitutional structure—in particular, by the mode of electing the United States Senate;[2] (2) the political and social forces that culminated in the adoption and ratification of the Seventeenth Amendment eliminated that crucial structural protection and thereby altered the very meaning of federalism itself; and (3) as a consequence, the original federal design has been amended out of existence and is no longer controlling—in the post-Seventeenth Amendment era, it is no more a part of the Constitution the Supreme Court is called upon to apply than, for example, in the post-Thirteenth Amendment era, the Constitution's original fugitive slave clause.[3]

The framers understood that federalism would be protected by the manner of electing (and, perhaps more importantly, reelecting) the Senate. This understanding was perfectly captured in a July 1789 letter to John

Adams in which Roger Sherman emphasized that "[t]he senators, being eligible by the legislatures of the several states, and dependent on them for reelection, will be vigilant in supporting their rights against infringement by the legislative or executive of the United States."[4] The adoption and ratification of the Seventeenth Amendment, providing for direct election of the Senate,[5] changed all that.

After an eighty-six-year campaign, the Seventeenth Amendment was approved by the United States Congress and ratified by the states to make the Constitution more democratic.[6] Progressives argued forcefully, persistently, and ultimately successfully that the democratic principle required the Senate to be elected directly by the people rather than indirectly through their state legislatures. The consequences of the ratification of the Seventeenth Amendment on federalism, however, went completely unexplored, and the people, in their desire to make the Constitution more democratic, inattentively abandoned what the framers regarded as the crucial constitutional means for protecting the federal-state balance and the interests of the states as states.[7]

Following ratification of the Seventeenth Amendment, there was a rapid growth of the power of the national government, with the Congress enacting measures that adversely affected the states as states[8]—measures that, quite simply, the Senate previously would never have approved.[9] Initially, i.e., during the period from the amendment's ratification in 1913 to *National Labor Relations Board* v. *Jones & Laughlin Steel Corporation*[10] in 1937, and then again since *National League of Cities* v. *Usery*[11] in 1976, the United States Supreme Court's frequent reaction to this congressional expansion of national power at the expense of the states was and has been to attempt to fill the gap created by the ratification of the Seventeenth Amendment and to protect the original federal design. It has done so by invalidating these congressional measures on the grounds that they violate the principles of dual federalism; go beyond the Court's narrow construction of the commerce clause; "commandeer" state officials to carry out certain federal mandates; exceed Congress's enforcement powers under Section 5 of the Fourteenth Amendment, or, most recently, trench on the states' sovereignty immunity. In so doing, it has repeatedly demonstrated its failure to appreciate that the Seventeenth Amendment not only eliminated the primary structural support for federalism but, in so doing, altered the very nature and meaning of federalism itself.

There is irony in all of this: An amendment, intended to promote democracy, even at the expense of federalism, has been undermined by an activist Court, intent on protecting federalism, even at the expense of the democratic principle. The irony is heightened when it is recalled that federalism was originally protected both structurally and democratically—the Senate, after all, was elected by popularly elected state legislatures. Today, federalism is protected neither structurally nor democratically—the ratification of the Seventeenth Amendment means that the fate of traditional state prerogatives depends entirely on either congressional sufferance (what the Court calls "legislative grace") or whether an occasional Supreme Court majority can be mustered.[12]

This book argues that federalism as it was understood by the framers—i.e., the "original federal design"—effectively died as a result of the social and political forces that resulted in the adoption and ratification of the Seventeenth Amendment. The Court, however, has had trouble learning this lesson—it took it until *Jones & Laughlin* in 1937 to learn it initially, and, since *National League of Cities* in 1976, it has repeatedly forgotten it. It argues that the Court—typically by the slimmest of majorities—has refused to acknowledge that its efforts to revive federalism—by drawing lines between federal and state power that the framers denied could be drawn and that they never intended for the Court to try to draw—are merely futile attempts to breathe life into a corpse.

Chapter 1 introduces the Supreme Court's efforts since 1976, and especially since 1992, to protect federalism by examining its reasoning in *National League of Cities* v. *Usery*,[13] *New York* v. *United States*,[14] *Lopez* v. *United States*,[15] *Seminole Tribe of Florida* v. *Florida*,[16] *City of Boerne* v. *Flores*,[17] *Printz* v. *United States*,[18] *Florida Prepaid Postsecondary Education Expense Board* v. *College Savings Bank*,[19] *College Savings Bank* v. *Florida Prepaid Postsecondary Education Expense Board*,[20] *Alden* v. *Maine*,[21] *Kimel* v. *Florida Board of Regents*,[22] *United States* v. *Morrison*,[23] and *Trustees of the University of Alabama* v. *Garrett*.[24] These decisions reveal an activist Court that has utterly failed to appreciate that the original federal design it is so committed to protecting is no longer a part of our constitutional system, as it was fundamentally altered by the Seventeenth Amendment.

Chapters 2 and 3 discuss why the framers valued federalism and how they understood that the mode of electing the Senate (rather than reliance on the Supreme Court) would be the principal means not only for protecting the interests of the states as states but also for identifying the line demarcating federal from state powers.

Chapter 4 provides three case studies from the First Congress that illustrate how well the framers' expectation that federalism would be protected by the mode of electing the Senate initially played out in practice. It examines the adoption of the Bill of Rights, the enactment of the Judiciary Act of 1789, and the passage of the act establishing the first Bank of the United States.

Chapter 5 shows how fully Chief Justice John Marshall appreciated the framers' understanding that federalism was to be protected structurally and not judicially. It argues that he felt free to construe Congress's enumerated powers broadly in cases such as *United States* v. *Fisher*,[25] *McCulloch* v. *Maryland*,[26] and *Gibbons* v. *Ogden*,[27] because he trusted that the Senate would be vigilant and not approve legislation that adversely affected the states as such.

Chapter 6 examines in detail the political and social forces at work in the states, and the legislative debates in the United States Congress, that ultimately led to the adoption and ratification of the Seventeenth Amendment and, thereby, to the public's inattentive alteration of the structural protection of federalism. It focuses on four interrelated factors: (1) legislative deadlocks over the election of senators brought about when one party controlled the state assembly or house and another the state senate; (2) scandals brought on by charges of bribery and corruption in the election of senators; (3) the growing strength of the Populist movement, with its deep-seated suspicion of wealth and influence and its penchant for describing the Senate as "an unrepresentative, unresponsive 'millionaires club,' high on partisanship but low in integrity";[28] and (4) the rise of Progressivism and its belief in "the redemptive powers of direct democracy,"[29] i.e., its conviction that the solution to all the problems of democracy was more democracy.

Chapter 7 reviews the post-Seventeenth Amendment congressional expansion of national power at the expense of the states as well as the Court's sporadic attempts to fill the gap created by the Seventeenth Amendment and to protect "the original federal design." It argues that judicial second-guessing of Congress's use of its plenary powers has never effectively protected federalism and never can, and that, as a consequence, the Court should announce that (1) federalism died with the ratification of the Seventeenth Amendment, (2) it is therefore explicitly withdrawing from attempting to draw lines between permissible and impermissible federal power, and (3) it will hereafter treat federalism questions as political questions, acknowledging in the language of *Baker* v. *Carr*,[30] that there are no "judicially discoverable and manageable standards for resolving" them and that the resolution of these questions is "constitutionally commit[ted]"[31] to the Congress alone. It includes a detailed and critical examination of *City of Boerne* v. *Flores,* the most blatant example to date of the Supreme Court's effort to protect a pre-Seventeenth Amendment understanding of federalism at the expense of the people's post-Seventeenth Amendment commitment to democracy. In *City of Boerne,* the Supreme Court, in the name of protecting the "federal balance," struck down the Religious Freedom Restoration Act of 1993, passed unanimously by the United States House of Representatives and by a vote of ninety-seven to three in the Senate and enthusiastically signed into law by President William J. Clinton. The Court asserted that the Congress unconstitutionally exceeded the powers conferred on it by Section 5 of the Fourteenth Amendment and thereby upset federalism. *City of Boerne* has quickly become an extremely influential precedent. The Court has subsequently relied on it to declare unconstitutional federal laws abrogating state sovereign immunity in cases in which the states were charged with violating trademark or patent laws or were sued by their own employees for discrimination on the basis of age or disability or for refusing to pay the minimum wage; it has also employed it to strike down a key provision of the Violence against Women Act. In each of these cases, the Court has perversely transformed Section 5 of the Fourteenth Amendment, intended by its drafters to be a sword by which Congress could protect individuals from constitutional violations of their rights by the states, into a shield by which state governments are protected from the consequences of their constitutional violations.

The conclusion offers a brief reflection on a passage in Abraham Lincoln's Lyceum Speech, in which he worried that the founding principles of the republic were "fading" from view and that, as a consequence, the "walls" of our Constitution would ultimately be "leveled" by "the silent artillery of time."[32] That passage perfectly describes the fate that has befallen the structural supports of federalism. The framers designed the Constitution so that federalism would be protected structurally through the election of the Senate by state legislatures. Over time, however, the public's understanding of the reasons for that structural protection "faded," and the walls of federalism were leveled by the "silent artillery of time," i.e., by an eighty-six-year campaign to make the Constitution more democratic resulting in the adoption and ratification of the Seventeenth Amendment.

Notes

1. In 1976, the Supreme Court invalidated Congress's 1974 amendments to the Fair Labor Standards Act, extending minimum wage/maximum hours requirements to employees of states and their political subdivisions. *National League of Cities* v. *Usery,* 426 U.S. 833 (1976). For the next sixteen years, the Court held its hand and, in fact, in 1985, reversed its 1976 decision in *Garcia* v. *San Antonio Metropolitan Transit Authority,* 469 U.S. 528 (1985). However, starting again in 1992, the Court has become very active, striking down eleven laws in ten years. It declared unconstitutional:

◊ in 1992, the Low-Level Radioactive Waste Policy Amendments Act of 1985, mandating that the states themselves must take title to radioactive waste within their borders if they fail otherwise to provide for its disposition, *New York* v. *United States,* 505 U.S. 144 (1992);

◊ in 1995, the Gun-Free School Zone Act of 1990, banning firearms within "a distance of 1,000 feet from the grounds of a public, parochial or private school," *Lopez* v. *United States,* 514 U.S. 549 (1995);

◊ in 1996, the provision of the Indian Gaming Regulatory Act of 1988 mandating the states to negotiate in good faith with Indian tribes to form compacts governing certain gaming activities and authorizing them to be sued by the tribes in federal court if they fail to do so, *Seminole Tribe of Florida* v. *Florida,* 517 U.S. 44 (1996);

◊ in 1997, both the Religious Freedom Restoration Act of 1993, barring all governments (federal, state, and local) from burdening the free exercise of religion without a compelling state interest, *City of Boerne* v. *Flores,* 521 U.S. 507 (1997), and a key provision of the Brady Handgun Violence Prevention Act of 1993, mandating state law-enforcement officers to conduct background checks for all individuals wishing to buy handguns, *Printz* v. *United States,* 521 U.S. 898 (1997);

◊ on a single day at the end of the Court's 1998-99 term, the Trademark Remedy Clarification Act of 1992 subjecting states to suit under the Trademark Act of 1946, *Florida Prepaid Postsecondary Education Expense Board.* v. *College Savings Bank,* 527 U.S. 627 (1999); the 1992 amendments to the Patent Remedy Act expressly abrogating state sovereign immunity in patent cases, *College Savings Bank* v. *Florida Prepaid Postsecondary Education Expense Board,* 527 U.S. 666 (1999); and those 1974 amendments to the Fair Labor Standards Act authorizing private actions against the states in their own courts without their consent, *Alden* v. *Maine,* 527 U.S. 706 (1999);

◊ in 2000, the provisions of the Age Discrimination in Employment Act of 1967 subjecting states to suits filed by state employees for age discrimination, *Kimel* v. *Florida Board of Regents,* 528 U.S. 62 (2000), and the provisions of the Violence against Women Act of 1994, allowing victims of gender-motivated violence to bring suit in federal court to recover compensatory and punitive damages for the injuries sustained, *United States* v. *Morrison*, 529 U.S. 598 (2000); and

◊ in 2001, the provisions of the Americans with Disabilities Act of 1990 allowing suits in federal court by state employees seeking to recover money damages by reason of a state's failure to comply with the Act's provisions, *Trustees of the University of Alabama* v. *Garrett*, 531 U.S. 356 (2001).

2. There are, of course, other structural protections of federalism in the Constitution—the states' involvement in the election of the president by the electoral college (Article II, Section 1) and in the amendment process (Article V) are two of them. This book focuses on the mode of electing the Senate, for it was that structural provision on which the framers placed most emphasis, and it is the only structural provision formally removed by constitutional amendment.

3. See Ralph A. Rossum, "The Irony of Constitutional Democracy: Federalism, the Supreme Court, and the Seventeenth Amendment," *San Diego Law Review* 36, no. 1 (August/September 1999): 671-741.

4. Philip B. Kurland and Ralph Lerner (eds.), *The Founders' Constitution*, 5 vols. (Chicago: University of Chicago Press, 1987), 2: 232.

5. The text of the Seventeenth Amendment is as follows:

> The Senate of the United States shall be composed of two Senators from each State, elected by the people thereof, for six years; and each Senator shall have one vote. The electors in each State shall have the qualifications requisite for electors of the most numerous branch of the State Legislatures.
>
> When vacancies happen in the representation of any State in the Senate, the executive authority of such State shall issue writs of election to fill such vacancies: Provided, That the Legislature of any State may empower the Executive thereof to make temporary appointments until the people fill the vacancies by election as the Legislature may direct.
>
> This amendment shall not be so construed as to affect the election or term of any Senator chosen before it becomes valid as part of the Constitution.

6. See Christopher H. Hoebeke, *The Road to Mass Democracy: Original Intent and the Seventeenth Amendment* (New Brunswick, N.J.: Transaction Publishers, 1995).

7. The phrase, "the interests of the states as states," refers to their interests as political rather than merely geographical entities. See Joseph Story, *Commentaries on the Constitution of the United States*, 3 vols. (New York: Hilliard & Gray, 1833), § 454, 1: 441. See also Jay S. Bybee, "Ulysses at the Mast: Democracy, Federalism, and the Sirens' Song of the Seventeenth Amendment," *Northwestern University Law Review* 91 (1997): 547.

8. Not only have these post-Seventeenth Amendment congressional measures increased in number and intrusiveness, they have also become, in Theodore J. Lowi's terms, more abstract, general, novel, discretionary, and prescriptive (in contrast to earlier pre-Seventeenth Amendment legislation that was more concrete, specific, traditional, rule-bound, and prospective). Lowi, *The End of Liberalism: Ideology, Policy, and the Crisis of Public Authority* (New York: W. W. Norton, 1969), 134-35. This development has led to what Lowi calls "policy without law." Lowi, *End of Liberalism*, 126. It has weakened not only the states but the Congress itself; with the Senate no longer answerable to state legislatures, it has felt increasingly free to join the House in legislating on every social, economic, or political problem it perceives as confronting the nation, even if the resulting measures are little more than blank checks of authority to the executive branch and the federal bureaucracy. See Vikram David Amar, "Indirect Effects of Direct Election: A Structural Examination of the Seventeenth Amendment," *Vanderbilt Law Review* 49 (1996): 1360-89.

9. It must be stressed that this is not a "cause and effect" argument; clearly, many factors account for the rapid expansion of the national government, with two world wars and the Cold War, continued industrial growth, and breakthroughs in transportation and electronic communications being chief among them. Moreover, as Bybee acknowledges, it is "a maddeningly difficult proposition to prove" the exact effects of direct election of senators. Bybee, "Ulysses at the Mast," 547. Nevertheless, it is clear that the ratification of the Seventeenth Amendment removed a previously existing constitutional brake on these centralizing tendencies, and that federalism, as Todd J. Zywicki has pointed out, has been reduced to "a pale imitation of its pre-Seventeenth Amendment vigor." Zywicki, "Beyond the Shell and Husk of History: The History of the Seventeenth Amendment and Its Implications for Current Reform Proposals," *Cleveland State Law Review* 45 (1997): 165, 212. See also 174-75: "Conventional wisdom states that the New Deal commenced a radical shift in the scope of the federal government. In fact, the growth in the federal government began almost immediately after the passage of the Progressive Era amendments. . . . The New Deal simply confirmed the constitutional revolution which had already transpired."

10. 301 U.S. 1 (1937).

11. 426 U.S. 833 (1976).

12. There is another irony as well that this book does not systematically explore: A majority of the Supreme Court is perfectly willing to deny the democratic principle and to protect federalism by invalidating what the popular branches have enacted, but it is unwilling to protect federalism and return vast areas of policy making to the states by repudiating its own earlier decisions that have held that the Fourteenth Amendment incorporates most of the provisions of the Bill of Rights and makes them applicable to the states. As Lino A. Graglia points out in *"United States* v. *Lopez:* Judicial Review under the Commerce Clause," *Texas Law Review* 74 (March 1996): 726, this loss of

state autonomy by the Court is simply impossible to justify, because it means "the loss not only of federalism but also of the rights of representative self-government, the removal of power not only from the states but from the ordinary political process."

13. 426 U.S. 833 (1976). *National League of Cities* was overturned by *Garcia v. San Antonio Metropolitan Transit Authority,* 469 U.S. 528 (1985), and so it will also be considered.

14. 505 U.S. 144 (1992).

15. 514 U.S. 549 (1995).

16. 517 U.S. 44 (1996).

17. 521 U.S. 507 (1997).

18. 521 U.S. 898 (1997).

19. 527 U.S. 627(1999).

20. 527 U.S. 666 (1999).

21. 527 U.S. 706 (1999).

22. 528 U.S. 62 (2000).

23. 529 U.S. 598 (2000).

24. 531 U.S. 356 (2001).

25. 6 U.S. 358 (1805).

26. 17 U.S. 316 1819).

27. 22 U.S. 1 (1824).

28. David E. Kyvig, *Explicit and Authentic Acts: Amending the U.S. Constitution, 1776-1995* (Lawrence: University Press of Kansas, 1996), 209. See also Hoebeke, *The Road to Mass Democracy,* 101.

29. Zywicki, "Beyond the Shell and Husk of History," 185.

30. 369 U.S. 186 (1962).

31. 369 U.S. at 217.

32. Richard N. Current (ed.), *The Political Thought of Abraham Lincoln* (New York: Bobbs-Merrill, 1967), 20.

Chapter 1

The Supreme Court, Judicial Activism, and the Protection of Federalism

For a generation, the foundational understanding among students of the United States Constitution was that federalism, as a viable constitutional principle capable of limiting the powers of the federal government, was dead; that the line demarcating those powers appropriately belonging to the federal government from those powers reserved to the states had been washed away by the flood of New Deal legislation initially rejected but eventually embraced by the Supreme Court; and that the Congress was free from Court interference to regulate any aspect of American life it chose to regulate. This understanding was based in large part on their reading of three landmark decisions of the Supreme Court: *National Labor Relations Board* v. *Jones & Laughlin Steel Corporation* (1937),[1] *United States* v. *Darby Lumber Company* (1941),[2] and *Wickard* v. *Filburn* (1942).[3]

Jones & Laughlin was a five-to-four decision handed down in the aftermath of President Franklin Delano Roosevelt's landslide reelection in 1936, amidst intense controversy over the Court's invalidation of much of his program for economic recovery, and in the face of Roosevelt's "court-packing" plan—a transparent attempt by the president to expand the size of the Supreme Court so that he could appoint justices who would uphold his New Deal program. In this decision, the Court abandoned its previous position that Congress could regulate production only if it had a "direct effect" on interstate commerce[4] and upheld Congress's power to pass the National Labor Relations Act (also called the Wagner Act), which was designed to protect the rights of workers to form unions and to bargain collectively.

The Wagner Act prohibited a variety of unfair labor practices and authorized the National Labor Relations Board (NLRB) to issue cease-and-desist orders to employers who engaged in such practices. Jones & Laughlin, one of the nation's largest steel producers, violated the Act by firing ten workers for engaging in union activities, and it then refused to comply with an NLRB order to reinstate these workers. Based on the Supreme Court's previous decisions, a federal appeals court declined to enforce the board's order, and the Supreme Court granted certiorari. Chief Justice Charles Evans Hughes found that Jones & Laughlin's discharge of these ten employees for union activities could result in "industrial strife [that] would have a most serious effect upon interstate commerce." Jones and Laughlin's "farflung activities," he insisted, "have such a close and intimate relation to interstate commerce as to make the presence of industrial strife a matter of the most urgent national concern." When industries organized themselves on a national scale and made their relation to interstate commerce the dominant factor in their activities, Hughes wondered how it could be "maintained that their industrial labor relations constitute a forbidden field into which Congress may not enter when it is necessary to protect interstate commerce from the paralyzing consequences of industrial war?"[5] Hughes argued that "the fundamental principle is that the power to regulate commerce is the power to enact 'all appropriate legislation' for its 'protection or advancement'; to adopt measures 'to promote its growth and insure its safety'; 'to foster, protect, control, and restrain.' That power is plenary and may be exerted to protect interstate commerce 'no matter what the source of the dangers which threaten it.'"[6]

Hughes insisted that while "activities may be intrastate in character when separately considered, if they have such a close and substantial relation to interstate commerce that their control is essential or appropriate to protect that commerce from burdens and obstructions, Congress cannot be denied the power to exercise that control." And, while conceding that "the scope of this power must be considered in the light of our dual system of government," he insisted that "[t]he question is necessarily one of degree" and, therefore, one for the Congress and not the Court to decide.[7] He quoted the Court's earlier language in *Board of Trade of City of Chicago* v. *Olsen*: "Whatever amounts to more or less constant practice, and threatens to obstruct or unduly to burden the freedom of interstate commerce is within the regulatory power of Congress under the commerce clause, and it is primarily for Congress to consider and decide the fact of the danger and to meet it."[8]

Jones & Laughlin was followed four years later by the unanimous decision in *Darby Lumber,* upholding the Fair Labor St Act's prohibition of shipment in interstate commerce of goods not pi in compliance with the Act's wage and hour requirements. Justice Harlan Fiske Stone declared that "[w]hile manufacture is not of itself interstate commerce the shipment of manufactured goods interstate is such commerce and the prohibition of such shipment by Congress is indubitably a regulation of the commerce." Quoting from Chief Justice Marshall's famous language in *Gibbons* v. *Ogden,*[9] he announced that "[t]he power to regulate commerce is the power 'to prescribe the rule by which commerce is to be governed,'" and that it "extends not 'only to those regulations which aid, foster and protect the commerce, but embraces those which prohibit it.'"[10] In response to the contention that, while the prohibition was "nominally a regulation of the commerce," "its motive or purpose" was in fact the "regulation of wages and hours of persons engaged in manufacture, the control of which has been reserved to the states,"[11] Stone maintained that "[t]he motive and purpose of a regulation of interstate commerce are matters for the legislative judgment upon the exercise of which the Constitution places no restriction and over which the courts are given no control. Whatever their motive and purpose, regulations of commerce which do not infringe some constitutional prohibition are within the plenary power conferred on Congress by the Commerce Clause."[12]

Congress, the unanimous Court held, could use its power under the Commerce Clause in any way that did "not infringe some constitutional prohibition." As Lino A. Graglia has pointed out, this effectively "eliminate[d] the notion of enumerated national powers and reserved state powers."[13] Those who believed that the Tenth Amendment—which provides that "[t]he powers not delegated to the United States by the Constitution, nor prohibited by it to the States, are reserved to the States respectively, or to the people"—represented such a "constitutional limitation" were quickly disabused of this belief. In Stone's memorable words, "The amendment states but a truism that all is retained which has not been surrendered."[14]

Wickard v. *Filburn* followed the next year. The Court, again unanimously, upheld a penalty imposed under the Agriculture Adjustment Act of 1938 on a farmer for growing 239 bushels of wheat in excess of his 1941 allotment of 223 bushels, even though the additional wheat was grown for consumption on his own farm.[15] Filburn had argued that the production for personal consumption of wheat was an activity beyond the reach of Congress's power under the Commerce Clause, since it was local in character, and its effects upon interstate commerce was at most "indirect."

In rejecting this claim, Justice Robert Jackson also relied heavily on language from *Gibbons*, pointing out that Marshall had not only "described the Federal commerce power with a breadth never yet exceeded" but had also "made emphatic the embracing and penetrating nature of this power by warning that effective restraints on its exercise must proceed from political rather than from judicial processes."[16] Jackson argued that even though Filburn's production of wheat for consumption on his own farm was "local" and even though "it may not be regarded as commerce, it may still, whatever its nature, be reached by Congress if it exerts a substantial economic effect on interstate commerce and this irrespective of whether such effect is what might at some earlier time have been defined as 'direct' or 'indirect.'"[17] How, one might ask, could Filburn's excess production of a mere 239 bushels of wheat have "a substantial economic effect on interstate commerce"? Jackson answered the question without hesitation: "The effect of the statute before us is to restrict the amount which may be produced for market and the extent as well to which one may forestall resort to the market by producing to meet his own needs. That appellee's [Filburn's] own contribution to the demand for wheat may be trivial by itself is not enough to remove him from the scope of federal regulation where, as here, his contribution, taken together with that of many others similarly situated, is far from trivial."[18]

The breadth of *Wickard*'s holding was breathtaking. If Congress could regulate, under the Commerce Clause, noncommercial activities that are local in character and trivial in effect, because, in the aggregate, they are not trivial and therefore have some effect on interstate commerce, there did not seem to be any limit to Congress's powers to trench upon what *The Federalist* had called the "inviolable and residuary sovereignty of the states."[19] As Graglia points out, *Wickard* confirmed and strengthened, as *Darby Lumber* had done the year before, the message of *Jones & Laughlin* that "the Court had withdrawn in all but name . . . from the role of protector of state autonomy. It was a role, events had shown, the Court was unable to perform and had no call to perform."[20] Federalism, indeed, seemed dead.

Further evidence of federalism's demise was furnished when the Court subsequently upheld Congress's employment of the Commerce Clause to protect civil rights and suppress crime. Relying on the Commerce Clause, Congress passed the Civil Rights Act of 1964, banning throughout the nation racial discrimination in public accommodations (restaurants, theaters, hotels, etc.). While the Court had previously declared such a ban to be unconstitutional in the *Civil Rights Cases of 1883*,[21] it upheld this ban in *Heart of Atlanta Motel* v. *United States*[22] and

Katzenbach v. *McClung*[23] as a valid exercise of Congress's power to regulate interstate commerce.[24]

Congress had concluded that racial discrimination by hotels, restaurants, and other public accommodations affected interstate commerce because it deterred interstate travel by blacks. For the Court, that provided Congress with all the reason it needed to pass the Act. And, as Justice Tom Clark wrote for a unanimous Court in *Heart of Atlanta Motel*,[25] while "[i]t may be argued that Congress could have pursued other methods to eliminate the obstructions it found in interstate commerce caused by racial discrimination. . . . [T]his is a matter of policy that rests entirely with the Congress not with the courts."[26] How obstructions in commerce are to be removed, and by what means, are "within the sound and exclusive discretion of the Congress" and are "subject only to one caveat—that the means chosen by it must be reasonably adapted to the end permitted by the Constitution. We cannot say that its choice here was not so adapted. The Constitution requires no more."[27]

While Clark referred to means that were "reasonably adapted" in *Heart of Atlanta Motel*, he spoke of the "rational basis " test in *Katzenbach*: "[W]here we find that the legislators, in light of the facts and testimony before them, have a rational basis for finding a chosen regulatory scheme necessary to the protection of commerce, our investigation is at an end."[28] The rational basis test is, of course, very difficult for the Congress to fail. "It is a test that as a practical matter cannot be failed, the purpose of which is to signify, without explicitly stating, the withdrawal of judicial review from the area in question."[29] The Court was thus clearly signaling that it would not strike down congressional measures for trenching on state sovereignty. However, not wanting to leave any doubt about the matter, Justice Clark continued: "The power of Congress in this field is broad and sweeping; where it keeps within its sphere and violates no express constitutional limitation it has been the rule of this Court, going back almost to the founding days of the Republic, not to interfere."[30] For the Court, the principle of federalism and the tautological Tenth Amendment clearly represented no such "express constitutional limitation." Graglia has put the matter well: "*Jones & Laughlin* signaled, and *Darby* and *Wickard* confirmed, the Court's de facto withdrawal from Commerce Clause review. *Katzenbach*'s pronouncement of the rational basis test made the withdrawal virtually *de jure*." After *Jones & Laughlin*, the Court "engaged in only pretend review"; after *Katzenbach*, the Court "hardly bothered to keep up the pretense."[31]

Just how little the Court bothered to keep up the pretense of reviewing congressional regulation under the Commerce Clause became readily apparent in *Perez* v. *United States*,[32] in which it sustained a provision of the

Consumer Credit Protection Act making loan-sharking or "extortionate credit transactions" (i.e., loans involving the threat of violence in their enforcement) a federal offense on the ground that it affects interstate commerce by supporting organized crime which "exacts millions from the pockets of people, coerces its victims into the commission of crimes against property, and causes the takeover by racketeers of legitimate business."[33] Justice William O. Douglas held for the Court that all that was needed for Congress to criminalize "extortionate credit transactions, though purely intrastate," was its judgment that they "affect interstate commerce."[34] In his solitary dissent, Justice Potter Stewart pointed out that, by similar reasoning, Congress could nationalize nearly all crime and, in the process, take over a core function of the states: Stewart demanded real review, even under the rational basis test: "In order to sustain this law we would, in my view, have to be able at the least to say that Congress could rationally have concluded that loan sharking is an activity with interstate attributes that distinguish it in some substantial respect from other local crime."[35] Because Stewart was "unable to discern any rational distinction between loan sharking and other local crime," he concluded that "this statute was beyond the power of Congress to enact. The definition and prosecution of local, intrastate crime are reserved to the States under the Ninth and Tenth Amendments."[36]

On this broad and deep foundation of judicial deference to Congress concerning the limits of its power, the Congress and the Court proceeded to build a mighty national edifice on what had previously been the exclusive territory of the states. In *Maryland* v. *Wirtz*,[37] for example, the Court upheld Congress's 1966 amendments to the Fair Labor Standards Act that applied its minimum-wage and maximum-hours provisions to schools and hospitals, even though neither shipped goods or competed in interstate commerce. According to the Court, not only did Congress's action pass the "rational basis test," in that schools and hospitals made purchases from out of state,[38] but it also addressed poor working conditions that might cause labor unrest and thereby "interrupt and burden the flow of goods across state lines."[39] In *Hodel* v. *Virginia Surface Mining & Reclamation Association*,[40] the Court upheld the Surface Mining Control and Reclamation Act of 1977, the purpose of which was stated by Congress to be the protection of "society and the environment." Objections that the Act violated the principles of federalism were met, as Graglia points out, "with the standard one-two punch: citation of *Gibbons*'s statement that Congress's commerce power is 'plenary' and *Katzenbach*'s statement that a congressional finding that an activity affects commerce must be upheld if it has 'any rational basis.'"[41] Congress had found that surface mining operations "adversely affected commerce" by, *inter alia*, "impairing natural beauty" and "degrading the quality of life in local communities."[42] Such concerns would seem to be local rather than national and, therefore, left up to the states to address. But Justice Thurgood Marshall held for the Court that there was not only a rational basis but "ample support" for these 'statutory findings."[43] In the companion case of *Hodel v. Indiana*,[44] the Court upheld provisions of the Surface Mining Act that required the restoration of mined "prime farmland" to at least the yield of surrounding non-mined land. Justice Marshall argued that there was a "rational basis" for Congress's finding "that the protection of prime farmland is a federal interest that may be addressed through Commerce Clause legislation."[45] The Court then abandoned its previous reluctance to rely on health and safety concerns to uphold commerce-power measures and held that Congress had power to protect not only agriculture and the environment but also "public health and safety" if injury to "any of these interests would have deleterious effect on interstate commerce."[46] If Congress is free to regulate intrastate commerce as a means of protecting life and property—a traditional state governmental function, then there really would seem to be no issue Congress could not reach. Any lingering doubt on this matter was removed when Marshall declared that it was unnecessary for all the "specific provisions challenged in this case . . . [to] be shown to be related to the congressional goal of preventing adverse effects on interstate commerce." As he observed, "[a] complex regulatory program such as established by the Act can survive a Commerce Clause challenge without a showing that every single facet of the program is independently and directly related to a valid congressional goal. It is enough that the challenged provisions are an integral part of the regulatory program and that the regulatory scheme when considered as a whole satisfies this test."[47] Clearly, the Court was arguing, whether Congress chooses to regulate a matter traditionally reserved to the states is a policy question for Congress alone to decide, not a constitutional question for the Court to address.

National League of Cities v. Usery

The ever-expanding national edifice Congress had been systematically building on the Commerce Clause for the thirty-nine years after *Jones & Laughlin* was suddenly shaken to its very foundations by the Court in *National League of Cities v. Usery*.[48] In this five-to-four decision, the Court invalidated Congress's 1974 amendments to the Fair Labor Standards Act applying the Act's minimum-wage and maximum-hours provisions to state governments and their political subdivisions; it did so on the grounds that this exercise of congressional power did not comport with the federal system of government embodied in the Constitution.

Justice William H. Rehnquist declared for the Court that these amendments would "significantly alter or displace the States' abilities to structure employer-employee relationships in such areas as fire prevention, police protection, sanitation, public health, and parks and recreation." Since he argued that these were the very functions that the state governments had been created to provide, "[i]f Congress may withdraw from the States the authority to make those fundamental employment decisions upon which their systems for performance of these functions must rest, we think there would be little left of the States' 'separate and independent existence.'"[49]

Rehnquist readily conceded that Congress's action was "undoubtedly within the scope of the Commerce Clause," but, he insisted, Congress could no more use its commerce power to usurp the states' right to carry out their traditional functions than it could to deny the right to trial by jury contained in the Sixth Amendment or violate the Due Process Clause of the Fifth Amendment.[50] He argued that the federal system imposes definite limits on Congress's power under the Commerce Clause to regulate the activities of the states as states, and that the Tenth Amendment contains "an express declaration of this limitation." Rehnquist quoted approvingly from *United States* v. *Fry*: "The Amendment expressly declares the constitutional policy that Congress may not exercise power in a fashion that impairs the States' integrity or their ability to function effectively in a federal system."[51] Since "the challenged amendments operate to directly displace the States' freedom to structure integral operations in areas of traditional governmental functions," he concluded that they violated the Tenth Amendment and "are not within the authority granted Congress by Article I, Section 8."[52] Moreover, since *Maryland* v. *Wirtz* had wrongly permitted Congress to interfere with hospitals and schools, "an integral portion of those governmental services which the States and their political subdivisions have traditionally afforded their citizens," he declared that it was now overruled.[53]

Justice William Brennan was filled with shock, dismay, and incredulity; in his dissent, he criticized the Court not only for departing from long-established precedent but also for engaging in judicial activism. He found it "surprising" that the Court "should choose this bicentennial year of our independence to repudiate principles governing judicial interpretation of our Constitution settled since the time of Mr. Chief Justice John Marshall, discarding his postulate that the Constitution contemplates that restraints upon exercise by Congress of its plenary commerce power lie in the political process and not in the judicial process."[54]

Brennan repeated Justice Stone's words from *Darby Lumber* that the Tenth Amendment is "but a truism" and vociferously denied that it constituted a "restraint based on state sovereignty requiring or permitting judicial enforcement."[55] He charged the majority with a "patent usurpation of the role reserved for the political process by their purported discovery in the Constitution of a restraint derived from the sovereignty of the States on Congress's exercise of the commerce power," and he dismissed their arguments "as a transparent cover for invalidating a congressional judgment with which they disagree."[56]

There is something incongruous about an opinion in which Justice Brennan criticizes others for judicial activism. However, the fact that he did not practice judicial self-restraint elsewhere is not grounds for simply dismissing his arguments out-of-hand. Brennan made two arguments for why the Court should practice judicial restraint on federalism questions. The first was based on prudence—on preserving judicial independence in the face of what might become once again an antagonistic and aroused Congress. Brennan argued that the reasoning in the majority opinion in *National League of Cities* resembled that "found in a line of opinions dealing with the Commerce Clause and the Tenth Amendment that ultimately provoked a constitutional crisis for the Court in the 1930s." While the Hughes Court weathered the storm, Brennan cautioned that "[i]t may have been the eventual abandonment of that overly restrictive construction of the commerce power that spelled defeat for the Court-packing plan, and preserved the integrity of this institution."[57]

It is not at all clear, however, that Brennan's prudential worries were justified. The Congress has shown no willingness whatsoever to sanction the Court for its recent activism, not even in the face of the justices' high-handed invalidation in 1997 of the Religious Freedom Restoration Act of 1993, a measure that had passed just four years before by a unanimous vote in the House and by a vote of ninety-seven to three in the Senate.

Brennan's second and more important argument on behalf of judicial restraint was based on his conviction that "[i]t is unacceptable that the judicial process should be thought superior to the political process in this area. Under the Constitution the Judiciary has no role to play beyond finding that Congress has not made an unreasonable legislative judgment respecting what is 'commerce.'"[58] Judicial restraint in the area of federalism, he argued, "merely recognizes that the political branches of our Government are structured to protect the interests of the States." Since Congress is "constituted of representatives in both the Senate and House *elected from the States*," he concluded that "[d]ecisions upon the extent of federal intervention under the Commerce Clause into the affairs of the States are in that sense decisions of the States themselves" and that a "[j]udicial redistribution of powers granted the National Government by the terms of the Constitution violates the fundamental tenet of our federalism that the extent of federal intervention into the States' affairs in the exercise of delegated powers shall be determined by the States' exercise of political power through their representatives in Congress."[59]

Brennan argued that the interests of the states are protected by the political process. On one level, his "process federalism" argument was not altogether wrong, for the framers of the Constitution clearly believed that the interests of the states as states would be protected by a political process in which the Senate was elected by state legislatures. On all the details, however, Brennan's argument was wide of the mark. To begin with, what was important to the framers was not what Brennan argued, namely, that the members of the House and Senate were "elected from the States," but rather that the members of the Senate were elected by state legislatures and were therefore to represent the interests of the states as such.[60] (By contrast, members of the House were elected by the people who, while they lived in the states, sent their representatives to the House to represent them on matters that affected the nation as a whole and to secure their interests as citizens of the United States, not their interests as citizens of a particular state.)

Moreover, while the states were protected in the original Constitution by a political process in which the Senate was elected by state legislatures, that process was fundamentally altered by the political and social forces that led to the adoption of the Seventeenth Amendment—something that Brennan completely ignored.[61] Since federalism was originally protected by the political process, and since the Seventeenth Amendment changed that process, one could plausibly argue that a different process—namely, judicial process—must be substituted to preserve federalism. That is implicitly the argument that Rehnquist made for the Court majority in *National League of Cities*.[62] For reasons that are developed at length in chapter 3, that argument ultimately fails, but it at least acknowledges the change brought about by the Seventeenth Amendment.

Alternatively, one could argue that, since federalism is never defined or even expressly mentioned in the Constitution and therefore has no existence apart from the structural means by which it was originally protected, and since the Seventeenth Amendment fundamentally altered that structure, federalism is no longer protected and, since no longer protected, no longer constitutes a viable constitutional restraint on Congress from trenching on what was once considered "the inviolable and residuary sovereignty of the states." That is the argument of this book, although it is couched exclusively in the language of constitutional structure rather than political process.

While these two arguments reach diametrically opposed conclusions concerning the impact of the Seventeenth Amendment on federalism, they both at least acknowledge that it had an impact, and they are, therefore, clearly superior to Brennan's anachronistic "process federalism" and its steadfast refusal to recognize formal constitutional change. Brennan, who on other occasions was quick to criticize those who "turn a blind eye to social progress and eschew adaptation of overarching principles to changes of social circumstances,"[63] insisted that the framers' original design for protecting federalism was still operative and was therefore to be honored. Brennan, who otherwise dismissed calls for the Court to adopt a "jurisprudence of original intention"[64] on the grounds that "it is arrogant to pretend that from our vantage we can gauge accurately the intent of the Framers on application of principle to specific contemporary questions,"[65] insisted that, in cases involving federalism, the Court was to apply "the intent of the Framers" and thereby embrace "process federalism." Given Brennan's customary disparagement of original-intent arguments, which he branded as "little more than arrogance cloaked as humility,"[66] his "process federalism" argument was shamelessly disingenuous and was subject to the same opprobrium he heaped on the majority opinion when he described it as nothing more than "a mirror" reflecting "its own conception of desirable governmental [policy]."[67]

Despite its many shortcomings, Brennan's "process-federalism" argument prevailed just eight years later in *Garcia* v. *San Antonio Metropolitan Transit Authority*,[68] in which the Court overruled *National League of Cities* and upheld the constitutionality of Congress's extension of the wage and hour provisions of the Fair Labor Standards Act to state and municipal governments, and, in this case, to a local transit authority. In *Garcia*, also a five-to-four decision, the Supreme Court declared that any "attempt to draw the boundaries of state regulatory immunity in terms of 'traditional governmental function' is not only unworkable but is also inconsistent with established principles of federalism."[69] Justice Harry Blackmun, who had joined the Court majority in *National League of Cities*, now wrote the opinion overturning it. He based his opinion for the Court solidly on "process federalism" arguments. "[T]he principal means chosen by the Framers to ensure the role of the States in the federal system lies in the structure of the Federal Government itself."[70]

Blackmun pointed out that while the states were given some role in the selection of the House through "their control of electoral qualifications" and of the president through "their role in Presidential elections," they were given "more direct influence in the Senate, where each State received equal representation and each Senator was to be selected by the legislature of his State."[71] Unlike Brennan in his dissent in *National League of Cities,* Blackmun conceded that "changes in the structure of the Federal Government have taken place since 1789, not the least of which has been the substitution of popular election of Senators by the adoption of the Seventeenth Amendment in 1913, and that these changes may work to alter the influence of the States in the federal political process."[72] However, while acknowledging that changes in structure had taken place, he denied that they had any significant effect, and he remained "convinced that the fundamental limitation that the constitutional scheme imposes on the Commerce Clause to protect the 'States as States' is one of process rather than one of result."[73] Only clear evidence of "failings in the national political process" could justify a departure from "process federalism,"[74] but, as Blackmun proceeded to demonstrate to his own satisfaction, clearly there was no failing in the political process in this case, as Congress, in the two decades since it first subjected state mass-transit systems to FLSA obligations, "had simultaneously provided extensive funding" totaling over "$22 billion in mass-transit aid to States and localities." In fact, the political process did not fail; it positively succeeded, for, thanks to congressional aid, state "mass-transit systems [were] better off than they would have been had Congress never intervened at all in the area."[75] Convinced of "the solicitude of the national political process for the continued vitality of the States," he saw no need for the judicial activism present in *National League of Cities*; since that decision "tried to repair what did not need repair," he declared it "overruled."[76]

Blackmun's opinion for the Court was met with vigorous dissents. Justice Lewis Powell objected that the majority opinion "reduces the Tenth Amendment to meaningless rhetoric when Congress acts pursuant to the Commerce Clause,"[77] and he vigorously denied that "the role of the States in the federal system may depend upon the grace of elected federal officials rather than on the Constitution as interpreted by this Court."[78] "The States' role in our system of government," he insisted, "is a matter of constitutional law, not of legislative grace."[79] (He would have spoken more accurately if he had said that the states' role was a matter of the original Constitution subsequently modified by the Seventeenth Amendment.) Powell repeatedly emphasized the "constitutionally mandated balance of power between the States and the Federal Government,"[80] and decried what he called the Court's "outright rejection" of "the intention of the Framers of the Constitution."[81] He seemed unwilling to acknowledge, however, that the original federal balance was altered by the direct election of senators and that the framers' original intentions were no longer controlling.

Justice Sandra Day O'Connor, worried that federalism was becoming "irrelevant,"[82] faulted the Court for its failure to interpret the "entire Constitution,"[83] by which she meant that the Court failed to take into account the "spirit of the Tenth Amendment."[84] She insisted that the Court must acknowledge "all the values to which the Constitution—as interpreted over time—gives expression."[85] That, however, would seem to include the public's preference for more direct democracy, even at the expense of federalism, as given expression in the Seventeenth Amendment, something she completely overlooked.

New York v. United States

In 1992, the Supreme Court, in a six-to-three decision in *New York* v. *United States*,[86] invalidated the "take title" provision of the Low-Level Radioactive Waste Policy Amendments Act of 1985. It did so on the grounds that it "infring[ed] upon the core of state sovereignty reserved by the Tenth Amendment" and was "inconsistent with the federal structure of our Government established by the Constitution."[87]

Confronting a dire shortage of disposal sites in thirty-one states for low-level radioactive waste generated by hospitals, research institutions, and various industries, Congress enacted the Low-Level Radioactive Waste Amendments Act of 1985. The Act was largely based on a proposal submitted by the National Governors' Association and embodied a compromise between sited and unsited states, in which the sited states agreed to extend for seven years the period in which they would accept low-level radioactive waste from other states and, in exchange, the unsited states agreed to end their reliance on the sited states by 1992. To ensure that these agreements were honored, the Act imposed on the states, alone or in "regional compacts" with other states, the obligation to provide for the disposal of waste generated within their borders, and it contained three provisions setting forth "incentives" to states to comply with that obligation. The first set of incentives was monetary; states with disposal sites were authorized to impose a surcharge on radioactive waste received from other states. The second set of incentives focused on access; states and regional compacts with disposal sites were authorized to increase gradually the cost of access to their sites and eventually to deny access altogether. The third incentive was a "take title" provision that specified that a state or regional compact that failed to provide for the disposal of all internally generated waste by 1992 had, upon the request of the waste's generator or owner, to take title to and possession of the waste and was thereupon liable for all damages suffered by the generator or owner as a result of the state's failure to take prompt possession.

New York state officials testified in Congress on behalf of the Act; Senator Daniel Patrick Moynihan spoke in support of the Act on the floor of the Senate; New York's state government took initial steps to comply with the Act's provisions; and the people of New York took full advantage of the import concession made by the sited states by exporting their low-level radioactive waste for the full seven-year extension period provided by Act. Nonetheless, in 1990, New York filed suit against the United States claiming the Act was unconstitutional under the Tenth Amendment. After losing at the district court and court of appeals levels, it scored a significant victory in the Supreme Court. While Justice O'Connor found for the Court that the first two incentives were "consistent with the Constitution's allocation of power to the Federal Government,"[88] she found the "take title" provision to be unconstitutional because it was either "outside Congress's enumerated powers" or "inconsistent with the federal structure of our Government established by the Constitution."[89] She saw no need to decide which it was, because, "[i]n the end, just as a cup may be half empty or half full, it makes no difference whether one views the question at issue in the case as one of ascertaining the limits of the power delegated to the Federal Government under the affirmative provisions of the Constitution or one of discerning the core of sovereignty retained by the States under the Tenth Amendment."[90]

While O'Connor admitted that the Tenth Amendment was a "truism" and "essentially a tautology," she insisted that it "confirms that the power of the Federal Government is subject to limits that may, in a given instance, reserve powers to the States. The Tenth Amendment thus directs us to determine, as in this case, whether an incident of state sovereignty is protected by a limitation on an Article I power."[91] That Court determination was to be made on the basis of an understanding of the "federal structure" as decided by the delegates to the Federal Convention (O'Connor spent several pages comparing and contrasting the Virginia and New Jersey Plans[92]) and as "set forth in the Constitution."[93] That federal structure, she insisted, has remained unchanged from 1787; while "the actual scope of the Federal Government's authority with respect to the States has changed over the years" (the result, she conceded, of "the Court's broad construction of Congress's power under the Commerce and Spending Clauses"[94]), "the constitutional structure underlying and limiting that authority has not."[95] In this respect, of course, O'Connor utterly failed to take account of the significant structural change brought about by the direct election of senators.

Seemingly unaware that she was protecting a "constitutional structure" no longer in effect because long since altered by the political and social forces that culminated in the ratification of the Seventeenth Amendment, O'Connor held that the federal government lacked the power to "conscript"[96] or "commandeer" state governments into either "accepting ownership of waste or regulating according to the instructions of Congress."[97] She was adamant on this point: "Whatever the outer limits of [state] sovereignty may be, one thing is clear: The Constitution . . . does not authorize Congress simply to direct the States to provide for the disposal of the radioactive waste generated within their borders."[98] Prohibiting such conscription, she insisted, would not frustrate congressional efforts to deal with the problem of disposing low-level radioactive waste. Congress could, she noted, "regulate matters directly and . . . preempt contrary state regulation."[99]

Justice Byron White filed a vigorous dissent that was based, for the most part, on the "process federalism" arguments of *Garcia*.[100] He did, however, raise two particularly interesting objections: First, he faulted the majority for its failure to recognize that the Act was the product of collective action by the states themselves and not an imposition placed on them by the federal government. Congress, in this instance, was merely playing the role of an arbiter of the disputes between sited and unsited states; as a consequence, the result was not federal commandeering but rather legislation that, as he put it, "reflected hard-fought agreements among States as refereed by Congress."[101] Second, White was perplexed how an opinion that relieved New York of its responsibilities served the cause of federalism. "The Court's refusal to force New York to accept responsibility for its own problem inevitably means that some other State's sovereignty will be impinged by it being forced, for public health reasons, to accept New York's low-level radioactive waste. I do not understand the principle of federalism to impede the National Government from acting as referee among the States to prohibit one from bullying another."[102]

In a brief dissent, Justice John Paul Stevens noted that, under the Articles of Confederation, the Federal Government had the "power to issue commands to the States," and that "nothing in the history [of the framing of the Constitution] suggests that the Federal Government may not also impose its will upon the several States as it did under the Articles. The Constitution enhanced, rather than diminished, the power of the Federal Government."[103] Under the Articles, use of that power required the unanimous approval the states, whose representatives in Congress were sent there as ambassadors to represent their interests. Under the original Constitution, use of that power would have required the concurrence of the

Senate, filled with individuals elected by state legislatures and therefore expected to protect the interests of states as states. The Seventeenth Amendment, of course, removed the structural check on the use of this power; Stevens's dissent no more acknowledges this structurally transforming amendment than does O'Connor's majority opinion.

United States v. *Lopez*

For the first time in almost six decades, the Supreme Court in *United States* v. *Lopez*[104] invalidated a federal law—in this case, the Gun-Free School Zones Act of 1990—for exceeding the scope of the Commerce Clause. Chief Justice William Rehnquist wrote for a five-member majority that the Act, which made it a federal offense "for any individual knowingly to possess a firearm at a place that the individual knows, or has reasonable cause to believe, is a school zone,"[105] "neither regulates a commercial activity nor contains a requirement that the possession be connected in any way to interstate commerce"; consequently, it "exceeds the authority of Congress 'to regulate Commerce . . . among the several States.'"[106]

Rehnquist began by answering what prior case law had left as a question, namely, for an activity to be within Congress's power to regulate under the Commerce Clause, is it enough that it merely "affect" interstate commerce, or must it affect it "substantially"? He concluded for the majority that the "proper test" was that the regulated activity must "substantially affect" interstate commerce.[107] Applying that test, he concluded that "the possession of a gun in a local school zone is in no sense an economic activity that might, through repetition elsewhere, substantially affect any sort of interstate commerce."[108]

Both the federal government in its argument to the Court and Justice Stephen Breyer in his dissent argued that the possession of a gun in a school zone did substantially affect commerce. Rehnquist summarized their argument as follows: "[T]he presence of guns in schools poses a substantial threat to the education process by threatening the learning environment. A handicapped education process, in turn, will result in a less productive citizenry. That, in turn, would have an adverse effect on the Nation's economic well-being."[109] The problem with that argument, as Rehnquist pointed out, is that it makes it impossible "to posit any activity by an individual that Congress is without power to regulate."[110] In fact, he continued, that argument "would bid fair to convert congressional authority under the Commerce Clause to a general police power of the sort retained by the States."[111] While admitting that "some of our prior cases have taken long steps down that road," he declined "to proceed any further."[112]

Justice Anthony Kennedy wrote a concurring opinion with decidedly more activist overtones; he emphasized the need for the Court to "ensure that the federal-state balance is not destroyed."[113] He found it strange that, "of the various structural elements in the Constitution, separation of powers, checks and balances, judicial review, and federalism, only concerning the last does there seem to be much uncertainty respecting the existence, and the content, of standards that allow the Judiciary to play a significant role in maintaining the design contemplated by the Framers."[114] However, had he understood that the framers depended not on the Court but on constitutional structure, i.e., the mode of electing the Senate, to protect federalism, he would have found it less strange. And, further, had he understood that the ratification of the Seventeenth Amendment removed the structural protection of federalism and therefore fundamentally shifted the federal-state balance, he would have appreciated both the futility and inappropriateness of his efforts to protect the framers' design, now amended out of the Constitution. Kennedy rightly sensed that "the absence of structural mechanisms" renders it difficult to maintain the federal balance, but he showed absolutely no awareness that the framers originally provided for such a mechanism—namely, the election of the Senate by state legislatures—or that, by their ratification of the Seventeenth Amendment, the people removed it. Rather, he simply concluded that the Court should be free "to intervene when one or the other level of Government has tipped the scales too far."[115]

Justice Clarence Thomas wrote a separate concurrence to comment on how far the Court's case law had drifted from the original understanding of the Commerce Clause and to distance himself from the "substantial effects" test. "Put simply, much if not all of Article I, section 8 (including portions of the Commerce Clause itself), would be surplusage if Congress had been given authority over all matters that substantially affect interstate commerce. An interpretation of clause 3 that makes the rest of section 8 superfluous simply cannot be correct. Yet this Court's Commerce Clause jurisprudence has endorsed just such an interpretation."[116] He criticized the dissenters for giving Congress "a blank check"[117] to regulate everything "under the guise of the Commerce Clause."[118] He failed to consider that this "blank check" was given, not by the Court but by the framers who were confident that it would not be abused because the mode they had provided for electing the Senate would protect the states as such.

The dissenters uniformly complained that the majority had abandoned "the practice of deferring to rationally based legislative judgments."[119] For

Justice David Souter, the "touchstone" of constitutionality" was "rational possibility,"[120] i.e., "whether the legislative judgment is within the realm of reason."[121] There was no evidence in the record that Congress had found that the presence of a gun within a school zone substantially affected interstate commerce, but, Souter insisted, "the legislation implies such a finding, and there is no reason to entertain claims that Congress acted *ultra vires* intentionally."[122] Justice Breyer reminded the majority that the Constitution requires the Court to judge "the connection between a regulated activity and interstate commerce, not directly, but at one remove." The Court must therefore give Congress "a degree of leeway" when determining whether there is a sufficiently "significant factual connection" between the two, not only because the Constitution "delegates the commerce power directly to Congress" but also because that determination "requires an empirical judgment of a kind that a legislature is more likely than a court to make with accuracy. The traditional words 'rational basis' capture this leeway."[123] Interestingly, Breyer was unwilling to give Congress as much "leeway" as Souter. While Souter inferred a connection between guns in school zones and their effect on interstate commerce from the fact that Congress had enacted the measure in question, Breyer felt obliged to prove the "empirical connection" that, while he claimed Congress could make with greater "accuracy," Congress had not bothered at all to make. Thus, Breyer spent six pages of his dissent (and added a fourteen-page appendix of citations)[124] to justify the "leeway" he was willing to give Congress that its unstated "empirical judgment" concerning the impact of guns on education and therefore on the economy was rational.

Seminole Tribe of Florida v. Florida

In *Seminole Tribe of Florida* v. *Florida*,[125] Chief Justice Rehnquist wrote for a five-member majority that Congress lacks power under the Commerce Clause to abrogate state sovereignty immunity protected by the Eleventh Amendment. Just as he declared in *National League of Cities* that the Tenth Amendment limits what Congress can regulate under the Interstate Commerce Clause, so also he declared in *Seminole Tribe* that the Eleventh Amendment limits what Congress can regulate under the Indian Commerce Clause.[126]

In 1988, pursuant to its powers under the Indian Commerce Clause, Congress passed the Indian Gaming Regulatory Act, which allowed Indian tribes to conduct certain gaming activities provided they are in conformity with the terms of a valid compact between the tribe and the state in which the gaming activities are located. Under the Act, Congress imposed on states a duty to negotiate in good faith with a tribe toward the formation of a compact and authorized the tribes to sue a state in federal court in order to compel performance of that duty. When the Seminole Tribe sued the State of Florida for its refusal to enter into good faith negotiations, Florida moved to dismiss the complaint on the ground that congressional authorization of the suit violated its sovereign immunity from suit in federal court. When the district court denied Florida's motion, the United States Court of Appeals for the Eleventh Circuit reversed, concluding that, under the Eleventh Amendment, the federal courts had no jurisdiction. An activist Supreme Court agreed.

Rehnquist's majority opinion had to overcome a major textual problem: By its terms, the Eleventh Amendment simply does not bar the kind of suit brought by the Seminole Tribe. It reads as follows: "The Judicial power of the United States shall not be construed to extend to any suit in law or equity, commenced or prosecuted against one of the United States by Citizens of another State, or by Citizens or Subjects of any Foreign State." The members of the Seminole Tribe were not "Citizens of another State, or . . . Citizens or Subjects of any Foreign State" bringing suit under the federal court's state-citizen diversity jurisdiction (granted by Article III in the original Constitution but then subsequently repealed by the Eleventh Amendment); rather they were bringing suit under the federal court's federal question (also known as "subject matter" or "arising under") jurisdiction (granted by Article III and left untouched by the Eleventh Amendment).

While the words of the Eleventh Amendment did not bar the suit filed by the Seminole Tribe, Rehnquist was undeterred, proclaiming that a "blind reliance upon the text of the Eleventh Amendment"[127] would be "overly exacting"[128] and would result in a "construction never imagined or dreamed of."[129] The Eleventh Amendment, he insisted, stands "not so much for what it says, as for the presupposition . . . which it confirms." That presupposition, he continued, has two parts: "[F]irst, that each State is a sovereign entity in our federal system; and second, that 'it is inherent in the nature of sovereignty not to be amenable to suit without its consent.'"[130]

The Eleventh Amendment was, Rehnquist pointed out, a reaction to "the now-discredited decision in *Chisholm* v. *Georgia*,"[131] in which the Supreme Court in 1793 had held that a state could be sued by a citizen of another state or by an alien. The Eleventh Amendment reversed that decision and, as Rehnquist emphasized, it "dealt in terms only with the problem presented" by *Chisholm*. Since the federal courts in 1793 did not have federal question jurisdiction and, in fact, would not have it until 1875, Rehnquist concluded that the authors of the Eleventh Amendment did not see a threat to the principle of state sovereign immunity coming from that quarter but rather only from suits brought under the federal court's diversity jurisdiction and, therefore, barred only those suits. Their goal, Rehnquist implied, was to protect the principle of state sovereign immunity from any threat; their means—in retrospective less comprehensive than they should have been—was to bar suits under the federal court's diversity jurisdiction.

Rehnquist went on to acknowledge that a state's sovereign immunity from suit is only a "presupposition" and is not absolute; Congress "may abrogate the States' sovereign immunity if it has 'unequivocally expressed its intent to abrogate the immunity' and has acted 'pursuant to a valid exercise of power.'"[132] The question for Rehnquist then became whether these two conditions had been met in this case. Rehnquist conceded that the Indian Gaming Regulatory Act had unequivocally expressed Congress's intent to lift Eleventh Amendment immunity to suits seeking to compel the states to negotiate in good faith to establish gaming compacts. Congressional power to abrogate, however, was less obvious than congressional intent to do so. The Court had previously found that Congress had power to abrogate under only two constitutional provisions: the Interstate Commerce Clause and Section 5 of the Fourteenth Amendment. In *Pennsylvania* v. *Union Gas Company*,[133] a plurality of the Court had found that the Interstate Commerce Clause granted Congress the power to abrogate state sovereign immunity, stating that the power to regulate interstate commerce would be "incomplete" without the power to hold states liable for damages. And in *Fitzpatrick* v. *Bitzer*,[134] the Court held that the Fourteenth Amendment had expanded federal power at the expense of the states; that, through it, federal power extended to "intrude upon the province of the Eleventh Amendment"; and that under Section 5 (giving Congress the "power to enforce, by appropriate legislation, the provisions of this article"), Congress has power to abrogate state sovereign immunity in order to enforce the rights spelled out in Section 1 of the Fourteenth Amendment.

Since the Court in *Union Gas* had found that Congress had power to lift Eleventh Amendment immunity under the Interstate Commerce Clause, the Seminole Tribe argued that it logically followed that Congress also had power to do so under the Indian Commerce Clause. Rehnquist concurred: "We agree . . . that the plurality opinion in *Union Gas* allows no principled distinction in favor of the States to be drawn between the Indian Commerce Clause and the Interstate Commerce Clause."[135] However, he and his colleagues in the majority refused to be bound by *Union Gas*, which they held to be a departure from "our established understanding of the Eleventh Amendment" and which they therefore overruled.[136] The Court in *Union Gas* had held, in effect, that the principle of state sovereign immunity embodied in the Eleventh Amendment could be limited through an appeal to the antecedent provisions of the Constitution. Rehnquist denied this and argued, to the contrary, that Congress's power to abrogate state sovereign immunity under the Commerce Clause was trumped, as it were, by the subsequent adoption of the Eleventh Amendment. Later amendments trump the original Constitution and earlier amendments; on the basis of that logic, Rehnquist held that the only constitutional provision authorizing Congress to abrogate state sovereign immunity was Section 5 of the Fourteenth Amendment—passed, of course, after the Eleventh Amendment and therefore able to trump its state protections. "[T]he Fourteenth Amendment, adopted well after the adoption of the Eleventh Amendment and the ratification of the Constitution, operates to alter the preexisting balance between the state and federal power achieved by Article III and the Eleventh Amendment."[137] Since Congress relied on the "Indian Commerce Clause" and not on its enforcement powers under Section 5 of the Fourteenth Amendment when it enacted the Indian Gaming Regulatory Act, Rehnquist concluded that Congress lacked the power to abrogate state sovereign immunity and affirmed the Court of Appeals' dismissal of the suit for want of jurisdiction.

Rehnquist's argument that subsequent amendments trump antecedent provisions and amendments was crucial to the outcome in *Seminole Tribe*. However, it also undermined his own opinion as well as much of the reasoning of the activists on the current Court who are eager to protect the original federal design from subsequent congressional alteration. Rehnquist acknowledged that the Fourteenth Amendment altered "the preexisting balance between state and federal power achieved by Article III and the Eleventh Amendment;" of course, so did the Seventeenth Amendment, which removed the primary structural feature of the Constitution intended by the framers to protect the interests of the states as such. If Rehnquist was willing to concede that the Fourteenth Amendment altered the original federal balance by trumping the original Constitution, then he and his colleagues should also have been willing to concede that the Seventeenth Amendment trumped and thereby profoundly altered federalism as well, and to recognize that their post-Seventeenth Amendment efforts to protect the original federal design are as inappropriate as efforts by the post-Eleventh Amendment Court plurality in *Union Gas* to protect Congress's power to abrogate state sovereign immunity under the Commerce Clause.

Justices Stevens and Souter wrote dissenting opinions. In the lead dissent joined by Justices Breyer and Ruth Bader Ginsburg, Justice Souter argued that *Chisholm* settled the question of whether the states could be sued not only under the federal court's citizen-state diversity jurisdiction but also, "by implication," under their federal question jurisdiction. "The constitutional text on federal-question jurisdiction, after all, was just as devoid of immunity language as it was on citizen-state diversity."[138] Yet, he pointed out, the Congress drafted the Eleventh Amendment to protect the states only from suits brought against them under the federal courts' diversity jurisdiction. As he went on to say: "If the Framers had meant the Amendment to bar federal-question suits as well, they could not only have made their intention clearer very easily, but could simply have adopted the first post-*Chisholm* proposal adopted by Theodore Sedgwick of Massachusetts on instructions from the Legislature of that Commonwealth." That proposal would have covered expressly what Rehnquist contended the Eleventh Amendment was intended to convey: "[N]o state shall be liable to be made a party defendant, in any of the judicial courts, established, or which shall be established under the authority of the United States, at the suit of any person or persons, whether a citizen or citizens, or a foreigner or foreigners, or any body politic or corporate, whether within or without the United States."[139]

Souter's argument has real power, but, just as with Rehnquist's majority opinion, it failed to confront the implications of the ratification of the Seventeenth Amendment. Souter argues that if the Congress had intended to bar federal question suits, it would have said so. But Congress simply never imagined that the Senate, elected by state legislatures, would ever pass a federal statute allowing states to be sued under the federal courts' federal question jurisdiction and, therefore, saw no need to protect against such a remote possibility. To this, it might be countered that it was the Senate that took the lead in drafting the Judiciary Act of 1789 and that granted the federal courts jurisdiction in cases between a state and citizens of other states or aliens. This counter, however, can, in turn, be rebutted. To begin with, Section 13, which granted state-citizen diversity, merely repeated the words of Article III, Section 2 of the Constitution. More significantly, however, a reasonable construction of Section 13 is that it merely allowed the states to sue, but not reciprocally to be sued by, citizens of other states or aliens; thereby demonstrating that the Senate fully recognized the principle of state sovereign immunity when it passed the Judiciary Act and that it had therefore acted in a manner to protect the interests of the states as such.[140]

City of Boerne v. Flores

In *City of Boerne* v. *Flores*,[141] an activist Supreme Court, by a vote of six to three, struck down the Religious Freedom Restoration Act of 1993 (RFRA), passed unanimously by the House of Representatives and by a vote of ninety-seven to three in the Senate, and signed enthusiastically into law by President Clinton. It did so, because it claimed that RFRA upset "the federal balance."[142]

In *Employment Division, Department of Human Resources of Oregon* v. *Smith*,[143] the Supreme Court held that the Free Exercise Clause of the First Amendment "does not relieve an individual of the obligation to comply with a 'valid and neutral law of general application on the ground that the law proscribes (or prescribes) conduct that his religion prescribes (or proscribes).'"[144] In so ruling, the Court declined to apply the balancing test, previously set forth by Justice Brennan in *Sherbert* v. *Verner*,[145] that asks whether the law at issue substantially burdens a religious practice and, if so, whether the burden is justified by a compelling government interest. In effect, *Smith* held that the Free Exercise Clause protects individuals only from intentional state discrimination on the basis of religion, not from state action that incidentally has a burdensome effect on religious exercise.

Congress enacted RFRA in direct response to the *Smith* decision, which was greeted with an overwhelming storm of protest that united fundamentalist religious groups on the right with the American Civil Liberties Union, Americans United for the Separation of Church and State, and the People for the American Way on the left. RFRA forbade "[g]overnment" from "substantially burden[ing] a person's exercise of religion," even if the burden results from a law of general applicability, unless it can demonstrate that the burden was "in furtherance of a compelling governmental interest" and was "the least restrictive means of furthering that interest." Its mandate applied to any branch of federal or state government and to all officials acting under color of law; its coverage was universal, including "all Federal or State law, and the implementation of that law, whether statutory or otherwise, and whether adopted before or after [RFRA's] enactment."[146] In effect, RFRA held that religious exercise was to be protected from incidental burdens no less than from intentional discrimination.

Congress presented RFRA as merely restoring the balancing test that the Court had been using in free exercise cases after *Sherbert* but that it had abandoned in *Smith*. In truth, however, RFRA went much further and mandated that the *Sherbert* balancing test be applied in all free exercise controversies, not merely in the two areas of law where the Court had previously applied it and which Congress expressly referenced in the statute itself (i.e., in unemployment compensation cases and in *Wisconsin* v. *Yoder*,[147] where the Court exempted the Amish from the need to comply with a state's mandatory school attendance law). RFRA was, in many ways, an ill-conceived measure;[148] nevertheless, a bad law is not necessarily an unconstitutional law, and the Court's invalidation of RFRA was much more problematic than the Act itself.

In imposing RFRA's requirements on the states, Congress had relied on its power under Section 5 of the Fourteenth Amendment "to enforce, by appropriate legislation," the Amendment's guarantee that no state shall deprive any person of "life, liberty, or property, without due process of law" or deny to any person the "equal protection of the laws." The respondent and the United States as *amicus* contended that RFRA was permissible enforcement legislation under Section 5, because it was enforcing the constitutional right to free exercise of religion, made applicable to the states by the Court itself in *Cantwell* v. *Connecticut*.[149] They cited two strong precedents in their favor.[150] First, in *Fitzpatrick* v. *Bitzer*,[151] the Court had upheld application of Title VII of the 1964 Civil Rights Act to state government employers as a legitimate exercise of Congress's Section 5 powers. Title VII gave employees a cause of action for facially neutral employment practices that had a disparate impact on racial minorities. The Court held that, even though the Equal Protection Clause of the Fourteenth Amendment recognized no such cause of action and in fact required a showing of intentional discrimination,[152] Congress had authority under its Section 5 powers to impose on public employers a disparate impact test as a way of "enforcing" the Equal Protection Clause. Second, in *City of Rome* v. *United States*,[153] the Court upheld a Voting Rights Act provision that prohibited state action that had the effect of diluting the votes of minorities, even where there was no intent on the part of the state to do so.[154] In both cases, the Court sustained Congress's enforcement powers to prohibit government conduct that had a disparate impact on minorities, even as it also held that the substantive constitutional provisions that these acts "enforced" were violated only by intentional discrimination. These cases provided what seemed a perfect defense of RFRA, which prohibited state action that had the effect of burdening religious exercise but that the Court had interpreted in *Smith* as permissible under the Free Exercise Clause because not intentionally discriminatory.

Justice Kennedy held for the majority, however, that Congress in this instance lacked the power to enforce such a prohibition against the states. He argued that Congress's enforcement power under Section 5 is merely "preventive" or "corrective" or "remedial, "not "definitional," and, therefore, does not extend to decreeing the substance of the Amendment's restrictions on the states.[155] Congress, he insisted, "does not enforce a constitutional right by changing what the right is. It has been given the power 'to enforce,' not the power to determine what constitutes a constitutional violation."[156] But, as David Cole points out, "the word 'enforce' cannot bear the weight of that claim; after all, it is just as natural to speak of the Court as 'enforcing' the Constitution when it 'determine[s] what constitutes a constitutional violation.'"[157] Moreover, Section 5 simply does not say that Congress has power only to "provide remedies for constitutional violations identified by the courts"; rather it says in much more expansive terms that Congress has power to enforce, by "appropriate" means, the provisions of Section 1. Cole underscores this point: "Had the Framers [of the Fourteenth Amendment] sought to restrict Congress's power to remedial measures, they could have done so expressly."[158]

Kennedy, however, was unmoved by either language or logic. Congress, he argued, has only remedial power under Section 5, and even when it exercises that power, "there must be a congruence and proportionality between the injury to be prevented or remedied and the means adopted to that end. Lacking such a connection, legislation may become substantive in operation and effect."[159] The Congress is limited to remedying only those problems that the Court itself considers serious enough to justify intervention. Religious bigotry, he continued was not a serious enough problem and, therefore, did not justify congressional remediation. He dismissed congressional hearings on the need for RFRA as focusing only on "incidental burdens of religion. Much of the discussion centered upon anecdotal evidence of autopsies performed on Jewish individuals and Hmong immigrants in violation of their religious beliefs."[160] From his vantage point inside the Marble Palace, he saw no "widespread pattern of religious discrimination in this country" sufficient to make RFRA an "appropriate" response. In fact, he railed, "RFRA is so out of proportion to a supposed remedial or preventive object that it cannot be understood as responsive to, or designed to prevent, unconstitutional behavior."[161]

Kennedy was quick to prohibit Congress from using its Section 5 powers to effect a shift in the federal-state balance.[162] Interestingly, however, he utterly failed to comprehend that Congress's assault on federalism in RFRA was trivial compared with (and even fundamentally-dependent upon) the Court's own earlier assault in *Cantwell* v. *Connecticut* in 1940 when it held that the Free Exercise Clause of the First Amendment was incorporated by the Fourteenth Amendment's Due Process Clause to apply to the states. [163] As Cole notes, "RFRA does not directly enforce Section 1 of the Fourteenth Amendment, but rather enforces the First Amendment as it has been incorporated and applied to the states through the Fourteenth Amendment's Due Process Clause. The paradoxical result is that an amendment expressly written to restrict Congress's own power to encroach on religious freedom has been transformed, via incorporation, into a positive authorization of congressional power to regulate the states."[164] The First Amendment begins "Congress shall make no law," but once the Court incorporated it to apply to the states, the sponsors of RFRA felt justified to read it, in the light of Section 5, as follows: "'Congress shall have the power to enforce, by appropriate legislation, the principle that the states shall make no law' burdening the free exercise of religion."[165] Since Congress merely "piggybacked" RFRA on *Cantwell*, the Court's eagerness to condemn Congress for what it perceived to be the harm that RFRA wrecked on federalism while remaining completely oblivious of the far-greater harm the Court itself has caused through its many incorporation decisions reminds one of nothing so much as the Biblical denunciation of hypocrisy: "Why beholdest thou the mote that is in thy brother's eye, but perceivest not the beam that is in thine own eye? . . . Thou hypocrite, cast out first the beam out of thine own eye, and then shalt thou see clearly to pull out the mote that is in thy brother's eye."[166]

Printz v. United States

The issue in *New York* v. *United States* of commandeering state officials surfaced again in *Printz* v. *United States*,[167] as the Court considered the constitutionality of those provisions of the Brady Handgun Violence Prevention Act that commanded the "chief law enforcement officer" (CLEO) of each local jurisdiction to conduct background checks on prospective handgun purchasers on an interim basis until a national instant background check system became operational in late 1998.[168] Justice Antonin Scalia held for a five-member majority that this congressional command was "fundamentally incompatible with our constitutional system of dual sovereignty" and was, therefore, unconstitutional.[169] Contrary to O'Connor in *New York*, Scalia acknowledged that there was no constitutional text, not even the Tenth Amendment, that spoke to the precise question of whether congressional action compelling state officers to execute federal laws was unconstitutional. Therefore, he turned for an answer to historical understanding and practice, the structure of the Constitution, and Court precedent.

Scalia began by researching historical understanding and practice. He reviewed the actions of the early Congresses, observed that they studiously "avoided use of this highly attractive power," and concluded that "the power was thought not to exist."[170] He would have been more precise if he had said that the power to commandeer state officials may indeed have existed but that the Senate, elected by state legislatures and therefore representing the interests of the states as states, simply refused to accede to its use.

Scalia then turned to the structure of the Constitution, where, most interestingly, he ultimately found federal commandeering of state officials to be unconstitutional not so much because it violated the principles of federalism but because it violated separation of powers. He noted that "[t]he Constitution does not leave to speculation who is to administer the laws enacted by Congress; the President, it says, 'shall take Care that the Laws be faithfully executed,' personally and through officers whom he appoints."[171] The Brady Act, however, effectively transferred this responsibility to thousands of state and local law-enforcement officers in the fifty states, who, as Scalia pointed out, "are left to implement the program without meaningful Presidential control (if indeed meaningful Presidential control is possible without the power to appoint and remove). The insistence of the Framers upon unity in the Federal Executive—to insure both vigor and accountability—is well known. That unity," Scalia concluded, "would be shattered, and the power of the President would be subject to reduction, if Congress could act as effectively without the President as with him, by simply requiring state officers to execute its laws."[172] This argument comes, of course, directly from his dissent in *Morrison* v. *Olson*,[173] in which he argued against the constitutionality of the independent counsel statute. In *Morrison*, Scalia wrote for himself alone; in *Printz*, however, by sugarcoating his separation-of-powers argument with a defense of federalism, he was able to write for a five-member majority.

Finally, Scalia turned to the Court's previous decisions on commandeering. He found them "conclusive,"[174] although, given the arm's-length distance he kept from the Tenth Amendment and in light of the separation-of-powers argument he had just made, perhaps not wholly persuasive.

In the lead dissent, Justice Stevens pointed out the irony of a decision intended to protect federalism that results in the further growth of the federal government: "Perversely, the majority's rul[ing] seems more likely to damage than to preserve the safeguards against tyranny provided by the existence of vital state governments. By limiting the ability of the Federal Government to enlist state officials in the implementation of its programs," Stevens noted that the Court simply created "incentives for the National Government to aggrandize itself. In the name of state's rights, the majority would have the Federal Government create vast national bureaucracies to implement its policies."[175] Stevens, of course, was only scoring debaters' points—the Congress was busily creating a "vast national bureaucrac[y]" to implement the Brady Act and had "enlist[ed] state officials" only on an interim basis. His better argument was his criticism of Scalia—the justice on the Court most closely associated with a textualist approach to constitutional interpretation[176]—for departing from the text: "There is not a clause, sentence, or paragraph in the entire text of the Constitution of the United States that supports the proposition that a local police officer can ignore a command contained in a statute enacted by Congress pursuant to an express delegation of power enumerated in Article I."[177]

Florida Prepaid Postsecondary Education Expense Board v. *College Savings Bank*

On June 23, 1999, the Court handed down three separate decisions striking down different provisions of federal law that abrogated state sovereign immunity. They were *Florida Prepaid Postsecondary Education Expense Board* v. *College Savings Bank*,[178] *College Savings Bank* v. *Florida Prepaid Postsecondary Education Expense Board*,[179] and *Alden* v. *Maine*.[180] Each of these cases was decided by the same five-to-four vote, with Chief Justice Rehnquist and Justices Kennedy, O'Connor, Scalia, and Thomas in the majority and Justices Breyer, Ginsburg, Souter, and Stevens in dissent. Each case is taken up in turn.

In *Florida Prepaid Postsecondary Education Expense Board* v. *College Savings Bank*, the Court invalidated the Patent Remedy Act of 1992 that expressly abrogated state sovereignty immunity from claims of patent infringement. College Savings Bank, a New Jersey institution, obtained a patent for the financing methodology of its "CollegeSure" certificate of deposit, an annuity contract for financing future college tuition expenses. When the Florida Prepaid Postsecondary Education Expense Board, a state-created entity, created a similar tuition prepayment contract available to Florida residents, College Saving brought suit in federal district court, claiming that Florida Prepaid had infringed on its patent. Florida Prepaid cited *Seminole Tribe* and moved to dismiss, arguing that the Patent Remedy Act was an unconstitutional attempt by Congress to use its Article I powers to abrogate state sovereign immunity. College Savings countered that Congress had exercised its power not under Article I but under Section 5 of the Fourteenth Amendment to enforce the guarantees of the Due Process Clause in Section I.

Agreeing with College Savings, the District Court for the District of New Jersey denied Florida Prepaid's motion to dismiss, and the Court of Appeals for the Federal Circuit affirmed.

In his majority opinion, Chief Justice Rehnquist rehearsed the three basic conclusions of his *Seminole Tribe* opinion: (1) The Eleventh Amendment stands "not so much for what it says, but for the presupposition . . . which it confirms"; (2) That presupposition precludes suits against a state in federal court under not only diversity but also federal question jurisdiction unless the state expressly consents to suit or unless Congress expressly abrogates state sovereign immunity; and (3) Congress has no power to abrogate sovereign immunity under Article I of the Constitution (which was trumped by the Eleventh Amendment) but has power to do so only under Section 5 of the Fourteenth Amendment (which, in turn, trumps the Eleventh Amendment).[181] To the conclusions of *Seminole Tribe* Rehnquist then added the conclusion of *City of Boerne*: Congress's enforcement power under Section 5 is merely "'remedial' in nature."[182]

Rehnquist then asked whether the Patent Remedy Act could be "viewed as remedial or preventive legislation aimed at securing the protections of the Fourteenth Amendment for patent owners."[183] He answered in the negative. The legislative record leading to the passage of the Patent Remedy Act established "no pattern of patent infringement by the States, let alone a pattern of constitutional violations."[184] In fact, he continued, "the evidence before Congress suggested that most state infringement was innocent or at worst negligent" and did not rise to the level of a violation of the Due Process Clause.[185] Consequently, the Act was "so out of proportion to the supposed remedial or preventive object" that it could not be understood as "designed to prevent unconstitutional behavior." Accordingly, it could not be sustained under Section 5.

With the abrogation-of-state-sovereign-immunity provision of the Patent Remedy Act declared unconstitutional, where could College Savings Bank go to seek protection from Florida Prepaid's infringement of its patent? Rehnquist suggested the Florida state courts, but that suggestion rang hollow, for he acknowledged that state remedies might well be "less convenient than federal remedies, and might undermine the uniformity of patent law."[186] He insisted, however, that the principle of state sovereign immunity was more important than convenience or uniformity. It would be time to consider whether it would be "appropriate" for Congress to remedy "arguable constitutional violations" by abrogating state sovereign immunity if a case arose in which a state were to refuse "to offer any state-court remedy for patent owners whose patents it had infringed."[187] As Justice Stevens pointed out in the dissent, however, such a congressional remedy was available only in theory.[188] To begin with, "Congress had long ago preempted state jurisdiction over patent infringement cases,"[189] and, as a result, "[s]tate judges have never had the exposure to patent litigation that federal judges have experienced for decades." Moreover, even if federal law were amended to "permit state courts to entertain infringement actions when a State is named as a defendant, given the Court's opinion in *Alden* v. *Maine* [discussed below], it is by no means clear that state courts would be required to hear these cases at all."[190]

In the name of federalism, the Court was willing to sacrifice the rights of patent holders. The Court majority, relying on its dubious conclusions in *Seminole Tribe* and *City of Boerne* to reach a conclusion here more dubious still, departed from the clear text of Article I, Section 8 authorizing Congress to secure "for limited times to authors and inventors the exclusive right to their respective writings and discoveries." It appeared so enamored with its formal logic that it forgot what Justice O'Connor claimed in *New York* v. *United States* was the "fundamental purpose" served by federalism: "The Constitution does not protect the sovereignty of States for the benefit of the States or state governments as abstract political entities.... To the contrary, the Constitution divides authority between federal and state governments for the protection of individuals. State sovereignty is not just an end in itself."[191]

College Savings Bank v.
Florida Prepaid Postsecondary Education Expense Board

College Savings Bank sued Florida Prepaid not only for patent infringement but also for violating the Trademark Remedy Clarification Act (TRCA), which subjected states to suits brought under the Trademark Act of 1946 for false and misleading advertising. College Savings alleged that Florida Prepaid was guilty of misrepresenting its own program. Florida Prepaid moved to dismiss this suit as well; it again argued that Congress's attempt to abrogate state sovereign immunity was unconstitutional because the TRCA, like the Patent Remedy Act, was enacted pursuant to Congress's Article I powers held by *Seminole Tribe* to have been trumped by the Eleventh Amendment. College Savings responded that the TRCA was constitutional because it was enacted not merely pursuant to Congress's powers under Article I but also pursuant to its Section 5 power to enforce the Due Process Clause of the Fourteenth Amendment. It also argued that, under the doctrine of constructive waiver, articulated by the Court in *Parden* v. *Terminal Railroad Company*,[192] Florida

Prepaid had voluntarily waived its immunity by engaging in interstate marketing and administration of its program after the TRCA made clear that such activity would subject it to suit. This time, however, the same District Court rejected College Savings' arguments and dismissed its suit. After the Court of Appeals for the Federal Circuit affirmed, the Supreme Court granted certiorari and held that federal courts have no jurisdiction to entertain this suit because Florida's sovereign immunity was neither constitutionally abrogated by the TRCA nor voluntarily waived.

In his opinion for the Court, Justice Scalia first denied College Savings Bank's claim that Congress had power under Section 5 to pass the TRCA to remedy and prevent state deprivations of property without due process. There simply is no property right, he insisted, to be free from a "competitor's false advertising about its own product";[193] there was, therefore, no constitutional violation for Congress to remedy and, hence, no power under Section 5 for Congress to abrogate state sovereign immunity.

Scalia then turned to the question of whether Florida had voluntarily waived its immunity by its activities in interstate commerce. College Savings had relied on the Court's 1964 decision in *Parden* to argue that Florida Prepaid had "'impliedly' or 'constructively' waived its immunity,"[194] since Congress had provided unambiguously in the TRCA that states would be subject to private suit if they engaged in certain federally regulated conduct and Florida Prepaid had thereafter voluntarily elected to engage in that conduct.

Parden, Scalia argued, was no longer good law; it stood "at the nadir of our waiver (and, for that matter, sovereign immunity) jurisprudence." Accordingly, he declared it to be "expressly overruled."[195] It could not be squared with the Court's "cases requiring that a state's express waiver be unequivocal"; as Scalia pointed out, "[t]here is a fundamental difference between a State's expressing unequivocally that it waives its immunity, and Congress's expressing unequivocally its intention that if the State takes certain action it shall be deemed to have waived that immunity."[196] Nor could it be squared with the principle that a state's waiver must be voluntary—he insisted that "the voluntariness of waiver" is destroyed "when what is attached to the refusal to waive is the exclusion of the State from otherwise lawful activity" such as, in the instant case, engaging in interstate marketing.[197]

In his dissent, Justice Stevens questioned the assumption that "Florida Prepaid is an 'arm of the State' of Florida." He noted that when the doctrine of sovereign immunity first arose in the eighteenth century, "sovereigns did not then play the kind of role in the commercial marketplace that they do today."[198] In the lead dissent, Justice Breyer developed this theme at length: "When a state engages in ordinary commercial ventures, it acts like a private person, outside the area of its 'core' responsibilities, and in a way unlikely to prove essential to the fulfillment of basic governmental obligations."[199] In fact, if Congress were to treat the states differently from their identically situated private competitors, it would place those competitors "at a significant disadvantage."[200] For Breyer, the conclusion was clear:

> These considerations make Congress's need to possess the power to condition entry into the market upon a waiver of sovereign immunity (as "necessary and proper" to the exercise of its commerce power) unusually strong, for to deny Congress that power would deny Congress the power effectively to regulate private conduct. At the same time they make a State's need to exercise sovereign immunity unusually weak, for the State is unlikely to have to supply what private firms already supply, nor may it fairly demand special treatment, even to protect the public purse, when it does so. Neither can one imagine what the Constitution's founders would have thought about the assertion of sovereign immunity in this special context.[201]

Since Breyer's argument above presupposed that Congress has power under the Commerce Clause to abrogate state sovereign immunity, a major portion of his dissent was an attack on the Court majority's reliance on *Seminole Tribe* (in which the Court denied that Congress has such a power) and its refusal to abide by the actual text of the Eleventh Amendment.[202] He also faulted the majority for its failure to appreciate that "courts cannot easily draw the proper lines of authority" between the states and national government: "[J]udicial rules that would allocate power are often far too broad. Legislatures, however, can write laws that more specifically embody that balance."[203] His statement certainly was true of the pre-Seventeenth Amendment Congress, with its senators elected by state legislatures and therefore keenly aware of the need to balance both the interests of the states they represented and the national government they served.

Alden v. Maine

Of the three sovereign immunity cases handed down by the Court on June 23, 1999, perhaps the most significant was *Alden* v. *Maine*. Whereas in the two *Florida Prepaid* cases (and *Seminole Tribe*, on which they were based), the Court stretched almost beyond recognition the text of the

Eleventh Amendment in order to hold that the federal courts have neither diversity nor federal question jurisdiction in cases in which a state is sued, in *Alden* it abandoned the text of the Eleventh Amendment altogether (since, after all, it spoke only of "the judicial power of the United States," not of the judicial power of the states) and held that state sovereign immunity, confirmed by the Eleventh Amendment, bars Congress from authorizing private actions against states in their own courts.

In *Alden*, a group of probation officers filed suit in 1992 in the United States District Court for the District of Maine against their employer, the State of Maine, for its failure to abide by the overtime provisions of the Fair Labor Standards Act of 1938, made applicable by Congress to the states in 1974 and upheld as constitutional by the Supreme Court in *Garcia* in 1984. Their suit was still pending when the Supreme Court held in *Seminole Tribe* that Congress lacked power under Article I of the Constitution to abrogate state sovereign immunity from suits in the federal courts. In light of *Seminole Tribe*, the district court dismissed their action, and the Court of Appeals for the First Circuit affirmed. The probation officers then filed the same action in state court, where the state trial court dismissed the suit on the basis of sovereign immunity and the Maine Supreme Judicial Court affirmed. The United States Supreme Court granted certiorari in order to address the question of the constitutionality of the provisions of the Fair Labor Standards Act authorizing private actions against states in their own courts without their consent.

In the majority opinion, Justice Kennedy admitted what the authors of the majority opinions in *Seminole Tribe* and the two *Florida Prepaid* refused to admit: There is no such thing as "Eleventh Amendment immunity." That phrase, he conceded, "is a convenient shorthand but something of a misnomer, for the sovereign immunity of the States neither derives from nor is limited by the terms of the Eleventh Amendment."[204] Rather, "the States' immunity from suit is a fundamental aspect of the sovereignty which the States enjoyed before the ratification of the Constitution"[205] and which was "confirm[ed]" by the Tenth Amendment.[206] The States, he continued, retain this immunity "today (either literally or by virtue of their admission into the Union upon an equal footing with the other States) except as altered by the plan of the Convention or certain constitutional amendments."[207]

Justice Kennedy observed that the question whether Congress has authority under Article I to abrogate a state's immunity from suit in its own courts was "a question of first impression" for which "the historical record gives no instruction as to the founding generation's intent."[208] He confidently asserted that "the founders' silence is best explained by the simple fact that no one, not even the Constitution's most ardent opponents, suggested the document might strip the States of the immunity."[209] He went so far as to declare that "it is difficult to conceive that the Constitution would have been adopted if it had been understood to strip the States of immunity from suit in their own courts."[210] Under the original Constitution, in which the Senate was elected by state legislatures and in which senators therefore both represented and protected the interests of the states as states, there was, of course, little reason to fear that the Congress would subject the states to private suits in their own courts. As Kennedy pointed out, "sovereign immunity derive[d] not from the Eleventh Amendment but from the structure of the original Constitution itself."[211] That structure, however, was radically altered by the adoption of the Seventeenth Amendment providing for direct election of the Senate. Kennedy, early in his opinion, acknowledged that immunity could be altered by subsequent constitutional amendments. He was thinking, of course, of the Fourteenth Amendment and Congress's power to authorize private suits against nonconsenting states pursuant to its Section 5 enforcement powers;[212] however, he failed altogether to consider the consequences of the adoption of the Seventeenth Amendment. Had he done so, he would have appreciated that this subsequent constitutional amendment altered the structure of the original Constitution and therefore altered state sovereign immunity; he would have recognized that what kept the Congress from initially authorizing private suits against the states in their own courts was not a lack of congressional power to abrogate state sovereign immunity but rather a refusal to do so, given the mode of electing the Senate.

Kennedy also offered another reason for why Congress could not abrogate a state's immunity from suit in its own courts: As a consequence of the Court's decisions in *Seminole Tribe* and the two *Florida Prepaid* cases, "Congress cannot abrogate the States' sovereign immunity in federal court; were the rule to be different here, the National Government would wield greater power in the state courts than in its own judicial instrumentalities."[213] For him, such a consequence was unthinkable, and he used this unthinkable consequence to justify his conclusion, not to call into question the very premises on which his and the Court majority's entire immunity jurisprudence was based.

Justice Souter wrote the dissent. He rehearsed at length what he had previously argued in *Seminole Tribe* concerning the meaning of *Chisholm v. Georgia*, prompting Justice Scalia to observe in his *Florida Prepaid* opinion that he engaged "in a degree of repetitive detail that has despoiled our northern woods."[214] He also delivered, however, a thoroughly devastating blow to Kennedy's opinion by his simple declaration that the

Supremacy Clause, "which requires state courts to enforce federal law and state-court judges to be bound by it, requires the Maine courts to entertain this federal cause of action."[215] The Court in *Garcia* had declared the Fair Labor Standards Act and its subsequent amendments to be constitutional, i.e., to be "made in pursuance" of the Constitution.[216] The Act was therefore "the supreme law of the law," and, according to the Supremacy Clause, it thereby bound the judges in every state, "any thing in the Constitution or laws of any state to the contrary notwithstanding." Souter drove this point home: State court judges were therefore bound by *Garcia* and by the clear textual language of the Supremacy Clause, not by the nontextual claims of state sovereign immunity.

Souter acknowledged that the framers would be no less "surprised to see States subjected to suit in their own courts under the commerce power" than they would be "astonished by the reach of Congress under the Commerce Clause generally."[217] For him, however, that is the consequence of a "living Constitution," and he quoted approvingly Justice Oliver Wendell Holmes's regrettable formulation in *Missouri* v. *Holland*[218] that "[w]hen we are dealing with words that also are a constituent act, like the Constitution of the United States, we must realize that they have called into life a being the development of which could not have been foreseen completely by the most gifted of its begetters. It was enough for them to realize that they had created an organism; it has taken a century and has cost their successors much sweat and blood to prove that they created a nation."[219] No less than his colleagues in the majority, Souter utterly failed to recognize that Congress always had power to abrogate state sovereign immunity—a power it has exercised with some regularity and ease once the original structural impediment to its use, namely a Senate elected by state legislatures, was removed by the Seventeenth Amendment.

Kimel v. *Florida Board of Regents*

In *Kimel* v. *Florida Board of Regents*,[220] the Supreme Court continued along the path it had laid out in *City of Boerne* and the two *Florida Prepaid* cases by holding that Congress exceeded its authority under Section 5 of the Fourteenth Amendment when it abrogated state sovereign immunity for suits charging states with discrimination because of an individual's age. In the Age Discrimination in Employment Act of 1967 (ADEA), as amended in 1974, Congress made it unlawful for an employer, including a state, "to fail or refuse to hire or to discharge any individual or otherwise discriminate against any individual because of such individual's age." While the Court had earlier found in *Equal Employment Opportunity Commission* v. *Wyoming*[221] that Congress's 1974 extension of the ADEA to state and local governments was a constitutional exercise of its powers under the Commerce Clause, it had not previously ruled on whether states could be sued without their consent for their refusal to abide by its provisions. In *Kimel*, by a five-to-four vote, it determined that they could not.

Following the argument laid out in the two *Florida Prepaid* cases, Justice O'Connor declared that an ADEA suit against a state could be maintained only if the Act were "appropriate legislation" under Section 5 of the Fourteenth Amendment. Relying on *City of Boerne*'s insistence that Section 5 gave Congress only the power to prevent or remedy violations of the Fourteenth Amendment but not to define its substance, and on its language that "[t]here must be a congruence and proportionality between the injury to be prevented or remedied and the means adopted to that end,"[222] O'Connor concluded that the ADEA was not "appropriate legislation." To begin with, she noted that age classifications that are rationally related to a legitimate state interest do not violate the Equal Protection Clause of the Fourteenth Amendment. Furthermore, Congress never identified any pattern of age discrimination by the states that would justify Congress in using its Section 5 enforcement powers to prevent or remedy such conduct. "In light of the indiscriminate scope of the Act's substantive requirements, and the lack of evidence of widespread and unconstitutional age discrimination by the States, we hold that the ADEA is not a valid exercise of Congress's power under Section 5 of the Fourteenth Amendment. The ADEA's purposed abrogation of the States' sovereign immunity is accordingly invalid."[223]

In his dissent, Justice Stevens attacked the Court for "the kind of judicial activism manifested" in *Kimel* and the Court's other recent sovereign immunity cases, which, he declared "represents such a radical departure from the proper role of this Court that it should be opposed whenever the opportunity arises."[224] He might have added as well how self-defeating the Court's activism in these cases was: In the name of protecting the principle of federalism, the Court unwittingly undercut the states' moral and political standing by allowing them to discriminate against older people and to violate patent and trademark laws, and by declaring that their courts are not bound under the Supremacy Clause to enforce the rights of employees as guaranteed in laws the Court concedes are constitutional. Stevens then unfortunately proceeded to undercut his principled opposition to activism by badly misstating the "process federalism" that he argued justifies judicial deference. "It is the Framers' compromise giving each State equal representation in the Senate that provides the principal structural protection for the sovereignty of the several States."[225] In truth, it was not equal representation that provided the structural protection for federalism, but rather the mode of electing the Senate. Moreover, in the post-Seventeenth Amendment era, it is simply wrong to speak of any remaining structural protection for federalism. Stevens should have argued that the Supreme Court should defer to what Congress enacts, not because the political process is protecting federalism, but because federalism as a viable constitutional principle is dead and, indeed, has been so for nearly a century.

United States v. *Morrison*

In *United States* v. *Morrison*,[226] the Supreme Court held, by still another five-to-four vote, that Congress lacked the constitutional authority to enact a key provision of the Violence Against Women Act (VAWA) of 1994 under either the original Constitution's Article I, Section 8 (the Commerce Clause) or Section 5 of the Fourteenth Amendment, both of which Congress had explicitly identified as sources of its authority to legislate in this area. Christy Brzonkala filed suit in the United States District Court for the Western District of Virginia, alleging that she was raped by two of her fellow students at the Virginia Polytechnic Institute and that this attack violated VAWA, which provided a federal civil remedy for victims of gender-motivated violence. When the respondents moved to dismiss, arguing that VAWA's civil remedy was unconstitutional, the United States intervened to defend its constitutionality. The district court and an *en banc* Court of Appeals for the Fourth Circuit, relying on the Supreme Court's decisions in *Lopez* and *City of Boerne*, agreed with the respondents and invalidated the statute. The Supreme Court granted certiorari.

In his majority opinion, Chief Justice Rehnquist expressed concern that if the Court were to uphold Congress's authority under the Commerce Clause to enact VAWA, the result would be "to completely obliterate the Constitution's distinction between national and local authority."

> The reasoning that petitioners advance seeks to follow the but-for causal chain from the initial occurrence of violent crime (the suppression of which has always been the prime object of the States' police power) to every attenuated effect upon interstate commerce. If accepted, petitioners' reasoning would allow Congress to regulate any crime as long as the nationwide, aggregated impact of that crime has substantial effects on employment, production, transit, or consumption. Indeed, if Congress may regulate gender-motivated violence, it would be able to regulate murder or any other type of violence since gender-

motivated violence, as a subset of all violent crime, is certain to have
lesser economic impacts than the larger class of which it is a part.[227]

Rehnquist feared that a Court decision affirming the constitutionality
of VAWA would provide Congress with authority to legislate on matters of
family law as well: "Petitioners' reasoning, moreover, will not limit Congress
to regulating violence but may . . . be applied equally as well to family law
and other areas of traditional state regulation since the aggregate effect of
marriage, divorce, and childrearing on the national economy is undoubtedly
significant. Congress may have recognized this specter when it expressly
precluded [VAWA] from being used in the family law context. Under our
written Constitution, however, the limitation of congressional authority is
not solely a matter of legislative grace."[228]

Rehnquist also rejected the argument that Congress had power under
Section 5 of the Fourteenth Amendment to enact VAWA. The United States
government had asserted that there was "pervasive bias" in various state justice
systems against victims of gender-motivated violence, an assertion it said was
supported by a voluminous congressional record. It argued that Congress had
received evidence that many state justice systems were perpetuating an array
of erroneous stereotypes and assumptions, and that Congress had concluded
on the basis of this evidence that these discriminatory stereotypes often resulted
in insufficient investigation and prosecution of gender-motivated crime,
inappropriate focus on the behavior and credibility of the victims of that crime,
and unacceptably lenient punishments for those who were actually convicted
of gender-motivated violence. It argued that this bias, in turn, denied victims
of gender-motivated violence the equal protection of the laws and that Congress
therefore had acted appropriately and in keeping with *City of Boerne* when it
enacted VAWA to remedy the states' bias and deter future instances of
discrimination in the state courts. Rehnquist responded, however, that the
framers of the Fourteenth Amendment placed "limitations" on Congress's power
to attack discriminatory conduct in order "to prevent the Fourteenth Amendment
from obliterating the Framers' carefully crafted balance of power between the
States and the National Government," and that "foremost among these
limitations" is the "time honored principle that the Fourteenth Amendment, by
its very terms, prohibits only state action."[229] He noted that VAWA's civil
remedies were not directed at "gender-based disparate treatment by state
authorities" but "at individuals who have committed criminal acts motivated
by gender bias." They visited "no consequences on any . . . public official" but
rather reached only private conduct. As a consequence, he concluded that

"Congress's power under Section 5 does not extend to the enactment" of VAWA.[230]

Justice Souter filed the principal dissent. He pointed out that the legislative record supporting the passage of VAWA was "far more voluminous than the record compiled by Congress and found sufficient" by the Court in upholding the 1964 Civil Rights Act. In both *Heart of Atlanta Motel, Inc.* v. *United States* and *Katzenbach* v. *McClung*, the Court referred to the anecdotal evidence on which Congress had relied to show the consequences of racial discrimination by motels and restaurants on interstate commerce. Souter pointed out that the Court found that evidence to be adequate and conclusive, even though "Congress did not, to my knowledge, calculate aggregate dollar values for the nationwide effects of racial discrimination in 1964." By contrast, in 1994, Congress did calculate the price the nation paid for "the harms caused by domestic violence and sexual assault, citing annual costs of $3 billion in 1990." Equally important for Souter in finding VAWA constitutional was the fact that "gender-based violence in the 1990s was shown to operate in a manner similar to racial discrimination in the 1960s in reducing the mobility of employees and their production and consumption of goods shipped in interstate commerce. Like racial discrimination, '[g]ender-based violence bars its most likely targets—women—from full partic[ipation] in the national economy.'"[231]

Souter's principal objection, however, was "the majority's rejection of the Founders' considered judgment that politics, not judicial review, should mediate between state and national interests."[232] Since the Founding, politics, he pointed out, had "markedly changed" the "relative powers of the two sovereign systems."[233] In particular, Souter noted, politics had led to the adoption and ratification of the Fourteenth and Seventeenth Amendments. He then drew the logical conclusion: "Amendments that alter the balance of power between the National and State Governments, like the Fourteenth, or that change the way the States are represented within the Federal Government, like the Seventeenth, are not rips in the fabric of the Framers' Constitution, inviting judicial repairs. The Seventeenth Amendment may indeed have lessened the enthusiasm of the Senate to represent the States as discrete sovereignties, but the Amendment did not convert the judiciary into an alternate shield against the commerce power."[234]

Trustees of the University of Alabama v. Garrett

Finally, in 2001, in *Trustees of the University of Alabama* v. *Garrett*,[235] the Supreme Court held, again by a vote of five to four (with Justices O'Connor, Scalia, Kennedy, and Thomas joining Chief Justice Rehnquist's majority opinion; and with Justices Stevens, Souter, and Ginsburg joining Justice Breyer's dissent), that Congress, when it passed the Americans with Disabilities Act of 1990 (ADA),[236] lacked the authority to abrogate state sovereign immunity and to allow state employees to recover monetary damages by reason of the state's failure to comply with the Act's provisions. Chief Justice Rehnquist no longer felt obliged even to recite the mantra that the Eleventh Amendment stands "not so much for what it says as for the presupposition . . . which it confirms."[237] Having become accustomed in so many recent cases to ignoring the actual text of the Eleventh Amendment, he was content simply to invoke precedent: "Although by its terms the Amendment applies only to suits against a State by citizens of another State, our cases have extended the Amendment's applicability to suits by citizens against their own States."[238]

Proceeding in an utterly formulaic manner, Rehnquist acknowledged that the Eleventh Amendment and the principle of state sovereignty which it embodies are necessarily limited by the enforcement provisions of Section 5 of the Fourteenth Amendment. However, he then repeated the assertions of the Court in *City of Boerne* that "it is the responsibility of this Court, not Congress, to define the substance of constitutional guarantees" and that any legislation that Congress passes under its Section 5 enforcement powers that reaches "beyond the scope of Section 1's actual guarantees must exhibit 'congruence and proportionality between the injury to be prevented or remedied and the means adopted to that end.'"[239] With these arguments in play, the question whether Congress could apply the provisions of the ADA to the states almost answered itself.

The Court, Rehnquist continued, had previously declared in *Cleburne* v. *Cleburne Living Center*[240] that state discrimination based on disability is not "suspect" and violates the Fourteenth Amendment only if it fails to pass the minimal "rational-basis" test. Therefore, Congress's attempt in the ADA to prohibit the states from "discriminating against a qualified individual with a disability" and to require that they make "reasonable accommodations to the known physical and mental limitations of an otherwise qualified individual" went beyond "the actual scope of Section 1's actual guarantees,"[241] because it was not irrational for states to refuse to hire the disabled. As Rehnquist noted: "[I]t would be entirely rational (and therefore constitutional) for a state employer to conserve scarce financial resources by hiring employees who are able to use existing facilities."[242]

Since the ADA's provisions went beyond "the actual scope of Section 1's actual guarantees," they could be upheld by the Court only if they were congruent and proportional means to the end of eliminating discrimination against the disabled by the states. But, in an argument reminiscent of O'Connor's in *Kimel*, Kennedy's in *City of Boerne*, and his own in *College Savings Bank*, Rehnquist denied that the ADA's provisions making it applicable to the states exhibited that necessary "congruence and proportionality." He reviewed the legislative record of the ADA and concluded that Congress had failed to identify a "pattern of irrational state discrimination in employment against the disabled"[243] that alone could justify the Act's application to the states—the record, he insisted, revealed no more than "half a dozen examples" and fell "far short of even suggesting the pattern of unconstitutional discrimination on which Section 5 legislation must be based."[244] Since there was no "pattern of discrimination by the States which violates the Fourteenth Amendment," the ADA's remedy of abrogating sovereign immunity and authorizing disabled state employees who have been discriminated against by their employers to bring suit against the state to recover money damages was not "congruent and proportional to the targeted violation" and was therefore an unconstitutional violation of the Eleventh Amendment.[245]

Justice Breyer's dissent attacked the majority opinion on three separate fronts. First, he denied that the remedy of allowing disabled state employees to sue their state employers lacked "congruence and proportionality." Rehnquist was wrong, he insisted, when he said there were only "half a dozen" instances of state discrimination. He attached to his opinion an appendix that listed 561 examples of discrimination by state and local governments that were submitted to a special task force that Congress created to assess the need for comprehensive disability legislation. Based on those examples, Breyer argued that "Congress could have reasonably believed" that there was a "widespread problem of unconstitutional discrimination" in need of a federal remedy.[246]

Second, Breyer challenged the Court's use of *Cleburne* and its "rational-basis" test to limit what Congress could do under its Section 5 powers. The "rational-basis" test, with "its presumptions favoring constitutionality," is an appropriate rule for judges, but, he insisted, it should not apply to "Congress when it exercises its Section 5 power."[247] "There is simply no reason to require Congress, seeking to determine facts relevant to the exercise of its Section 5 authority, to adopt rules or presumptions that reflect a court's institutional limitations."[248] He drew several clear distinctions between courts and the Congress:

Unlike courts, Congress can gather facts from across the Nation, assess the magnitude of a problem, and more easily find an appropriate remedy. Unlike courts, Congress directly reflects public attitudes and beliefs, enabling Congress better to understand where, and to what extent, refusals to accommodate a disability amount to behavior that is callous and unreasonable to the point of lacking constitutional justification. Unlike judges, Members of Congress can directly obtain information from constituents who have first-hand experience with discrimination and related issues. Moreover, unlike judges, Members of Congress are elected. . . . To apply a rule designed to restrict courts as if it restricted Congress' legislative power is to stand the underlying principle—a principle of judicial restraint—on its head.[249]

Third, Breyer accused the majority of adopting "[r]ules for interpreting Section 5" that "run counter to the very object of the Fourteenth Amendment." That Amendment was intended to prohibit states "from denying their citizens equal protection of the laws," not to provide them "with special protections" when they do so. He saw a constitutional irony in how the Court stood this principle, too, on its head. "[I]ronically, the greater the obstacle the Eleventh Amendment poses to the creation by Congress of the kind of remedy at issue here—the decentralized remedy of private damage actions—the more Congress, seeking to cure important national problems, such as the problem of disability discrimination before us, will have to rely on more uniform remedies, such as federal standards and court injunctions, which are sometimes draconian and typically more intrusive."[250]

* * * * *

In *Morrison*, Souter complained that an activist Court had come to view its role as the defender of the original federal design. In *Garrett*, Breyer charged that the Court had come to treat the Fourteenth Amendment as a shield, protecting the states from federal legislation, rather than as a sword, protecting the people from constitutional violations by the states. What underlies their criticisms is their conviction that the current Court has failed to appreciate that the framers relied on politics and not the judiciary to protect the federal balance. Chapters 2 and 3 take up the framers' understanding of how federalism was to be protected. Chapter 2 discusses why and how the framers relied on structural means to secure the ends of the Constitution. Chapter 3 then shows how they understood that the mode of electing the Senate (and not, as some on the Court have asserted, equal representation of all states in the Senate) was to be the principal structural means for securing federalism and demarcating the line between federal and state powers. It also argues that the framers never contemplated that the interests of the states as such were to be protected by the Court, and that they would have rejected out of hand the judicial activism the current Court has routinely displayed in the name of federalism.

Notes

1. 301 U.S. 1 (1937). As David P. Currie has written, "constitutional federalism died" with the Court's decision in *Jones & Laughlin*. David P. Currie, *The Constitution in the Supreme Court: The Second Century, 1888-1986* (Chicago: University of Chicago Press, 1990), 238.

2. 312 U.S. 100 (1941).

3. 317 U.S. 111 (1942).

4. This previous position was originally articulated in *United States* v. *E.C. Knight Co.*, 156 U.S. 1 (1895) and had been most recently employed by the Court in *Schechter Poultry Corporation* v. *United States*, 295 U.S. 495 (1935), *United States* v. *Butler*, 297 U.S. 1 (1935), and *Carter* v. *Carter Coal Company*, 298 U.S. 238 (1936).

5. 301 U.S. at 41.

6. 301 U.S. at 36-37.

7. 301 U.S. at 37.

8. 262 U.S. 1, 37 (1923).

9. 22 U.S. 1 (1824).

10. 312 U.S. at 113.

11. 312 U.S. at 113.

12. With this argument, the Court explicitly overruled *Hammer* v. *Dagenhart*, 247 U.S. 251 (1918), in which the Court had held that Congress lacked the power to ban the interstate shipment of goods produced by child labor, because Congress's motive was not the regulation of commerce but rather the regulation of child labor—a matter reserved to the states to regulate as they chose under their police powers to protect the health, safety, and welfare of their residents. See 312 U.S. at 117.

13. Lino A. Graglia, "*United States* v. *Lopez*: Judicial Review under the Commerce Clause," *Texas Law Review* 74 (March 1996): 719, 740.

14. 312 U.S. at 124. "There is nothing in the history of its adoption to suggest that it was more than declaratory of the relationship between the national and state governments as it had been established by the Constitution before the amendment or that its purpose was other than to allay fears that the new national government might seek to exercise powers not granted, and that the states might not be able to exercise fully their reserved powers. From the beginning and for many years the amendment has been construed as not depriving the national government of authority to resort to all means for the exercise of a granted power which are appropriate and plainly adapted to the permitted end."

15. Under the terms of the Act, these extra bushels constituted "farm marketing excess" and subjected Filburn to a penalty of $117.11. 317 U.S. at 115. The penalty was 49 cents a bushel at time when the average price for a bushel of wheat was $1.16. 317 U.S. at 126.

16. 317 U.S. at 121.

17. 317 U.S. at 125.

18. 317 U.S. at 127-28. As Jackson continued, "But if we assume that it is never marketed, it supplies a need of the man who grew it which would otherwise be reflected by purchases in the open market. Home-grown wheat in this sense competes with wheat in commerce. The stimulation of commerce is a use of the regulatory function quite as definitely as prohibitions or restrictions thereon. This record leaves us in no doubt that Congress may properly have considered that wheat consumed on the farm where grown if wholly outside the scheme of regulation would have a substantial effect in defeating and obstructing its purpose to stimulate trade therein at increased prices." 317 U.S. at 128-29.

19. The phrase is from *Federalist* No. 39. James Madison, Alexander Hamilton, and John Jay, *The Federalist,* ed. Jacob E. Cooke (New York: World Publishing Company, 1961), 256.

20. Graglia, *"United States* v. *Lopez,"* 741.

21. 109 U.S. 3 (1883). The Court held that Congress, which had relied on its enforcement powers under Section 5 of the Fourteenth Amendment for authority to pass the Civil Rights Act of 1875, lacked the power under that amendment to prohibit any person from denying a citizen "the full and equal enjoyment of the accommodations, advantages, facilities, and privileges of inns, public conveyances on land and water, theatres, and other places of public amusement," because Section 1 of the Fourteenth Amendment prohibited only "state action" that denied equal protection and not "individual invasion of individual rights." The Commerce Clause was never addressed by the Court in 1883, because neither the Congress nor the Court believed that racial discrimination was a part of commerce.

22. 379 U.S. 241 (1964).

23. 379 U.S. 294 (1964).

24. The Court distinguished the *Civil Rights Cases* as follows in *Heart of Atlanta Motel*:

> [T]he fact that certain kinds of businesses may not in 1875 have been sufficiently involved in interstate commerce to warrant bringing them within the ambit of the commerce power is not necessarily dispositive of the same question today. Our populace had not reached its present mobility, nor were facilities, goods and services circulating as readily in interstate commerce as they are today. Although the principles which we apply today are those first formulated by Chief Justice Marshall in *Gibbons* v. *Ogden* (1824), the conditions of transportation and commerce have changed dramatically, and we must apply those principles to the present state of commerce. The sheer increase in volume of interstate traffic alone would give discriminatory practices which inhibit travel a far larger impact upon the Nation's commerce than such practices had on the economy of another day. Finally, there is language in the *Civil Rights Cases* which indicates that the Court did not fully consider whether the 1875 Act could be sustained as an

exercise of the commerce power. Though the Court observed that "no one will contend that the power to pass it was contained in the Constitution before the adoption of the last three amendments [Thirteenth, Fourteenth, and Fifteenth]," the Court went on specifically to note that the Act was not "conceived" in terms of the commerce power and expressly pointed [that]out. 379 U.S. at 251.

25. Justices Black and Douglas wrote concurring opinions in *Heart of Atlanta Motel*. Justice Douglas in particular was "somewhat reluctant" to have the Court rest its decision "solely on the Commerce Clause." "I would prefer to rest on the assertion of legislative power contained in Section 5 of the Fourteenth Amendment which states: 'The Congress shall have power to enforce, by appropriate legislation, the provisions of this article'—a power which the Court concedes was exercised at least in part in this Act. A decision based on the Fourteenth Amendment would have a more settling effect, making unnecessary litigation over whether a particular restaurant or inn is within the commerce definitions of the Act or whether a particular customer is an interstate traveler." 379 U.S. at 280.

26. 379 U.S. at 261.

27. 379 U.S. at 261-62.

28. 379 U.S. at 303-4.

29. Graglia, "*United States* v. *Lopez*," 726.

30. 379 U.S. at 305.

31. Graglia, "*United States* v. *Lopez*," 746.

32. 402 U.S. 146 (1971).

33. 402 U.S. at 156.

34. 402 U.S. at 153-54. He went out of his way to deny "that Congress need make particularized findings in order to legislate." 402 U.S. at 156.

35. 402 U.S. at 157.

36. 402 U.S. at 158.

37. 392 U.S. 183 (1968). That same year, Congress passed the Civil Obedience Act of 1968 that prohibited teaching the use of a firearm, explosive, or incendiary device for use in a "civil disorder" or interfering with public safety officers (e.g., firemen or police officers) during a civil disorder which "may in any way or degree obstruct, delay, or adversely affect commerce or the movement of any article or commodity in commerce."

38. 392 U.S. at 194-95.

39. 392 U.S. at 195.

40. 452 U.S. 264 (1981).

41. Graglia, "*United States* v. *Lopez*," 746. The following discussion of *Hodel* v. *Virginia Surface Mining & Reclamation Association* and *Hodel* v. *Indiana* is heavily dependent on Graglia's analysis.

42. 452 U.S. at 277.

43. 452 U.S. at 277.

44. 452 U.S. 314 (1981).

45. 452 U.S. at 324.

46. 452 U.S. at 329.

47. 452 U.S. at 329, n. 17.

48. 426 U.S. 833 (1976).

49. 426 U.S. at 851.

50. 426 U.S. at 841.

51. 426 U.S. at 843.

52. 426 U.S. at 852.

53. 426 U.S. at 855.

54. 452 U.S. at 857.

55. 452 U.S. at 863, 858. "The reliance of my Brethren upon the Tenth Amendment as 'an express declaration of [a state sovereignty] limitation' not only suggests that they overrule governing decisions of this Court that address this question but must astound scholars of the Constitution." 426 U.S. at 861-62.

56. 452 U.S. at 858, 867.

57. 452 U.S. at 868.

58. 452 U.S. at 876.

59. 426 U.S. at 876-77. Emphasis in the original. At this point in his argument, Brennan cited Herbert Wechsler, "The Political Safeguards of Federalism: The Role of the States in the Composition and Selection of the National Government," *Columbia Law Review* 54 (1954): 543. Wechsler was the first to propound what has been called the theory of "process federalism," which contends that "the balance between the states and federal government can safely be left to the self-correcting powers of the political process." See Michael S. Greve, *Real Federalism: Why It Matters, How It Could Happen* (Washington, D.C.: AEI Press, 1999), 17. In fact, a better name would be "structural federalism," as the framers intended that federalism would be protected by constitutional structure—in particular, the mode of electing the Senate. See chapter 2 for an extended discussion of the framers' reliance on structure and self-interest.

60. This argument is developed at length in chapter 3.

61. See Jesse H. Choper, *Judicial Review and the National Political Process: A Functional Reconsideration of the Role of the Supreme Court* (Chicago: University of Chicago Press, 1980), who argues for "the dispensability of judicial review" on the grounds of "process federalism" and who likewise never even mentions the Seventeenth Amendment.

62. This is also the implicit argument made by the Court from the Seventeenth Amendment's ratification in 1913 to *Jones & Laughlin*. While the argument is made implicitly by Rehnquist in *National League of Cities* and by the earlier members of the Court, it is made explicitly by Roger G. Brooks in "*Garcia*, The Seventeenth Amendment, and the Role of the Supreme Court in Defending Federalism," *Harvard Journal of Law and Public Policy* 10 (1987): 189.

63. William J. Brennan, "The Constitution of the United States: Contemporary Ratifications," presentation at the Text and Teaching Symposium, Georgetown University, Washington, D.C., October 12, 1985, 5.

64. Address of Attorney General Edwin Meese III before the American Bar Association, Washington, D.C., July 9, 1985; a revised and expanded version of this speech was published as "Toward a Jurisprudence of Original Intention" in *Benchmark* 2, no. 1 (January/February, 1986): 1-10.

65. Brennan, "The Constitution of the United States: Contemporary Ratifications," 4.

66. Brennan, "The Constitution of the United States: Contemporary Ratifications," 4.

67. 426 U.S. at 875.

68. 469 U.S. 528 (1984).

69. 469 U.S. at 530.

70. 469 U.S. at 550.

71. 469 U.S. at 551.

72. 469 U.S. at 554. Strangely, Blackmun cites Choper's *Judicial Review and the National Political Process* at this point in his argument, even though Choper never even mentions the Seventeenth Amendment.

73. 469 U.S. at 554.

74. 469 U.S. at 554.

75. 469 U.S. at 555.

76. 469 U.S. at 556.

77. 469 U.S. at 560.

78. 469 U.S. at 560-61.

79. 469 U.S. at 567.

80. 469 U.S. at 572.

81. 469 U.S. at 577.

82. 469 U.S. at 588.

83. 469 U.S. at 586.

84. 469 U.S. at 585.

85. 469 U.S. at 586. Justice O'Connor was quoting from Terrance Sandalow, "Constitutional Interpretation," *Michigan Law Review* 79 (1981): 1055.

86. 505 U.S. 144 (1992).

87. 505 U.S. at 177.

88. 505 U.S. at 149.

89. 505 U.S. at 177.

90. 505 U.S. at 159.

91. 505 U.S. at 156-57.

92. 505 U.S. at 164-67.

93. 505 U.S. at 157.

94. 505 U.S. at 158.

95. 505 U.S. at 159.

96. 505 U.S. at 178.

97. 505 U.S. at 175.

98. 505 U.S. at 188.

99. 505 U.S. at 178.

100. 505 U.S. at 205.

101. 505 U.S. at 194.

102. 505 U.S. at 199.

103. 505 U.S. at 210.

104. 514 U.S. 549 (1995).

105. 18 U.S.C. § 922(q)(1)(A), 1988 ed., Supp. V. A "school zone" was defined as "in, or on the grounds of, a public, parochial, or private school" or "within a distance of 1,000 feet from the grounds of a public, parochial or private school." 18 USC § 921(a)(25).

106. 514 U.S. at 551.

107. 514 U.S. at 559.

108. 514 U.S. at 567. The Act, Rehnquist argued, "has nothing to do with 'commerce' or any sort of economic enterprise, however broadly one might define those terms." It "is not an essential part of a larger regulation of economic activity, in which the regulatory scheme could be undercut unless the intrastate activity were regulated. It cannot, therefore, be sustained under our cases upholding regulations of activities that arise out of or are connected with a commercial transaction, which viewed in the aggregate, substantially affects interstate commerce." 514 U.S. at 561.

109. 514 U.S. at 563.

110. 514 U.S. at 564.

111. 514 U.S. at 567.

112. 514 U.S. at 567.

113. 514 U.S. at 581.

114. 514 U.S. at 575. Kennedy commented that "there is an irony in this, because of the four structural elements in the Constitution just mentioned, federalism was the unique contribution to political science and political theory." 514 U.S. at 575. By his failure to appreciate that federalism was to be secured by the mode of electing the Senate, Kennedy demonstrated his failure to grasp what was unique about American federalism. See chapter 3 for details of how the framers employed the mode of electing the Senate as the principal means of protecting the interests of the states as such.

115. 514 U.S. at 578.

116. 514 U.S. at 589.

117. 514 U.S. at 602.

118. 514 U.S. at 600.

119. 514 U.S. at 600.

119. 514 U.S. at 604. Justice Souter dissenting.

120. 514 U.S. 614.

121. 514 U.S. at 613.

122. 514 U.S. at 613.

123. 514 U.S. at 616-17. Breyer asserted, but without much apparent conviction, that "[t]o hold this statute constitutional is not to 'obliterate' the 'distinction between what is national and what is local'; nor is it to hold that the Commerce Clause permits the Federal Government to 'regulate any activity that it found was related to the economic productivity of individual citizens,' to regulate 'marriage, divorce, and child custody,' or to regulate any and all aspects of education." 514 U.S. at 624.

124. See 514 U.S. at 619-25, 631-44.

125. 517 U.S. 44 (1996). See Daniel J. Meltzer, "The *Seminole* Decision and State Sovereign Immunity," in Dennis J. Hutchinson, David A. Strauss, and Geoffrey R. Stone (eds.), *1996 Supreme Court Review* (Chicago: University of Chicago Press, 1997), 1-65.

126. The Indian Commerce Clause, found in Article I, Section 8, ¶ 3, reads: "Congress shall have power . . . to regulate Commerce . . . with the Indian Tribes."

127. 517 U.S. at 69.

128. 517 U.S. at 70.

129. 517 U.S. at 69.

130. 517 U.S. at 54.

131. 2 U.S. 419 (1793).

132. 517 U.S. at 44.

133. 491 U.S. 1 (1989).

134. 427 U.S. 445 (1976).

135. 517 U.S. at 63.

136. 517 U.S. at 66.

137. 517 U.S. at 65-66.

138. 517 U.S. at 107-8.

139. 517 U.S. at 111. See also his argument at 517 U.S. at 158.

140. See Clyde E. Jacobs, *The Eleventh Amendment and Sovereign Immunity* (Westport, Conn.: Greenwood Press, 1972), 42.

141. 521 U.S. 507 (1997).

142. 521 U.S. at 536. The Court also claimed that *City of Boerne* violated separation of powers, in that it asserted that Congress was attempting to contradict the Court's previous interpretation of the Free Exercise Clause in *Employment Division, Department of Human Resources of Oregon* v. *Smith*, discussed below. However, as David Cole argues in "The Value of Seeing Things Differently: *Boerne* v. *Flores* and the Congressional Enforcement of the Bill of Rights," in Dennis J. Hutchinson, David A. Strauss, and Geoffrey R. Stone (eds.), *1997 Supreme Court*

Review (Chicago: University of Chicago Press, 1998), 31-77, 41: "The [Court's] separation of powers argument . . . is easily rebutted. The argument's premise is that, in enacting RFRA, Congress sought to 'alter the Fourteenth Amendment's meaning.' But it did no such thing. RFRA provided a statutory right, not a constitutional right. It did not change the Constitution, but only the United States Code. It cannot possibly be inconsistent with the separation of powers for Congress to protect, by statute, rights not protected by the Constitution. Innumerable federal statutes—directed at private and government conduct alike—do precisely that." The real question in *City of Boerne*, therefore, was not whether Congress was free to disagree with the Court concerning how much protection should be afforded to religious liberty, but whether Congress had the power to impose such an expanded understanding on the states—that is to say, the real question is a question of federalism. Accordingly, the discussion that follows focuses exclusively on the federalism aspects of *City of Boerne*. See Bonnie I. Robin-Vergeer, "Disposing of the Red Herrings: A Defense of the Religious Freedom Restoration Act," *Southern California Law Review* 69 (January 1996): 589, 679. "In sum, RFRA presents no conflict at all between Congress and the Supreme Court. The serious issue it raises is whether Congress has the power to impose RFRA's requirement of strict scrutiny on the states—an issue that concerns not the separation of powers between the federal branches, but federalism."

143. 494 U.S. 872 (1990).

144. 494 U.S. at 879.

145. 374 U.S. 398 (1963).

146. Public Law No. 103-141, 107 Stat. 1488 (1993).

147. 406 U.S. 205 (1972).

148. Its impact on the administration of prisons was especially perverse. See, for example, Lino A. Graglia, "*Church of Lukumi Babalu Aye:* Of Animal Sacrifice and Religious Persecution," *Georgetown Law Journal* 85 (November 1996): 1, 60-69. See also Christopher L. Eisgruber and Lawrence G. Sager, "Congressional Power and Religious Liberty after *City of Boerne* v. *Flores*," in Dennis J. Hutchinson, David A. Strauss, and Geoffrey R. Stone (eds.), *1997 Supreme Court Review* (Chicago: University of Chicago Press, 1998), 79-139.

149. 310 U.S. 296 (1940).

150. The following discussion relies heavily on Cole, "The Value of Seeing Things Differently," 44-49.

151. 427 U.S. 445 (1976).

152. See also *Washington* v. *Davis*, 416 U.S. 229 (1976).

153. 446 U.S. 156 (1980).

154. At stake in *City of Rome* was not Congress's power to enforce the Fourteenth Amendment (under its Section 5) but rather its power to enforce the Fifteenth Amendment (under comparable enforcement language in its Section 2).

155. 521 U.S. at 525, 532.

156. 521 U.S. at 519.

157. Cole, "The Value of Seeing Things Differently," 49.

158. Cole, "The Value of Seeing Things Differently," 49.

159. 521 U.S. at 520. See Michael W. McConnell, "The Supreme Court, 1996 Term: Comment: Institutions and Interpretation: A Critique of *Boerne* v. *Flores*," *Harvard Law Review* 111 (November 1997): 153, 165, 170.

160. 521 U.S. at 530-31.

161. 521 U.S. at 532.

162. It should be noted that none of the dissenting opinions addressed the federalism issue. Justice O'Connor dissented because she believed that *Smith* was wrongly decided and was therefore an inappropriate "yardstick for measuring the constitutionality of RFRA." 521 U.S. at 544-45. She acknowledged that she agreed "with much of the reasoning set forth" by Kennedy and declared that "if I agreed with the Court's standards in *Smith*, I would join the opinion." 521 U.S. at 545. Justice Souter dissented because he considered the writ of certiorari to have been "improvidently granted," 521 U.S. at 566, and Justice Breyer simply wished to withhold any judgment until *Smith* was reargued. 521 U.S. at 566.

163. 310 U.S. 296 (1940).

164. Cole, "The Value of Seeing Things Differently," 54.

165. Cole, "The Value of Seeing Things Differently," 54; see also 55: "Incorporation effected a major shift in federal-state power, but once incorporation has been established, there is no independent ground beyond Section 5 for distinguishing between the federal court's power to enforce the incorporated provisions of the Bill of Rights against the states and Congress's power to do so."

166. *Luke* 6: 41-42.

167. 521 U.S. 898 (1997).

168. "[K]nowingly violat[ing]" the Act subjected CLEOs to a potential fine or a term of imprisonment "for no more than one year, or both." 18 U.S.C. § 924(a)(5).

169. 521 U.S. at 935.

170. 521 U.S. at 905.

171. 521 U.S. at 922.

172. 521 U.S. at 922-23.

173. 487 U.S. 654 (1988).

174. 521 U.S. at 925.

175. 521 U.S. at 958.

176. See Antonin Scalia, *A Matter of Interpretation: Federal Courts and the Law* (Princeton: Princeton University Press, 1997). See also Ralph A. Rossum, "The Textualist Jurisprudence of Justice Scalia," *Perspectives on Political Science* 28 (winter 1999): 5-10.

177. 521 U.S. at 944. In that respect, see *Reno* v. *Condon*, 528 U.S. 141, 120 S.Ct. 666 (2000), in which the Supreme Court unanimously reversed the United States Court of Appeals for the Fourth Circuit and held that Congress's enactment

of the Driver's Privacy Protection Act of 1994 (DPPA), which established a regulatory scheme restricting a state's ability to disclose a driver's personal information without the driver's consent, did not run afoul of the federalism principles enunciated in *New York* v. *United States* and *Printz* v. *United States*. In Chief Justice Rehnquist's words: "[T]he DPPA does not require the States in their sovereign capacity to regulate their own citizens. The DPPA regulates the States as the owners of databases. It does not require the South Carolina Legislature [the respondent in this case] to enact any laws or regulations, and it does not require state officials to assist in the enforcement of federal statues regulating private individuals." 528 U.S. at 151.

178. 527 U.S. 627 (1999).

179. 527 U.S. 666 (1999).

180. 527 U.S. 706 (1999).

181. 527 U.S. at 634-35.

182. 527 U.S. at 638.

183. 527 U.S. at 639.

184. 527 U.S. at 640.

185. 527 U.S. at 645. Rehnquist concluded that "[t]he statute's more basic aims were to provide a uniform remedy for patent infringement and to place States on the same footing as private parties under that regime. These are proper Article I concerns, but that Article does not give Congress the power to enact such legislation after *Seminole Tribe*." 527 U.S. at 648.

186. 527 U.S. at 644.

187. 527 U.S. at 647.

188. 527 U.S. at 658.

189. 527 U.S. at 658.

190. 527 U.S. at 659.

191. 505 U.S. at 181.

192. 377 U.S. 184 (1964).

193. 527 U.S. at 672.

194. 527 U.S. at 676.

195. 527 U.S. at 676, 680.

196. 527 U.S. at 681.

197. 527 U.S. at 687.

198. 527 U.S. at 692.

199. 527 U.S. at 694.

200. 527 U.S. at 695.

201. 527 U.S. at 695.

202. 527 U.S. at 700.

203. 527 U.S. at 704.

204. 527 U.S. at 713.

205. 527 U.S. at 713.

206. 527 U.S. at 713. This prompted Justice Souter to remark in his dissent: "As a consequence, *Seminole Tribe*'s contorted reliance on the Eleventh Amendment and its background was presumably unnecessary; the Tenth would have done the work with an economy that the majority in *Seminole Tribe* would have welcomed. Indeed, if the Court's current reasoning is correct, the Eleventh Amendment itself was unnecessary." 527 U.S. at 761.

207. 527 U.S. at 713.

208. 527 U.S. at 741.

209. 527 U.S. at 741.

210. 527 U.S. at 743.

211. 527 U.S. at 728.

212. 527 U.S. at 756.

213. 527 U.S. at 752.

214. 527 U.S. at 688.

215. 527 U.S. at 801.

216. 527 U.S. at 806.

217. 527 U.S. at 807.

218. 252 U.S. 416, 433 (1920). For a sustained critique of the "living Constitution" argument, see Raoul Berger, "A Lawyer Lectures a Judge," *Harvard Journal of Law and Public Policy* 18 (1995): 851-65.

219. 527 U.S. at 807.

220. 528 U.S. 62 (2000).

221. 460 U.S. 226 (1983).

222. The language from *City of Boerne* is from 521 U.S. at 520. It is quoted in *Kimel* at 528 U.S. at 81.

223. 528 U.S. at 91.

224. 528 U.S. at 99.

225. 528 U.S. at 93.

226. 529 U.S. 598 (2000).

227. 529 U.S. at 615.

228. 529 U.S. at 615-16.

229. 529 U.S. at 621.

230. 529 U.S. at 627.

231. 529 U.S. at 636.

232. 529 U.S. at 647.

233. 529 U.S. at 650.

234. 529 U.S. at 652.

235. 531 U.S. 356, 121 S.Ct. 955 (2001).

236. 104 Stat. 330 (1990).

237. See *Kimel* v. *Florida Board of Regents*, 528 U.S. at 72-73; *College Savings Bank* v. *Florida Prepaid*, 527 U.S. at 634-35; and *Seminole Tribe of Florida* v. *Florida*, 517 U.S. at 54.

238. 121 S.Ct. at 962.

239. 121 S.Ct. at 963.

240. 473 U.S. 432 (1985).

241. 121 S.Ct. at 962.

242. 121 S.Ct. at 966. "States are not required by the Fourteenth Amendment to make special accommodations for the disabled, so long as their actions towards such individuals are rational. They could quite hard headedly—and perhaps hardheartedly—hold to job-qualification requirements which do not make allowance for the disabled. If special accommodations for the disabled are to be required, they have to come from positive law and not through the Equal Protection Clause." 121 S.Ct. at 964.

243. 121 S.Ct. at 965.

244. 121 S.Ct. at 965.

245. 121 S.Ct. at 967-68.

246. 121 S.Ct. at 972.

247. 121 S.Ct. at 972. Breyer quoted *Oregon* v. *Mitchell*, 400 U.S. 112, 248: "Limitations stemming from the nature of the judicial process . . . have no application to Congress."

248. 121 S.Ct. at 973.

249. 121 S.Ct. at 973. See McConnell, "Institutions and Interpretation: A Critique of *Boerne* v. *Flores*," 153, 165, 170.

250. 121 S.Ct. at 975.

Chapter 2

Constitutional Structure, Federalism, and the Securing of Liberty

---

Near the end of her three-volume *History of the Rise, Progress, and Termination of the American Revolution*, Mercy Warren observed that Americans enjoyed and "will probably long retain a greater share of freedom than can be found in any other part of the civilized world." She worried, however, that this was "more the result of [their] local situation, than from [their] superior policy or moderation," for she bluntly asserted that "most of the inhabitants of America" are "too proud for monarchy, yet too poor for nobility, and it is to be feared, too selfish and avaricious for a virtuous republic."[1]

Her animadversions underscored the crucial problem faced by the founding generation: Once independence had been achieved, how could it be preserved? How could good and decent government consistent with the principles of the Declaration of Independence be established and sustained by such people?

The founding generation rejected monarchy and nobility not because they believed that Americans were too proud for the former or too poor for the latter and not even because they understood these forms of government to be incompatible with the Declaration of Independence;[2] rather, they rejected them because they were inconsistent with "the fixt genius of the people of America."[3] That left them with some form of popular, i.e., republican, government. But how could republican government composed of individuals as selfish and avaricious as Warren described them be made virtuous—or less ambitiously, how could it be rendered safe and secure?

The Declaration of Independence formulated two criteria for judging whether any government is good or legitimate. First, it must be derived from the consent of the governed, and second, it must secure men's inalienable rights to life, liberty, and the pursuit of happiness. Between these two criteria, a tension exists: The governed may consent to governmental actions that jeopardize these rights. This tension is heightened in republican governments, for not only are they instituted on the basis of consent but they operate thereafter on that principle as well. How could this tension be reduced, if not eliminated? How could the Declaration's two criteria of good government be made to complement rather than to contradict each other?

For Warren, the answer to these questions was found in the promotion of religious belief[4] and civic virtue.[5] Warren insisted that "profligacy, tyranny, and the wanton exercise of arbitrary sway" inevitably result "when the checks of conscience are thrown aside, or the moral sense weakened by the sudden acquisition of wealth or power."[6] For her, "ambition and avarice are the leading springs" that actuate mankind;[7] if these forces were ever freed from the constraints of religion and virtue, they would reduce the "inhabitants of America" to "a degenerate, servile race of beings, corrupted by wealth, effeminated by luxury, impoverished by licentiousness, and become the automatons of intoxicated ambition."[8]

For the framers of the Constitution,[9] the answer to these questions was altogether different. Rejecting Warren's reliance on religion and virtue (on what they termed the "weaker springs of the human character"[10]), they depended instead on constitutional structure (on what *Federalist* No. 51 called "inventions of prudence"[11] and on what Tocqueville called the "utility of forms"[12]) to channel and direct "ambition and avarice" so that they would serve rather than threaten free government.

Why the Framers Relied on Constitutional Structure

The framers fully appreciated that for "the spirit and form of popular government" to be preserved in practice, i.e., for republican government to succeed, "the public good and private rights" would have to be secured against the dangers of majority tyranny.[13] Madison in *Federalist* No. 10 described this as "the great object" to which all of their inquiries were directed, and, he added, "it is the desideratum by which alone this form of government can be rescued from the opprobrium under which it has so long labored and be recommended to the esteem and adoption of mankind."[14]

As the framers well knew, the "great object" of their inquiries posed enormous difficulties. They were irrevocably committed to republican government, but historically, republican governments had led invariably to majority tyranny. In them, measures were decided "not according to the rules of justice, and the rights of the minor party; but by the superior force of an interested and overbearing majority."[15] Minority rights were disregarded, as were "the permanent and aggregate interests of the community."[16] Republican governments too easily allowed for "unjust combinations of the majority as a whole"[17] and therefore proved to be "incompatible with personal security, or the rights of property."[18] This was the "opprobrium" under which they had "so long labored."

The most commonly prescribed palliative for the problem of majority tyranny was to render the government powerless. However eager those in the majority might be to "concert and carry into effect their schemes of oppression,"[19] if their governing institutions were sufficiently impotent, they would pose little real threat. William Symmes reflected this point of view in the Massachusetts Ratifying Convention: "I hold to this maxim that power was never given, but it was exercised; nor ever exercised but it was finally abused."[20] For him and those of like mind, the implication was clear: To prevent abuses, power had to be jealously withheld. This view, however, rendered government inept and prompted Alexander Hamilton in the New York Ratifying Convention to observe that while the object of "secur[ing] ourselves from despotism" was certainly "a valuable one, and deserved our utmost attention," there was "another object, equally important, and which our enthusiasm rendered us little capable of regarding: I mean the principle of *strength* and *stability* in the organization of our government, and *vigor* in its operations."[21]

The framers understood that a strong and stable government was necessary not only to cope with the problems that society faces but also to render liberty more secure. For republican government to be "recommended to the esteem and adoption of mankind," they realized that they would have to solve the rival defects to which majority rule seemed inevitably destined and establish a constitution capable of avoiding majority tyranny on the one hand and democratic ineptitude on the other.[22] These rival defects had overwhelmed the federal and state governments under the Articles of Confederation and led to the calling of the Federal Convention. Under the Articles, the individual states were so powerful and their legislatures so dominant and unchecked that the tyrannical impulses that surged through the majority continually jeopardized the rights and liberties of their citizens,

and the central federal authority was so infirm and its responsibilities so
few and limited that, as Hamilton noted in *Federalist* No. 15, it was reduced
"to the last stage of national humiliation."[23]

The framers fully appreciated the challenge they faced. As James
Madison formulated it in *Federalist* No. 51: "In framing a government to
be administered by men over men, the great difficulty lies in this: You must
first enable the government to control the governed, and in the next place,
oblige it to control itself."[24] Nevertheless, they believed that they had met
this challenge. Their solution to the problem of republican government was
based on their assessment of human nature. Rather than rely on religion
and virtue, they would depend instead on the rather ignoble but reliable
inclination of men to follow their own "sober second thoughts of self-
interest"[25] as a means of ensuring good government. They would establish
a republic in which the public good is advanced in the same way that
commercial prosperity is achieved—through individuals pursuing their own
self-interest.[26] They would create, in short, a commercial as opposed to a
virtuous republic.[27] As Noah Webster forthrightly declared in his
"Examination into the Leading Principles of the Federal Constitution," "The
system of the great Montesquieu will ever be erroneous, till the words
property or lands in fee simple are substituted for *virtue*, throughout his
Spirit of Laws."[28]

The framers of the Constitution shared Warren's assessment of human
nature.[29] They, too, understood mankind to be driven by self-interest and
consumed by the desire for distinction and the love of honor; they, too,
pictured men as "ambitious, rapacious, and vindictive."[30] Among the
framers, Gouverneur Morris painted perhaps the most graphic portrait: Men,
he wrote, are but "poor reptiles! It is with them a vernal morning; they are
struggling to cast off their winter's slough, they bask in the sunshine, and
ere noon they will bite."[31] "Human selfishness" and "the love of power"[32]
are so powerful and basic, the framers continued, that it is folly to expect to
control them by traditional republican reliance on patriotism, respect for
character, conscience or religion, or even the not-very-lofty maxim that
"honesty is the best policy."[33] Such "remote considerations of policy, utility
or justice" can never provide adequate control over man's "momentary
passions and immediate interests."[34] Rather, avarice and the "lust of power"
will prevail and "divide mankind into parties," inflame them with "mutual
animosity," and render them "much more disposed to vex and oppress each
other than to cooperate for their common good."[35] This propensity of
mankind to fall into mutual animosity is so powerful, they argued, that
"where no substantial occasion presents itself, the most frivolous and fanciful
distinctions . . . [will be] sufficient to kindle their unfriendly passions and

excite their most violent conflicts."[36] Men are predictable in such matters; they will have their factions, whether or not there are substantial reasons for them. Their passions will, as a consequence, lead them in ways inconsistent with "the dictates of reason and justice."[37] In fact, their reason typically ends up in service of their passions, providing them with arguments for self-indulgence rather than incentives to virtue.[38]

Given this assessment, the framers placed little faith in improving human nature through moral reformation or in the activities of "enlightened statesmen."[39] The only hope for republican government, they believed, was the establishment of constitutional structures that, by accommodating "the ordinary depravity of mankind,"[40] would make it in the interest, even of bad men, to act for the public good. Self-interest, the framers earnestly believed, was the one check that nothing could overcome and the principal hope for security and stability in republican government.[41]

Thomas Wait, a Massachusetts Anti-Federalist, warned that the framers' reliance on constitutional structure was wholly unrealistic. "You might as well attempt to rule Hell by prayer," he declared.[42] As Herbert J. Storing has pointed out, the framers' response was, in effect, to argue that what was unrealistic was to expect that men, any more than Hell, could be ruled by prayer—by moral exhortation, by religion, or by appeals to conscience.[43] "Men," Hamilton argued in the New York Ratifying Convention, "will pursue their interests. It is as easy to change human nature as to oppose the strong current of the selfish passions. A wise legislator will gently divert the channel, and direct it, if possible, to the public good."[44]

The framers appreciated the power of self-interest. They did not attempt to stifle or contain it with "parchment barriers,"[45] i.e., with prescriptive and proscriptive words in a constitution. To begin with, such an attempt would be extraordinarily difficult, given the imprecision of language. As Madison observed in *Federalist* No. 37:

> Besides the obscurity arising from the complexity of objects, and the imperfection of the human faculties, the medium through which the conceptions of men are conveyed to each other adds a fresh embarrassment. . . . Hence, it must happen, that however accurately objects may be discriminated in themselves, and however accurately the discrimination may be considered, the definition of them may be rendered inaccurate by the inaccuracy of the terms in which it is delivered. And this unavoidable inaccuracy must be greater or less, according to the complexity and novelty of the objects defined. When the Almighty himself condescends to address mankind in their own language, his meaning, luminous as it must be, is rendered dim and doubtful, by the cloudy medium through which it is communicated.[46]

However, even if the difficulty of language could be overcome, the framers were convinced that the use of "parchment barriers" would still be in vain. They had been warned by Cesare Beccaria that the fate of such provisions "is the same as that of dikes set up directly against the course of a river; either they break down immediately and are overrun or a whirlpool which they themselves form corrodes and undermines them imperceptibly."[47] Thus, they did not seek to block or dam these interests through, for example, the inclusion of a bill of rights[48] but rather designed constitutional structures to direct and channel them through the process of mutual checking so that the federal and state governments could control the governed while at the same time being obliged to control themselves. Gouverneur Morris articulated this strategy in the Federal Convention: "The vices as they exist, must be turned against each other."[49] As the perceptive Alexis de Tocqueville would later describe it, the framers relied on institutional mechanisms to "check one personal interest by another" and used "to direct the passions the very same instrument that excites them."[50] The constitutional structures they designed were based on the "great improvements" they had made during the Convention itself to the "science of politics";[51] they included a novel reliance on the ameliorative effects of an extended republic, a new form of separation of powers, and a new form of federalism.

The next section focuses on these constitutional structures, paying particular attention to federalism. It shows why Madison was able to proclaim proudly in *Federalist* No. 10 that, through their ingenious reliance on "the extent and proper structure of the Union," the framers had provided "a Republican remedy for the diseases most incident to Republican Government."[52]

The Key Structural Provisions of the Constitution

The Extended Republic

The multiplicity of interests present in the extended commercial republic established by the Constitution represents one of the principal mechanisms by which the framers sought to avoid the rival defects of majority tyranny and democratic ineptitude. The advantages of an extended republic can be best seen by examining the defects of a small republic. As Madison noted in *Federalist* No. 10, the smaller the republic, "the fewer probably will be the distinct parties and interests composing it; the fewer the distinct parties and interests, the more frequently will a majority be found of the same party; and the smaller the compass within which they are placed, the more easily will they concert and execute their plans of oppression." Thus the prospect for democratic tyranny arises, which can be prevented only by rendering the government impotent and thereby fostering democratic ineptitude. In contrast, the larger the republic, the greater the variety of interests, parties, and sects present within it and the more moderate and diffused the conflict. In the words of *Federalist* No. 10, "Extend the sphere, and you take in a greater variety of parties and interests; you make it less probable that a majority of the whole will have a common motive to invade the rights of other citizens; or if such a common motive exists, it will be more difficult for all who feel it to discover their own strength, and to act in unison with each other."[53] Because of the "greater variety" of economic, geographic, religious, political, cultural, and ethnic interests that an extended republic takes in, rule by a majority is effectively replaced by rule by ever-changing coalitions of minorities that come together on a particular issue to act as a majority but that break up on the next. For example, the coalition of minorities that acts as a majority on the issue of import duties is not likely to remain intact on the issue of internal improvements. The very real possibility that allies in one coalition may be opponents in the next encourages a certain moderation in politics, in terms of both the political objectives sought and the political tactics employed. Political interests become reluctant to raise the political stakes too high: By scoring too decisive a political victory on one issue, an interest may find that it has only weakened itself by devastating a potential ally and thus rendering itself vulnerable to similar treatment in the future. Accordingly, politics is moderated, not through idle appeals to conscience and good will but rather through reliance on the inclination of individuals to look after their own self-interest. As Madison observed in *Federalist* No. 51, this diversity of interests assures that "a coalition of a majority of the whole society" will seldom take place "on any other principles than those of justice and the common good."[54] The advantages of an extended republic thus helped to make it possible for the framers to give the national government sufficient power to prevent democratic ineptitude without raising the spectre of democratic tyranny.

The framers' recognition of and reliance on the moderating effects brought about by an extended republic is apparent in such constitutional provisions as the Contract Clause in Article I, Section 10, which prohibits any state from passing laws "impairing the obligation of contracts." Note that only the states are restrained, the federal government is not—and for good reasons. It was thought that no state, however large, was or would be extensive enough to contain a variety of interests wide enough to prevent majorities from acting oppressively and using their legislative power to nullify contracts for their own advantage. Consequently they had to have their power to do so limited by the Constitution. The federal government, by contrast, was large enough and contained the multiplicity of interests necessary to prevent oppression of this sort, and so had no need of constitutional constraint. Thus could majority tyranny be avoided simply by relying on the popular principle to operate naturally in an extended republic.

Separation of Powers and Checks and Balances

For the framers, the "great desideratum of politics" was the formation of a "government that will, at the same time, deserve the seemingly opposite epithets—efficient and free."[55] The extended republic was one means by which they sought to realize this objective; separation of powers and checks and balances were another. They were aware that "the accumulation of all powers legislative, executive, and judiciary in the same hands, whether of one, a few, or many, and whether hereditary, self-appointed, or elective may justly be pronounced the very definition of tyranny," and therefore that "the preservation of liberty requires that the three great departments of power should be separate and distinct."[56] Thus, they established a government consisting of three coordinate and equal branches, with each performing a blend of functions, thereby balancing governmental powers. No one has described the complex and balanced government provided by the Constitution with greater perspicuity than Herbert J. Storing; it is, he said, "fundamentally a balance of constitutional orders or powers, blended with a constitutional differentiation of functions, formed by the makers of the Constitution and requiring only the impulse of popular consent to breathe life into it and the private interests and ambitions of citizens and representatives to keep it in motion."[57]

The framers' new understanding of separation of powers, developed during their deliberations at the Constitutional Convention, contrasted sharply with two traditional understandings of separation of powers extant at the time: the understanding present in the British regime and the understanding present in many of the early state constitutions.

In Great Britain, power was separated among the three departments of government according to the principle of rule that each department embodied. Thus, the Crown had the powers it did because they were powers associated with the principle of rule by the one, monarchy; the House of

Lords had the powers it did because they were associated with the principle of rule by the few, aristocracy; and the House of Commons had the powers it did because they were associated with the principle of rule by the many, democracy. The result of this British understanding was not a functional separation of powers but rather a balance of powers described by Sir William Blackstone in his *Commentaries on the Laws of England*[58] as "the true excellence of the English government." Blackstone explained the advantages of this checking and balancing as follows: "Like three distinct powers in mechanics, they jointly impel the machine of government in a direction different from what either, acting by itself, would have done; but at the same time in the direction partaking of each, and formed out of all; a direction which constitutes the true line of the liberty and happiness of the community."[59]

The understanding of separation of powers present in many of the early state constitutions was entirely different. These constitutions were drafted in the hope of keeping the legislative, executive, and judicial departments totally separate and distinct from each other. Each department was understood to have a separate and distinct function and was to exercise only the powers associated with that function. As it is put in the Massachusetts Constitution: "The legislative department shall never exercise the executive and judicial powers, or either of them: The executive shall never exercise the legislative and judicial powers, or either of them: The judicial shall never exercise the legislative and executive powers, or either of them."[60] Since tyranny was understood to consist of the accumulation of all power in one branch of the government, this rigid, functional separation of powers—secured through absolute constitutional prohibitions—was seen by many who helped draft these early state constitutions as an essential means for the preservation of liberty.

The framers rejected both of these traditional understandings. They rejected the British understanding of separation of powers, despite its ability to check and balance powers, because it was impossible to duplicate in America. The United States lacked the social raw materials necessary to bring it into existence—viz., a millennium's experience with aristocracy and monarchy. They also rejected the understanding of a rigid, functional separation of powers present in the state constitutions as unable to prevent any branch of government from tyrannizing the people, or the majority from tyrannizing the minority.

Rather, the framers sought to structure the government so that the three branches would "by their mutual relations, be the means of keeping each other in their proper places,"[61] and this they succeeded in doing. They began by giving most legislative power to the Congress, most executive power to the President, and most judicial power to the Supreme Court and to such inferior federal courts as Congress might establish. But they then set out to "divide and arrange" the remaining powers in such a manner that each branch could be "a check on the others." They checked the Congress by introducing the principle of bicameralism, according to which Congress was divided into the House of Representatives and the Senate, and by arranging for the President to exercise certain important legislative powers by requiring of him annual addresses on the State of the Union and by providing him with a conditional veto power.[62] They kept the President in check by requiring senatorial confirmation of executive appointees and judicial nominees, mandating that the Senate advise on and consent to treaties, and allowing for impeachment by the Congress. Finally, they supplied the means for keeping the Supreme Court in its "proper place" by giving the Congress budgetary control over the judiciary, the power of impeachment, and the power to make exceptions to and regulate the Court's appellate jurisdiction. While they were aware that the various branches of the government, even though popularly elected, might from time to time be activated by "an official sentiment opposed to that of the General Government and perhaps to that of the people themselves,"[63] they were confident that separation of powers would ensure the fidelity of these popular agents. Separation of powers would provide, they argued, for a "balance of the parts" that would consist "in the independent exercise of their separate powers and, when their powers are separately exercised, then in their mutual influence and operation on one another. Each part acts and is acted upon, supports and is supported, regulates and is regulated by the rest." This balance would assure that even if these separate parts were to become activated by separate interests, they would nonetheless move "in a line of direction somewhat different from that, which each acting by itself, would have taken; but, at the same time, in a line partaking of the natural direction of each, and formed out of the natural direction of the whole—the true line of publick [sic] liberty and happiness."[64]

The framers introduced separation and balancing of powers not only to prevent any branch of government from tyrannizing the people but also to thwart the majority of the people from tyrannizing the minority. By creating an independent executive and judiciary, by establishing a bicameral legislature, and by providing for staggered terms of office (two years for the House, four years for the President, six years for the Senate, and tenure "for good behavior" for the judiciary), the framers provided the means for temporarily blocking the will of tyrannical majorities. Thus, although separation of powers cannot permanently frustrate the wishes of the people, on those occasions when "the interests of the people are at variance with their inclinations," it so structures these institutions that they are able to "withstand the temporary delusions" of people, in order to give them "time and opportunity for more cool and sedate reflection."[65] The prospects for democratic tyranny are dimmed accordingly.

The framers relied on separation of powers not only to prevent tyranny but also to render the government efficient, thereby minimizing the prospects for democratic ineptitude. This objective has largely mystified subsequent generations. Justice Louis Brandeis clearly articulated the modern misunderstanding in his dissent in *Myers* v. *United States*: "The doctrine of separation of powers was adopted by the Convention of 1787, not to promote efficiency but to preclude the exercise of arbitrary power. The purpose was, not to avoid friction, but, by means of the inevitable friction incident to the distribution of government powers among the three departments, to save the people from autocracy."[66] The framers, however, knew better; they knew that government would be more efficient if its various functions were performed by separate and distinct bodies. James Wilson, a leading member of the Constitutional Convention, defended the creation of an independent and energetic executive on this exact basis:

> In planning, forming, and arranging laws, deliberation is always becoming, and always useful. But in the active scenes of government, there are emergencies, in which the man . . . who deliberates is lost. Secrecy may be equally necessary as dispatch. But can either secrecy or dispatch be expected, when, to every enterprise, mutual communication, mutual consultation, and mutual agreement among men, perhaps of discordant views, of discordant tempers, and discordant interests, are indispensably necessary? How much time will be consumed! and when it is consumed, how little business will be done! . . . If, on the other hand, the executive power of government is placed in the hands of one person, who is to direct all the subordinate officers of that department; is there not reason to expect, in his plans and conduct, promptitude, activity, firmness, consistency, and energy?[67]

Generalizing on Wilson's point and expanding it to take into account all three branches, Herbert J. Storing has ruminated: "The legislative function requires large numbers, more or less public gatherings, procedures to foster deliberation, etc. The executive function requires, as was said so often, secrecy, energy, and dispatch. Judging requires manifest impartiality and special training in the artificial reasoning of the law." With each branch separate and distinct from each other, "each can perform its function in its appropriate way. This division is not aimed primarily at mutual checking but at the efficient performance of certain kinds of tasks."[68]

Federalism

The American constitutional system rests on a federal arrangement in which power is shared by the national government and the states. The primary purpose of this arrangement was to provide for a strong central government. The framers considered this to be essential, for the "imbecility" of the central government under the Articles of Confederation was so great that, in the words of *Federalist* No. 15, "there is scarcely any thing that can wound the pride, or degrade the character of an independent nation, which we do not experience."[69] There was obviously a need for a "more perfect union" and for new arrangements capable of rendering the political structure "adequate to the exigencies of Government and the preservation of the Union."[70]

The new federalism created by the framers eliminated the ineptitude and imbecility that existed under the Articles of Confederation. To begin with, the power of the new federal government was enhanced considerably. Not only could it now operate directly on the individual citizen, just as the state governments could, but it could also deal with internal matters: For example, it now could regulate commerce among the several states, establish uniform rules of bankruptcy, coin money, establish a postal system, tax, and borrow money. Moreover, the federal government was made supreme over the states on those matters to which it had been delegated power. As Article VI spelled out: "This Constitution, and the laws of the United States which shall be made in pursuance thereof . . . shall be the supreme law of the land."

If the federalism the framers created strengthened the central government, it also helped to avoid majority tyranny by preserving the presence of powerful states capable of checking and controlling not only the central government but each other as well. Federalism granted the new central government only those powers expressly or implicitly delegated to it in the Constitution and allowed the states to retain all powers not prohibited to them. The states were permitted to regulate intrastate commerce and the health, safety, and welfare of the citizenry (i.e., the police power) and were even authorized to exercise certain powers concurrently with the central government—for example the power of taxation and the power to regulate interstate commerce—so long as these powers were not exercised in a manner inconsistent with constitutional limitations or federal regulations. Finally, the framers' federalism also reduced the prospects for majority tyranny by blending federal elements into the structure and procedures of the central government itself.[71] To take only the most obvious example, it mixed into the Senate the federal principle of equal representation of all the states. When joined with bicameralism and separation of powers, this principle serves, in the words of *Federalist* No. 62, as "an additional impediment . . . against improper acts of legislation."[72] Thus, for a measure to become law, it must pass the Senate where, because of the federal principle of equal representation of all the states, the presence of a nationally distributed majority (with the moderating tendencies that provides) is virtually guaranteed.[73]

This division of power between the federal and state governments also provided another remedy for the ills of democratic ineptitude. As James Wilson emphasized, with two levels of government at their disposal, the people were placed in a position to assign their sovereign power to whichever level they believed to be more productive in promoting the common good. Moreover, efficiency is gained in still another way. The federal system permits the states to serve, in the words of Justice John Marshall Harlan, as "experimental social laboratories"[74] in which new policies and procedures can be implemented. If these experiments prove to be successful, they can be adopted elsewhere; if they fail, the damage is limited to the particular state in question. Since the risks are lessened, experimentation is encouraged, and the chances of positive reform and better governance are increased accordingly.[75] In a wholly national system, on the other hand, experimentation can take place only on a national scale, and social inertia and a commitment to the status quo are encouraged. The enhanced efficiency of the federal system, in turn, dims the prospect of democratic tyranny. As Madison observed in *Federalist* No. 20, "Tyranny has perhaps oftener grown out of the assumptions of power, called for, on pressing exigencies, by a defective constitution, than by the full exercise of the largest constitutional authorities."[76]

The framers created a constitution that was, "in strictness, neither a national nor a federal Constitution, but a composition of both."[77] They created what James Madison termed a "compound system"—a system that, he continued, must "be explained by itself, and not by similitudes or analogies."[78]

It is essential for understanding the federalism created by the framers to appreciate that they went into the Convention recognizing only two fundamental modes, or elements, of political organization—the federal and the national[79]—and that they thought that they had succeeded for the first time in combining these two elements into a compound system. Today, in contrast, it is commonplace to speak of three elemental forms: confederal, federal, and national or unitary. This modern typology treats the confederal and national forms as the extremes, with a confederation preserving the primacy and autonomy of the states and with a nation giving unimpeded primacy to the government of the whole society. Federalism, in this view, stands between these two poles and combines the best characteristics of each. Specifically, federalism is thought to combine states, which confederally retain sovereignty within a certain sphere, with a central body that nationally possesses sovereignty within another sphere.

The framers, however, saw no more difference between confederal and federal than we see, for example, between the words *inflammable* and *flammable*: Nothing more was involved than the accidental presence or absence of a nonsignifying prefix. For them, the confederal or federal was opposed to the unitary or national, and they viewed the constitution they had created as a composition of both elemental modes. Today, we regard as a third fundamental mode or element what they regarded as a mere compound, bestowing the simple word *federal* on what they considered to be a composition of both confederal or federal and national elements.

The founding generation's idea of confederal or federal arrangements, as represented in the Articles of Confederation, was characterized by three operative principles, each of which drastically limited the power of the federal authority and preserved the primacy of the member states.[80] First, the central federal authority did not govern individual citizens; it dealt only with the individual states that composed the federal system and operated primarily by the voluntary consent of those states. Second, the central government had no authority to deal with the internal affairs of the member states; rather, its rule was narrowly confined to certain external tasks of mutual interest to all—for example, diplomacy, war, and common defense. Third, each member state had an exact equality of suffrage—an equal vote derived from the equal sovereignty possessed by each state, regardless of size, strength, or wealth.[81]

By contrast, in the framers' conception of a unitary or national government, all power resided in the central authority, and local units of government, if retained at all, were mere subdivisions that existed for administrative purposes only. Such powers as these localities possessed were delegated by the national government and could be overridden or withdrawn altogether at its will. The national authority, then, extended to all matters of internal administration and acted directly, through its own officials, not merely on the local governments but upon every citizen as well. Finally, since the national government was independent of the local units, it could continue in existence even if they were to disappear.

Given a choice between these two modes, those who favored republican government invariably had preferred a confederal or federal arrangement; they regarded it as the only way by which the advantages of size could be combined with the blessings of republicanism. Proponents of this view argued, first of all, that only small countries with homogeneous populations could possess republican government, for only small countries could secure the public's voluntary attachment to the government and voluntary obedience to the laws; and, second, that when such small republics would seek the advantages and safety of greater size, as inevitably they would, they could preserve their republican character only by uniting in a federal manner. Federalism was, for them, the protective husk that preserved the kernels of free government.[82]

The leading framers countered, however, that the traditional republican embrace of federalism, as incorporated in the Articles of Confederation, had humiliated the people and degraded the character of the nation. The principles of federalism, they asserted, had rendered the Articles so weak that the situation "sometimes border[ed] on anarchy."[83] Nor was the government's "imbecility"[84] limited to the realm of foreign affairs; they pointed out how, domestically, the "infirmities of the existing federal system"[85] rendered precarious the "security of private rights" and the "steady dispensation of justice."[86] Convinced of the need for a more powerful government, many delegates to the Constitutional Convention supported the Virginia Plan. As amended, that plan declared that "a Union of the States merely federal will not accomplish the objects proposed by the Articles of Confederation, namely common defense, security of liberty, and general welfare" and proposed, therefore, that "a *national* Government ought to be established consisting of a *supreme* Legislative, Executive and Judiciary."[87]

At this juncture, a serious question arose: Could a national government be formed without jeopardizing republican liberty? Those who favored the establishment of such a government had to persuade their contemporaries that the proposed plan was also compatible with republican government— that federalism as it had been understood to that time was not indispensable to republicanism. To do so, they chose to undermine the prevailing notion that without federalism, only small countries could possess republican governments. Madison's "extended-republic" arguments—made on June 6 in the Convention and repeated in *Federalist* No. 10, were decisive in this respect. Turning the small-republic view on its head, Madison contended that smallness, not largeness, was fatal to republican liberty. History demonstrated that small republics continuously were racked with faction and oppression; indeed, the Constitutional Convention itself had been instigated by the fear for liberty in the small American states. "Was it to be supposed that republican liberty could long exist under the abuses of it practiced in some of the States? . . . Were we not thence admonished to enlarge the sphere as far as the nature of the government would admit?" Because smallness had proven fatal to republicanism, "the only remedy is to enlarge the sphere, and thereby divide the community into so great a number of interests and parties, that in the first place a majority will not be likely at the same moment to have a common interest separate from that of the whole or of the minority; and in the second place, that in case they should have such an interest, they may not be apt to unite in the pursuit of it."[88] The multiplicity of interests present in a large republic thus was the true guardian of republican liberty.[89]

While Madison's arguments on behalf of a large extended republic effectively demolished the small-republic argument, they failed to convince the Convention to adopt a wholly national government.[90] Most of the delegates were reluctant to abolish the states altogether and sought some means for preserving their existence and agency. Increasingly, they came to recognize that because, as William Johnson of Connecticut pointed out, the states were both distinct "political societies" and "districts of people composing one political society,"[91] neither a wholly federal nor a wholly national constitution was appropriate. Spurred on by George Mason of Virginia and others, they realized that it was possible for the people to create and assign power to more than "one set of immediate representatives."[92] The people could not only preserve the states while at the same time establishing a new national government, but they could also have a political structure in which both levels of government operated over the same geographic area. Power would be divided between these two levels according to a simple yet elegant formula: Any object of government confined in operation and effect wholly within the bounds of a particular state would belong to the government of that state, and any object of government extended in its operation and effect beyond the bounds of the particular state would belong to the government of the United States.

Beyond this straightforward division of power between the central government and the states, federalism to the framers also came to mean the presence of federal elements in the central government itself. They came to recognize, in the words of William Davie, that the new constitution would "in some respects operate on the states, in others on the people,"[93] and since the new central government would act upon both the states and the people, they concluded that both ought to be represented in the new government. Accordingly, they mixed together varying proportions of federal and national elements to create a composition that was neither wholly federal nor wholly national. This blend of federal elements in the central government is apparent in the equal representation of the states in the Senate, in the election of the Senate by state legislatures, and in the assignment to the Senate alone of such traditional federal functions as approval of treaties. It is also apparent in such other constitutional provisions as the mode by which the Constitution was to be ratified, the amending process, and the electoral college.

When Tocqueville examined the American Constitution, he described it as "neither exactly national nor exactly federal; but the new word which ought to express this novel thing does not yet exist."[94] While he was correct in declaring that a new word had not been devised, a familiar term from the beginning had been pressed into service to express this novel thing: the term was *federal*. Well aware that federalism was generally thought to be essential for a republican government, the framers seized the word for themselves and called their new compound arrangement federalism. This stratagem proved to be of considerable value during the ratification campaign, as it enabled them to present themselves as the defenders of federalism and to refer to the adherents of federalism as it had been traditionally understood as Anti-Federalists.[95] But the framers' identification of their compound government as federal, although an effective ploy at the time, has been the source of much subsequent confusion concerning exactly what federalism means and concerning what mode of government the American Constitution establishes. Such confusion, however, can be avoided by reference to the Constitution's Preamble.[96] The Constitution was intended neither to provide for a perfect union (i.e., a wholly national government), nor to preserve the radically imperfect union of the Articles of Confederation; rather, it was ordained and established "in order to form a more perfect Union." The phrase, "a more perfect Union," is no grammatical solecism; to the contrary, it is an accurate description of the compound government—made up of both federal and national elements—that the Convention had devised.

The framers incorporated this federal design into the Constitution, but without ever defining federalism or expressly mentioning it.[97] This design, however, would seem to be inherently unstable; the precarious balance between national and federal elements would seem inevitably to shift over time, tilting the government toward becoming either more national or more federal. And, when that shift occurred, given the widely recognized need for a more powerful national government as well as the actual powers delegated to it in Article I, Section 8, the tilt would seen necessarily to be in the direction of making the government more national. How could the balance of national and federal elements be maintained, and how could the original federal design be preserved? The framers' answer to these questions was not to employ the "cloudy medium" of words or to erect ineffectual "parchment barriers" in an attempt to prohibit such a tilt but rather to rely on constitutional structure. In this case, they relied on the mode of electing the U.S. Senate. As chapter 3 develops at length, the fact that senators were elected (and re-elected) by state legislatures made it in their self-interest to preserve the original federal design and to protect the interests of states as states.

Notes

1. Mercy Warren, *History of the Rise, Progress, and Termination of the American Revolution,* 3 vols. (Boston: Manning and Loring, 1805), 3: 370.

2. See Paul Eidelberg, *A Discourse on Statesmanship: The Design and Transformation of the American Polity* (Urbana: University of Illinois Press, 1974), 447. "The word democracy does not appear in the Declaration. Besides, what the Declaration emphasizes is not the *forms* but the *ends* of government. In its own words: 'whenever *any* Form of Government becomes destructive of these ends, it is the Right of the People to alter or to abolish it.' From this it follows that there are legitimate forms of government other than democracy, for example, constitutional monarchy."

3. The words are Edmund Randolph's from the Federal Convention. See Max Farrand (ed.), *The Records of the Federal Convention of 1787,* 4 vols. (New Haven: Yale University Press, 1937), 1: 66. (Hereafter cited as Farrand, *Records.*) See also the statements of John Dickinson (87), George Mason (101), and James Wilson (153). See also Alexander Hamilton, James Madison, and John Jay, *The Federalist,* ed. Jacob E. Cooke (New York: World Publishing Company, 1961), No. 39, 250: "It is evident that no other form [of government] would be reconcilable with the genius of the people of America."

4. Warren characterized religion as the "grand palladium" of republican institutions. Warren, *History,* 3: 403.

5. Warren argued that to maintain their independence, Americans needed to adhere strictly to "the principles of the revolution, and the practice of every public, social, and domestic virtue." *History,* 3: 429.

6. Warren, *History,* 1: 2.

7. Warren, *History,* 1: 2.

8. Warren, *History,* 3: 377.

9. By the framers, I mean that subset of the founding generation that participated actively in the drafting and ratification of the Constitution.

10. *Federalist* No. 34, 212.

11. *Federalist* No. 51, 349.

12. Alexis de Tocqueville, *Democracy in America,* trans. Henry Reeve, ed. Phillips Bradley, 2 vols. (New York: Random House, 1945), 2: 344.

13. *Federalist* No. 10, 61.

14. *Federalist* No. 10, 61.

15. *Federalist* No. 10, 57.

16. *Federalist* No. 10, 57.

17. *Federalist* No. 51, 351.

18. *Federalist* No. 10, 61. See also James Madison, "Vices of the Political System of the United States," in Marvin Meyers (ed.), *The Mind of the Founder:*

Sources of the Political Thought of James Madison, Rev. ed. (Hanover, N.H.: Brandeis University Press, 1981), 57-65.

19. *Federalist* No. 10, 61, 64.

20. Jonathan Elliot (ed.), *The Debates in the Several State Conventions on the Adoption of the Federal Constitution as Recommended by the General Convention in Philadelphia in 1787*, 5 vols. (Philadelphia: J. B. Lippincott, 1863), 2: 74. (Hereafter cited as Elliot, *Debates*.) See the comments of "An Old Whig," writing in Philadelphia's *Independent Gazetteer*: "It is justly observed that the possession of sovereign power is a temptation too great for human nature to resist; and although we have read in history of one or two illustrious characters who have refused to enslave their country when it was in their power—and although we have seen one illustrious character in our own times resisting the possession of power when set in competition with his duty to his country, yet these instances are so very rare, that it would be worse than madness to trust to the chance of their being often repeated." Herbert J. Storing (ed.), *The Complete Anti-Federalist*, 7 vols. (Chicago: University of Chicago Press, 1981), 3: 23.

21. Elliot, *Debates*, 2: 301. Emphasis in the original.

22. *Federalist* No. 9, 50.

23. *Federalist* No. 15, 91. The United States was, indeed, going through a "critical period." See Herbert J. Storing, *What the Anti-Federalists Were For: The Political Thought of the Opponents of the Constitution* (Chicago: University of Chicago Press, 1981), 25-26. This volume was published separately and also as volume 1 of Storing, *The Complete Anti-Federalist*.

24. *Federalist* No. 51, 349.

25. The phrase comes from Frederick Douglass, "The Destiny of Colored Americans," *The North Star*, November 16, 1849, reprinted in Herbert J. Storing (ed.), *What Country Have I? Political Writings of Black Americans* (New York: St. Martin's Press, 1970), 40.

26. In the words of *Federalist* No. 51, 349, they designed the institutions of government so that "the private interest of every individual may be a centinel over the public rights."

27. As Alexander Hamilton had previously observed: "[N]o wise statesman will reject the good from an apprehension of the ill. The truth is in human affairs, there is no good, pure and unmixed; every advantage has two sides, and wisdom consists in availing ourselves of the good and guarding as much as possible against the bad." Letter to Robert Morris, April 30, 1781, in Harold C. Syrett and Jacob E. Cooke (eds.), *The Papers of Alexander Hamilton*, 26 vols. (New York: Columbia University Press, 1961), 2: 618. It was this strategy, however, that drove Mercy Warren into the Anti-Federalist camp. See her "Observations on the New Constitution and on the Federal and State Conventions by a Columbia Patriot," in Storing, *The Complete Anti-Federalist*, 4: 270-87. See also Jean Fritz, *Cast for a Revolution: 1728-1814* (Boston: Houghton Mifflin, 1972), 246-48.

28. Noah Webster, "An Examination into the Leading Principles of the Federal Constitution," in Paul Leicester Ford (ed.), *Pamphlets on the Constitution of the United States* (Brooklyn, N.Y.: Historical Printing Club, 1888), 59. Emphasis in the original. Webster wrote his "Examination" under the pseudonym of "A Citizen of America." Webster continued as follows: "*Virtue*, patriotism, or love of country, never was and never will be, till men's natures are changed, a fixed, permanent principle and support of government." Emphasis in the original.

29. Warren began her *History*, 1: 2, with the following commentary: "The study of the human character opens at once a beautiful and a deformed picture of the soul. We there find a noble principle implanted in the nature of man, that pants for distinction. This principle operates in every bosom, and when kept under the control of reason, and the influence of humanity, it produces the most benevolent effects. But when the checks of conscience are thrown aside, or the moral sense weakened by the sudden acquisition of wealth or power, humanity is obscured, and if the favorable coincidence of circumstances permits, this love of distinction often exhibits the most mortifying instances of profligacy, tyranny, and the wanton exercise of arbitrary sway. Thus when we look over the theatre of human action, scrutinize the windings of the heart, and survey the transactions of man from the earliest to the present period, it must be acknowledged that ambition and avarice are the leading springs which generally actuate the restless mind. From these primary sources of corruption have arisen all the rapine and confusion, the depredation and ruin, that have spread distress over the face of the earth from the days of Nimrod."

30. See *Federalist* No. 10, 59, and No. 6, 28.

31. Quoted in Merrill Jenson, *The Articles of Confederation* (Madison: University of Wisconsin Press, 1962), 34.

32. *Federalist* No. 15, 98, 97.

33. On June 6 in the Federal Convention, anticipating his argument in *Federalist* No. 10, Madison asked "what motives are to restrain" mankind; he then proceeded to answer his question as follows: "A prudent regard to the maxim that honesty is the best policy is found by experience to be as little regarded by bodies of men as by individuals. Respect for character is always diminished in proportion to the number among whom the blame or praise is to be divided. Conscience, the only remaining tie, is known to be inadequate in individuals; in large numbers, little is to be expected from it. Besides, Religion itself may become a motive to persecution & oppression." Farrand, *Records*, 1: 135. See *Federalist* No. 10, 61, in which Madison declared, "If the impulse and the opportunity" to carry "into effect schemes of oppression . . . be suffered to coincide, we well know that neither moral nor religious motives can be relied on as an adequate control."

34. *Federalist* No. 6, 31.

35. *Federalist* No. 61, 412, No. 10, 59.

36. *Federalist* No. 10, 59.

37. *Federalist* No. 15, 96.

38. *Federalist* No. 48, 334. Nonetheless, as *Federalist* No. 49, 340, continued, while "the reason of man, like man himself, is timid and cautious, when left alone," it "acquires firmness and confidence in proportion to the number with which it is associated." *Federalist* No. 63, 425, reinforces this point by arguing that with adequate institutional assistance, reason can ensure that the "cool and deliberate sense of the community" will prevail. Perhaps the most unusual compliment the framers paid to the rationality of the public was in asking them to acknowledge, without indignation or rancor, that all men are prone to impulse and passion and are therefore in need of constitutional structure to channel their avarice and appetites so that they strengthen rather than jeopardize free government. See Benjamin F. Wright, *"The Federalist* on the Nature of Political Man," *Ethics: An International Journal of Social, Political, and Legal Philosophy*, vol. 59, no. 2 (January 1949): 28.

39. "It is in vain to say that enlightened statesmen will be able to adjust these clashing interests, and render them all subservient to the public good. Enlightened statesmen will not always be at the helm." *Federalist* No. 10, 60.

40. *Federalist* No. 78, 529-30.

41. See Patrick Henry's speech on June 9, 1788, before the Virginia Ratifying Convention when he objected to the framers' failure to ground the Constitution adequately on self-interest. "Tell me not of checks on paper; but tell me of checks founded on self-love. The English Government is founded on self-love. ... Have you a resting place like the British Government? Where is the rock of your salvation? The real rock of political salvation is self-love perpetuated from age to age in every human breast, and manifested in every action.... In the British Government there are real balances and checks. In this system, there are only ideal balances. Till I am convinced that there are actual efficient checks, I will not give my assent to its establishment." Storing, *The Complete Anti-Federalist*, 5: 33-34.

42. Letter to George Thatcher, November 22, 1787. Quoted in Jackson Turner Main, *The Antifederalists: Critics of the Constitution, 1781-1788* (Chicago: Quadrangle Books, 1961), 129.

43. Storing, *What the Anti-Federalists Were For*, 47.

44. Elliot, *Debates*, 2: 320.

45. "Will it be sufficient to mark, with precision, the boundaries of these departments, in the constitution of the government, and to trust to these parchment barriers against the encroaching spirit of power? This is the security which appears to have been principally relied on by the compilers of most of the American constitutions. But experience assures us, that the efficacy of the provision has been greatly overrated; and that some more adequate defense is indispensably necessary for the more feeble, against the more powerful, members of the government." *Federalist* No. 48, 332-33.

46. *Federalist* No. 37, 236-37.

47. Cesare Beccaria, *On Crimes and Punishments*, trans. Henry Paolucci (New York: Bobbs-Merrill, 1963), 29.

48. No mention was made during the Federal Convention of a bill of rights until September 12, just five days before the Convention adjourned. On that date, George Mason declared that "[h]e wished the plan had been prefaced with a Bill of Rights & would second a Motion if made for the purpose. It would give great quiet to the people, and with the aid of the State declarations, a bill might be prepared in a few hours." Mason's suggestion was quickly defeated. Upon Elbridge Gerry's formal motion and Mason's second, it was rejected by the Convention by a vote of 0 states "yes," 10 states "no," 1 state absent. Farrand, *Records,* 2: 587. When on June 8, 1789, James Madison subsequently proposed the adoption of a Bill of Rights in the First Congress, he stressed that his proposed language did no more than "expressly declare the great rights of mankind secured under this constitution." Helen E. Veit, Kenneth R. Bowling, and Charlene Bangs Bickford (eds.), *Creating the Bill of Rights: The Documentary Record from the First Federal Congress* (Baltimore: Johns Hopkins University Press, 1991), 78. He thereby clearly conveyed his understanding that the "great rights of mankind" proclaimed in his proposed Bill of Rights were secured not by parchment barriers but by constitutional structure. See Robert A. Goldwin, *From Parchment to Power: How James Madison Used the Bill of Rights to Save the Constitution* (Washington, D.C.: AEI Press, 1997) and Ralph A. Rossum, "*The Federalist*'s Understanding of the Constitution as a Bill of Rights," in Charles R. Kesler (ed.), *Saving the Revolution: The Federalist Papers and the American Founding* (New York: Free Press, 1987), 219-33.

49. Farrand, *Records,* 1: 512. See also *Federalist* No. 51, 349: "Ambition must be made to counteract ambition," and No. 72, 489: "His avarice might be a guard upon his avarice."

50. Tocqueville, *Democracy in America,* 2: 131.

51. *Federalist* No. 9, 51.

52. *Federalist* No. 10, 65.

53. *Federalist* No. 10, 63-64.

54. *Federalist* No. 51, 353.

55. The words are James Wilson's. Robert Green McCloskey (ed.), *The Works of James Wilson* (Cambridge: Belknap Press of Harvard University Press, 1967), 791.

56. *Federalist* No. 47, 324.

57. Storing, *What the Anti-Federalists Were For,* 62.

58. Sir William Blackstone, *Commentaries on the Laws of England,* 4 vols. (Oxford: Clarendon, 1765), 1: 151.

59. Blackstone, *Commentaries,* 1: 151. See also 1: 51-53.

60. Massachusetts Constitution of 1780, Part the First: A Declaration of the Rights of the Inhabitants of the Commonwealth of Massachusetts, Article XXX.

61. *Federalist* No. 51, 347-48.

62. The ability of the courts (and especially the Supreme Court) to check and restrain the Congress through the power of judicial review is not mentioned here, because it is not mentioned in the Constitution. See the discussion of the Supreme Court in chapter 3. Those who contend that the Court legitimately has the power of

judicial review argue inferentially. They argue that the way in which the Constitution provides for a separation of powers that, in the words of *Federalist* No. 48, 332, so "connects" and "blends" the three departments of government "as to give to each a constitutional control over the others" implies the appropriateness, nay the necessity, of judicial review. This power, they contend, simply gives the Court a means of checking and restraining the popular branches and thereby of protecting itself from their encroachments, much as the popular branches—through such constitutional controls as impeachment and congressional appropriation of money for the judicial branch—have means at their disposal for restraining the courts. The Constitution, however, simply does not make explicit provision for judicial review, while it does explicitly provide for impeachment; congressional control of the Court's appellate jurisdiction; congressional determination of the size, shape, and composition of the entire federal judiciary; presidential appointment of judges subject to Senate confirmation; congressional appropriations for the courts; etc. Separation of powers, from which judicial review is inferred, is itself never explicitly mentioned in the Constitution; rather it is inferred from the specific powers that the Constitution assigns to the branches. Judicial review is no more than an inference drawn from an inference. See Ralph A. Rossum, "The Least Dangerous Branch?" in Peter Augustine Lawler and Robert Martin Schaefer (eds.), *The American Experiment: Essays on the Theory and Practice of Liberty* (Lanham, Md.: Rowman & Littlefield, 1994), 248, 252.

63. Farrand, *Records*, 1: 359.

64. McCloskey, *The Works of James Wilson*, 300.

65. *Federalist* No. 71, 482-83.

66. 272 U.S. 52, 293 (1926). Justice Brandeis dissenting.

67. McCloskey, *The Works of James Wilson*, 294, 296.

68. Storing, *What the Anti-Federalists Were For*, 60. See Harvey Flaumenhaft, "Hamilton on the Foundation of Good Government," *Political Science Reviewer* 6 (Fall 1976): 211. "The device to decrease the danger can be employed against inefficacy; government can be energized by the very safeguard against government oppression."

69. *Federalist* No. 15, 91.

70. Resolution of the Congress calling for the Federal Convention of 1787, in Farrand, *Records*, 3: 14.

71. See Martin Diamond, "*The Federalist* on Federalism: Neither a National nor a Federal Constitution, but a Composition of Both," *Yale Law Journal* 86, no. 6 (May 1977): 1273-85.

72. *Federalist* No. 62, 417.

73. "No law or resolution can now be passed without the concurrence first of a majority of the people, and then of a majority of the states." *Federalist* No. 62, 417.

74. *Roth* v. *United States*, 354 U.S. 476, 505 (1957). Justice Harlan dissenting. See also *New State Ice Co.* v. *Liebmann*, 258 U.S. 262, 311 (1932), Justice Brandeis dissenting: "It is one of the happy incidents of the federal system that a single courageous state may, if its citizens choose, serve as a laboratory; and try novel social and economic experiments without risk to the rest of the country."

75. See Justice Sandra Day O'Connor's opinion for the Court in *Gregory* v. *Ashcroft*, 501 U.S. 452, 458 (1991): "The federalist structure of joint sovereigns preserves to the people numerous advantages. It assures a decentralized government that will be more sensitive to the diverse needs of a heterogeneous society; it increases opportunity for citizen involvement in democratic processes; it allows for more innovation and experimentation in government; and it makes government more responsive by putting the States in competition for a mobile citizenry."

76. *Federalist* No. 20, 127.

77. *Federalist* No. 39, 257.

78. James Madison, "Outline," in Gaillard Hunt (ed.), *The Writings of James Madison*, 9 vols. (New York: G. P. Putnam's Sons, 1910), 9: 246.

79. This discussion relies heavily on Martin Diamond, "What the Framers Meant by Federalism" in Robert A. Goldwin (ed.), *A Nation of States*, 2d ed. (Chicago: Rand McNally, 1974).

80. See Martin Diamond, "The Ends of Federalism," *Publius* 3, no. 2 (Fall 1973): 131-32.

81. See also Diamond, "What the Framers Meant by Federalism," 25-42.

82. Herbert J. Storing, "Foreword," in Paul Eidelberg, *The Philosophy of the American Constitution* (New York: Free Press, 1968), xi.

83. *Federalist* No. 22, 141.

84. *Federalist* No. 15, 92.

85. *Federalist* No. 22, 145.

86. Farrand, *Records*, 1: 134.

87. Farrand, *Records*, 1: 33. Emphasis in the original.

88. Farrand, *Records*, 1: 134-36.

89. *Federalist* No. 10, 64.

90. They have even have failed completely to convince Madison. See his statement in *Federalist* No. 51, 354: "It is no less certain than it is important, notwithstanding the contrary opinions which have been entertained, that the larger the society, provided it lie within a practicable sphere, the more duly capable it will be of self-government. And happily for the republican cause, the practicable sphere may be carried to a very great extent, by the *judicious modification and mixture of the federal principle*." Emphasis added.

91. Farrand, *Records*, 1: 461.

92. Farrand, *Records*, 1: 339.

93. Farrand, *Records*, 1: 488.

94. Tocqueville, *Democracy in America*, 1: 165.

95. It was, in truth, more than a stratagem. They could legitimately claim to be Federalists, because they sought to strengthen the federal government, if at the expense of the federal principle.

96. In this respect, see Justice Story: "The importance of examining the preamble, for the purpose of expounding the language of a statute, has been long

felt, and universally conceded in all juridical discussions. It is an admitted maxim in the ordinary course of the administration of justice, that the preamble of a statute is a key to open the mind of the makers, as to the mischiefs, which are to be remedied, and the objects, which are to be accomplished by the provisions of the statute. . . . There does not seem any reason why, in a fundamental law or constitution of government, an equal attention should not be given to the intention of the framers, as stated in the preamble." Joseph Story, *Commentaries on the Constitution of the United States*, 3 vols. (New York: Hilliard & Gray, 1833), Sections 459-60, 1: 444.

97. The same, of course, can be said of separation of powers. See Justice Scalia: "Indeed, with an economy of expression that many would urge as a model for modern judicial opinions, the principle of separation of powers is found only in the structure of the [Constitution,] which successively describes where the legislative, executive, and judicial powers shall reside." Antonin Scalia, "The Doctrine of Standing as an Essential Element of the Separation of Powers," *Suffolk University Law Review* 17 (1983): 881.

Chapter 3

How the Framers Protected Federalism

The framers understood that federalism would be protected structurally—the mode of electing (and reelecting) the Senate making it in the self-interest of senators to preserve the original federal design and to protect the interests of states as states.[1] The debates in the Constitutional Convention make this abundantly clear.

The Mode of Electing the Senate as a Means of Protecting the States as States

On May 31, 1787, very early in the Constitutional Convention, the delegates rejected Resolution 5 of the Virginia Plan that proposed that the "second branch of the National Legislature ought to be elected by those of the first," doing so by a vote of seven states "no," three states "yes."[2] Instead on June 7, they unanimously accepted a motion made by John Dickinson and seconded by Roger Sherman providing for the appointment of the Senate by the state legislatures.[3]

The delegates were apparently persuaded by Dickinson's argument that the "sense of the States would be better collected through their Governments than immediately from the people at large"[4] and by George Mason's observation that election of the Senate by state legislatures would provide the states with "some means of defending themselves against encroachments of the National Government. In every other department, we have studiously endeavored to provide for its self-defense. Shall we leave the States alone unprovided with the means for this purpose? And what better means can we provide than giving them some share in, or rather making them a constituent part of, the Nat'l Establishment?"[5] Even when the delegates subsequently agreed on June 11 to some form of proportional representation in the Senate,[6] they still remained firmly committed to the election of the Senate by the state legislatures.

On June 20, James Wilson, a passionate nationalist,[7] warned his fellow delegates that "a jealousy would exist between the State Legislatures & the General Legislature." He observed "that the members of the former would have views & feelings very distinct in this respect from their constituents. A private Citizen of a State is indifferent whether power be exercised by the Genl. or State Legislatures, provided it be exercised most for his happiness." On the other hand, "[h]is representative has an interest in its being exercised by the body to which he belongs. He will therefore view the National Legisl. with the eye of a jealous rival."[8] On June 25, he continued his attack on the election of the Senate by state legislatures, charging that "the election of the second branch by the Legislatures will introduce and cherish local interests and local prejudices."[9] Wilson's attack, however, utterly failed, not because the delegates disputed his analysis but because they approved the outcome.[10] Since they were committed to preserving the states as political entities, they found persuasive Mason's assertions that the states would need the "power of self-defense"[11] and that "the only mode left of giving it to them was by allowing them to appoint the second branch of the National Legislature."[12] Accordingly, on that day, the Convention affirmed its previous decision to elect the Senate by state legislatures by a vote of nine states "yes," two states "no."[13]

Other Possible "Modes" of Providing the States with the "Power of Self-Defense"

Mason's assertion that the appointment of senators by state legislatures was the "only mode" of providing the states with the "power of self-defense" seems, on first impression, to be an exaggeration. The delegates were clearly aware of other "modes" they also could have incorporated into the Constitution that would have helped to defend the interests of the states as states. To mention the four most obvious, they could have (1) specified that the Senate delegation from a state vote as a block, (2) made explicit provision for the instruction of senators by state legislatures, (3) allowed the states to recall their senators, and (4) required rotation in office.[14] For a variety of reasons, however, the framers, declined to adopt these other "modes."

Block Voting

The Great Compromise, accepted by the Convention on July 16, 1787, gave each state equal representation in the Senate and proportional representation in the House. It did not, however, specify the number of senators each state would have; it only declared that "each state shall have an equal vote."[15] This issue was resolved on July 23, when Gouverneur Morris and Rufus King moved "that the representation in the second branch consist of [   ] members from each State, who shall vote per capita."[16] Morris then moved "to fill the blank with three" because "he wished the Senate to be a pretty numerous body," but his motion was defeated by a vote of one state "yes," eight states "no." The Convention then took up Nathaniel Gorham's motion that each state have two senators, which he defended on the grounds that "a small number was more convenient for deciding on peace & war, &c. which he expected would be vested in the 2d. branch," and passed it unanimously.[17] It then turned to the question of per capita voting. Oliver Ellsworth, a delegate from Connecticut whose diplomatic skills were instrumental in gaining approval of the Great Compromise, immediately indicated that "he had always approved of voting in that mode." Hugh Williamson from North Carolina concurred. Luther Martin from Maryland objected, however, declaring that he was "opposed to voting per Capita, as departing from the idea of the *States* being represented in the 2d. branch."[18] Daniel Carroll, also of Maryland, indicated that while he had no "objection agst. the mode, he did not wish so hastily to make so material an innovation." Nonetheless, at the conclusion of his speech, the Convention adopted the "whole motion, viz, the 2d. b. to consist of 2 members from each State and to vote per capita," by a vote of nine states "yes," one state (Martin and Carroll's home state of Maryland) "no."[19]

Carroll was indeed correct in describing the decision to have a state's senators vote per capita as a material innovation. Article V of the Articles of Confederation had specified that, while states could be represented in Congress by not "less than two, nor by more than seven Members," when it came to "determining questions in the united states, in Congress, assembled, each state shall have one vote."[20] The Convention's decision was a clear departure from the current practice. Having acquiesced to the demands of the small states that the Articles were to be followed with regard to the equal representation of the states in the Senate, the Convention then proceeded, with very little discussion, to depart from the Articles and allow a state's two senators to vote independently, thereby potentially splitting their votes. As Jay S. Bybee notes, "That action seems contrary to the idea of state representation."[21] Yet, this material innovation prompted little debate, either in the Convention or during the ratification process. Why?

As Bybee argues, "the reasons for approving per capita voting may have had more to do with the delegates' practical experience than with a desire to undermine state representation." The framers knew from experience that caucuses had gone unrepresented because of an evenly divided vote. "Per capita voting ensured that states would be represented, even if they were not represented consistently."[22] It also ensured that divided state delegations would not be forced to abstain and, by so doing, frustrate the Senate from acting at all.

The framers also appreciated that per capita voting could often represent a state's interests better than block voting, even if occasionally that state's senators split their vote. Since their six-year terms of office were to be staggered, and since they were elected by state legislatures that, as Madison observed in *Federalist* No. 63, were continuously "regenerate[d]" by "the periodic change of members,"[23] a state's two senators would be able to represent somewhat different political moods and sentiments. Elected by shifting majorities in the state legislature, the two senators, voting per capita, would be able to reflect more accurately the shifting political sentiments of the people in their home states than if they were required to vote as a block. Interestingly, the only time the framers departed from per capita voting in the Constitution was the one time they are spared the need to take account of shifting political sentiments: Article II, Section 1 provides that when the election of the President is thrown into the House of Representatives (all of whose members were elected at the same time and who could not, therefore, reflect shifting political sentiments), "the votes shall be taken by States, the Representation from each State having one Vote."[24]

Instruction of Senators

The ability of state legislatures to instruct senators was mentioned frequently during the Constitutional Convention and the state ratifying conventions and was always assumed to exist.[25] An exchange on August 24 during the Constitutional Convention as the delegates debated the

Appointments Clause[26] is telling in this respect. The Convention had just accepted John Dickinson's motion that the President "shall appoint to all offices established by the Constitution, except in cases herein otherwise provided for, and to all offices which may hereafter be created by law."[27] Edmund Randolph worried aloud, however, that the power of appointments was "a formidable one both in the Executive & Legislative hands—and suggested whether the Legislature should not be left at liberty to refer appointments in some cases, to some State authority."[28] When Dickinson then moved language to that effect, James Wilson intervened: "If this be agreed to it will soon be a standing instruction from the State Legislatures to pass no law creating offices unless the appts. be referred to them," whereupon Dickinson's motion "was negatived without a Count of the States."[29] Wilson's assertion that the state legislatures would instruct their senators to vote in a certain way not only went unchallenged but clearly proved persuasive.

The state ratifying conventions shared the same understanding of the state legislature's ability to instruct senators. In Massachusetts, Rufus King argued that "the state legislatures, if they find their delegates erring, can and will instruct them. Will not this be a check? When they hear the voice of the people solemnly dictating to them their duty, they will be bold men indeed to act contrary to it." These instructions, he pointed out, will not be sent to the state's senators "in a private letter, which can be put in their pockets; they will be public instructions, which all the country will see, and they will be hardy men indeed to violate them."[30] In New York, Alexander Hamilton responded to the charge that the House of Representatives, initially consisting of sixty-five members, was too small by observing that "[i]f the general voice of the people be for an increase, it undoubtedly must take place. They have it in their power to instruct their representatives; and the state legislatures, which appoint the senators, may enjoin it also upon them."[31] John Jay acknowledged the advantages of a "large representation" in the national legislature but thought the ability of state legislatures to instruct senators achieved much the same goal: "The Senate is to be composed of men appointed by the state legislatures: they will certainly choose those who are most distinguished for their general knowledge. I presume they will also instruct them, that there will be a constant correspondence between the senators and the state executives, who will be able, from time to time, to afford them all that particular information which particular circumstances may require."[32] And, in Virginia, Patrick Henry complained that, while state legislatures could instruct their senators, they could not enforce those instructions by recalling them: "But can you in this government recall your senators? Or can you instruct them? You

cannot recall them. You may instruct them, and offer your opinions; but if
they think them improper, they may disregard them."[33]

The first Congress also assumed that state legislatures could issue
instructions, as is apparent from what the *Daily Advertiser* characterized as
the "long debate"[34] that took place on August 15, 1789, as the members of
the House considered the proposed Bill of Rights.[35] Representative Thomas
Tudor Tucker of South Carolina proposed that, after the words "the right of
the people peaceably to assemble," there be inserted the words "to instruct
their Representatives."[36] Tucker's motion generated a most interesting
exchange. George Clymer of Pennsylvania hoped "the amendment will not
be adopted, but if our constituents chuse [*sic*] to instruct us, that they may
be left at liberty to do so." He worried that, "if they have a constitutional
right to instruct us, it infers we are bound by those instructions," which he
labeled a "most dangerous principle, utterly destructive of all ideas of an
independent and deliberative body."[37] Elbridge Gerry of Massachusetts
denied that the language would bind the members of Congress. "I do not
conceive that this necessarily follows: I think the representative, not
withstanding the insertion of these words, would be at liberty to act as he
pleased; if he declined to pursue such measures as he was directed to attain,
the people would have a right to refuse him their suffrages at a future
election."[38] Madison, the author of the language that Tucker sought to
amend, then joined the debate and opposed Tucker's motion, fearing the
predicament confronting representatives who would consider their
instructions as binding: "Suppose they instruct a representative by his vote
to violate the constitution, is he at liberty to obey such instructions?"[39]
This, however, prompted a sharp rebuke from Gerry: "Can we conceive
that our constituents would be so absurd as to instruct us to violate our
oath, and act directly contrary to the principles of a government ordained
by themselves? We must look upon them to be absolutely abandoned and
false to their own interests to suppose them capable of giving such
instructions."[40] Madison was more successful when he opposed Tucker's
motion as unnecessary. After he observed that, if instructions meant "nothing
more than this, that the people have a right to express and communicate
their sentiments and wishes, we have provided for it already,"[41] the debate
became, in the words of the reporter for the *Congressional Register*,
increasingly "desultory," and Tucker's motion was eventually defeated by
a vote of forty-one to ten.[42]

State legislatures not only were assumed to have the power to instruct
their senators[43] but immediately began to exercise that power once the new
government was established. In the very first Congress, Virginia, in response
to the Senate's refusal to deliberate in public, instructed its senators to secure

"one of the important privileges of the people" by obtaining their "free admission" to the Senate. When Virginia's resolution was ignored, Maryland, New York, North Carolina, South Carolina, and Virginia instructed their senators to propose again that the Senate conduct its business in public. When the senators from those states refused to act on these instructions, Maryland, North Carolina, South Carolina, and Virginia reissued their instructions, asserting that their senators were "bound by the instructions of the legislature . . . where such instructions are not repugnant to the constitution of the United States" and condemning their senators' refusal to act on them. The senators from Maryland and South Carolina continued to ignore their instructions, prompting Maryland to issue a vote of censure. These state instructions, however, ultimately were heeded, and, when the Senate agreed to open its meetings in 1794, it identified itself in its resolution of approval as "the Representatives of the sovereignties of the individual states."[44]

The next issue that prompted state legislatures to instruct their senators was the Supreme Court's refusal to acknowledge the doctrine of state sovereign immunity in *Chisholm* v. *Georgia*.[45] Both Virginia and Massachusetts passed resolutions instructing their senators and requesting their representatives[46] to adopt an amendment depriving federal courts of jurisdiction over suits by private individuals against the states (what became the Eleventh Amendment).[47] These instructions were followed in quick succession by Kentucky's instruction to its senators, through the Kentucky Resolutions of 1798, to procure the repeal of the "unconstitutional and obnoxious" Sedition Act;[48] by instructions from New York, Massachusetts, and Vermont to change the mode of electing the President and Vice President (what became the Twelfth Amendment);[49] and by instructions from Pennsylvania and Virginia to oppose rechartering the Bank of the United States.[50] State legislatures thereafter issued instructions on a wide range of subjects, including the compensation of members of Congress (Massachusetts); the construction of bridges (Ohio and Pennsylvania); cod fishing and whaling (Massachusetts); pensions (Massachusetts); futures (Mississippi); free coinage of silver (Mississippi); the admission of Kansas, California, West Virginia, and New Mexico as states (Virginia, Tennessee, Vermont); slavery (Vermont); and presidential censure (Maine, New Jersey, Ohio).[51] The practice of issuing instructions diminished somewhat after the Civil War[52] but survived until the adoption and ratification of the Seventeenth Amendment—an amendment that nine states instructed their senators to support.[53]

Not only did state legislatures take seriously their ability to issue instructions, but the senators who received them generally took them seriously as well. In 1809, John Quincy Adams, then a U.S. senator from

Massachusetts, resigned his seat rather than follow the antiembargo instructions he had received from the Massachusetts General Court.[54] In 1814, Senator David Stone of North Carolina, "upon being informed that the General Assembly had by a large majority resolved that he had incurred its disapprobation" for voting with the New England Federalists, resigned at once.[55] In 1835, Senator Peleg Sprague of Maine resigned after voting contrary to the Maine Legislature, which had instructed him to oppose the restoration of governmental deposits and the renewal of the charter of the Bank of the United States.[56] And one final illustration: In the aftermath of the Senate's censure of President Andrew Jackson for crippling the Bank of the United States by ordering the withdrawal of all U.S. funds from it, several southern state legislatures instructed their senators to seek to have the censure expunged from the Senate records, prompting seven southern senators (Alexander Porter of Louisiana; Bedford Brown, Robert Strange, and Willie Mangum of North Carolina; Hugh White of Tennessee; and William Rives and John Tyler of Virginia) to resign their offices rather than accede to their instructions.[57]

Clearly the lack of an express constitutional provision on instruction did not prevent its use by those states so inclined. (And, to the extent that their senators heeded their instructions, the consequences of per capita voting were overcome.) The framers treated the issue of instruction in much the same way that they treated the issue of who could vote for members of Congress under the new Constitution—by leaving it up to the states to determine for themselves.[58] By so doing, the framers showed respect for the "inviolable and residuary sovereignty of the states."[59]

Recall

Authorizing a state legislature to recall its senators if they voted contrary to the state's interest or failed to follow instructions would have been still another mode of providing the states with "the power of self-defense." And, as Patrick Henry's statement above makes clear, it is closely related to the ability to issue instructions. Recall was authorized under the Articles of Confederation[60] and, interestingly, was also provided for in the Virginia Plan, which proposed in Resolution 4 that "the members of the first branch of the National Legislature ought . . . to be subject to recall"; since the members of the second branch were "to be elected by those of the first," the drafters of the Virginia Plan apparently saw no need to subject them to recall.[61] The Convention, however, quickly rejected the idea; on June 12,

Charles Pinckney's motion to strike the language on recall passed unanimously.[62]

Once the Convention finally determined that the Senate would be elected by state legislatures, the need to reconsider the possible utility of recall and its ability to assist in protecting the interests of states as states would have seemed obvious, but the records of the Convention's deliberations show no such discussion. Jay S. Bybee suggests a reason: Granting the states the power to recall their senators would have been inconsistent with the decision to have senators serve for the relatively lengthy term of six years. "Had the Constitution granted states the recall power, then each succeeding legislature might select its own delegates to the Senate, perhaps making the Senate as subject to the winds of political change as the House."[63] The framers intended the Senate to protect federalism and to secure the interests of states as such, but they also intended it to be a repository of "wisdom and stability."[64] Recall would have undermined the ability of the Senate to check "the mischievous effects of mutable government" and advance "the collective and permanent welfare" of the country.[65] The framers were willing to live with this trade-off, depending on the state legislatures' power to provide instructions and to refuse to reelect disobedient senators to protect state interests. As Wilson Nicholas declared in the Virginia Ratifying Convention: "We cannot recall our senators. We can give them instructions; and if they manifestly neglect our interest, we have sufficient security against them. The dread of being recalled would impair their independence and firmness."[66]

Rotation in Office

Rotation in office was another mode considered by the framers to ensure the fidelity of the states' representatives. The principle of rotation was found in the Articles of Confederation, which declared that "[n]o person shall be capable of being a delegate for more than three years in any term of six years."[67] Resolution 4 of the Virginia Plan made members of the first branch "incapable of reelection for a space of [ ] years after the expiration of their term of service," which the delegates struck without discussion.[68] As the Convention considered the length of the term of office for the Senate, James Wilson proposed "9 years with a rotation" and with one-third "go[ing] out triennially" as a means of gaining from foreign nations negotiating commercial treaties with the United States the necessary "confidence in the stability and efficacy of our Government," but his motion was defeated by a vote of eight states "no," three states "yes."[69]

The most fulsome debate on the merits of rotation occurred in the New York State Ratifying Convention. There, Gilbert Livingston faulted the Constitution for not providing for rotation and argued that, without it, senators would serve "as long as they please. Indeed, in my view, it will amount nearly to an appointment for life."[70] He animadverted on the deleterious effects that the "federal town" (i.e., the nation's capital) would have on senators serving indefinitely: "In this Eden will they reside with their families, distant from the observation of the people. In such a situation, men are apt to forget their dependence, lose their sympathy, . . . contract selfish habits, . . . and thus become strangers to the condition of the common people." Rotation, he insisted, would "revive their sense of dependence." It would impress "on their minds that they are soon to return to the level whence the suffrages of the people raised them." It would incline them to "consider their interests as the same with those of their constituents, and that they legislate for themselves as well as others. They will not conceive themselves made to receive, enjoy, and rule, nor the people solely to earn, pay, and submit."[71]

This defense of rotation did not go unchallenged. "The people," Robert R. Livingston argued, "are the best judges of who ought to represent them. To dictate and control them, to tell them whom they shall not elect, is to abridge their natural rights." He branded rotation as "an absurd species of ostracism—a mode of proscribing eminent merit, and banishing from stations of trust those who have filled them with the greatest faithfulness. Besides, it takes away the strongest stimulus to public virtue—the hope of honors and rewards." He declared that "[t]he acquisition of abilities is hardly worth the trouble, unless one is to enjoy the satisfaction of employing them for the good of one's country." Moreover, "We all know that experience is indispensably necessary to good government." He concluded by asking: "Shall we, then, drive experience into obscurity? I repeat that this is an absolute abridgment of the people's rights."[72]

While powerful arguments could be made on both sides of the rotation question, the framers chose not to make it a constitutional provision. They were aware that any state legislature persuaded by the arguments in its favor could practice rotation on its own by simply refusing to reelect an incumbent senator after one term—or after what it would consider to be an appropriate number of terms. They were also aware that, by refusing to impose rotation on the states, they were actually protecting the interests of the states as states by allowing them to exercise discretion on this matter as they saw fit.

How the Mode of Electing the Senate Was Understood during the Ratification Debates and in the New Republic

The service rendered to federalism by the mode of electing the Senate was repeatedly acknowledged and proclaimed during the ratification debates. Examples abound and are listed here in chronological order.

In "An Examination of the Constitution of the United States," Tench Coxe, writing under the pseudonym of "An American Citizen" in Philadelphia's *Independent Gazetteer*, noted that the members of the Senate will "feel a considerable check from the constitutional powers of the state legislatures, whose rights they will not be disposed to infringe, since they are the bodies to which they owe their existence."[73] In the Pennsylvania Ratifying Convention, in a speech brimming with sarcasm, James Wilson, now reconciled to the Constitution's mode of electing the Senate, responded to those who charged that the new government would "abolish the independence and sovereignty of the states individually"[74] by declaring: "In the system before you, the senators, sir—those tyrants that are to devour the legislatures of the states—are to be chosen by the state legislatures themselves. Need any thing more be said on this subject?"[75]

In the Connecticut Ratifying Convention, Oliver Wolcott noted that "[t]he Constitution effectually secures the states in their several rights. It must secure them for its own sake; for they are the pillars which uphold the general system. The Senate, a constituent branch of the general legislature, without whose assent no public act can be made, are appointed by the states, and will secure the rights of the several states."[76] In the Massachusetts Ratifying Convention, Fisher Ames described senators elected by their state legislatures as "ambassadors of the states"[77] and explained how they could be trusted to protect state interests: "A third part is to retire from office every two years. By this means, while the senators are seated for six years, they are admonished of their responsibility to the state legislatures. If one third new members are introduced, who feel the sentiments of their states, they will awe that third whose term will be near expiring. This article seems to be an excellence of the Constitution, and affords just ground to believe that it will be, in practice as in theory, a federal republic."[78] Rufus King in the same convention then shrewdly observed that "the senators will have a powerful check in those men [i.e., those state legislators] who wish for their seats, who will watch their whole conduct in the general government, and will give alarm in case of misbehavior."[79]

In *Federalist* No. 45, Madison declared that, since "[t]he Senate will be elected absolutely and exclusively by the State Legislatures," it "will owe its existence more or less to the favor of the State Governments, and

must consequently feel a dependence, which [he candidly regretted] is much
more likely to beget a disposition too obsequious, than too overbearing
towards them."[80] In *Federalist* No. 46, he further noted that, if the House
of Representatives were to sponsor legislation that encroached on the
authority of the states, "a few representatives of the people would be opposed
to the people themselves; or rather one set of representatives would be
contending against thirteen sets of representatives, with the whole body of
their common constituents on the side of the latter."[81] The Senate, he assured
his readers, would be "disinclined to invade the rights of the individual
States, or the prerogatives of their governments."[82]

In *Federalist* No. 59, Alexander Hamilton likewise emphasized that the
appointment of senators by state legislatures secured "a place in the organization
of the National Government" for the "States in their political capacities."[83] He
continued: "So far as [the mode of electing the Senate] . . . may expose the
Union to the possibility of injury from the State legislatures, it is an evil;
but it is an evil which could not have been avoided without excluding the
States, in their political capacities, wholly from a place in the organization
of the national government. If this had been done, it would doubtless have
been interpreted into an entire dereliction of the federal principle; and would
certainly have deprived the State governments of that absolute safeguard
which they will enjoy under this provision."[84] Finally, in *Federalist* No.
62, Madison praised "the appointment of senators by state legislatures" as
not only "the most congenial with the public opinion" but also "giving to
state governments such an agency in the formation of the federal
government, as must secure the authority of the former."[85]

During the New York Ratifying Convention in 1788, Hamilton explicitly
connected the mode of electing the Senate with the protection of the interests
of the states as states. "When you take a view of all the circumstances
which have been recited, you will certainly see that the senators will
constantly look up to the state governments with an eye of dependence and
affection. If they are ambitious to continue in office, they will make every
prudent arrangement for this purpose, and, whatever may be their private
sentiments or politics, they will be convinced that the surest means of
obtaining reelection will be a uniform attachment to the interests of their
several states."[86] He also declared: "Sir, the senators will constantly be
attended with a reflection, that their future existence is absolutely in the
power of the states. Will not this form a powerful check?"[87] And finally,
during North Carolina's first ratifying convention in 1788, James Iredell
also noted that "[t]he manner in which our Senate is to be chosen gives us
an additional security. . . . There is every probability that men elected in
this manner will, in general, do their duty faithfully. It may be expected,

therefore, that they will cooperate in every laudable act, but strenuously resist those of a contrary nature."[88]

This same argument was also made repeatedly in the early days of the new republic. For example, in a July 1789 letter to John Adams, Roger Sherman emphasized that "[t]he senators, being eligible by the legislatures of the several states, and dependent on them for reelection, will be vigilant in supporting their rights against infringement by the legislative or executive of the United States."[89] In his 1803 edition of *Blackstone's Commentaries*, St. George Tucker declared that "the senate are chosen to represent the states in their sovereign capacity"[90] and that, if a senator abuses the confidence of "the individual state which he represents," he "will be sure to be displaced."[91] James Kent in his *Commentaries on American Law* noted that "[t]he election of the Senate by the state legislatures is also a recognition of their separate and independent existence, and renders them absolutely essential to the operation of the national government."[92] And Joseph Story in his *Commentaries on the Constitution of the United States* observed that one of the "main grounds" for the mode of appointing the Senate was that it "would introduce a powerful check upon rash legislation" and "would increase public confidence by securing the national government from undue encroachments on the powers of the states."[93]

The Mode of Electing the Senate as a Means of Partitioning Federal and State Power

The framers favored election of the Senate by state legislatures not simply because it was, as Madison put it in *Federalist* No. 62, "the most congenial with the public opinion"[94] and not simply because it provided, in Hamilton's words from *Federalist* No. 59, incentives for senators to remain vigilant in their protection of the "States in their political capacities."[95] They also favored this mode of election because it helped them sidestep what Madison described in *Federalist* No. 37 as the "arduous" task of "marking the proper line of partition, between the authority of the general, and that of the State Governments."[96]

An episode at the very outset of the Convention is most telling on this point. On May 31, the Convention, meeting as a committee of the whole, had just taken up Resolution 6 of the Virginia Plan that proposed, *inter alia*, that "the National Legislature ought to be empowered . . . to legislate in all cases to which the separate States were incompetent." Charles Pinckney and John Rutledge "objected to the vagueness of the term *incompetent,* and said they could not well decide how to vote until they should see an exact enumeration of the powers comprehended by this definition."[97] While Edmund Randolph quickly "disclaimed any intention to give indefinite powers to the national Legislature,"[98] Madison took a different tack—one he would repeat in *The Federalist*. He expressed his "doubts concerning [the] practicality" of "an enumeration and definition of the powers necessary to be exercised by the national Legislature." Despite coming into the Convention with a "strong bias in favor of an enumeration," he owned that, during the weeks before a quorum gathered in Philadelphia (during which he and his fellow Virginia delegates drafted the Virginia Plan, including the language in Resolution 6), "his doubts had become stronger." He declared that he would "shrink from nothing," including, he implied, abandoning any attempt to enumerate the specific powers of the national government, "which should be found essential to such a form of Government as would provide for the safety, liberty, and happiness of the community. This being the end of all our deliberations, all the necessary means for attaining it must, however reluctantly, be submitted to."[99] Madison would later elaborate on this same "means-ends" argument in *Federalist* No. 41, in which he declared that "[i]t is vain to oppose constitutional barriers to the impulse of self-preservation. It is worse than in vain; because it plants in the Constitution itself necessary usurpations of power, every precedent of which is a germ of unnecessary and multiplied repetitions."[100]

On May 31, Madison merely foreshadowed the argument he would later develop more fully in *Federalist* No. 51, viz., that the power of the new federal government was to be controlled, not through an exact enumeration, i.e., through the use of "parchment barriers,"[101] but by "so contriving the interior structure of the government, as that its several constituent parts may, by their mutual relations, be the means of keeping each other in their proper places."[102] Nonetheless, his words were obviously reassuring, for the Convention voted at the conclusion of his speech to accept that portion of Resolution 6 by a vote of nine states "yes," one state "divided."[103]

The Convention apparently shared Madison's doubts about the "practicality" of partitioning power between the federal government and the states through an enumeration of the powers of the former. Spending almost no time debating what specific powers the federal government should have, it focused instead and almost exclusively on the question of constitutional structure. Thus, the only resolution pertaining to the powers of the federal government forwarded by the delegates to the Committee of Detail (charged with taking "the proceedings of the Convention for the establishment of a Natl. Govt." and "prepar[ing] and report[ing] a Constitution conformable thereto"[104]) stated only that "the Legislature of the United States ought to possess the legislative Rights vested in Congress by the Articles of Confederation; and moreover to legislate in all Cases for the general Interests of the Union, and also in those Cases to which the States are separately incompetent, or in which the Harmony of the United States may be interrupted by the Exercise of individual Legislation."[105]

Not even when the Committee of Detail created out of whole cloth what ultimately became Article I, Section 8,[106] did the Convention systematically scrutinize the powers enumerated therein. Thus, for example, on August 16, when the language of the Committee of Detail concerning "commerce" first came up for discussion, Madison simply reported in his notes: "Clause for regulating commerce with foreign nations, &c. agreed to nem. con."[107] There was no discussion of Congress's power to regulate commerce "among the several States," and, interestingly, Madison does not even allude to that portion of what will become the Interstate Commerce Clause but mentions only foreign commerce. Not even when, very late in the Convention, Madison confesses, first, that "[w]hether the States are now restrained from laying tonnage duties depends on the extent of the power 'to regulate commerce.' These terms are vague but seem to exclude this power of the States," and, further, that "[h]e was more & more convinced that the regulation of Commerce was in its nature indivisible and ought to be wholly under one authority," did his fellow delegates seek clarification or assurance.[108]

The delegates did not even object to the proposed Necessary and Proper Clause. On August 20, when the Convention first took up the language proposed by the Committee of Detail that Congress have power "to make all laws necessary and proper for carrying into execution the foregoing powers, and all other powers vested, by this Constitution, in the Government of the U.S. or any department or officer thereof," the only discussion centered on a motion by James Madison and Charles Pinckney "to insert between 'laws' and 'necessary' 'and establish all offices,' it appearing to them liable to cavil that the latter was not included in the former." Madison reports in his Notes that "Mr. Govr. Morris, Mr. Wilson, Mr. Rutlidge and Mr. Elseworth urged that the amendment could not be necessary," and it was defeated by a vote of nine states "no," two states "yes." With that matter resolved, Madison then reports that "[t]he clause as reported was then agreed to nem con."[109]

The conclusion is clear: Rather than rely on precisely drawn lines demarcating the powers of the federal and state governments, the framers preferred instead to rely on such structural arrangements as the election of the Senate by the state legislatures to ensure that the vast powers they provided to the national government would not be abused and that the federal design would be preserved.

The Supreme Court and the Original Federal Design

One point concerning how the framers protected federalism needs to be underscored. They relied on constitutional structure and the self-interest of senators, not on the Supreme Court. They drafted a constitution that protected the interests of the states as states not only structurally but also democratically—the state legislators who would elect the senators were, after all, elected by the people of the states. They clearly did not intend that the undemocratic Supreme Court would protect the original federal design or that it would interfere with Congress's decision of where to draw the line between federal and state powers.[110]

Just how modest were the framers' designs for the federal judiciary on this matter (or on any other as well) can be appreciated by simply noting the placement, brevity, and generality of the judicial article. To begin with, Article III, establishing the federal judiciary, follows Article I, establishing the legislative branch, and Article II, establishing the executive branch. By so arranging the articles, the framers addressed each branch, in the words of James Wilson, a member of the Constitutional Convention and an original justice on the Supreme Court, "as its greatness deserves to be considered."[111] Further, Article III is only about a sixth as long as the legislative article, and only about a third as long as the executive article. Moreover, Article I specifies in great detail the qualifications of representatives and senators (including age and citizenship requirements), the sizes of the two houses of Congress, the procedures they must follow, and the powers they are authorized or prohibited to exercise. Article II is likewise quite detailed in its discussion of the President's qualifications, mode of appointment, powers, and responsibilities. By contrast, Article III merely vests the judicial power of the United States in one Supreme Court of unspecified size and in "such inferior Courts as the Congress may from time to time ordain and establish." Article III outlines no procedures the courts are obliged to follow, and it imposes no qualifications on judges, not even the requirement of citizenship.[112]

More specific evidence that the framers did not expect the Court to protect federalism is also available. Thus, they understood that drawing a line between federal and state powers involves prudential considerations beyond the Court's legal capacity to pass judgment. They understood that, to the extent that the Constitution authorized the Court to exercise the power of judicial review (and whether it did was itself a major question),[113] it was only in those cases in which the popular branches had acted, in the words of *Federalist* No. 78, "contrary to the *manifest tenor* of the Constitution."[114] The Court was not to invalidate congressional measures in close cases. As

James Wilson, a vigorous defender of judicial review,[115] acknowledged in the Constitutional Convention: "Laws may be unjust, may be unwise, may be dangerous, may be destructive; and yet may not be *so unconstitutional* as to justify the Judges in refusing to give them effect."[116] Rather, as Hamilton makes clear in *Federalist* No. 78, the Court was to invalidate measures only in cases in which Congress's disregard for "certain specified exceptions to the legislative authority" was akin to its passage of a bill of attainder or an ex post facto law.[117] Decisions by Congress regarding where federal power ends and state power begins were of a different character; they did not implicate "specified exceptions" to Congress's legislative authority but, rather, merely involved prudential judgments, agreed to by a Senate elected by state legislatures, concerning the outer reaches of delegated congressional powers. As a consequence, these decisions could never be held unconstitutional by the Court, because they never could be regarded as clearly contrary to the Constitution's "manifest tenor."

Hamilton's discussion in *Federalist* No. 33 of the Necessary and Proper Clause,[118] regarded by many Anti-Federalists as a source of unlimited power for Congress, is most instructive in this regard, for, in it, he did not so much as allude to the Supreme Court when he answered his own question of "who is to judge the necessity and propriety of the laws to be passed for executing the powers of the Union?" For Hamilton, Congress was to judge "in the first instance the proper exercise of its powers; and its constituents [and for the Senate, that meant the state legislatures] in the last." If Congress were to use the Necessary and Proper Clause "to overpass the just bounds of its authority and make a tyrannical use of its powers," Hamilton argued that "the people whose creature it is must appeal to the standard they have formed, and take such measures to redress the injury done to the constitution, as the exigency may suggest and prudence justify."[119] Again, he made no reference to the Supreme Court exercising judicial review to negative such congressional actions.

Quite apart from these prudential considerations, the framers did not expect the Court to protect federalism, because they recognized that they could not make it in the Court's self-interest to do so. As the Anti-Federalist Brutus had shrewdly remarked, it would never be in the self-interest of the Court to strike down federal laws trenching on the "inviolable and residuary sovereignty" of the states, because "[e]very extension of the power of the general legislature, as well as of the judicial powers, will increase the powers of the courts." Brutus insisted that it will be in the interest of the judges "to extend their power and to increase their rights; this of itself will operate strongly upon the courts to give such a meaning to the constitution in all cases where it can possibly be done as will enlarge the sphere of their own authority," and he concluded, "[f]rom these considerations the judges will be interested to extend the powers of the courts, and to construe the constitution as much as possible in such a way as to favour it."[120] The framers made no effort to contradict Brutus's assessment and thus concurred *sub silentio*.[121]

In fact, while Brutus emphasized that it was always in the Court's self-interest to uphold the growth of federal power at the expense of the states, the framers focused on the other side of the coin of self-interest and drafted Article III so as to make it decidedly contrary to the Court's self-interest to interfere with Congress's decisions concerning where to draw the line between federal and state power. Thus, while they gave Congress the power to create, if it so chose, virtually the entire federal judiciary, they also gave it the power to tear down, if sufficiently motivated, what it had created. They drafted Article III in such a way that it is possible for a sufficiently outraged Congress to reduce the entire federal judiciary to a Supreme Court consisting only of a chief justice[122] and possessing only original jurisdiction, i.e., jurisdiction in "cases affecting Ambassadors, other public Ministers and Consuls, and those in which a State shall be Party."[123]

They also gave Congress other powers over the Court as well. In *Federalist* No. 80, Hamilton discussed one of them. He observed that, "[i]f some partial inconveniences should appear to be connected with the incorporation of any of [the powers of the judiciary] . . . into the plan," e.g., if the Court were ever to interfere with where Congress had drawn the line between federal and states powers, "it ought to be recollected that the national legislature will have ample authority to make such exceptions, and to prescribe such regulations as will be calculated to obviate or remove these inconveniences."[124] In *Federalist* No. 81, he discussed another. He spoke of "the important constitutional check which the power of instituting impeachments in one part of the legislative body, and of determining upon them in the other, would give to that body upon the members of the judicial department. This is alone," he continued, "a complete security. There never can be danger that the judges, by a series of deliberate usurpations on the authority of the legislature, would hazard the united resentment of the body intrusted with it, while this body was possessed of the means of punishing their presumption, by degrading them from their stations." Hamilton concluded with an observation that has particular relevance to the question of federalism: "While this ought to remove all apprehensions on the subject, it affords, at the same time, a cogent argument for constituting the *Senate* a court for the trial of impeachments."[125]

One final point concerning the framers' intentions for the Court: As they did not see it in the self-interest of the Court to protect federalism, so also they did not regard it as in the best interest of federalism for it to be protected by the Court. The framers wanted the people to have maximum flexibility to draw the line between federal and state powers where they wished. They recognized, as Madison argued in *Federalist* No. 46, that the people might "in [the] future become more partial to the federal than to the State governments, . . . and in that case, the people ought not surely to be precluded from giving most of their confidence where they may discover it to be most due." They were confident that such a "change [could] only result from such manifest and irresistible proofs of a better administration [by the federal government], as will overcome all [the people's] antecedent propensities";[126] nevertheless, if such a change of public attitude did come about, they wanted to accommodate the people's wishes to draw the line between federal and state power where their representatives in the House and their states' representatives in the Senate wanted them, not where the Supreme Court might determine.

Notes

1. The framers also relied on the composition of the Senate. Composition here means, in the words of Oliver Ellsworth, "that in the second branch each state have an equal vote," resulting thereby in a "general government *partly federal and partly national.*" Max Farrand (ed.), *The Records of the Federal Convention of 1787, Rev. ed.,* 4 vols. (New Haven: Yale University Press, 1937), 1: 474. Emphasis in the original. (Hereafter cited as Farrand, *Records.*) This, of course, is the description James Madison will apply to the new federal structure created by the Constitutional Convention in *Federalist* No. 39. James Madison, Alexander Hamilton, and John Jay, *The Federalist,* ed. Jacob E. Cooke (New York: World Publishing Company, 1961), 257. Had all states not been equally represented in the Senate, the ability of the smaller states to protect their interests as such would have been seriously impaired. See also Todd J. Zywicki, "Beyond the Shell and Husk of History: The History of the Seventeenth Amendment and Its Implications for Current Reform Proposals," *Cleveland State Law Review* 45 (1997): 165, 176-79, for an excellent discussion of how bicameralism also served to preserve the interests of the states as states. The focus of this chapter is not on the composition of the Senate (or on how equal representation of the states and bicameralism advance the interests of federalism) but only on the manner by which the Senate is elected.

2. Farrand, *Records,* 1: 52. On that same day, Richard Spaight of North Carolina proposed "that the 2d branch ought to be chosen by the State legislatures" and moved an amendment to that effect. However, when Rufus King argued that Spaight's motion "would be impracticable, unless it [the Senate] was to be very numerous, or the idea of proportion among the States was to be disregarded," Spaight "withdrew his motion." Farrand, *Records,* 1: 51-52.

3. Farrand, *Records,* 1: 156.

4. Farrand, *Records,* 1: 150. See also Sherman's argument: "[T]he particular States would thus become interested in supporting the National Government, and . . . a due harmony between the two Governments would be maintained." Farrand, *Records,* 1: 150.

5. Farrand, *Records,* 1: 155. In Robert Yates's "Notes" for the same day, John Dickinson observed that "this mode will more intimately connect the state governments with the national legislature," and George Mason is reported as saying: "[T]he second branch of the national legislature should flow from the legislature of each state, to prevent the encroachments on each other, and to harmonize the whole." Farrand, *Records,* 1: 157. Rufus King recorded Mason as follows: "The Danger is that the national, will swallow up the State Legislatures—what will be a reasonable guard agt. this Danger, and operate in favor of the State authorities—The answer seems to me to be this, let the State Legislatures appoint the Senate." Farrand, *Records,* 1: 160. Unavailing were Edmund Randolph's objection that state legislatures were marked by "the turbulence and follies of democracy" and Madison's animadversions that election by state legislatures was not "the best choice" because "the great evils complained of were that the State Legislatures run

into schemes of paper money, etc., whenever solicited by the people, and sometimes without even the sanction of the people." Farrand, *Records,* 1: 51, 154.

6. Farrand, *Records,* 1: 202. This decision was, of course, subsequently overturned on July 16 when the Convention accepted what is often called either the "Great Compromise" or the "Connecticut Compromise" and agreed that the states would be proportionately represented in the House of Representatives (based on population) and equally represented in the Senate. Farrand, *Records,* 2: 15.

7. See Ralph A. Rossum, "James Wilson and the 'Pyramid of Government': The Federal Republic," *Political Science Reviewer* 6 (1976): 113-42.

8. Farrand, *Records,* 1: 343-44.

9. Farrand, *Records,* 1: 406.

10. Roger G. Brooks, "*Garcia,* the Seventeenth Amendment, and the Role of the Supreme Court in Defending Federalism," *Harvard Journal of Law & Public Policy* 10 (1987): 189, 193.

11. Farrand, *Records,* 1: 407. Roger Sherman had already made much the same argument on June 6: "If it were in view to abolish the State Govts. the elections ought to be by the people. If the State Govts. are to be continued, it is necessary in order to preserve harmony between the National & State Govts. that the elections to the former shd. be made by the latter." Farrand, *Records,* 1: 133.

12. Farrand, *Records,* 1: 407. The delegates flatly rejected Wilson's plea that in forming "the Genl. Govt.," they "ought to proceed by abstracting as much as possible from the idea of State Govts. With respect to the province & objects of the Gen'l Govt. they should be considered as having no existence. . . . The Gen'l Govt. is not an assemblage of States, but of individuals for certain political purposes—it is not meant for the States, but for the individuals composing them: the individuals therefore not the States, ought to be represented in it." Farrand, *Records,* 1: 406.

13. Farrand, *Records,* 1: 408. The importance of having the state legislatures elect the Senate appears, in fact, to have motivated some delegates ultimately to favor equal representation of the states in the Senate. See William Davie's speech of June 30: "The Report of the Committee allowing the Legislatures to choose the Senate, and establishing a proportional representation in it, seemed to be impracticable. There will according to this rule be ninety members in the outset, and the number will increase as new States are added. It was impossible that so numerous a body could possess the activity and other qualities required in it. Were he to vote on the comparative merits of the report as it stood, and the amendment [providing for equal representation of the states in the Senate], he should be constrained to prefer the latter." Farrand, *Records,* 1: 487.

14. See Elaine K. Swift, *The Making of the American Senate: Reconstitutive Change in Congress, 1787-1841* (Ann Arbor: University of Michigan Press, 1996), 39-45, and John C. Yoo, "The Judicial Safeguards of Federalism," *Southern California Law Review* 70 (1997): 1311, 1369-71.

15. Farrand, *Records,* 2: 16.

16. Farrand, *Records,* 2: 94.

17. Farrand, *Records*, 2: 94.

18. Farrand, *Records*, 2: 94. Emphasis in the original.

19. Farrand, *Records,* 2: 95.

20. Articles of Confederation, Article V.

21. Jay S. Bybee, "Ulysses at the Mast: Democracy, Federalism, and the Sirens' Song of the Seventeenth Amendment," *Northwestern University Law Review* 91 (Winter 1997), 500, 514. See the views of George Clinton before the New York Ratifying Convention: "In the Senate, indeed, they are equally represented, and in this instance it would appear to partake of the principles of a confederate government, but this feature of federalism is destroyed, as the mode of voting in the Senate is not by states but by voices, in the latter way the States may not be able to express their will for having two members who may vote differently on the same question, they may have two wills, a negative and a positive one." "Notes of Speeches Given by George Clinton before the New York Ratifying Convention," in Herbert J. Storing (ed.), *The Complete Anti-Federalist,* 7 vols. (Chicago: University of Chicago Press, 1981), 2: 183. These remarks of Governor Clinton were not reported in the newspapers and, therefore, not included in Jonathan Elliot (ed.), *The Debates in the Several State Conventions on the Adoption of the Federal Constitution as Recommended by the General Convention at Philadelphia in 1787,* 5 vols. (Philadelphia: J. B. Lippincott, 1845). (Hereafter cited as Elliot, *Debates.*)

22. Bybee, "Ulysses at the Mast," 214.

23. *Federalist* No. 63, 429.

24. Of course, there were other reasons as well for having the state delegations in the House cast one vote. See Farrand, *Records,* 2: 513, 526-29.

25. At the time of the Federal Convention, five states (Pennsylvania, North Carolina, Vermont, Massachusetts, and New Hampshire) explicitly recognized the right of instructions in their constitutions, and two states (Virginia and Maryland) recognized that right implicitly. While Pennsylvania thereupon dropped such language in its Constitution of 1790, Tennessee (1796), Ohio (1802), Indiana (1816), Illinois (1818), Maine (1819), Michigan (1835), Arkansas (1836), New Jersey (1844), Iowa (1846), California (1849), Kansas (1855), Oregon (1857), Nevada (1864), Florida (1868), West Virginia (1872), and Idaho (1889) subsequently added language to their state constitutions providing for the right of instruction. Robert Luce, *Legislative Principles: The History and Theory of Lawmaking by Representative Government* (Boston: Houghton Mifflin, 1930), 452-55.

26. U.S. Constitution, Article II, §2, clause 2.

27. Farrand, *Records*, 2: 405. The vote was six states "yes," four states "no," and one state "absent."

28. Farrand, *Records,* 2: 405.

29. Farrand, *Records*, 2: 406.

30. Elliot, *Debates,* 2: 47.

31. Elliot, *Debates,* 2: 252.

32. Elliot, *Debates,* 2: 283.

33. Elliot, *Debates*, 3: 355.

34. Helen E. Veit, Kenneth R. Bowling, and Charlene Bang Bickford (eds.), *Creating the Bill of Rights: The Documentary Record of the First Federal Congress* (Baltimore: Johns Hopkins University Press, 1991), 151

35. For a fuller discussion of the first Congress and the Bill of Rights, see chapter 4.

36. *Annals of Congress*, 1st Cong., 1st Sess., 761 (1789).

37. *Annals of Congress*, 1st Cong., 1st Sess., 763 (1789).

38. *Annals of Congress*, 1st Cong., 1st Sess., 765 (1789).

39. *Annals of Congress*, 1st Cong., 1st Sess., 766 (1789).

40. *Annals of Congress*, 1st Cong., 1st Sess., 769 (1789).

41. *Annals of Congress*, 1st Cong., 1st Sess., 766 (1789). The *Daily Advertiser* reported Madison's words as follows: "If by instructions were meant a given advice, or expressing the wishes of the people, the proposition was true, but still unnecessary, since that right was provided for already." Veit et al., *Creating the Bill of Rights*, 152.

42. *Annals of Congress*, 1st Cong., 1st Sess., 776 (1789).

43. Although, for a contrary point of view, see "An Argument on the Right of the Constituent to Instruct His Representative in Congress," *The American Review of History and Politics* 6 (1812): 137-71.

44. Bybee, "Ulysses at the Mast," 524-25.

45. 2 U.S. 419 (1793).

46. The practice of states' instructing their senators but only requesting their representatives was, as Robert Luce has pointed out, "no accident. It followed the theory that the Legislatures were the constituents of the Senators, but that the Legislatures had no control over the members of the lower House." Luce, *Legislative Principles*, 461. See also George H. Haynes, *The Senate of the United States: Its History and Practice*, 2 vols. (Boston: Houghton Mifflin, 1938), 2: 1027: "The basis for this distinction between instructing and requesting disappeared, of course, with the ratification of the Seventeenth Amendment."

47. Clyde E. Jacobs, *The Eleventh Amendment and Sovereign Immunity* (Westport, Conn.: Greenwood Press, 1972), 59, 62.

48. Not all scholars agree that the Kentucky Resolution was in the form of an instruction to its senators. Compare William H. Riker, "The Senate and American Federalism," *American Political Science Review* 49 (1955), 457, who argues that it was, with Wayne D. Moore, "Reconceiving Interpretive Authority: Insights from the Virginia and Kentucky Resolutions," *Constitutional Commentary* 11 (1994), 322, who argues that it was not.

49. Luce, *Legislative Principles*, 462-63.

50. Pennsylvania's instruction read: "Resolved, by the Senate and House of Representatives of the Commonwealth of Pennsylvania, in General Assembly met, That the Senators of this State in the Senate of the United States be and are hereby instructed, and the Representatives of this State, in the House of Representatives of the United States be, and they hereby are, requested to use every exertion in

their power to prevent the charter of the Bank of the United States from being renewed, or any other bank from being chartered by Congress, designed to have operation within the jurisdiction of any State, without first having obtained the consent of the Legislature of such State." *Annals of Congress,* 11th Cong., 3rd Sess., 153 (1811). New York's instruction was somewhat more brief: "Resolved, That the Senators of this State, in the Congress of the United States, be instructed and our Representatives most earnestly requested, in the execution of their duties, as faithful representatives of their country, to use their best efforts in opposing by every means in their power the renewal of the charter of the Bank of the United States." *Annals of Congress,* 11th Cong., 3rd Sess., 201 (1811).

51. Luce, *Legislative Principles,* 463-77. See also Bybee, "Ulysses at the Mast," 524-25.

52. "The practice of instructing Senators was more prevalent during the second quarter of the nineteenth century than at any other period of our history." Haynes, *The Senate of the United States,* 2: 1027.

53. Bybee, "Ulysses at the Mast," 527. "The last refusal of a Senator to comply with a legislature's instruction prior to the adoption of popular election of Senators was that of Heyburn (Idaho), who refused to vote for the Seventeenth Amendment, a measure which he had persistently opposed." Haynes, *The Senate of the United States,* 2: 1030.

54. Luce, *Legislative Principles,* 463.

55. Luce, *Legislative Principles,* 466.

56. Luce, *Legislative Principles,* 468.

57. See Haynes, *The Senate of the United States,* 2: 1025-29.

58. See U.S. Constitution, Article I, §2: "The House of Representatives shall be composed of Members chosen every second Year by the People of the several States, and the Electors in each State shall have the Qualifications requisite for Electors of the most numerous Branch of the State Legislature."

59. The phrase is from *Federalist* No. 39, 256. "Residuary sovereignty" is also mentioned in No. 43, 296 and No. 62, 417.

60. Articles of Confederation, Article V: "[D]elegates shall be annually appointed in such manner as the legislature of each state shall direct, to meet in Congress on the first Monday in November, in every year, with a power reserved to each state to recall its delegates, or any of them, at any time within the year, and to send others in their stead, for the remainder of the Year."

61. Farrand, *Records,* 1: 20.

62. Farrand, *Records,* 1: 217.

63. Bybee, "Ulysses at the Mast," 530.

64. *Federalist* No. 62, 420. See also No. 63, 424-25, in which Madison says that a "well-constructed Senate . . . may be sometimes necessary as a defense to the people against their own temporary errors and delusions. As the cool and deliberate sense of the community ought, in all governments, and actually will, in all free governments, ultimately prevail over the views of its rulers; so there are particular moments in

public affairs when the people, stimulated by some irregular passion, or some illicit advantage, or misled by the artful misrepresentations of interested men, may call for measures which they themselves will afterwards be the most ready to lament and condemn. In these critical moments, how salutary will be the interference of some temperate and respectable body of citizens, in order to check the misguided career, and to suspend the blow meditated by the people against themselves, until reason, justice, and truth can regain their authority over the public mind?"

65. *Federalist* No. 62, 420, No. 63, 424.

66. Elliot, *Debates*, 3: 360. See also Haynes, *The Senate of the United States*, 2: 1023-25.

67. Articles of Confederation, Article V.

68. Farrand, *Records,* 1: 20, 217.

69. Farrand, *Records*, 1: 426.

70. Elliot, *Debates*, 2: 287. Brutus had earlier made much the same argument. "It is not probable that senators once chosen for a state will, as the system now stands, continue in office for life. The office will be honorable if not lucrative. The persons who occupy it will probably wish to continue in it, and therefore use all their influence and that of their friends, to continue in office.—Their friends will be numerous and powerful, for they will have it in their power to confer great favors; besides it will before long be considered as disgraceful not to be reelected. It will therefore be considered a matter of delicacy to the character of the senator not to return him again." "The Essays of Brutus," in Storing (ed.), *The Complete Anti-Federalist*, Essay 11, 2: 444-45.

71. Elliot, *Debates*, 2: 287-88.

72. Elliot, *Debates*, 2: 292-93. See also Richard Harrison's argument that rotation actually limited senatorial accountability: "If the senator is conscious that his reelection depends only on the will of the people, and is not lettered by any law, he will feel an ambition to deserve well of the public. On the contrary, if he knows that no meritorious exertions of his own can procure a reappointment, he will become more unambitious, and regardless of the public opinion. The love of power, in a republican government, is ever attended by a proportionable sense of dependence." Elliot, *Debates*, 2: 298.

73. "An American Citizen" (Tench Coxe), "An Examination of the Constitution of the United States," reprinted in Colleen A. Sheehan and Gary L. McDowell (eds.), *Friends of the Constitution: Writings of the "Other" Federalists: 1787-1788* (Indianapolis: Liberty Fund, 1998), 466. See also Coxe's "An American Citizen IV: On the Federal Government," also published in the *Independent Gazetteer*, in *The Documentary History of the Ratification of the Constitution*, Vol. 13: *Commentaries on the Constitution: Public and Private, Vol. 1: 21 February to 7 November 1787*, ed. John P. Kaminski and Gaspare J. Saladino (Madison: State Historical Society of Wisconsin, 1981), 436-37, in which he denies that "a majority of the Senate, each of whom will be chosen by the legislature of a free, sovereign, and independent state . . . can destroy our liberties."

74. The words are from Robert Whitehill, whose speech is not recorded in Elliot's *Debates*. See "The Pennsylvania Convention," in *The Documentary History of the Ratification of the Constitution*, Vol. 2: *Ratification of the Constitution by the States: Pennsylvania*, ed. Merrill Jensen (Madison: State Historical Society of Wisconsin, 1976), 393.

75. Elliot, *Debates*, 2: 439.

76. Elliot, *Debates*, 2: 202.

77. Elliot, *Debates*, 2: 46. Interestingly enough, certain members of the House of Representatives were still using similar language as late as 1898: The states "as sovereign [are] . . . entitled . . . to have a separate branch of Congress to which they could . . . send their ambassadors." "Election of Senators," *House Reports*, No. 1456, 50th Cong., 1st Sess. 4 (1898). See also Luce, *Legislative Principles*, 455: "Our first Congresses were distinctly gatherings of ambassadors, or agents who felt themselves dependent on the will of their principals."

78. Elliot, *Debates*, 2: 46-47.

79. Elliot, *Debates*, 2: 47.

80. *Federalist* No. 45, 311.

81. *Federalist* No. 46, 320.

82. *Federalist* No. 46, 319.

83. *Federalist* No. 59, 400-401.

84. *Federalist* No. 59, 401.

85. *Federalist* No. 62, 416.

86. Elliot, *Debates*, 2: 306.

87. Elliot, *Debates*, 2: 317-18.

88. Elliot, *Debates*, 4: 40. See also Iredell's "Answers to Mr. Mason's Objections to the New Constitution, Recommended by the Late Convention," in Paul Leicester Ford (ed.), *Pamphlets on the Constitution of the United States* (Brooklyn, 1888), 340: "They [Senators] have no permanent interest as a body to detach them from the general welfare, since six years is the utmost period of their existence, unless their respective legislatures are sufficiently pleased with their conduct to reelect them. This power of reelection is itself a great check upon abuse, because if they have ambition to continue members of the Senate they can only gratify this ambition by acting agreeably to the opinion of their constituents."

89. Philip B. Kurland and Ralph Lerner (eds.), *The Founders' Constitution*, 5 vols. (Chicago: University of Chicago Press, 1987), 2: 232.

90. St. George Tucker, *Blackstone's Commentaries: With Notes of Reference to the Constitution and Laws of the Federal Government of the United States and the Commonwealth of Virginia*, 5 vols. (Philadelphia, 1803), 1: 195.

91. Tucker, *Blackstone's Commentaries*, 1: 244.

92. James Kent, *Commentaries on American Law*, 4 vols. (New York: O. Halsted, 1826), 1: 211.

93. Joseph Story, *Commentaries on the Constitution of the United States*, 3 vols. (New York: Hilliard & Gray, 1833), 2: 183.

94. *Federalist* No. 62, 416.

95. *Federalist* No. 59, 401.

96. *Federalist* No. 37, 234.

97. Farrand, *Records*, 1: 53. Emphasis in the original.

98. Farrand, *Records*, 1: 53.

99. Farrand, *Records*, 1: 53. Madison appreciated the difficulty of attempting to put into words a precise enumeration. As he argued in *Federalist* No. 37, 236-37, even "[w]hen the Almighty himself condescends to address mankind in their own language, his meaning, luminous as it must be, is rendered dim and doubtful, by the cloudy medium through which it is communicated." See chapter 2 for a fuller discussion of the framers' reluctance to rely on words and parchment barriers.

100. *Federalist* No. 41, 270. See also Alexander Hamilton's similar statements in *Federalist* No. 31, 194, in which Hamilton describes as "maxims in ethics and politics . . . that the means ought to be proportioned to the end; that every power ought to be commensurate with this object, [and] that there ought to be no limitation of a power destined to effect a purpose, which is itself incapable of limitation."

101. *Federalist* No. 48, 333.

102. *Federalist* No. 51, 347-48. The mode of electing the Senate was obviously one such contrivance that the framers employed to keep the general government in its proper place.

103. Farrand, *Records*, 1: 54. This same debate was largely repeated on July 16, after the Convention had agreed to equal representation of the states in the Senate and proportionate representation of the states in the House. When the delegates again considered Congress's power "to legislate in all cases to which the separate States were incompetent," Pierce Butler called for "some explanation of the extent of this power; particularly the word *incompetent*. The vagueness of the terms," he contended, "rendered it impossible for any precise judgment to be formed." Nathaniel Gorham defended the vagueness: "The vagueness of the terms constitutes the propriety of them. We are now establishing general principles, to be extended hereafter into details which will be precise & explicit." John Rutlidge, who had raised Butler's precise objection on May 31, "urged the objection started by Mr. Butler and moved that the clause should be committed to the end that a specification of the powers comprised in the general terms, might be reported." His motion, however, failed when the states divided equally. Farrand, *Records*, 2: 17. Emphasis in the original.

104. Farrand, *Records*, 2: 95.

105. Farrand, *Records*, 2: 131-32.

106. The Committee of Detail took the brief and general language just quoted in the text and transformed it into the following provisions, as reported in Farrand, *Records*, 2: 181.

Sect. 1. The Legislature of the United States shall have the power to
lay and collect taxes, duties, imposts and excises;

To regulate commerce with foreign nations, and among the several
States;

To establish an uniform rule of naturalization throughout the United
States;

To coin money;

To regulate the value of foreign coin;

To fix the standard of weights and measures;

To establish Post-offices;

To borrow money, and emit bills on the credit of the United States;

To appoint a Treasurer by ballot;

To constitute tribunals inferior to the Supreme Court;

To make rules concerning captures on land and water;

To declare the law and punishment of piracies and felonies committed
on the high seas, and the punishment of counterfeiting the coin of the
United States, and of offences against the law of nations;

To subdue a rebellion in any State, on the application of its legislature;

To make war;

To raise armies;

To build and equip fleets;

To call forth the aid of the militia, in order to execute the laws of the
Union, enforce treaties, suppress insurrections, and repel invasions;

And to make all laws that shall be necessary and proper for carrying
into execution the foregoing powers, and all other powers vested, by this
Constitution, in the government of the United States, or in any department
or officer thereof.

107. Farrand, *Records,* 2: 308.

108. Farrand, *Records,* 2: 625. Madison's comments are made on September
15, just two days before the Convention adjourns sine die. Madison's failure to
clarify the exact meaning of the Commerce Clause would come back to haunt him.
See his letter of February 13, 1829, to J. C. Cabell: "For a like reason, I made no
reference to the 'power to regulate commerce among the several States.' I always
foresaw that difficulties might be started in relation to that power which could not
be fully explained without recurring to views of it, which, however just, might
give birth to specious though unsound objections. Being in the same terms with
the power over foreign commerce, the same extent, if taken literally, would belong
to it. Yet it is very certain that it grew out of the abuse of the power by the importing
States in taxing the nonimporting, and was intended as a negative and preventive
provision against injustice among the States themselves, rather than as a power to
be used for the positive purposes of the General Government, in which alone,
however, the remedial power could be lodged." Farrand, *Records,* 3: 478.

109. Farrand, *Records,* 2: 344-45. While both Edmund Randolph and Elbridge
Gerry eventually mentioned the Necessary and Proper Clause among their reasons

for refusing to sign the Constitution, they never objected to its wording or sought its elimination when the Convention was reviewing the work of the Committee of Detail. See Farrand, *Records*, 2: 563, 632.

110. See, however, Brooks, "*Garcia*, the Seventeenth Amendment, and the Role of the Supreme Court in Defending Federalism," 197, and Yoo, "The Judicial Safeguards of Federalism," 1375.

111. Robert Green McCloskey (ed.), *The Works of James Wilson* (Cambridge: Belknap Press of Harvard University Press, 1967), 290.

112. See Ralph A. Rossum, "The Courts and the Judicial Power," in Leonard W. Levy and Dennis J. Mahoney (eds.), *The Framing and Ratification of the Constitution* (New York: Macmillan, 1987), 222.

113. Several delegates to the Convention clearly believed that the Court would have the power of judicial review. Gouverneur Morris, for one, observed that the judiciary should not "be bound to say that a direct violation of the Constitution was law." Farrand, *Records*, 2: 299. Luther Martin, for another, argued against a proposed Council of Revision on the grounds that "the constitutionality of laws . . . will come before the judges in their official character. In this character, they have a negative on the laws." Farrand, *Records*, 2: 76. See also Gerry's comments at Farrand, *Records*, 2: 97. The problem with these statements, however, is that they imply neither a general power to expound the Constitution nor an obligation on the part of the other branches to regard a judicial decision on the constitutionality of their actions as binding. Moreover, statements were also made by other Convention delegates unequivocally rejecting judicial review. Thus, for example, John Mercer "disapproved of the doctrine that the judges as expositors of the Constitution should have authority to declare a law void. He thought laws ought to be well and cautiously made, and then to be uncontrollable." Farrand, *Records*, 2: 298. So, too, did Dickinson, who argued that, "as to the power of the Judges to set aside the law, . . . no such power ought to exist." Farrand, *Records*, 2: 299. See George Anastaplo, *The Constitution of 1787: A Commentary* (Baltimore: Johns Hopkins University Press, 1989), 47-48, who, by proceeding "section by section" through the Constitution, concludes that the Constitution tends toward legislative supremacy and that judicial review is highly suspect; noting the "complete silence in the Constitution about judicial review," he wonders "if it is likely . . . that judicial review was indeed anticipated, when nothing was said about it, considering the care with which [for example] executive review is provided for." See also Ralph A. Rossum, "The Least Dangerous Branch?" in Peter Augustine Lawler and Robert Martin Schaefer (eds.), *The American Experiment: Essays on the Theory and Practice of Liberty* (Lanham, Md.: Rowman & Littlefield, 1994), 241-58.

114. *Federalist* No. 78, 524. Emphasis added.

115. Rossum, "James Wilson and the 'Pyramid of Government,'" 133-34.

116. Farrand, *Records*, 2: 73. Emphasis added.

117. *Federalist* No. 78, 524. Here is the entire passage: "The complete independence of the courts of justice is peculiarly essential in a limited Constitution. By a limited Constitution, I understand one which contains certain specified exceptions to the legislative authority; such, for instance, as that it shall pass no bills of attainder, no ex-post-facto laws, and the like. Limitations of this kind can

be preserved in practice no other way than through the medium of courts of justice, whose duty it must be to declare all acts contrary to the manifest tenor of the Constitution void. Without this, all the reservations of particular rights or privileges would amount to nothing."

118. U.S. Constitution, Article I, §8. "Congress shall have power . . . to make all laws which shall be necessary and proper for carrying into Execution the foregoing Powers, and all other Powers vested by this Constitution in the Government of the United States, or in any Department or Officer thereof."

119. *Federalist* No. 33, 206. As Hamilton made clear in both *Federalist* No. 59 and during the New York Ratifying Convention, Elliot, *Debates*, 2: 306, 317-18, one way the people could "redress the injury" caused by congressional infringement on the "residuary sovereignty" of the States was by electing state legislators who would hold senators responsible for this infringement.

120. "The Essays of Brutus," in Storing, *The Complete Anti-Federalist*, Essay 11, 2: 421.

> Every body of men invested with office are tenacious of power; they feel interested, and hence it has become a kind of maxim to hand down their offices, with all its rights and privileges, unimpared [*sic*] to their successors; the same principle will influence them to extend their power and to increase their rights; this of itself will operate strongly upon the courts to give such a meaning to the constitution in all cases where it can possibly be done as will enlarge the sphere of their own authority. Every extension of the power of the general legislature, as well as of the judicial powers, will increase the powers of the courts; and the dignity and importance of the judges will be in proportion to the extent and magnitude of the powers they exercise. I add, it is highly probable the emolument of the judges will be increased, with the increase of the business they will have to transact and its importance. From these considerations the judges will be interested to extend the powers of the courts, and to construe the constitution as much as possible in such a way as to favour it; and that they will do it, appears probable.

See also Todd Zywicki, "Beyond the Shell and Husk of History," 228, who discusses the Supreme Court's "inherent conflict-of-interest in enforcing federalism," and Lino A. Graglia, "*United States* v. *Lopez*: Judicial Review under the Commerce Clause," *Texas Law Review* 74 (March 1996), 719, 770, who notes that states are forced to rely on a national court to enforce limitations on national power.

121. See Gary L. McDowell, "Were the Anti-Federalists Right?" *Publius: The Journal of Federalism* 12 (1982): 99-108.

122. U.S. Constitution, Article I, Section 3 requires a chief justice to preside in the Senate in cases of the impeachment of the president.

123. U.S. Constitution, Article III, Section 2.

124. *Federalist* No. 80, 541. U.S. Constitution, Article III, Section 2 placed the Court's appellate jurisdiction under the complete control of the Congress. See also Hamilton's argument in *Federalist* No. 81, 552: "To avoid all inconveniences, it will be safest to declare generally that the Supreme Court shall possess appellate jurisdiction both as to law and fact, and that this jurisdiction shall be subject to such exceptions and regulations as the national legislature shall prescribe. This will enable the government to modify it in such a manner as will best answer the ends of public justice and security." In the Virginia Ratifying Convention, John Marshall, later the author of *Marbury* v. *Madison*, 5 U.S. 137 (1803), made very much the same argument: "Congress is empowered to make exceptions to the appellate jurisdiction, as to law and fact, of the Supreme Court. These exceptions certainly go as far as the legislature may think proper for the interest of liberty and the people." Elliot, *Debates*, 3: 560. In the Pennsylvania Ratifying Convention, the only other convention that specifically discussed the Exceptions Clause, Wilson, chairman of the Federal Convention's Committee of Detail, likewise noted that if the Court's powers under its appellate jurisdiction "shall be attended with inconvenience, the Congress can alter them as soon as discovered." John Bach McMaster and Frederick D. Stone (eds.), *Pennsylvania and the Federal Constitution* (Philadelphia: Historical Society of Pennsylvania, 1888), 359. See Ralph A. Rossum, *Congressional Control of the Judiciary: The Article III Option* (Washington, D.C.: Center for Judicial Studies, 1988), and "Congress, the Constitution, and the Appellate Jurisdiction of the Supreme Court: The Letter and Spirit of the Exceptions Clause," *William and Mary Law Review* 24 (1983): 385-428.

125. *Federalist* No. 81, 545-46. Emphasis added.

126. *Federalist* No. 46, 317. See, however, No. 39, 256, in which Madison seems to argue to the contrary. He speaks there of a "tribunal" that is to resolve "controversies relating to the boundary between the two jurisdictions." He argues that "the proposed government cannot be deemed a national one; since its jurisdiction extends to certain enumerated objects only, and leaves to the several States a residuary and inviolable sovereignty over all other objects. It is true that in controversies relating to the boundary between the two jurisdictions, the tribunal which is ultimately to decide, is to be established under the general government. But this does not change the principle of the case. The decision is to be impartially made, according to the rules of the Constitution; and all the usual and most effectual precautions are taken to secure this impartiality. Some such tribunal is clearly essential to prevent an appeal to the sword and a dissolution of the compact; and that it ought to be established under the general rather than under the local governments, or, to speak more properly, that it could be safely established under the first alone, is a position not likely to be combated." It is not at all clear, however, that the "tribunal" to which Madison was referring was not the Senate. See George W. Carey, *In Defense of the Constitution* (Indianapolis: Liberty Fund, 1995), 104-5, who argues that "Madison looked upon the disputes surrounding state-national relations as primarily political issues to be settled through distinctly political, not judicial . . . processes."

Chapter 4

The Senate's Protection of Federalism in the First Congress

This chapter provides three case studies from the First Congress that shed light on how the framers' expectation that federalism would be protected by the mode of electing the Senate played out in practice. They involve the adoption of the Bill of Rights, the passage of the Judiciary Act of 1789, and the passage of the act chartering the first Bank of the United States.

David P. Currie has described the First Congress as "a sort of continuing constitutional convention."[1] Not only did it include among its members many prominent individuals who helped to draft and ratify the Constitution (e.g., James Madison, Oliver Ellsworth, Elbridge Gerry, Rufus King, Robert Morris, Pierce Butler, William Johnson, and William Paterson) but the First Congress was also responsible for taking the generalities of the Constitution—what Chief Justice John Marshall later called its "great outlines"[2]—and translating them into concrete and functioning institutions. As Currie points out, the First Congress determined its own procedures; established the great executive departments of War, State, Justice, and Treasury; set up the federal judiciary; enacted a system of taxation; provided for payment of Revolutionary War debts; created a national bank; provided for national defense; regulated relations with Indian tribes; advised the president on foreign affairs (the Senate); passed statutes regarding naturalization, patents, copyrights, and federal crimes; regulated relations with existing states and admitted new ones; provided for the administration of the territories; established a permanent seat of government; and adopted a bill of rights.[3] By the time the First Congress adjourned on March 3, 1791, "the country had a much clearer idea of what the Constitution meant than it had when that body had first met in 1789."[4] It is not surprising that, two months into the Second Congress, Fisher Ames, a Massachusetts Congressman, lamented in a November 24, 1791, letter to William Tudor that "Congress is not engaged in very interesting work. The first acts were the pillars of the federal edifice. Now we have only to keep the sparks from catching the shavings; we must watch the broom, that it is not set behind the door with fire on it, etc. etc. Nobody cares much for us now, except the enemies of the excise law, who remonstrate and make a noise."[5] Case studies from the First Congress of how the Senate protected federalism are therefore most appropriate; they illustrate how well the members of this "continuing constitutional convention" acted in conformity with the understanding of the delegates to the Philadelphia Convention.

The Adoption of the Bill of Rights

On June 8, 1789, James Madison proposed to the House of Representatives a series of amendments to the Constitution, many of which eventually became part of what we call the Bill of Rights.[6] Madison's sponsorship of the Bill of Rights requires some explanation, for, during the Constitutional Convention, he believed that the new Constitution the delegates were drafting, marked as it was by a new understanding of separation of powers and federalism and operating as it would over a large, differentiated, commercial republic, was the complete remedy for the diseases of republican government. He saw no need for a bill of rights, as the Constitution was itself a full defense of liberty. Neither, apparently, did most of his fellow delegates; more than three months passed before it even occurred to anyone to include a bill of rights, and, when, on September 12 (just five days before the Convention adjourned) George Mason proposed that the Constitution be "prefaced with a Bill of Rights," his motion was defeated by a unanimous "no" vote of ten states.[7]

The view of the framers was well stated by Alexander Hamilton, who argued in *Federalist* No. 84 that the Constitution was "itself in every rational sense and to every useful purpose, A BILL OF RIGHTS."[8] Hamilton insisted that "bills of rights, in the sense and to the extent in which they [we]re contended" by Mason in the Convention and the Anti-Federalists during the ratification process, were not only "unnecessary" but also "dangerous" in that "they would contain exceptions to powers which are not granted; and on this very account, would afford a colorable pretext to claim more than were granted."[9] Finally, Hamilton and the other framers argued, they were ineffectual. They were merely "parchment barriers" that had been demonstrated by history to be unable to control the acts of overbearing majorities; as James Madison himself had remarked, "experience proves the inefficacy of a bill of rights on those occasions when its control is most needed."[10]

Nevertheless, in the First Congress, Madison served as principal sponsor of a series of amendments that, when ratified, became the Bill of Rights. The question, of course, is why? The answer is revealed in part in a letter Madison wrote to Thomas Jefferson, in which he noted that "[i]t is a melancholy reflection that liberty should be equally exposed to danger whether the Government have too much or too little power"[11] Madison believed that the Constitution struck the proper balance but that a bill of rights, if properly framed, would not jeopardize that balance and, in fact, could help preserve it. It could win the support of many who mistakenly thought a bill of rights was necessary for the protection of their liberties, and it could silence the Anti-Federalists' call for a general convention as well as thwart their attempts to revise the basic structure and powers of the new federal government.[12] "We have in this way," he candidly confessed to his fellow members of the House of Representatives, "something to gain, and, if we proceed with caution, nothing to lose."[13]

During the ratification struggle, pressure mounted to add a bill of rights—its absence provided the Anti-Federalists with convenient and readily understandable grounds for objecting to the new constitution. Massachusetts, South Carolina, New Hampshire, Virginia, and New York all ratified the Constitution on the understanding that a series of widely desired amendments to the Constitution would be proposed by the First Congress and submitted to the states for ratification.[14] Madison argued against these amendments so long as the Constitution remained unratified. As he wrote to George Eve in 1789:

> I freely own that I have never seen in the Constitution as it now stands those dangers which have alarmed many respectable Citizens. Accordingly, whilst it remained unratified, and it was necessary to unite the States in some one plan, I opposed all previous alterations as calculated to throw the States into dangerous contentions, and to furnish the secret enemies of the Union with an opportunity of promoting its dissolution.[15]

Once the Constitution was ratified, however, Madison became the principal sponsor of the Bill of Rights. He explained his apparent change of heart in a letter he wrote to Thomas Jefferson: "I have never thought the omission (of a bill of rights) a material defect, nor been anxious to supply it even by subsequent amendment, for any other reason than that it is anxiously desired by others. I have favored it because I supposed it might be of use, and, if properly executed, could not be of disservice."[16]

Madison labored persistently on behalf of the Bill of Rights, not because he thought it essential but because *others* did. In much the same way that the Constitution he helped to design channels and directs the self-interest and passions of the citizenry in directions that serve the public good and happiness, so, too, Madison channeled the public's desire for a bill of rights into a set of amendments that gave "satisfaction to the doubting part of our fellow-citizens"[17] but without "endangering any part of the Constitution, which is considered as essential to the existence of the Government by those who promoted its adoption."[18]

On June 8, 1789, Madison addressed the House of Representatives and introduced a series of amendments, most of which were ultimately ratified as the Bill of Rights. It is significant that, in this crucial speech, Madison never argued on behalf of these amendments in his own name. He proposed these amendments, he said, so that "those who had been friendly to the adoption of this Constitution may have the opportunity of proving to those who were opposed to it that they were as sincerely devoted to liberty and a Republican Government, as those who charged them with wishing the adoption of this Constitution in order to lay the foundation of an aristocracy or despotism."[19] Those who believed that the Constitution was deficient because it lacked a bill of rights were "mistaken," but, he continued, "there is a great body of the people falling under this description, who at present feel much inclined to join their support to the cause of Federalism, if they were satisfied on this one point." Accordingly, he urged the Congress "not to disregard their inclination, but, on principles of amity and moderation, conform to their wishes, and *expressly declare the great rights of mankind secured under this Constitution.*"[20] (Notice that he saw the Bill of Rights not as securing rights—and certainly not as creating them—but as simply declaring rights already secured, not by parchment barriers but by structure, under the Constitution.) A bill of rights would, he argued, reassure "a great number of our fellow-citizens who think these securities necessary."[21] It would "satisfy the public mind that their liberties will be perpetual."[22]

The people wanted a bill of rights, and even though there was no need for it, Madison was prepared to give it to them—but only if it were "properly executed." Only then could there be "something to gain" and "nothing to lose." Thus, Madison proposed amendments that were "of such a nature as will not injure the Constitution."[23] He did not seek to alter the structure of the federal government (by imposing, for example, a council on the president, as many Anti-Federalists wanted). Neither did he seek to restrict its powers (by prohibiting standing armies and the granting of monopolies or suspending the writ of habeas corpus, as Jefferson urged).[24] These measures would have undermined the constitutional scheme and sapped the vigor and capacity of the government. Rather, he sought measures that relied on the principles of, and restated the rights secured by, the Constitution. Thus, the words comprising what became the first eight amendments merely made explicit the rights that Madison believed were already secured by separation of powers, federalism, and the operation of an extensive commercial republic. The Ninth Amendment merely stated that other rights, in addition to those specifically enumerated, were also protected by these same institutional arrangements. The Tenth Amendment met the objection *The Federalist* itself had raised to a bill of rights—that its presence would suggest that the federal government was one of reserved rather than delegated powers—and, again, was wholly consistent with the original constitutional scheme.

Only one of Madison's proposed amendments represented an attempt to alter substantively the original constitutional design; interestingly, however, it was directed against the states and, consistent with Madison's plan to incorporate the amendments into the body of the Constitution itself, would have been included in Article I, Section 10 along with other prohibitions on state action. It read: "No state shall violate the equal rights of conscience, or the freedom of the press, or the trial by jury in criminal cases."[25] It was one of the very few of his proposed amendments that was ultimately rejected by the Congress.

During the debate on this provision, Representative Thomas Tudor Tucker, an Anti-Federalist from South Carolina, argued for its defeat, observing that, while it was offered as an amendment to the Constitution, "it goes only to the alteration of the constitutions of particular states." He argued that "it will be much better . . . to leave the state governments to themselves, and not to interfere with them more than we already do, and that is thought by many to be rather too much." He therefore moved to "strike out these words."[26] Madison defended his proposal, declaring that he "conceived this to be the most valuable amendment on the whole list; if there was any reason to restrain the government of the United States from infringing on these essential rights, it was equally necessary that they should be secured against the state governments."[27] By a voice vote, Tucker's motion was rejected, and Madison's limitation of state governments made its way into the House Resolution and Articles of Amendment, which were approved on August 24 and thereafter transmitted to the Senate for its consideration.[28]

Madison's proposed amendment easily passed the House, but it was defeated in the Senate. While no Senate debates exist because the Senate met in secret,[29] we do know that the Senate "disagreed" to this particular provision on September 7.[30] In a letter to Patrick Henry, Senator William Grayson of Virginia suggested that this was because "this disgusted the Senate."[31] The Senate appears to have understood this proposed amendment as Tucker understood it—as an interference with the residuary sovereignty of the states. But whatever its motivation, the Senate acted clearly and decisively to protect the interests of the states as states. George Anastaplo has reflected on the Senate's action as follows:

> The Senate's constitutional function, then, is to insist upon protecting state sovereignty and power, even against demands that that power be sacrificed to what is declared to be a good cause. This function was performed . . . when the Senate refused to accept the amendment limiting the states. We cannot claim, the Founders would concede, that all these particular effects were foreseen; but we did foresee and plan that such effects would result, and we left it to the working of self-interest to contribute to the achievement of the desirable results.[32]

Madison bitterly complained to Edmund Pendleton that the Senate's action struck at one of "the most salutary articles."[33] Madison's disappointment that the Senate seemed interested only in protecting the interests of the states as political entities was possibly assuaged, however, by his gratitude for what the Senate also rejected. While it refused to assent to his proposed amendment that would have altered the constitutions of the individual states, it also refused to assent to amendments that would have altered the very structure of the Constitution itself. It rejected, for example, proposed Anti-Federalist amendments that would have required that any treaty "ceding, contracting, restraining, or suspending the territorial rights or claims of the United States, or any of them, or any of their rights or claims to fishing in the American Seas, or navigating the American Rivers" be approved by "three fourths of the whole number of the members of both Houses" and that would have required that any navigation law or law regulating commerce be passed by "two thirds of the members present in both Houses."[34] In short, the Senate acted to preserve the original federal/ state balance, neither agreeing to further restrictions on the states' "residuary sovereignty" nor embracing measures that would have weakened the federal government.

The Judiciary Act of 1789

The passage of the Judiciary Act of 1789[35] also demonstrates that the framers' faith that the mode of electing the Senate would protect the original federal design was not misplaced. While Article III of the Constitution vested the judicial power of the United States in "one supreme Court, and in such inferior Courts as the Congress may from time to time ordain and establish," provided that federal judges should hold their offices during good behavior, and outlined the kinds of jurisdiction the federal courts could entertain, it was not "self-executing" and needed "legislation to bring it to life."[36] That legislation was the Judiciary Act of 1789, which, as Wythe Holt reminds us, "endures essentially to this day as the framework of the national judiciary."[37] Interestingly, it was crafted almost exclusively by the Senate.[38]

Article III was as brief and general as it is because the framers were not especially concerned about the judiciary. Hamilton reflected the prevailing opinion when he described it as "beyond comparison the weakest of the three departments of power."[39] Accordingly, they spent almost no time considering it. Discussion of the judicial branch consumed, in total, only about two days of the seventeen-week Federal Convention.

Resolution 9 of the Virginia Plan provided for a federal judiciary. It proposed that

> a National Judiciary be established to consist of one or more supreme tribunals, and of inferior tribunals to be chosen by the National Legislature, to hold their offices during good behavior; and to receive punctually at stated times fixed compensation for their services, in which no increase or diminution shall be made so as to affect the persons actually in office at the time of such increase or diminution.

It further proposed that

> the jurisdiction of the inferior tribunals shall be to hear and determine in the first instance, and of the supreme tribunal to hear and determine in the dernier resort, all piracies and felonies on the high seas, captures from any enemy; cases in which foreigners or citizens of other States applying to such jurisdictions may be interested, or which respect the collection of the National revenue; impeachments of any National officers, and questions which may involve the national peace and harmony.

This resolution generated almost no controversy or debate, and the delegates quickly agreed to the creation of one "supreme tribunal" on June 4.[40] Likewise, while the delegates initially differed among themselves concerning the mode of appointing judges (with a majority voting repeatedly from early June through late August for appointment by the Senate), they eventually accepted, unanimously and without debate, language supplied in early September by the Committee of Eleven that (without prior authorization from the Convention) changed the mode to appointment by the president with the advice and consent of the Senate.[41] They accepted from the outset that the judges should serve during good behavior and that their compensation should be free from political interference. They also accepted without controversy and with little discussion substitute language from the Committee of Detail specifying the Supreme Court's original jurisdiction and subjecting the Court's appellate jurisdiction to such exceptions and regulations as the Congress would make.[42]

The only part of Resolution 9 to generate any sustained debate was its language mandating the creation of "inferior tribunals." John Rutledge was representative of a majority of the delegates; he insisted "that the State Tribunals might and ought to be left in all cases to decide in the first instance, the right to appeal to the supreme national tribunal being sufficient to secure the national rights and uniformity of judgments."[43] Madison made the case for Resolution 9 as presented; he observed that, unless inferior tribunals were dispersed throughout the new republic, with final jurisdiction in many cases, "appeals would be multiplied to a most oppressive degree." Besides, without lower federal courts, an appeal would typically provide no remedy. "What was to be done," Madison queried, "after improper Verdicts in State tribunals obtained under the biassed directions of a dependent Judge, or the local prejudices of an undirected Jury? To remand the cause for a new trial would answer no purpose," for it would presumably end in no better verdict. Madison pleaded that "an effective Judiciary establishment commensurate to the legislative authority was essential. A Government without a proper Executive and Judiciary would be a mere trunk of a body without arms or legs to act or move."[44] His plea, however, was unavailing, and all he could eventually secure was the delegates' consent to provide the National Legislature with the option "to institute inferior tribunals" if it should choose to do so.[45]

While Article III generated little controversy in the Philadelphia Convention, that all changed during the ratification debates. The judicial article was perceived by the Anti-Federalists as a threat both to democracy and to the continued existence of the states.

It was viewed as a threat to democracy, because it vested enormous power over the vital daily concerns of men in a small group of unelected judges serving for good behavior. As Brutus declared, "I question whether the world ever saw, in any period of it, a court of justice invested with such immense powers, and yet placed in a situation so little responsible."[46] The Anti-Federalists recognized that "there is no feature in a free government more difficult to be well formed" than the judiciary.[47] This was so because of the nature of the judicial function. As the "Federal Farmer" observed:

> It is true, the laws are made by the legislature: but the judges and juries, in their interpretations, and in directing the execution of them, have a very extensive influence for preserving or destroying liberty, and for changing the nature of the government. It is an observation of an approved writer, that when we have ascertained and fixed its limits with all the caution and precision we can, it will yet be formidable, somewhat arbitrary and despotic—that is, after all our cares, we must leave a vast deal to the discretion and interpretation—to the wisdom, integrity, and politics of the judges.[48]

While the Anti-Federalists recognized that judicial discretion was inevitable under any constitution, they faulted the framers for failing to fix any limits on it. Article III, after all, was both brief and incomplete and, while it did provide Congress with powers to check judicial encroachments, the Anti-Federalists expected that Congress would be loathe to restrain the judiciary, for the courts would be the principal means of consolidating all power into the general government and thereby enhancing the powers of Congress.

Moreover, Article III extended federal court jurisdiction to "all cases in law and equity" arising under the Constitution and laws of the United States. Equity—the power to dispense with the harsh rigor of the law and to formulate decrees of relief in certain cases as the court deems necessary—was seen by the Anti-Federalists as posing a particular threat to liberty in that, in the words of the "Federal Farmer," it enhanced "an arbitrary power of discretion in the judges, to decide as their conscience, their opinions, their caprice, or their politics" might dictate.[49] While England had established, through the centuries, a system for drawing the line between law and equity that was rooted in tradition and bound by precedent, the United States had no such system.[50] Further, with political separation from England had also come legal separation from the binding precedents of the English common law. As the "Federal Farmer" warned: "We have no precedents in this country, as yet, to regulate the divisions of equity as in Great Britain; equity, therefore, in the Supreme Court for many years will be mere discretion."[51] In any government dedicated to the rule of law, such discretion is inherently dangerous, and the Anti-Federalists charged that the Constitution's lack of precision in defining the limits of equity was a serious defect. "It is a very dangerous thing," the "Federal Farmer" warned, "to vest in the same judge power to decide on the law, and also general powers in equity; for if the law restrain him, he is only to step into his shoes of equity, and give what judgment his reason or opinion may dictate."[52]

The Anti-Federalists particularly feared this vast judicial discretion because, unlike legislative or executive abuse, judicial abuse would be difficult for the people fully to discern. Judicial proceedings are, the "Federal Farmer" sagaciously noted, "far more intricate, complex, and out of the . . . [people's] immediate view." Thus, "bad law immediately excites a general alarm," but "a bad judicial determination, though no less pernicious in its consequences," does not, for it is "immediately felt, probably, by a single individual only, and noticed only by his neighbors, and a few spectators in the Court."[53] Thus, the Anti-Federalists concluded—in direct contradiction to Hamilton's claim in *Federalist* No. 78—that "we are more in danger of sowing the seeds of arbitrary government in this department than in any other."[54]

The Anti-Federalists also perceived the judicial article as a threat to democracy because of the way in which it weakened that most democratic of institutions: trial by jury. While Article III, Section 2 guaranteed the right to trial by jury in criminal cases, it did not in civil cases. Moreover, even in criminal cases, it conferred upon the Supreme Court appellate jurisdiction "both as to law and fact," thereby prompting many Anti-Federalists to fear that the Supreme Court could overturn verdicts of acquittal returned by juries. As Luther Martin complained in his "Genuine Information":

> The appellate jurisdiction extends, as I have observed, to cases criminal as well as to civil, and on the appeal the Court is to decide not only on the law but on the facts; if therefore, even in criminal cases the general government is not satisfied with the verdict of the jury, its officer may remove the prosecution to the supreme court, and there the verdict of the jury is to be of no effect, but the judges of this court are to decide upon the facts as well as the law, the same as in civil cases.[55]

Martin's objections were part of a more general Anti-Federalist objection to the Court's appellate jurisdiction. They saw in it the spectre of aristocracy. As "A Friend to the Rights of the People" observed, the Court's appellate jurisdiction "extends to all cases and disputes which may happen between man and man; and so may prove, in the issue, a source of mischief and ruin to thousands—The rich and wilful citizen may," he warned darkly, "after passing through the lower forms of law, appeal up to this federal court, at four, or five hundred miles distance; there the other party must repair, at an amazing expence, or else lose his case however just and righteoce [*sic*]—Hereby the course of public justice may be much obstructed, the poor, oppressed, and many undone—Every door therefore against such a pernicious effect, ought to be shut in the Constitution."[56] Brutus was in full agreement. Expecting that the Supreme Court would hold its session "at the seat of the general government," thereby obligating the parties to "travel many hundred miles, with their witnesses and lawyers to prosecute or defend a suit," he anticipated that "no man of midling fortune" could sustain the expense of such a lawsuit and "therefore the poorer and midling class of citizen will be under the necessity of submitting to the demands of the rich and the lordly, in cases that will come under the cognizance of this court."[57]

Finally, the Anti-Federalists perceived Article III as a threat to the continued existence of the states. They feared with Brutus that the Court would "operate to effect, in the most certain, but yet silent and imperceptible manner, what is evidently the tendency of the constitution: I mean, an entire subversion of the legislative, executive, and judicial powers of the individual states."[58] The judges would "lean strongly in favor of the general government" and would rule in such a way as "will favor an extension of its jurisdiction" not only because the Constitution's provisions permit it—they were "conceived in general and indefinite terms, which are either equivocal, ambiguous, or which require long definitions to unfold the extent of their meaning"—but also because it will "enlarge the sphere of their own authority." Brutus was quick to point out that "every extension of the power of the general legislature, as well as of the judicial powers, will increase the powers of the courts; and the dignity and importance of the judges, will be in proportion to the extent and magnitude of the powers they exercise."[59]

This outpouring of criticism led the various state ratifying conventions officially or unofficially to propose sixteen substantive alterations to Article III. Wythe Holt has summarized them as follows:

> Some proposals would have guaranteed jury trials in noncriminal cases, and some would have limited or eliminated federal question jurisdiction. New York, Virginia, and Pennsylvania would have restricted the lower federal courts to admiralty jurisdiction; New York, Virginia, North Carolina, and the minority in Pennsylvania would have eliminated diversity and alienage jurisdiction altogether; and Massachusetts, New Hampshire, and Maryland would have placed a minimum amount-in-controversy limitation on diversity cases and a higher limit on appeals. Maryland would have required trials by jury in all actions on debts or contracts. Virginia proposed that national jurisdiction should "extend to no case where the

cause of action shall have originated before the ratification of this Constitution."[60]

It was against this backdrop that the first Senate, on April 7, 1789, just one day after it had a quorum to organize itself,[61] created a committee "to bring in a bill for organizing the Judiciary of the United States."[62] Under the leadership of Oliver Ellsworth,[63] the committee's task was "to cater to these demands" of the state ratifying conventions, but to do so "without seriously crippling the national judiciary."[64] The Judiciary Committee rose to the occasion and completed a detailed draft of the proposed legislation by late May, which was readily approved at the committee level on June 12 and by the full Senate on July 17.[65] The House thereupon overwhelmingly approved the Senate bill with "no material alterations"[66] on September 17, and President George Washington signed it into law on September 24.

What the Senate proposed, and the House readily accepted, was the following: There would be a Supreme Court—consisting of a chief justice and five associate justices—with power, under Section 25, to hear appeals whenever the highest state court having jurisdiction of the case ruled against the constitutionality of a federal law or treaty, in favor of the validity of a state act that had been challenged as contrary to the Constitution or federal law, or against a right or privilege claimed under the Constitution or federal law.

The Senate also exercised the Congress's constitutional option to establish a system of inferior federal courts. It did so for two principal reasons. First, it believed an effective maritime commerce (essential to the new nation) needed a dependable body of admiralty and maritime law,[67] and that the most reliable method to assure its development would be to entrust it to a new set of federal courts. As John Frank has remarked: "The experience of the Confederation convinced virtually every conscientious patriot of the 1780s that the admiralty jurisdiction ought to be totally, effectively, and completely in the hands of the national government, and an extended search has not revealed a criticism from any contemporary source of the constitution granting federal admiralty jurisdiction."[68] The need for district courts with admiralty jurisdiction, in turn, "opened the door for somewhat broader jurisdiction, since it effectively surrendered the argument over the expense of federal district courts."[69]

Second, the Senate exercised Congress's option to create lower federal courts because at least one state, Virginia, had adopted legislation, sponsored by Patrick Henry,[70] prohibiting its judges from "executing federal functions." As Senator Caleb Strong noted: "The State of Virginia by a Law passed since their Adoption of the Constitution, have prohibited their Officers from holding Offices under the United States, and their Courts from having Jurisdiction of

Causes arising under the Laws of the Union; by such Laws every State would be able to defeat the Provisions of Congress if the Judiciary powers of the Genl. Government were directed to be exercised by the State Courts."[71]

Having determined to establish lower federal courts, the Senate next had to decide on their organization and jurisdiction. It began by proposing the creation of a federal district court, consisting of a single judge, to sit in each state. However, attentive not only to the needs of the "Genl. Government" but also to the interests of the states, it then proposed to limit the jurisdiction of these federal district courts to admiralty cases, petty criminal offenses, and custom cases—i.e., "to areas where the state courts had never had jurisdiction or could not appropriately take jurisdiction,"[72]— and to allow state courts to have jurisdiction over many areas of potential federal jurisdiction, including most cases arising under the Constitution, federal laws, and treaties. As Henry Bourguignon has put it, "[f]ederal district court jurisdiction, therefore, consisted of precisely charted islands in the vast sea of state court jurisdiction."[73]

To avoid the appearance of denigrating the states by creating a strong federal district court with broad jurisdiction in each state, the Senate also proposed the creation of circuit courts that would hear cases in the three circuits into which the country was to be divided.[74] The circuit courts— consisting of two Supreme Court justices, who literally would ride the circuit, and the district judge of the district where they were sitting—would have some appellate jurisdiction over the district courts, thus making them "traveling mini-Supreme Court[s]."[75] They would also have original jurisdiction over all federal crimes, over cases between foreign parties and citizens, and over cases between citizens of different states (alienage and diversity jurisdiction). With greater jurisdiction, territorial reach, and prestige than the district courts, they would bring federal judicial power into all of the states. In deference to the states, the Senate also provided in Section 34—what has come to be known as the Rules of Decision Act—that "the laws of the several States, except where the Constitution, treaties, or statutes of the United States shall otherwise require or provide, shall be regarded as rules of decision in trials at common law in the courts of the United States in cases where they apply."[76] In a further nod to the states, the Senate included a $500 jurisdictional minimum for the circuit court's diversity and alienage jurisdiction, thus leaving most cases in state courts. The Senate carved out even more space for state courts by restricting the federal courts' admiralty and maritime jurisdiction to "significant" seizures, i.e., to seizures made "on waters which are navigable from the Sea by Vessels of ten or more tons burthen," and by "Saving to Suitors, in all cases, the right of a common law remedy where the common law is competent to give it," i.e., the right to seek relief in the state courts.[77] Finally, the Senate limited appeals from the circuit courts to the Supreme Court to legal issues only (the sole mode of appeal it provided was the writ of error which prevented issues of fact resolved by juries from being reexamined), and it subjected even those issues to a $2000 jurisdictional minimum.

Much of what the Senate proposed in the Judiciary Act of 1789 was intended to address the concerns about Article III expressed during the ratification debates and to avoid offending state sensibilities. Ellsworth summed it up this way in a letter to Richard Law once the Senate had completed its work:

> To annex to State Courts jurisdictions which they had not before, as of admiralty cases, & perhaps of offenses against the United States, would be constituting the Judges of them, *pro tanto*, federal Judges, & of course they would continue such during good behavior & and on fixed sales, which in many cases, would illy comport with their present tenures of office. Besides, if the State Courts as such could take cognizance of those offenses, it might not be safe for the generall [*sic*] government to put the trial & punishment of them entirely out of its own hands. One federal judge at least, resident in each State, appears unavoidable. And, without creating any more, or much enhancing the expense, there may be circuit courts, which would give system to the department, uniformity to the proceedings, settle many cases in the States that would otherwise go to the Supreme Court, & provide for the higher grade of offenses. Without this arrangement there must be many appeals or writs of error from the supreme courts of the States, which by placing them in a Subordinate scituation [*sic*], & Subjecting their decissions [*sic*] to frequent reversals, would probably hurt their feelings & their influence, than to divide the ground with them at first & leave it optional with the parties entitled to federal jurisdiction, where the causes are of considerable magnitude to take their remedy in which line of courts they pleased.[78]

Bourguignon has written that "the principles of federalism permeated the Judiciary Act of 1789."[79] He is certainly correct. The Senate went out of its way to protect the original federal design.[80] Thus, the Senate followed state boundaries in establishing districts for the new federal courts. It imposed state procedures and state common law on the federal courts hearing cases in the states. It severely restricted the jurisdiction of the district and circuit courts, and it allowed the state courts to retain a "great deal of that jurisdiction many had thought to be rendered exclusively federal by the Constitution."[81] It imposed a $500 jurisdictional minimum on the circuit courts, thereby preventing "the poorer and midling class of citizen" from being brought into federal court and "excluding a huge number of the British debt claims." It limited alienage jurisdiction so that cases brought by British creditors that were already pending in state courts could not be transferred to federal court. It imposed a $2000 jurisdictional minimum on the Supreme Court, saving many litigants from having to travel to the seat of the federal government for appeals. Finally, the Senate provided state courts maximum concurrent jurisdiction with the federal courts, and it granted them exclusive jurisdiction over most cases arising under federal law, treaties, and the Constitution. As Bourguignon notes, the omission of general federal questions jurisdiction from the judicial powers granted to the federal courts was no "oversight." While the district courts were "little more than admiralty courts" and, therefore, unlikely candidates to receive general federal question jurisdiction, the circuit courts "would seem to have been the ideal courts to receive this important area of jurisdiction, but they did not." Bourguignon attributes this "enormous concession of federal judicial power to the often distrusted state courts" to the Senate's desire to protect the interests of the states as states.[82]

The Judiciary Act pleased the erstwhile critics of Article III. Senator Richard Henry Lee, an Anti-Federalist from Virginia, was able to write to Patrick Henry that "so far as this has gone, I am satisfied to see a spirit prevailing that promises to send this system out free from those vexations and abuses that might have been warranted by the terms of the constitution."[83] This accommodation, however, infuriated James Madison. Madison, whose bid to use the Bill of Rights to improve state constitutions was frustrated by the Senate when it rejected his proposed amendment mandating the states to protect rights of conscience, free press, and trial by jury, was again frustrated by the Senate's solicitous regard for the states. He complained in a letter to Edmund Pendleton that the Judiciary Act was "defective both in its general structure, and many of its particular regulations."[84] Clearly, he believed it had failed to provide the federal government with the strong "arms and legs" for which he had argued in the Federal Convention.

The First Bank Act

A third case study, the passage of the act chartering the first Bank of the United States, also shows the founding generation's appreciation for the way in which the mode of electing the Senate protected state interests. On December 14, 1790, Secretary of the Treasury Alexander Hamilton transmitted a report to the House of Representatives proposing the creation of a "National Bank," describing it as "an institution of primary importance to the prosperous administration of the [new nation's] finances."[85]

Hamilton's report was a response to a House order that he detail "such further provision as may, in his opinion, be necessary for establishing the public credit."[86] Hamilton's report focused on what he called "considerations of public advantage."[87] In it, he reviewed the "principal advantages of a bank,"[88] addressed its "disadvantages, real or supposed,"[89] discussed the relation of the proposed bank to the "three banks in the United States" then in existence (the Bank of North America—originally established by Congress under the Articles of Confederation but subsequently chartered by Pennsylvania, the Bank of New York, and the Bank of Massachusetts),[90] outlined "the principles upon which a national bank ought to be organized,"[91] and spelled out twenty-four specific provisions for its operation.[92] In those twenty-four provisions, Hamilton proposed the creation of a private banking corporation, the Bank of the United States, with close links to the federal government. Its stock would be sold by subscription under the supervision of persons appointed by the president. Three-fourths of the payments for private subscriptions were to be made in public securities; the United States, however, was to be permitted to pay for its subscription (totaling one-fifth of the Bank's capital stock) by borrowing from the Bank. The Bank's notes and bills of credit were to be generally negotiable and acceptable as payment for any debts due the federal government—Hamilton's intention was to render them a de facto circulating medium. The Bank's directors were to be elected by the stockholders (including the United States) rather than appointed by the government, but their operations were to be subject to close review by the Secretary of the Treasury.

Hamilton's report was devoid of any constitutional arguments addressing Congress's power under the Constitution to charter such a bank. It may well be, however, that he thought it obvious that Congress had this power. This was the view of Representative John Laurance, a Federalist from New York, who would later argue on the floor of the House: "Under the late confederation, the . . . Bank of North America was instituted." He "presumed that it would not be controverted that the present government is vested with powers equal to those of the late confederation."[93]

On December 23, the House delivered a copy of Hamilton's report to the Senate, which took the lead and quickly passed a bill incorporating the Bank of the United States on January 20, 1791, by a vote of sixteen to six. While the Senate deliberations were not open to the public, its journals reveal that most of the Senate debate centered on the length of the term of the Bank's incorporation, an issue that Hamilton had not addressed. Motions to limit its term of incorporation to seven or ten years were rejected; so, too, was a motion to extend it all the way to 1815. Ultimately, the Senate agreed to a twenty-year term, with the Bank's charter set to expire on March 4, 1811.[94]

On January 21, the bill was referred to the House, which began its consideration of the Bank on February 1. On February 8, the House likewise approved the measure but only after a heated debate, led by James Madison, over its constitutionality.[95] Madison argued, first, that the Convention had explicitly rejected a motion to give the Congress power to issue charters of incorporation, and, second, that the Necessary and Proper Clause could not be read so broadly as to justify incorporating the Bank.

Concerning the actions of the Federal Convention, Madison attempted to use his personal knowledge of what transpired during its secret deliberations in an effort to "deny the authority of Congress" to pass the Bank. As he told his fellow congressmen, "he well recollected that a power to grant charters of incorporation had been proposed in the general convention, and rejected."[96]

Madison's attempt to speak for the Convention did not go unchallenged. Elbridge Gerry had also been in attendance, and he confronted Madison directly. Gerry argued that it was "improper" to "depend on the memory of the gentleman [Madison] for an history of their debates, and from thence to collect their sense." It was "improper" because "the memories of different gentlemen would probably vary, as they have already done, with respect to those facts; and, if not, the opinions of the individual members, who debated, are not to be considered the opinions of the convention." However, if they were to be so considered, Gerry wanted the members of Congress to know that his opinions differed from Madison's: "[N]o motion was made in that convention, and, therefore, none could be rejected for establishing a national bank. And the measure which the gentleman has referred to was a proposition merely to enable Congress to erect commercial corporations, which was, and always ought to be, negatived."[97]

With his first argument against the Bank effectively parried, Madison launched an attack on the whole doctrine of implied powers.

> The doctrine of implication is always a tender one. The danger of it has been felt in other Governments. The delicacy was felt in the adoption of our own; the danger may also be felt, if we do not keep close to our chartered authorities.

> Mark the reasoning on which the validity of the bill depends. To borrow money is made the *end*, and the accumulation of capital *implied* as the *means*. The accumulation of capital is, then, the *end*, and a bank implied as the *means*. The bank is then the *end*, and a charter of incorporation . . .

implied as the *means*.[98]

Supporters of the Bank Act responded to Madison's attack on implied powers in several different ways. Representative William Loughton Smith of South Carolina found it strange that Madison would now deny the doctrine of implication, as he had previously employed an implied powers argument to assert that the President alone had the power to remove members of the executive branch. "[T]he principles advanced by Mr. Madison, in the debate on the power of removability . . . , he conceived, applied very aptly to the present subject. Matters of a fiscal nature necessarily devolve on the General Government, and he urged, that every power resulting from the acknowledged right of Congress to control finances of this country, must be as necessarily implied, as in the case of the power of removability."[99]

Other members quoted the Preamble of the Constitution and defended the Bank as a means for achieving the "common defense and general welfare."[100] Fisher Ames argued that the Bank was constitutional even under Madison's narrow reading of the Necessary and Proper Clause. "The most orderly governments in Europe have banks. They are considered as *indispensably* necessary; these examples are not to be supposed to have been unnoticed."[101]

Congressman Smith of South Carolina also made another and especially profound argument. "It would be a deplorable thing," he said, "if this Government should enact a law subversive of the constitution, or that so enlightened a body as the Senate of the United States should, by so great a majority as were in favor of this bill, pass a law hostile to the liberties of this country, as the opposition to this measure have suggested the bank system to be."[102] Smith's argument showed keen insight. The Senate, whose mode of election ensured the protection of the interests of the states as states, did not regard its reliance on implied powers to pass the Bank Act as a threat to the "residuary sovereignty" of the states; rather, it considered the Bank as necessary and proper for carrying into execution the enumerated powers of Article I, Section 8 and for achieving the "great objects" spelled out in the Preamble. Smith, in effect, argued that questions of what is permissible under the Constitution are not convincingly resolved by relying on an interpretation of its words, as Madison's equivocations on the Necessary and Proper Clause clearly demonstrated, but rather are effectively resolved only by relying on constitutional structure, which allows the self-interest of the various branches to determine the answer.

Elbridge Gerry would build on Smith's argument. "The interpretation of the constitution, like the prerogative of a sovereign, may be abused, but from hence the disuse of either cannot be inferred. In the exercise of prerogative, the minister is responsible for his advice to his sovereign, and the members of either House are responsible to their constituents for their conduct in construing the constitution. We act at our peril: if our conduct is directed to the attainment of the great objects of Government, it will be approved."[103] The state legislatures were, of course, the constituents of the Senate, and, as Gerry made clear, it was for them to judge whether the Senate, through its use of implied powers, was serving "the great objects of Government" or jeopardizing the original federal design.

Madison's arguments that the Congress lacked the power to charter the Bank of the United States and that it was invading the reserved powers of the states were unavailing in the House, which approved the Bank Act by a vote of thirty-nine to twenty.[104] They did, however, sufficiently concern President George Washington that, when the measure was sent to him for approval, he referred it to Attorney General Edmund Randolph[105] and Secretary of State Thomas Jefferson for their opinions. In brief statements, both agreed that the bank bill was contrary to the Constitution and urged Washington to veto it.

Randolph, who wrote first, prepared two separate memoranda: As he explained in his transmittal letter to Washington, in the first, he stated affirmatively his own constitutional analysis of the bill's invalidity while, in the second, he addressed "a minor class of arguments against the bill, which I have received through the public prints & other sources of communication."[106]

In his first memorandum, Randolph argued that the implied powers argument of the Bank's supporters "would beget a doctrine so indefinite as to grasp every power"[107] and would "stretch the arm of Congress into the whole circle of State legislation."[108] Concerning the Necessary and Proper Clause, Randolph offered contradictory advice, and all in the same paragraph: After initially insisting that it "does not enlarge the powers of Congress, but rather restricts them," he quickly reversed field and concluded that, "as the friends of the bill ought not to claim any advantage from this clause, so ought not the enemies to it, to quote the clause as having a restrictive effect. Both ought to consider it among the surplusage which as often proceeds from inattention as caution."[109]

In his second memorandum, Randolph addressed, inter alia, the contention "that even the infirm old Congress incorporated a bank; and can a less power be presumed to be vested in the Federal Government, which has been formed to remedy their weakness?"[110] This question was clearly of more than academic interest to Randolph, as he had drafted the 1781 ordinance by which the Confederation Congress chartered the first national bank, the Bank of North America, and he was the author of the committee report to Congress justifying its creation.[111] His answer was, in effect, that the Bank of North America was unconstitutional but, at the time, absolutely necessary. "This argument [that, if the Confederation Congress could charter a bank, so, too, could the Congress under the Constitution] is so indefinite, the time of the incorporation was so pressing, and the States had such an unlimited command over Congress and their acts, that the public acquiescence ought not to be the basis of such a power under the present circumstances."[112] Randolph also took up and rejected Madison's contention that the Bank was unconstitutional because the Constitutional Convention had refused to grant the Congress power to issues charters of incorporation. Madison had claimed special knowledge as a delegate to the Convention, but both Randolph and Washington had been in attendance as well, prompting Randolph to remark. "An appeal has been also made by the enemies of the bill to what passed in the federal convention on the subject. But ought not the constitution to be decided on by the import of its own expressions? What may not be the consequence if an almost unknown history should govern the construction."[113]

Jefferson argued in his opinion that the Bank Act went beyond the boundaries "specifically drawn around the powers of Congress" and took "possession of a boundless field of power, no longer susceptible to any definition."[114] He would later protest in similar fashion against the efforts of the federal government in 1800 to charter a company to mine copper in New Jersey, employing what would become memorable language: "Congress are authorized to defend the nation. Ships are necessary for defence; copper is necessary for ships; mines necessary for copper; a company necessary to work the mines; and who can doubt this reasoning who has ever played at 'This is the House that Jack Built'? Under such a process of filiation of necessities the sweeping clause makes clean work."[115]

Jefferson insisted in his opinion to Washington that the Constitution should be read to "lace Congress up straitly within the enumerated powers; and those without which, as means, those powers could not be carried into effect."[116] The Necessary and Proper Clause, therefore, had to be understood as limiting the Congress to "those means, without which the grant of power would be nugatory."[117] Interestingly for one who had not actually attended the Convention, Jefferson repeated Madison's contention that the Federal Convention had rejected conferring on Congress the power to grant charters of incorporation.

It is known that the very power now proposed as a *means*, was rejected *as an end* by the convention which formed the constitution: a proposition was made to them to authorize Congress to open canals, and an amendatory one to empower them to incorporate; but the whole was rejected, and one of the reasons of rejection urged in the debate was, that then they would have power to erect a bank, which would render the great cities, where there were prejudices or jealousies on this subject, adverse to the reception of the constitution.[118]

Walter Dellinger and H. Jefferson Powell characterize Jefferson's view of congressional authority as "crabbed";[119] to Jefferson's credit, however, he concluded his opinion to Washington with these words: "It must be added, however, that, unless the President's mind, on a view of every thing, which is urged for and against this bill, is tolerably clear that it is unauthorized by the constitution; if the pro and the con hang so even as to balance his judgment, a just respect for the wisdom of the Legislature, would naturally decide the balance in favor of their opinion."[120]

Randolph's and Jefferson's opinions troubled Washington, prompting him to ask Hamilton for "his sentiments" on the "validity and propriety" of the Act. Hamilton's opinion was lengthy and detailed.[121] In it, he advanced a powerful "means-ends" argument much like the one Madison had made earlier during the Constitutional Convention (when he "doubt[ed] the practicality" of enumerating the powers of the federal government) and the one that Hamilton had previously made in *Federalist* No. 31.[122] While conceding that "difficulties on this point are inherent in the nature of the federal constitution," resulting as "inevitably" they must "from a division of legislative power," Hamilton proceeded to offer "a criterion of what is constitutional, and of what is not so. This criterion is the *end* to which the measures relates as a *mean.* If the end be clearly comprehended within any of the specified powers, and if the measure have an obvious relation to that end, and is not forbidden by any particular provision of the constitution, it may safely be deemed to come within the compass of the national authority."[123] Washington was ultimately persuaded by Hamilton's argument,[124] and, rather than deliver the veto message he had asked Madison to prepare,[125] he signed the act incorporating the Bank on February 25, 1791.

Notes

1. David P. Currie, *The Constitution in Congress: The Federalist Period, 1789-1801* (Chicago: University of Chicago Press, 1997), 3.

2. *McCulloch* v. *Maryland*, 17 U.S. 316, 407 (1819).

3. Currie, *The Constitution in Congress*, 4.

4. Currie, *The Constitution in Congress*, 5.

5. W. B. Allen (ed.), *Works of Fisher Ames*, 2 vols. (Indianapolis: Liberty Fund, 1983), 2: 877.

6. See Robert A. Goldwin, *From Parchment to Power: How James Madison Used the Bill of Rights to Save the Constitution* (Washington, D.C.: AEI Press, 1997).

7. Max Farrand (ed.), *The Records of the Federal Convention of 1787, Rev. ed.*, 4 vols. (New Haven: Yale University Press, 1937), 2: 587-88. (Hereafter cited as Farrand, *Records*.)

8. James Madison, Alexander Hamilton, and John Jay, *The Federalist*, ed. Jacob E. Cooke (New York: World Publishing Company, 1961), No. 84, 581. Emphasis in the original.

9. *Federalist* No. 84, 579.

10. Letter to Thomas Jefferson, October 17, 1788. In Gaillard Hunt (ed.), *The Writings of James Madison*, 9 vols. (New York: Putnam, 1904), 5: 271-75.

11. Hunt, *The Writings of James Madison*, 5: 271-75.

12. In a letter of August 19, 1789, to Richard Peters, Madison referred to "the nauseous project of amendments," but defended his sponsorship of them, saying: "If amendts. had not been proposed from the federal side of the House, the proposition would have come within three days, from the adverse side. It is certainly best that they should appear to be the free gift of the friends of the Constitution rather than to be extorted by the address & weight of its enemies. It will kill the opposition every where, and by putting an end to the disaffection to the Govt. itself, enable the administration to venture on measures not otherwise safe." In Helen E. Veit, Kenneth R. Bowling, and Charlene Bang Bickford (eds.), *Creating the Bill of Rights: The Documentary Record of the First Federal Congress* (Baltimore: Johns Hopkins University Press, 1991), 281-82.

13. Veit et al., *Creating the Bill of Rights*, 79.

14. See Veit et al., *Creating the Bill of Rights*, 14-28, for the text of the proposed amendments from these five states.

15. Letter to George Eve, January 2, 1789, in Hunt, *The Writings of James Madison*, 5: 319.

16. Letter to Thomas Jefferson, October 17, 1788, in Hunt, *The Writings of James Madison*, 5: 271-72. The following analysis has benefited greatly from Herbert J. Storing, "The Constitution and the Bill of Rights," in Ralph A. Rossum and Gary L. McDowell (eds.), *The American Founding: Politics, Statesmanship, and the Constitution* (Port Washington, N.Y., Kennikat, 1981), 29-45.

17. Veit et al., *Creating the Bill of Rights*, 78.

18. Veit et al., *Creating the Bill of Rights*, 79-80.

19. Veit et al., *Creating the Bill of Rights*, 78.

20. Veit et al., *Creating the Bill of Rights*, 78. Emphasis in the original.

21. Veit et al., *Creating the Bill of Rights*, 78.

22. Veit et al., *Creating the Bill of Rights*, 79-80.

23. Veit et al., *Creating the Bill of Rights*, 78.

24. Letter to James Madison, December 20, 1787, in Julian Bond (ed.), *The Papers of Thomas Jefferson*, 18 vols. (Princeton: Princeton University Press, 1955), 12: 440.

25. Veit et al., *Creating the Bill of Rights*, 13.

26. Veit et al., *Creating the Bill of Rights*, 188.

27. Veit et al., *Creating the Bill of Rights*, 188. In truth, given his "extended republic" argument in *Federalist* No. 10, Madison should have said that it was even more necessary that these rights should be secured against the states.

28. Veit et al., *Creating the Bill of Rights*, 37-41.

29. Veit et al., *Creating the Bill of Rights*, xix.

30. Veit et al., *Creating the Bill of Rights*, 41.

31. Letter of William Grayson to Patrick Henry, September 29, 1789, in Veit, *Creating the Bill of Rights*, 300.

32. George Anastaplo, *The Constitutionalist: Notes on the First Amendment* (Dallas: Southern Methodist University Press, 1971), 174. See also Julius Goebel Jr., *The Oliver Wendell Holmes Devise History of the Supreme Court of the United States*, Vol. 1: *Antecedents and Beginnings to 1801* (New York: Macmillan, 1971), 448. "Since the Senators represented the states, the . . . rejection [of this provision] was forseeable."

33. Letter of James Madison to Edmund Pendleton, September 14, 1789, in Veit et al., *Creating the Bill of Rights*, 296. Fisher Ames wrote that "[t]he Amendments too have been amended by the Senate, & many in our house, Mr. Madison, in particular, thinks, that they have lost much of their seductive Virtue by the alteration." Letter of Fisher Ames to Caleb Strong, September 15, 1789, Veit et al., *Creating the Bill of Rights*, 297. Senator Payne Wingate wrote that "[a]s to amendments to the Constitution, Madison says he had rather have none than those agreed to by the Senate." Letter of Paine Wingate to John Landgon, September 17, 1789, in Veit et al., *Creating the Bill of Rights*, 297. Not all Federalist House members, however, were disappointed with the Senate's actions. Roger Sherman thought the Senate had "altered for the better" the House's proposals. Letter of Roger Sherman to Samuel Huntington, September 17, 1789, in Veit et al., *Creating the Bill of Rights*, 297.

34. Veit et al., *Creating the Bill of Rights*, 44.

35. 1 Stat. 73 (1789).

36. Paul Bator, "Judiciary Act of 1789," in Leonard W. Levy, Kenneth L. Karst, and Dennis J. Mahoney (eds.), *Encyclopedia of the American Constitution*, 5 vols. (New York: Macmillan, 1986), 3: 1075.

37. Wythe Holt, "'To Establish Justice': Politics, the Judiciary Act of 1789, and the Invention of the Federal Courts," *Duke Law Journal* 1989 (1989): 1421, 1478.

38. As Wilfred J. Ritz writes: "By a decision process that is unknown, the new Senate undertook as its first order of business the formidable task of constructing an act that would establish the third branch of government, the judiciary. This division of labor was apparently agreeable to the House of Representatives, but we do not know how this agreement was negotiated." Ritz, *Rewriting the History of the Judiciary Act of 1789: Exposing Myths, Challenging Premises, and Using New Evidence*, ed. Wythe Holt and L. H. LaRue (Norman: University of Oklahoma Press, 1990), 13. Holt suggests the following basis for this division of labor: "In the important task of building a government, the House first took up the problems of revenue [because the Constitution requires that money bills originate in the House], while the Senate undertook to fashion a judiciary." Holt, "To Establish Justice," 1478.

39. *Federalist* No. 78, 523. Hamilton also described it as "the least dangerous" branch, "because it will be least in a capacity to annoy or injure" the "political rights of the constitution." No. 78, 522.

40. Farrand, *Records*, 1: 105.

41. Farrand, *Records*, 2: 539.

42. Farrand, *Records*, 2: 431-32.

43. Farrand, *Records*, 1: 124.

44. Farrand, *Records*, 1: 124.

45. Farrand, *Records*, 1: 125.

46. "The Essays of Brutus," in Herbert J. Storing (ed.), *The Complete Anti-Federalist*, 7 vols. (Chicago: University of Chicago Press, 1981), 2: 438.

47. "The Letters from the Federal Farmer," in Storing (ed.), *The Complete Anti-Federalist*, 2: 315.

48. "The Letters from the Federal Farmer," 2: 315.

49. "The Letters from the Federal Farmer," 2: 322-23.

50. A few states—New York in particular—did have such a system. See James Kent, *Commentaries on American Law*, 4 vols. (New York: O. Halsted, 1826), and Gary L. McDowell, *Equity and the Constitution: The Supreme Court, Equitable Relief, and Public Policy* (Chicago: University of Chicago Press, 1982).

51. "The Letters from the Federal Farmer," 2: 244.

52. "The Letters from the Federal Farmer," 2: 244.

53. "The Letters from the Federal Farmer," 2: 316.

54. "The Letters from the Federal Farmer," 2: 316.

55. Luther Martin, "Genuine Information," in Storing, *The Complete Anti-Federalist*, 2: 70.

56. "A Friend to the Rights of the People," in Storing, *The Complete Anti-Federalist*, 4: 241.

57. "The Essays of Brutus," 2: 434.

58. "The Essays of Brutus," 2: 420.

59. "The Essays of Brutus," 2: 421.

60. "More than two hundred amendments to the Constitution, embodying approximately eighty different substantive changes, were suggested by the various state ratification conventions. Sixteen of the eighty proposed important alternations in the national judiciary." Holt, "To Establish Justice," 1477.

61. The First Congress was to assemble and commence business on March 4, 1789; however, on that appointed day, only thirteen of the thirty representatives and eight of the twelve senators needed to constitute quorums had arrived. The Senate did not have a quorum until Richard Henry Lee of Virginia arrived on April 6. Holt, "To Establish Justice," 1478.

62. Henry J. Bourguignon, "The Federal Key to the Judiciary Act of 1789," *South Carolina Law Review* 46 (1995): 647, 666.

63. Ellsworth was a member of the Constitutional Convention, had served as a judge of the Connecticut Superior Court, and had considerable knowledge of the problems of federal appellate authority from his service on the Standing Committee of the Continental Congress for appeals in cases of prize. See Goebel, *History of the Supreme Court,* 459. "Ellsworth clearly deserves the encomiums he has received as the father of the Judiciary Act of 1789. Like a good lawyer, he had thoroughly digested the situation and considered his proposed solution; he knew when to yield but forcefully presented his complex and apt plan; and he worked ceaselessly to obtain adoption of it." Holt, "To Establish Justice," 1483. For its first six years, the Senate met in secret, and so we have no record of the Senate's debate on the Judiciary Act. We do have, however, the detailed diary of William Maclay, a Federalist senator from Pennsylvania. See Kenneth R. Bowling and Helen E. Veit (eds.), *The Diary of William Maclay and Other Notes on Senate Debates: March 4, 1789-March 3, 1791* (Baltimore: Johns Hopkins University Press, 1988). Maclay was much less laudatory of Ellsworth than Holt; see his disparaging remarks of Ellsworth and "this Vile Bill" which Maclay describes as "a child of his, and he defends it with the Care of a parent, even in wrath and anger." Bowling and Veit, *Diary of William Maclay,* 93. Maclay's objection was not that the Bill was either too national or too federal, but that it was too expensive and too likely to give advantage to the lawyerly class. While Maclay had served as a Common Pleas judge in Pennsylvania, he had only a hornbook acquaintance with the law and considerable suspicion of lawyers, prompting him to remark at one point: "This day, the Lawyers shewed plainly the Cloven foot of their intentions. . . ." Bowling and Veit, *Diary of William Maclay,* 105.

64. Ritz, *Rewriting the History of the Judiciary Act of 1789,* 20. "Ellsworth combined the tenacious qualities of a Connecticut Yankee lawyer and judge, including tirelessness, with a debating technique that overwhelmed opponents through systematic and repetitious defense of his position. His blunt but effective statesmanship grew from a grudging but serious understanding of how important it was to make drastic concessions to the position . . . [represented by those who drafted the various proposed amendments to Article III in the state ratifying conventions] while maintaining the essential strength of the federal judiciary." Holt, "To Establish Justice," 1481.

65. Ritz, *Rewriting the History of the Judiciary Act of 1789,* 17.

66. Holt reports that "[m]ost observers agreed with Congressman Benjamin Goodhue that 'no material alterations' had been made in 'the Judicial bill . . . as it came from the Senate.'" Holt, "To Establish Justice," 1516, n. 348. See also Ritz, *Rewriting the History of the Judiciary Act of 1789,* 18. See Goebel, *History of the Supreme Court,* 504-7, for a discussion of four "novel" but not material alternations made by the House.

67. Bator, "Judiciary Act of 1789," 1075.

68. John Frank, "Historical Bases of the Federal Judicial System," *Law and Contemporary Problems* 13 (1948): 3, 9. They recognized that admiralty jurisdiction had international ramifications and that uncontrolled state admiralty courts hearing prize disputes had already generated interstate and international resentment. Holt, "To Establish Justice," 1427-30.

69. Bourguignon, "The Federal Key to the Judiciary Act of 1789," 688.

70. Goebel, *History of the Supreme Court,* 462.

71. Maeva Marcus et al. (eds.), *Documentary History of the Supreme Court of the United States, 1789-1800: Organizing the Federal Judiciary: Legislation and Commentaries* (New York: Columbia University Press, 1992), 4: 395-96. This prompted Goebel to remark: "Clearly the Virginians had been hoist by their own petard." Goebel, *History of the Supreme Court,* 462.

72. Bourguignon, "The Federal Key to the Judiciary Act of 1789," 679.

73. Bourguignon, "The Federal Key to the Judiciary Act of 1789," 682.

74. The Senate rejected a motion by William Samuel Johnson of Connecticut to replace the district and circuit courts with a system of *nisi prius* courts—the system then in use in Massachusetts, New York, and Great Britain. With a *nisi prius* system, a large group of judges would ride, singly or in small groups, into the countryside to try cases but return to the center of government for deliberation, consultation, and resolution of difficult or novel questions of law. Those favoring *nisi prius* courts argued that they would be less expensive, would save the costs of travel to the center of government for parties and witnesses, and would create uniformity in decisions. Holt, "To Establish Justice," 1481, 1492.

75. Bourguignon, "The Federal Key to the Judiciary Act of 1789," 669.

76. In the same legislative session, Congress passed the Act to Regulate Processes in the Courts of the United States, known as the Process Act, 1 Stat. 93 (1789). This Act was drafted by the same Judiciary Committee in the Senate that wrote the Judiciary Act. As Julius Goebel has written: "It supplemented the Judiciary Act and . . . projected into another area the political principle of section 34," i.e., it embodied the judgment of "those who conceived that in each district state forms and modes of process should prevail" rather than those "who favored creation of a uniform procedure for the new federal courts." Goebel, *History of the Supreme Court,* 509, 510.

77. Judiciary Act of 1789, Chapter 20, Section 9.

78. Letter from Oliver Ellsworth to Richard Law, August 4, 1789, in Marcus et al., *Documentary History of the Supreme Court of the United States,* 4: 495.

79. Bourguignon, "The Federal Key to the Judiciary Act of 1789," 700. Wythe Holt goes even further: "The judiciary bill's passage through Congress significantly blunted the momentum of the drive to amend the Constitution." Holt, "To Establish Justice," 1513.

80. Wythe Holt again goes further and argues that the Judiciary Act solved "most of the large problems with Article III put forward by the opponents of the Constitution." Holt, "To Establish Justice," 1487.

81. Holt, "To Establish Justice," 1487.

82. Bourguignon, "The Federal Key to the Judiciary Act of 1789," 694.

83. Undated letter from Richard Henry Lee to Patrick Henry, in Marcus et al., *Documentary History of the Supreme Court of the United States,* 4: 400. Compare these sentiments with those expressed by the "Federal Farmer" (generally supposed to have been written by Lee); see especially, "Letters from the Federal Farmer," No. XV, in Storing, *The Complete Anti-Federalist,* 2: 315-23. Arthur Lee, brother of Richard Henry Lee, concurred: "It is difficult to say how . . . [the Judiciary Act] could have been framed less exceptionable." Letter from Arthur Lee to Tench Coxe, August 4, 1789, quoted in Holt, "To Establish Justice," 1517. However, see also the notes of Pierce Butler's speech, delivered on the floor of the Senate on July 17, 1789, in which he argued that "the ultimate tendency" of the Judiciary Act "manifestly will be to destroy, to Cut up at the Root the State Judiciaries." Bowling and Veit, *The Diary of William Maclay,* 455. Butler was so troubled by the Act that, immediately prior to its final approval in the Senate, he moved "[t]hat on the final question upon a bill or resolve, any Member shall have a right to enter his Protest or dissent on the Journal, with reasons in support of such dissent, provided the same be offered within two days after the determination of such final question." His motion "passed in the negative." Linda Grant De Pauw, Charlene Bangs Bickford, and LaVonne Marlene Siegel (eds.), *Senate Legislative Journal,* Vol. 1: *Documentary History of the First Federal Congress of the United States of America* (Baltimore: Johns Hopkins University Press, 1972), 84.

84. Letter from James Madison to Edmund Pendleton, September 14, 1789, quoted in Holt, "To Establish Justice," 1516-17.

85. M. St. Clair Clarke and D. A. Hall (eds.), *Legislative and Documentary History of the Bank of the United States* (Washington, D.C.: Gales and Seaton, 1832), 15. (Hereafter cited as Clarke and Hall, *Documentary History of the Bank.*)

86. Clarke and Hall, *Documentary History of the Bank,* 15.

87. Clarke and Hall, *Documentary History of the Bank,* 29.

88. Clarke and Hall, *Documentary History of the Bank,* 16-18.

89. Clarke and Hall, *Documentary History of the Bank,* 18-22.

90. Clarke and Hall, *Documentary History of the Bank,* 25-28.

91. Clarke and Hall, *Documentary History of the Bank,* 28-31.

92. Clarke and Hall, *Documentary History of the Bank,* 31-33.

93. Clarke and Hall, *Documentary History of the Bank,* 38. See also Elbridge Gerry's argument at Clarke and Hall, *Documentary History of the Bank,* 80.

94. Clarke and Hall, *Documentary History of the Bank*, 36.

95. Much speculation has arisen as to Madison's opposition to the Bank of the United States. His opposition, after all, seems inconsistent with his views on the Bill of Rights and the Judiciary Act. See George W. Carey, *In Defense of the Constitution* (Indianapolis: Liberty Fund, 1995), 91-94, for an excellent discussion of what might have "caused Madison's change of heart."

96. Clarke and Hall, *Documentary History of the Bank*, 40.

97. Clarke and Hall, *Documentary History of the Bank*, 79-80. What Madison wrote in his notes for September 14 concerning the Convention's decision on Congress's power to issue charters of incorporation is as follows:

Docr. Franklin moved to add after the words "post roads" Art. I; Sect. 8. "a power to provide for cutting canals where deemed necessary." Wilson 2ded. the motion.

Mr. Sherman objected. The expence in such cases will fall on the U— States, and the benefit accrue to the places where the canals may be cut.

Mr. Wilson. Instead of being an expence to the U.S. they may be made a source of revenue.

Mr. Madison suggested an enlargement of the motion into a power "to grant charters of incorporation where the interest of the U.S. might require & the legislative provisions of individual States may be incompetent." His primary object was however to secure an easy communication between the States which the free intercourse now to be opened, seemed to call for— The political obstacles being removed, a removal of the natural ones as far as possible ought to follow. Mr. Randolph 2ded. the proposition.

Mr. King thought the power unnecessary.

Mr. Wilson. It is necessary to prevent a State from obstructing the general welfare.

Mr. King— The States will be prejudiced and divided into parties by it— In Philada. & New York, It will be referred to the establishment of a Bank, which has been a subject of contention in those Cities. In other places it will be referred to mercantile monopolies.

Mr. Wilson mentioned the importance of facilitating by canals, the communication with the Western Settlements— As to Banks he did not think with Mr. King that the power in that point of view would excite the prejudices & parties apprehended. As to mercantile monopolies they are already included in the power to regulate trade.

Col. Mason was for limiting the power to the single case of Canals. He was afraid of monopolies of every sort, which he did not think were by any means already implied by the Constitution as supposed by Mr. Wilson.

The motion being so modified as to admit a distinct question specifying & limited to the case of canals.

N— H— no— Mas. no. Ct. no— N— J— no— Pa ay. Del. no— Md. no. Va. ay. N— C— no— S—C. no— Geo. ay. [Ayes — 3; noes — 8.]

The other part fell of course, as including the power rejected.

Farrand, *Records*, 2: 615-16.

98. Clarke and Hall, *Documentary History of the Bank*, 42. Emphasis in the original by Madison.

99. Clarke and Hall, *Documentary History of the Bank*, 63.

100. See the speeches of Fisher Ames, Clarke and Hall, *Documentary History of the Bank*, 49, 58; and the speech of Elbridge Gerry, 76.

101. Clarke and Hall, *Documentary History of the Bank*, 47. Emphasis in the original. In a letter of February 7, 1791, to Thomas Dwight, Congressman Fisher Ames wrote the following: "Mr. Madison has made a great speech against it [the bank]. I am not an impartial judge of it. Take my opinion with due allowance;—it is, that his speech was full of casuistry and sophistry. He read a long time out of books of debates on the Constitution when considered in the several states, in order to show that the powers were to be construed strictly. This was a dull piece of business, and very little to the purpose, as no man would pretend to give Congress the power, against a fair construction of the Constitution." Allen, *Works of Fisher Ames*, 2: 862.

102. Clarke and Hall, *Documentary History of the Bank*, 63.

103. Clarke and Hall, *Documentary History of the Bank*, 78.

104. Clarke and Hall, *Documentary History of the Bank*, 85.

105. See Walter Dellinger and H. Jefferson Powell, "The Constitutionality of the Bank Bill: The Attorney General's First Constitutional Law Opinions," *Duke Law Journal* 44 (1994): 110.

106. Dellinger and Powell, "The Constitutionality of the Bank Bill," 121.

107. Clarke and Hall, *Documentary History of the Bank*, 86.

108. Clarke and Hall, *Documentary History of the Bank*, 89.

109. Clarke and Hall, *Documentary History of the Bank*, 89.

110. Clarke and Hall, *Documentary History of the Bank*, 91.

111. Dellinger and Powell, "The Constitutionality of the Bank Bill," 115.

112. Clarke and Hall, *Documentary History of the Bank*, 91.

113. Clarke and Hall, *Documentary History of the Bank*, 90.

114. Clarke and Hall, *Documentary History of the Bank*, 91.

115. David P. Currie, *The Constitution in the Supreme Court: The First Hundred Years, 1789-1888* (Chicago: University of Chicago Press, 1985), 163. See also G. Edward White, *The Oliver Wendell Holmes Devise History of the Supreme Court of the United States*, Vols. 3-4: *The Marshall Court and Cultural Change, 1815-35* (New York: Macmillan, 1988), 550.

116. Clarke and Hall, *Documentary History of the Bank*, 92. See also H. Jefferson Powell, *Languages of Power: A Sourcebook of Early American Constitutional History* (Durham, N.C.: Carolina Academic Press, 1991): 43.

117. Clarke and Hall, *Documentary History of the Bank*, 93.

118. Clarke and Hall, *Documentary History of the Bank*, 92. Emphasis in the original.

119. Dellinger and Powell, "The Constitutionality of the Bank Bill," 119.

120. Clarke and Hall, *Documentary History of the Bank*, 94.

121. Hamilton's opinion was over 15,000 words in length, compared to Randolph's two opinions totaling approximately 4,500 words and Jefferson's opinion totaling approximately 2,500 words.

122. In *Federalist* No. 31, 194, Hamilton described as "maxims in ethics and politics" "that the means ought to be proportioned to the end; that every power ought to be commensurate with its object, [and] that there ought to be no limitation of a power destined to effect a purpose, which is itself incapable of limitation."

123. Clarke and Hall, *Documentary History of the Bank*, 99. Emphasis in the original. In the last sentence just quoted, Hamilton clearly anticipated Chief Justice John Marshall's famous passage in *McCulloch* v. *Maryland*, 17 U.S. 316, 421 (1819): "Let the end be legitimate, let it be within the scope of the Constitution, and all means which are appropriate, which are plainly adapted to that end, which are not prohibited, but consist with the letter and spirit of the Constitution, are Constitutional." Hamilton repeatedly employed this "means-ends" argument in his opinion: He declared that "every power vested in a government is in its nature sovereign and includes, by force of the term, a right to employ all the means requisite and fairly applicable to the attainment of the ends of such power, and which are not precluded by restrictions and exceptions specified in the constitution, or not immoral, or not contrary to the essential ends of political society." Clarke and Hall, *Documentary History of the Bank*, 95. And he proclaimed that "[t]he degree in which a measure is necessary, can never be a test of the *legal right* to adopt it. That must be a matter of opinion, and can only be a test of expediency. The relation between the *measure* and the *end*; between the *nature* of the *mean* employed towards the execution of a power, and the *object* of that power; must be the criterion of constitutionality; not the more or less of necessity or utility." Clarke and Hall, *Documentary History of the Bank*, 98. Emphasis in the original.

124. In his opinion to Washington, Hamilton also addressed the issue of what had transpired in the Convention concerning Congress's power to grant charters of incorporation: Responding directly to Jefferson's contentions, Hamilton wrote:

Another argument made use of by the Secretary of State is, the rejection, by the convention, of a proposition to empower Congress to make corporations, either generally or for some special purpose. What was the precise nature or extent of this proposition, or what the reasons for refusing it, is not ascertained by any authentic document, or even by accurate recollections. As far as any such document exists, it specifies only canals. If this was the amount of it, it would, at most, only prove, that it was thought inexpedient to give a power to incorporate for the purpose of opening canals; for which purpose a special power would have been necessary, except with regard to the Western territory; there being nothing in any part of the constitution respecting the regulation of canals. It must be confessed, however, that very different accounts are given of the import of the proposition, and of the motives for rejecting it. Some affirm that it was confined to the opening of canals and obstructions in rivers; others, that it embraced banks; and others, that it extended to the power of incorporating generally. Some again allege, that it was disagreed to, because it was thought improper to vest in Congress a power of erecting corporations; others, because it was thought unnecessary to specify the power, and inexpedient to furnish an additional topic of objection to the constitution. In this state of the matter, no inference whatever can be drawn from it.

Clarke and Hall, *Documentary History of the Bank*, 101.

125. For Madison's draft of the veto message, see Charles Hobson and Robert A. Rutland (eds.), *The Papers of James Madison: January 20, 1790 to March 31, 1791*, 17 vols. (Charlottesville: University Press of Virginia, 1981), 13: 395.

Chapter 5

Marshall's Understanding of the Original Federal Design

The framers' understanding that federalism would be protected structurally, i.e., by the manner of electing the Senate, appears to have been fully appreciated by Chief Justice John Marshall when he read expansively the Necessary and Proper Clause in *United States* v. *Fisher*[1] and *McCulloch* v. *Maryland*[2] and the Commerce Clause in *Gibbons* v. *Ogden*.[3] He did not fear that a broad construction of Congress's enumerated powers would destroy the original federal design, because he understood that the Senate would not approve legislation that adversely affected the states as such. The Court could be appropriately restrained in its review of congressional measures because the Senate could be trusted to be vigilant.

United States v. *Fisher*

While *McCulloch* v. *Maryland*, decided in 1819, is Marshall's most famous consideration of the Necessary and Proper Clause, it was not his first.[4] In 1805 in *United States* v. *Fisher*, he had occasion to address the meaning of the Clause as the Court determined the constitutionality of a 1797 statute that gave the United States priority in bankruptcy cases. The act, entitled "an Act to Provide More Effectually for the Settlement of Accounts between the United States and Receivers of Public Money," declared that "where any revenue officer, or other person, hereafter becoming indebted to the United States, by bond or otherwise, shall become insolvent, or where the estate of any deceased debtor, in the hands of executors or administrators, shall be insufficient to pay all the debts due from the deceased, the debt due to the United States shall be first satisfied."[5]

When the United States attached the property of the bankrupt Peter Blight that was in the hands of the revenue collector of Newport, Rhode Island, Fisher and other assignees of Blight brought suit against the United States, claiming, inter alia, that the law giving it priority of payment was unconstitutional. "Besides the destruction of private credit, and the ruin of individuals, it would repeal all the state laws of distribution of intestate estates; it would prostrate all state priority, which in those cases has been long established. It would produce a collision between the prerogative of the states, and of the United States."[6] When the issue came before the Supreme Court, Jared Ingersoll, one of the attorneys for Fisher, asked the justices during oral argument: "Under what clause of the constitution is such a power given to Congress? Is it under the general power to make all laws necessary and proper for carrying into execution the particular powers specified? If so, where is the necessity or where the propriety of such a provision, and to the exercise of what other power is it necessary?"[7]

In reply, Alexander J. Dallas, the United States Attorney for Pennsylvania and a Jefferson appointee,[8] squarely addressed the question of constitutionality. He argued first that "the inconvenience or impolicy of a law are not arguments to a judicial tribunal, if the words of the law are plain and express. Such arguments must be reserved for legislative consideration."[9] He articulated what James Bradley Thayer was subsequently to call the "reasonable doubt test":[10] "They [the courts] are bound to decide an act to be unconstitutional, if the case is clear of doubt, but not on the ground of inconvenience, inexpediency, or impolicy. It must be a case in which the act and the constitution are in plain conflict with each other. If the question be doubtful, the court will presume that the legislature has not exceeded its powers." Congress, Dallas continued, "have duties and powers expressly given, and a right to make all laws necessary to enable them to perform those duties, and to exercise those powers. They have power to borrow money, and it is their duty to provide for its payment. For this purpose, they must raise a revenue, and, to protect that revenue from frauds, a power is necessary to claim a priority of payment."[11]

Marshall delivered the opinion of the Court, upholding both the constitutionality of the law and its application to the case at hand. While he began his discussion of the law's constitutionality by acknowledging that "under a constitution conferring specific powers, the power contended for must be granted, or it cannot be exercised," he immediately noted that among the specific powers conferred on Congress was the "authority to make all laws which shall be necessary and proper to carry into execution the powers vested by the Constitution in the government of the United States."[12] And, he continued, "in construing this clause it would be incorrect and produce endless difficulties, if the opinion should be maintained that no law was authorized which was not indispensably necessary to give effect to a specified power." He noted that, "where various systems might be adopted for that purpose, it might be said with respect to each, that it was not necessary because the end might be obtained by other means." But, in the most deferential of language, he insisted that "Congress must possess the choice of means, and must be empowered to use any means which are in fact conducive to the exercise of a power granted by the Constitution." Applying that language to the 1797 law under challenge, he declared: "The government is to pay the debt of the union, and must be authorized to use the means which appear to itself most eligible to effect that object. It has consequently a right to make remittances by bills or otherwise, and to take those precautions which will render the transaction safe."[13] Addressing the complaint that, by giving priority to the claims of the United States, the law will "interfere with the right of the state sovereignties respecting the dignity of debts, and will defeat the measures they have adopted to secure themselves against the delinquencies on the part of their own revenue officers," Marshall bluntly asserted: "[T]his is an objection to the Constitution itself. The mischief suggested, so far as it can really happen, is the necessary consequence of the supremacy of the laws of the United States on all subjects to which the legislative power of Congress extends."[14]

Marshall's assertion had an interesting qualifier—"the mischief, so far as it can really happen." Marshall did not believe that "mischief" would result from giving the Congress free rein, for he implicitly trusted the Senate not to approve of such "mischief." The senators were, he would later say, "the representatives of the state sovereignties."[15] Given the mode of electing senators, Marshall could confidently construe the Necessary and Proper Clause as conferring on Congress "any means which are in fact conducive to the exercise of a power granted by the Constitution" without worrying that this power would be abused. While Marshall only hints at this argument in *Fisher*, in *McCulloch*, he makes it expressly.[16]

McCulloch v. Maryland

In *McCulloch* v. *Maryland*, the Supreme Court recognized Congress's power to charter the second Bank of the United States and invalidated a Maryland tax on that bank. The first Bank, chartered for a period of twenty years, expired in 1811 when legislation to reauthorize it failed by one vote in each house.[17] The disorganization of the country's finances during the War of 1812, however, prompted James Madison, now serving as President, to take a very different stance from the one he took in the First Congress and to propose a second Bank of the United States,[18] which, after several false starts, was agreed to by Congress[19] and signed into law by Madison on April 10, 1816.

With the lapse of the first Bank, state banks emerged as the principal depositories of currency and issued their own bank notes. When the second Bank began to do business in January of 1817, it immediately established branches in several of the states, loaned money, and actively competed with the state banks in what was a thriving economy. Its reputation was soon sullied, however, during the Panic of 1818. Those hardest hit by this severe depression "found a highly visible, tempting target in the Bank, that economic colossus in which the government had only a minority interest, that nationwide commercial bank whose loans constituted the major source of credit and whose notes provided the major medium of exchange."[20]

Several states, resentful of the federal presence it symbolized and the stiff competition it provided, took advantage of the public's general hostility to the Bank and passed measures designed to regulate or prohibit its operations within their borders.[21] Maryland was one such state; on February 11, 1818, it passed a stamp tax on all notes issued by any bank established "without authority from the State." The tax ranged from ten cents for every five dollar note issued by such a bank to twenty dollars for every thousand dollar note. The stamp tax could be avoided only "by paying, in advance to the Treasurer of the Western Shore, for the use of the State, the [annual] sum of fifteen thousand dollars."[22] Maryland's statute went into effect in May of that year and was immediately challenged by the Baltimore branch of the Bank. A case was arranged in which the cashier for the branch, James William McCulloch, having refused to pay in advance the fifteen thousand dollars which would have relieved the branch from the operation of the stamp tax, issued a bank note to a George Williams that was not "issued on stamped paper in the manner prescribed by the act."[23] Maryland's enforcement of its "practically annihilatory tax"[24] on the Maryland branch of the Bank gave John Marshall the opportunity to address the question of the reach of Congress's powers under Article I, Section 8.[25] His answer, consistent with his earlier opinion in *Fisher*, can be summarized as follows: What Congress can do under its enumerated powers—i.e., what powers are delegated to it as opposed to reserved to the states—is a question for Congress alone to decide.[26]

Marshall began by observing that Congress's power to incorporate a bank could "scarcely be considered as an open question entirely unprejudiced by the former proceedings of the Nation respecting it. The principle now contested was introduced at a very early period of our history, has been recognized by many successive legislatures, and has been acted upon by the Judicial Department, in cases of peculiar delicacy, as a law of undoubted obligation."[27] He acknowledged that "a bold and daring usurpation" would surely have to be resisted even "after an acquiescence still longer and more complete than this." Nonetheless, he continued, federalism questions posed no danger of such a usurpation as they "are not concerned" with "*the great principles of liberty*" but only with how "*the respective powers of those who are equally the representatives of the people, are to be adjusted.*"[28] Consequently, on these matters, the Court would have to defer to congressional practice. As Marshall had noted in his earlier discussion of the Necessary and Proper Clause in *Fisher,* if Congress's decision where to draw the line between its powers and those of the states "interferes with the right of the state sovereignties," it "is the necessary consequence of the supremacy of the laws of the United States on all subjects to which the legislative power of Congress extends," and any objection to this outcome should not be directed to the Court but should be understood to be "an objection to the Constitution itself."[29]

Marshall reminded the parties that "[t]he power now contested was exercised by the first Congress elected under the present Constitution." And he stressed that the question of the first Bank's constitutionality was fully debated at the time: "The bill for incorporating the Bank of the United States did not steal upon an unsuspecting legislature and pass unobserved. Its principle was completely understood, and was opposed with equal zeal and ability. After being resisted first in the fair and open field of debate, and afterwards in the executive cabinet, with as much persevering talent as any measure has ever experienced, and being supported by arguments which convinced minds as pure and as intelligent as this country can boast, it became a law." Marshall then turned to the Bank's more recent history: While "[t]he original act was permitted to expire, . . . a short experience of the embarrassments to which the refusal to revive it exposed the Government convinced those who were most prejudiced against the measure of its necessity, and induced the passage of the present law." All of this prompted him to remark that "[i]t would require no ordinary share of intrepidity to assert that a measure adopted under these circumstances was a bold and plain usurpation to which the Constitution gave no countenance."[30]

Marshall made it clear that, when "the respective powers" of the federal and state governments were involved, the Court would defer to the Congress.[31] The House and the Senate were, as he pointed out, as "equally" representative of the people and therefore of the states as the state legislatures themselves. Therefore, so long as Congress did not engage in "a bold and daring usurpation" by trenching on "the great principles of liberty" as they were practiced in the states, something highly unlikely given the composition and mode of electing the Senate,[32] the Court would not "tread on legislative ground."[33] Marshall repeated the same "means-ends" argument that Madison made in the Convention and that Alexander Hamilton offered in his defense of the Bank bill when he proclaimed that "the sound construction of the Constitution must allow to the national legislature that discretion with respect to the means by which the powers it confers are to be carried into execution which will enable that body to perform the high duties assigned to it in the manner most beneficial to the people."[34]

Here again, he was merely repeating his earlier words from *Fisher*: "Congress must possess the choice of means, and must be empowered to use any means which are in fact conducive to the exercise of a power granted by the constitution."[35] In *Fisher*, Marshall had rejected a narrow construction of the Necessary and Proper Clause: "In construing this clause it would be incorrect and would produce endless difficulties, if the opinion should be maintained that no law was authorized which was not indispensably necessary to give effect to a specified power."[36] In *McCulloch*, he was able to construe the Clause affirmatively and broadly and to declare that it authorized the Congress to adopt all measures that are "convenient or useful" for carrying into execution its enumerated powers.[37] In what is probably the most-famous rule of constitutional interpretation ever uttered by a Supreme Court justice, Marshall declared: "Let the end be legitimate, let it be within the scope of the Constitution, and all means which are appropriate, which are plainly adapted to that end, which are not prohibited, but consist with the letter and spirit of the Constitution, are constitutional."[38]

During oral argument, Joseph Hopkinson, one of Maryland's attorneys, invited the Court to become a perpetual calibrator of necessity and circumstance. He rather ingeniously suggested to the justices that "a power, growing out of a necessity, which may not be permanent, may also not be permanent." Necessity, he argued, "has a relation to circumstances which change; in a state of things which may exist at one period, and not at another."

Thus, he continued, "[t]he argument might have been perfectly good, to show the necessity of a bank for the operation of revenue, in 1791, and entirely fail now, when so many facilities for money transactions abound, which were wanting then."[39] Hopkinson reminded the Court that "necessity was the plea and justification of the first Bank of the United States. If the same necessity existed when the second was established, it will afford the same justification; otherwise, it will stand without justification, as no other is pretended."[40] With this premise in place, he then proceeded to review for the Court the "experience of the five years since the expiration of the old charter of the bank" in order to show that the state banks had proven themselves fully capable of serving "all the purposes and uses alleged as reasons for erecting that bank in 1791." He considered "[t]he loans to the government by the State banks, in the emergencies spoken of; the accommodation to individuals, to enable them to pay their duties and taxes; the creation of a circulating currency; and the facility of transmitting money from place to place," and judged them all to have "been effected, as largely and beneficially, by the State banks, as they could have been done by a bank incorporated by Congress." His conclusion: "The change in the country, in relation to banks, and an experience that was depended upon, concur in proving, that whatever might have been the truth and force of the bank argument in 1791, they were wholly wanting in 1816."[41]

Marshall, however, declined Hopkinson's invitation, proclaiming that it was for Congress only to "inquire into the degree of its necessity" and, if the Court were to follow Hopkinson's suggestion and do so, it "would pass the line which circumscribes the judicial department."[42] He insisted that "Congress alone can make the election"[43] of where "the respective powers"[44] of the federal government end and the states begin.[45] The Court, he continued, "disclaims all pretensions to such a power."[46] And when the Court's refusal to gainsay Congress's decision that the Bank was necessary and that its incorporation was a legitimate exercise of federal power was attacked out-of-doors, Marshall took up his pen and reminded the Court's critics that even the members of the Senate, whom he described as "the representatives of the state sovereignties,"[47] had found the Bank to be necessary. He argued that, to the extent that necessity and circumstances were to be calibrated, it was to be done, not by the Court, but by the state legislatures as they contemplated the election or reelection of their senators. "At the elections," they would be able to communicate what was necessary and what was not. As Marshall put it, "under the pretext of them [i.e., measures that enhanced federal power] being unnecessary," the state legislatures could "control the legislative will and direct its understanding."[48]

McCulloch presented the Court with two questions: Had Congress acted within its constitutional powers in establishing the Bank? If so, could Maryland constitutionally tax the activities of one of its branches? Marshall answered the first question in the affirmative and the second in the negative. He argued that the Bank was constitutional because the Constitution should be expounded broadly and flexibly; because otherwise such a document would have to "partake of the prolixity of a legal code" to contain within it "an accurate detail of all the subdivisions of which its great powers will admit, and of all the means by which they may be carried into execution;"[49] and because the Congress, consisting of a House elected by the people and a Senate elected by state legislatures, legitimately has broad discretion, affirmed by the Necessary and Proper Clause, to select means to achieve the ends listed in the enumerated powers of Article I, Section 8. Marshall's answer to the first question clearly showed his appreciation for the framers' understanding of how federalism would be protected and revealed as well the grounds for his deferential review of Congress's exercise of its enumerated powers.

Marshall's answer to the second question, the constitutionality of Maryland's tax on the Bank, likewise showed his keen insight into the framers' reliance on constitutional structure and the operation of self-interest. In their appearance before the Court, Joseph Hopkinson and Luther Martin, the Attorney General of Maryland, had argued that Maryland's tax on the Bank was constitutional because the states were free to exercise any of their reserved powers not prohibited by the Constitution and the Constitution had barred the states from imposing only two kinds of taxes: "In the 10th section of the 1st article, it is declared that 'no state shall, without the consent of Congress, lay any imposts or duties, on imports or exports, except what may be absolutely necessary for executing its inspection laws.' And there is a like prohibition to laying any duty of tonnage. Here, then is the whole restriction, or limitation, attempted to be imposed by the Constitution, on the power of the States to raise revenue."[50]

Marshall rejected Maryland's argument on two grounds. The first was based on the Supremacy Clause. Marshall began by reciting three "propositions not to be denied": "That the power to tax involves the power to destroy; that the power to destroy may defeat and render useless the power to create; that there is a plain repugnance, in conferring on one government a power to control the constitutional measures of another, which other, with respect to those very measures, is declared to be supreme over that which exerts the control."[51] Maryland's argument that its tax was constitutional was contradicted by those undeniable propositions. If

Maryland's argument were allowed to prevail, "we shall find it capable of arresting all the measures of the government, and of prostrating it at the foot of the States. The American people have declared their Constitution, and the laws made in pursuance thereof, to be supreme, but this principle [i.e., Maryland's argument] would transfer the supremacy, in fact, to the States. If the States may tax one instrument, employed by the government in the execution of its powers, they may tax any and every other instrument." Relying on examples supplied him during oral argument by William Pinckney, one of the attorneys representing the Bank, Marshall continued, "They may tax the mail, they may tax the mint, they may tax patent rights; they may tax the papers of the custom-house; they may tax judicial process; they may tax all the means employed by the government, to an excess which would defeat all the ends of government. This was not intended by the American people. They did not design to make their government dependent on the States."[52]

The second ground for Marshall's rejection of Maryland's argument was based on the fact that the federal government was not represented in the state governments. For the same reason that Marshall is willing to allow Congress to determine the outer limits of its enumerated powers—because the interests of the states as states are represented in the Senate, he is unwilling to allow state legislatures to tax or otherwise burden the federal government—because the interests of the federal government are wholly unrepresented and therefore unprotected in their halls. William Pinckney had made this argument before the Court: He began by observing that "Congress exercises the power of the people. The whole acts on the whole. But the State tax is a part acting on the whole." He then launched into his main point: "The people of the United States, and the sovereignties of the several States, have no control over the taxing power of a particular State. But they have a control over the taxing power of the United States, in the responsibility of the members of the House of Representatives to the people of the State which sends them, and of the senators to the legislature by whom they are chosen." By contrast, "there is no correspondent responsibility of the local legislature of Maryland, for example, to the people of the other States of the Union. The people of other States are not represented in the legislature of Maryland, and can have no control, directly or indirectly, over its proceedings. The legislature of Maryland is responsible only to the people of that State."[53]

Marshall built on Pinckney's argument, tying it directly to the issues of constitutional structure and self-interest.

It is admitted that the power of taxing the people and their property is essential to the very existence of government, and may be legitimately exercised on the objects to which it is applicable, to the utmost extent to which the government may chuse to carry it. The only security against the abuse of this power, is found in the structure of the government itself. In imposing a tax the legislature acts upon its constituents. This is in general a sufficient security against erroneous and oppressive taxation.

The people of a State, therefore, give to their government a right of taxing themselves and their property, and as the exigencies of government cannot be limited, they prescribe no limits on the exercise of this right, resting confidently on the interest of the legislator, and on the influence of the constituents over their representative, to guard against its abuse.[54]

For Marshall, constitutional structure and the self-interest of the legislator protected the people from "erroneous and oppressive taxation." That structural protection, however, did not exist beyond the boundaries of the state itself. The people of other states were not represented in its assemblies and were not protected by the self-interest of the legislators. As Marshall continued, "The people of all the States have created the general government, and have conferred upon it the general power of taxation. The people of all the States, and the States themselves, are represented in Congress, and, by their representatives, exercise this power." When the House and Senate tax the chartered institutions of the states, he observed that they tax their own constituents and, further, that "these taxes must be uniform."[55] By contrast, however, when a state taxes the operations of the federal government, "it acts upon institutions created, not by their own constituents, but by people over whom they claim no control. It acts upon the measures of a government created by others as well as themselves, for the benefit of others in common with themselves." For Marshall, these two cases were completely different, and that difference was "that which always exists, and always must exist, between the action of the whole on a part, and the action of a part on the whole—between the laws of a government declared to be supreme, and those of a government which, when in opposition to those laws, is not supreme."[56]

The whole can be trusted to protect the parts that compose it and that are represented in it, while the parts cannot be trusted to protect the whole. That principle explains Marshall's answers to both questions in *McCulloch*—why it was constitutional for Congress to charter the Bank and unconstitutional for Maryland to tax it. It also explains not only why Marshall found it inappropriate to inquire whether Congress was correct when it determined that a Bank was necessary but also why he found it unnecessary to investigate whether Maryland's tax was, in fact, confiscatory. "We are not driven to the perplexing inquiry, so unfit for the judicial department, what degree of taxation is the legitimate use, and what degree may amount to the abuse of the power. The attempt to use it on the means employed by the government of the Union, in pursuance of the Constitution, is itself an abuse, because it is the usurpation of a power which the people of a single State cannot give."[57]

Gibbons v. Ogden

Marshall's seminal treatment of the Commerce Clause is found in his opinion for the Court in *Gibbons* v. *Ogden*. In it, he held that Congress's power to regulate commerce extended to the regulation of navigation and that the laws of New York granting to Robert R. Livingston and Robert Fulton the exclusive right to operate steamboats in the waters of that state collided with and therefore had to yield to a 1793 federal law regulating the coasting trade, which, being made pursuant to the Constitution's delegation to the Congress of the power to regulate commerce among the several states, was supreme.

Aaron Ogden, former governor of New Jersey, had secured a franchise from the heirs of Livingston and Fulton to operate steam ferryboats across the Hudson River from Staten and Manhattan Islands in New York to Elizabethtown, New Jersey. Ogden found, however, that his boats were facing unauthorized competition from a passenger steamboat owned by Thomas Gibbons and operated by Cornelius Vanderbilt of subsequent railroad fame.[58] The penalty for Gibbons and other unauthorized competitors for infringing on New York's monopoly law was high: confiscation of their vessels and their forfeiture to the franchise holder.[59] Nevertheless, Vanderbilt managed to elude New York authorities and to continue in operation, thereby cutting Ogden's profits. The quarrel between Ogden and Gibbons became so heated and personal that Gibbons finally challenged Ogden to a duel, and Ogden sued Gibbons, successfully, for $8,000 for trespass.[60]

Ogden also responded to the competition of Gibbons's steamboat by securing in 1819 an injunction against Gibbons's operation from the New York Court of Chancery. Chancellor James Kent rejected Gibbons's contention that he was free to compete against Ogden, because, under the 1793 federal law, he had a coasting license from the United States government to "navigate the waters of any particular state by steamboats." Kent argued that the federal coasting law was not intended to regulate commerce but only to raise revenue and to designate ships as "American," thereby reducing the tonnage duty they were obliged to pay. Kent held that the states had a concurrent power to regulate interstate commerce in the absence of an explicit federal declaration preempting state action and that the 1793 law in question contained no such declaration. Gibbons then appealed to the United States Supreme Court on a writ of error and dispatched Vanderbilt to Washington to secure the services of Daniel Webster to argue his case.[61]

Because of procedural complications, the case was not argued before the Supreme Court until February of 1824. The attorneys for Ogden, Thomas Emmet and Thomas Oakley, advanced three principal arguments in support of the constitutionality of New York's steamboat monopoly statute.[62] They argued, first of all, that the states have a concurrent power to regulate interstate commerce when Congress has not acted. They drew a distinction between two kinds of concurrent powers: "those where, from their nature, when Congress has acted on the subject matter, the States cannot legislate at all in any degree" (e.g., "the power to fix the standard of weights and measures") and "those where the States may legislate, though Congress has previously legislated on the same subject matter."[63] For them, the power to regulate commerce was an example of the latter. Commerce, Oakley insisted, "is a concurrent power." "It was fully possessed by the States, after the declaration of independence, and constantly exercised. It is one of the attributes of sovereignty, specifically designated in that instrument 'to establish commerce.' It is not granted, in exclusive terms, to Congress. It is not prohibited, generally to the States."[64] The states, therefore, have a concurrent power to regulate commerce "in all cases where its regulations do not actually conflict with those of Congress."[65]

Second, they argued that New York's steamboat monopoly did not conflict with any federal law. The 1793 federal coasting law on which Gibbons was relying provided him "only a license to carry on the coasting trade, without making entry or paying tonnage duties, conformably to the laws of Congress in other cases." As Emmet asserted, "It gives no right to enter, nor to trade, nor to navigate the waters of the United States; it only enables the licensed vessel to do those things, in certain cases, on cheaper and easier terms than other vessels could, who, nevertheless, had equal rights to carry on the same trade, though with less advantages."[66] Oakley summarized the case for Ogden, arguing that Congress had "made no regulations," "that all the regulations of the State, therefore, which operate within its own limits, are binding upon all who come within its jurisdiction, and that if Congress deems such regulations to be injurious, it may control them by express provisions, operating directly upon the case."[67]

Their third argument, however, took away from what they had just conceded, for they insisted that Congress had no power under the Commerce Clause to regulate transportation of passengers. Invoking the rule of interpretation laid down by St. George Tucker in his edition of *Blackstone's*

Commentaries that "the powers delegated to the federal government are, in all cases, to receive the most strict construction that the instrument will bear, where the rights of a State, or of the people, either collectively or individually, may be drawn in question,"[68] they argued that "the correct definition of commerce is, the transportation and sale of commodities," and that Congress lacked the power under the Commerce Clause to license or in any other way to regulate the "transportation of persons or passengers for hire."[69]

Daniel Webster, Gibbons' attorney, and William Wirt, United States Attorney General, responded to each of these arguments. Concerning the "doctrine of a general concurrent power in the States," Webster labeled it "insidious and dangerous."[70] He declared that "[w]e do not find, in the history of the formulation and adoption of the Constitution, that any man speaks of a general concurrent power, in the regulation of foreign and domestic trade, as still residing in the States. The very object intended, more than any other, was to take away such power. If it had not so provided, the Constitution would not have been worth accepting."[71] Wirt reinforced this point, noting that New York's law was "precisely [like] those which the States had been passing, and which mainly led to the adoption of the Constitution."[72] Webster's conclusion was direct and unequivocal: The commerce power "should be considered as exclusively vested in Congress."[73]

Moreover, they continued, even if the Court were to reject their contention and recognize the concurrent power of the states to regulate commerce in the absence of congressional action, they insisted that Congress had acted and, therefore, had preempted the field with its passage of the 1793 coasting act. Webster argued that the "whole object of the act regulating the coasting trade, was to declare what vessels shall enjoy the benefit of being used in the coasting trade. To secure this use of certain vessels, and to deny it to others, was precisely the purpose for which the act was passed." He faulted Chancellor Kent and the New York Court of Chancery for "having thought, that although Congress might act, it had not yet acted, in such a way as to confer a right of the appellant: whereas, if a right was not given by this law, it never could be given; no law could be more express."[74] Congress's action, no less than its inaction, preempted state efforts to regulate.

Finally, they rejected a "strict construction" of the Constitution in favor of a "reasonable" one,[75] and contended that commerce "always implies intercom-munication and intercourse." As Wirt argued, "This is the sense in which the Constitution uses it; and the great national object was, to regulate the terms on which intercourse between foreigners and this country, and between the different States of the Union, should be carried on."

Carefully responding to each point raised by opposing counsel, Wirt went on to say: "If freight be the test of commerce, this vessel was earning freight, for what is freight, but the compensation paid for the use of a ship? The compensation for the carrying of passengers may be insured as freight."[76]

In his opinion for the Court, Marshall largely reiterated the arguments of Webster and Wirt as he broadly construed Congress's powers under the Commerce Clause; however, he made their arguments his own by the way in which he revealed his confidence that Congress would not abuse the great powers that he insisted the Constitution had delegated to it.

Marshall began by rejecting "strict construction" as "the rule by which the Constitution is to be expounded," declaring that it "cripple[s] the government and render[s] it unequal to the object for which it is declared to be instituted."[77] Employing a "means-ends" argument similar to the one he employed in *McCulloch*, he asserted that, with respect to the extent of any given power (in this case, the power of Congress to "regulate commerce . . . among the several States"), "it is a well settled rule that the objects for which it was given, especially when those objects are expressed in the instrument itself, should have great influence in the construction." He saw "no reason for excluding this rule from the present case. The grant does not convey power which might be beneficial to the grantor if retained by himself, or which can enure [*sic*] solely to the benefit of the grantee, but is an investment of power for the general advantage, in the hands of agents selected for that purpose, which power can never be exercised by the people themselves, but must be placed in the hands of agents, or lie dormant."[78] Thus, Marshall concluded, "[w]e know of no rule for construing the extent to such powers, other than is given by the language of the instrument which confers them, taken in connexion with the purposes for which they were conferred."[79]

Relying on that rule to construe the meaning of the word "commerce," he refused to "limit it to traffic, to buying and selling, or the interchange of commodities" and rejected the claim that it did not "comprehend navigation," claiming that to do so "would restrict a general term, applicable to many objects, to one of its significations." Commerce, he argued, was more than traffic, it was "intercourse," and, therefore, the "object" of the Commerce Clause was to empower Congress to regulate all "commercial intercourse between nations, and parts of nations, in all its branches."[80] Marshall had no doubt that the Commerce Clause extended to navigation. As he declared, "[t]he mind can scarcely conceive a system for regulating commerce between nations which shall exclude all laws concerning navigation, which shall be silent on the admission of the vessels of the one nation into the ports of the other, and be confined to prescribing rules for the conduct of individuals in the actual employment of buying and selling or of barter."[81]

Marshall then proceeded to observe, again in a manner reminiscent of his *McCulloch* opinion, that the Congress's exercise of the power to regulate navigation under the Commerce Clause was longstanding. It was "exercised from the commencement of the government" and "with the consent of all."[82] Among the acts of Congress regulating navigation was the 1793 coasting act, which allowed vessels to be enrolled as American—thereby conferring on them certain privileges with regard to tonnage duties—and, once enrolled, to be licensed "to carry on the coasting trade."[83]

Having concluded that the 1793 coasting act was a valid exercise of Congress's power under the Commerce Clause, Marshall could have ended his opinion. After all, given the Supremacy Clause, the New York statute granting the exclusive right to operate steamboats in its waters clearly conflicted with, and thereby fell before, the right of a federally licensed vessel to carry on the coasting trade.[84] However, Marshall was unable to put down his pen, for he had to address as well the whole issue whether, in the absence of federal legislation, the states had a concurrent power to regulate commerce.

Daniel Webster had argued unequivocally that they did not.

> As the word "to regulate" implies in its nature, full power over the thing to be regulated, it excludes, necessarily, the action of all others that would perform the same operation on the same thing. That regulation is designed for the entire result, applying to those parts which remain as they were, as well as to those which are altered. It produced a uniform whole, which is as much disturbed and deranged by changing what the regulating power designs to leave untouched, as that on which it has operated.[85]

Marshall made it clear that he was in fundamental agreement. He declared that "[t]here is great force in this argument, and the Court is not satisfied that it has been refuted."[86] Marshall accepted without qualification Webster's assertion that "full power to regulate a particular subject [in this case commerce], implies the whole power, and leaves no residuum, that a grant of the whole is incompatible with the existence of a right in another to any part of it."[87] In so doing, he was also able to establish that what separated him from Justice William Johnson, who concurred separately, was only a matter of statutory construction, not constitutional interpretation.

Johnson rejected Marshall's conclusion that the license granted under the 1793 coasting act conferred on a vessel the right to carry on the coastal trade. Arguing that it was only intended "to confer on her American privileges, as contradistinguished from foreign, and to preserve the government from fraud by foreigners, in surreptitiously intruding themselves into the American commercial marine, as well as frauds upon the revenue, in the trade coastwise,"[88] he denied that the New York steamboat monopoly conflicted with any federal regulation. For Johnson, however, that was of no consequence, for he denied that the states had a concurrent power to regulate commerce. With the ratification of the Constitution, he declared, all state commercial regulations "dropped lifeless from their statute books, for want of the sustaining power, that had been relinquished to Congress."[89] That fact prompted him to declare that "I cannot overcome the conviction, that if the licensing act was repealed tomorrow, the rights of the appellant to a reversal of the decision complained of, would be as strong as it is under this license."[90]

Marshall distinguished Congress's exclusive power to regulate commerce from the state's concurrent power to tax, which he had previously recognized in *McCulloch*. The power to tax, he argued, is "indispensable" to the states' existence and "is capable of residing in, and being exercised by, different authorities at the same time." He went on to express what is now the quaint notion that "[t]axation is the simple operation of taking small portions from a perpetually accumulating mass."[91] Noting that "a power in one to take what is necessary for certain purposes, is not, in its nature, incompatible with a power in another to take what is necessary for other purposes," he concluded that "[t]here is no analogy, then, between the power of taxation and the power of regulating commerce."[92]

Marshall also parried Ogden's argument that a 1789 federal statute permitting the states to regulate the conduct of harbor pilots "acknowledged a concurrent power in the States" to regulate commerce with foreign nations and among the states. He observed that, "[a]lthough Congress cannot enable a State to legislate, Congress may adopt the provisions of a State on any subject." Noting that when the Constitution was adopted, a system for the regulation of harbor pilots existed "in full force in every State," Marshall remarked that the 1789 federal act merely adopted this system and gave it "the same validity as if its provisions had been specially made by Congress." That did not mean, however, that Congress could not preempt state regulation of pilots through the enactment of legislation imposing uniform regulations for all pilots or prohibiting their regulation altogether—itself a form of regulation. As Marshall pointedly declared, the 1789 act was "prospective also, and the adoption of laws to be made in future, presupposes the right in the maker to legislate on the subject."[93]

Marshall in *Gibbons* thus gave a very broad construction to Congress's power under the Commerce Clause. He defined commerce to include navigation and all "commercial intercourse between nations and parts of nations, and all its branches";[94] he argued that Congress's power to "regulate commerce with foreign nations, and among the several States, and with the Indian tribes" was exclusive and not shared with the states and that it "did not stop at the external boundary line of each State, but may be introduced into the interior";[95] he limited the power of the states to regulate only that commerce "which is completely internal, which is carried on between man and man in a State, or between different parts of the same State, and which does not *extend to or affect* other States";[96] and he stressed that it was up to the Congress, and not the Court, to draw the line between what the federal government could regulate and what was reserved for state control. This final point was Marshall's own; it was not supplied by counsel but rather was consistent with his understanding, already expressed in *McCulloch*, that the only effective check on Congress was constitutional structure. The Commerce Clause, he argued, is an "investment of power for the general advantage" placed "in the hands of agents selected for that purpose,"[97] i.e., the members of the House, representing the people, and the Senate, representing the interests of states as states. Since both sets of agents were subject to reelection, Marshall had full confidence in their ability to regulate commerce for "the general advantage." He reminded his readers that "[t]he wisdom and the discretion of Congress, their identity with the people, and the influence which their constituents possess at elections are, in this, as in many other instances, as that, for example, of declaring war, the sole restraints on which they have relied, to secure them from its abuse. They are the restraints on which the people must often rely solely, in all representative governments."[98] As Marshall well appreciated, the "constituents" of the Senate were the state legislatures, and, as Elbridge Gerry had observed in the debate over the Bank Act in the First Congress, the senators would therefore feel their "influence" at reelection time and would disregard the interests of their state only at their peril.[99]

Notes

1. 6 U.S. 358, 397 (1805).

2. 17 U.S. 316 (1819).

3. 22 U.S. 1 (1824).

4. *Fisher* was the Supreme Court's first consideration of the Necessary and Proper Clause. See Ronald D. Rotunda, John E. Nowak, and J. Nelson Young, *Treatise on Constitutional Law: Substance and Procedure,* 3 vols. (St. Paul: West Publishing, 1986), 1: 204.

5. 3 Stat. 423 (1797).

6. 6 U.S. at 377.

7. 6 U.S. at 378.

8. George Lee Haskins and Herbert A. Johnson, *The Oliver Wendell Holmes Devise History of the Supreme Court of the United States,* Vol. 2: *Foundations of Power: John Marshall, 1801-15* (New York: Macmillan, 1981), 335.

9. 6 U.S. at 382.

10. James Bradley Thayer, "The Origin and Scope of the American Doctrine of Constitutional Law," *Harvard Law Review* 7 (1893): 129-56.

11. 6 U.S. at 384.

12. 6 U.S. at 396.

13. 6 U.S. at 396.

14. 6 U.S. at 397.

15. John Marshall writing as "A Friend of the Constitution," in Gerald Gunther (ed.), *John Marshall's Defense of McCulloch v. Maryland* (Stanford, Calif.: Stanford University Press, 1969), 209.

16. See David P. Currie, *The Constitution in the Supreme Court: The First Hundred Years, 1789-1888* (Chicago: University of Chicago Press, 1985), 163, who argues that *McCulloch* does more than make explicit the argument implicit in *Fisher* but in fact represents a "vast improvement upon *Fisher*" by requiring that the means Congress employs must be "plainly adapted" and not merely "conducive" to the ends they serve. Currie does not entertain the idea that the primary constitutional check on the federal government from trenching on the "residuary sovereignty" of the states is constitutional structure based on self-interest, not "the cloudy medium of words" as interpreted by the Supreme Court.

17. Bray Hammond, *Banks and Politics in America: From the Revolution to the Civil War* (Princeton: Princeton University Press, 1957), 222.

18. In his Seventh Annual Message to Congress on December 5, 1815, Madison declared: "It is, however, essential to every modification of the finances that the benefits of an uniform national currency should be restored to the community. The absence of the precious metals will, it is believed, be a temporary evil, but until they can again be rendered the general medium of exchange it devolves on the wisdom of Congress to provide a substitute which shall equally engage the

confidence and accommodate the wants of the citizens throughout the Union. If the operation of the State banks can not produce this result, the probable operation of a national bank will merit consideration." James D. Richardson (ed.), *A Compilation of the Messages and Papers of the Presidents, 1789-1897* (Washington, D.C.: Government Printing Office, 1896), 1: 565. Regarding his earlier arguments that the Bank was unconstitutional, Madison declared that they were "precluded . . . by repeated recognitions, under varied circumstances, of the validity of such an institution, in acts of the legislative, executive, and judicial branches of the government, accompanied by indications in different modes of a concurrence of the general will of the nation." Quoted in Hammond, *Banks and Politics in America*, 223-34.

19. The Senate approved the second Bank bill by a vote of twenty-two to twelve, the House by a vote of ninety to sixty-one. Hammond, *Banks and Politics in America*, 240.

20. Gunther, *John Marshall's Defense of McCulloch v. Maryland*, 3.

21. G. Edward White, *The Oliver Wendell Holmes Devise History of the Supreme Court of the United States*, Vols. 3-4: *The Marshall Court and Cultural Change, 1815-35* (New York: Macmillan, 1988), 543.

22. 17 U.S. at 320-21.

23. 17 U.S. at 318-19.

24. Hammond, *Banks and Politics in America*, 263. Tennessee, Georgia, North Carolina, Kentucky, and Ohio had also imposed confiscatory taxes on the Bank, and others were considering doing so.

25. As G. Edward White points out, Marshall's discussion of federal power was "widely perceived by contemporaries" as of great significance not only "because in a time of economic instability it tested the legitimacy of the most powerful and controversial economic institution in the country, the Second Bank of the United States," but also "because observers regarded it as a kind of advisory opinion for two other issues of even greater potential importance, the constitutionality of federally sponsored internal improvements projects and the constitutionality of federal slavery legislation." White, *History of the Supreme Court of the United States*, 542.

26. Lino A. Graglia, "*United States* v. *Lopez*: Judicial Review under the Commerce Clause," *Texas Law Review*, 74 (1996): 725.

27. 17 U.S. at 401. Marshall's argument here, as throughout the entire opinion, drew heavily on the arguments made before the High Court by Daniel Webster and William Pinckney. See 17 U.S. at 322-30, 377-400.

28. 17 U.S. at 401. Emphasis added.

29. 6 U.S. at 397. Interestingly, Marshall does not cite *Fisher* in his *McCulloch* opinion, but, as Currie notes, "It was typical of Marshall not to cite even his own opinions although they squarely supported him. . . . As far as the report reveals, counsel [in *McCulloch*] had not invoked *Fisher*, and maybe nobody remembered it. That decision had not raised much dust in 1805; that was a long time before *McCulloch*, and the indexing of cases was not what it is today." Currie, *The Constitution in the Supreme Court*, 163.

30. 17 U.S. at 402.

31. For Marshall, "adjust[ing]" the "respective powers" of the federal and state governments was different from preserving the separation of powers within the federal government itself. See *Marbury* v. *Madison*, 5 U.S. 137 (1803), in which Marshall insisted that "[i]t is emphatically the provision and duty of the judicial department to say what the law is," and, on that basis, struck down, on behalf of a unanimous Court, an offending provision of Section 13 of the Judiciary Act of 1789.

32. See *Federalist* No. 62, 417.

33. 17 U.S. at 423.

34. 17 U.S. at 421.

35. 6 U.S. at 396.

36. 6 U.S. at 396.

37. 17 U.S. at 413.

38. 17 U.S. at 421. Graglia has written that *McCulloch*

adopted what was later called the "rational basis" test: A challenged statute is valid if it can be said to have any relation, regardless of degree, to an end or purpose acknowledged as legitimate. It is a test that as a practical matter cannot be failed. The purpose of which is to signify, without explicitly stating, the withdrawal of judicial review from the area in question. It was not unrealistic to expect that the national court would be an instrument for the limitation of national power, and *McCulloch* made clear that it would not be. Although the decision was the subject of bitter protest by advocates of state autonomy, it has remained definitive. It should certainly be congenial to proponents . . . of judicial restraint. Questions of the scope of national power are usually or always questions of degree— that is, involving trade-offs and policy judgments—and such judgments in our system are for legislators, not judges.

Graglia, "*United States* v. *Lopez*," 726.

39. 17 U.S. at 331.

40. 17 U.S. at 332.

41. 17 U.S. at 333.

42. 17 U.S. at 423.

43. 17 U.S. at 421.

44. 17 U.S. at 401.

45. Marshall, of course, did insist that, "[s]hould Congress, in the execution of its powers, adopt measures which are prohibited by the Constitution, or should Congress, under the pretext of executing its powers, pass laws for the accomplishment of objects not intrusted to the Government, it would become the painful duty of this tribunal, should a case requiring such a decision come before it, to say that such an act was not the law of the land." 17 U.S. at 423. But this merely repeats the theme he introduced early in his opinion when he distinguished between measures that threaten

"the great principles of liberty" and measures that merely demarcate the line between federal and state power. Moreover, he prefaced that statement with these words: "But were its [the Bank's] necessity less apparent, none can deny its being an appropriate measure." For Marshall, even if the Court were appropriately to review questions of line drawing, i.e., if it were constitutionally authorized to second-guess Congress's decision of where its enumerated powers end, this was not even a close case. Marshall could rattle his judicial-review sword secure in the knowledge that the mode of electing the Senate spared him of the need to draw it to protect federalism.

46. 17 U.S. at 423.

47. Gunther, *John Marshall's Defense of McCulloch v. Maryland,* 209. The phrase comes from Marshall's reply to Spencer Roane's "Hampden" Essays, which Marshall wrote under the pseudonym of "A Friend of the Constitution."

48. Gunther, *John Marshall's Defense of McCulloch v. Maryland,* 173.

49. 17 U.S. at 407.

50. 17 U.S. at 343. They did not address the question whether Congress could have immunized the Bank from state taxation by statute, because the charter law was silent on the matter. See Currie, *The Constitution in the Supreme Court,* 166.

51. 17 U.S. at 431.

52. 17 U.S. at 432.

53. 17 U.S. at 398.

54. 17 U.S. at 428-29.

55. This was clearly a response to Luther Martin, who had argued: "But it is said that a right to tax, in this case, implies a right to destroy; that it is impossible to draw the line of discrimination between a tax fairly laid for the purposes of revenue, and one imposed for the purpose of prohibition. We answer, that the same objection would equally apply to the right of Congress to tax the State banks; since the same difficulty of discriminating occurs in the exercise of that right." 22 U.S. at 385.

56. 17 U.S. at 435-36. By returning to the principle of federal supremacy, Marshall thus joined his two grounds for rejecting Maryland's argument that its tax on the Bank was constitutional.

57. 17 U.S. at 430.

58. White, *History of the Supreme Court of the United States,* 569.

59. 22 U.S. at 10.

60. White, *History of the Supreme Court of the United States,* 570.

61. White, *History of the Supreme Court of the United States,* 570.

62. This discussion addresses only the Commerce Clause dimensions of *Gibbons* and leaves altogether unexplored the lengthy arguments presented to the Court concerning Congress's power to promote the progress of science and the useful arts. It leaves them unexplored, because the Court also left them unexplored. See 22 U.S. at 221.

63. 22 U.S. at 39.

64. 22 U.S. at 60.

65. 22 U.S. at 70-71.

66. 22 U.S. at 137-38.

67. 22 U.S. at 71.

68. 22 U.S. at 86-87, 95.

69. 22 U.S. at 76. In Emmet's words, "The power of Congress could only be extended to fair cases of trading, within the purview of the Constitution, and not to the mere transportation of passengers, nor to any colourable pretence of trading, as a cover for carrying passengers." 22 U.S. at 89. See also Emmet's argument at 22 U.S. at 96: "[T]he powers of Congress have nothing to say to the carrying of passengers."

70. 22 U.S. at 17.

71. 22 U.S. at 13.

72. 22 U.S. at 180. See also Webster's remarks at 22 U.S. at 11. "Few things were better known, than the immediate causes which led to the adoption of the present Constitution; and he thought nothing clearer, than that the prevailing motive was to regulate commerce, to rescue it from the embarrassing and destructive consequences, resulting from the legislation of so many different States, and to place it under the protection of a uniform law."

73. 22 U.S. at 14, 16.

74. 22 U.S. at 28-29.

75. 22 U.S. at 14.

76. 22 U.S. at 183.

77. 22 U.S. at 188.

78. 22 U.S. at 188-89.

79. 22 U.S. at 189. Continuing in his discourse on how the Constitution is to be interpreted, Marshall proclaimed:

> It is a rule of construction, acknowledged by all, that the exceptions from a power mark its extent; for it would be absurd, as well as useless, to except from a granted power, that which was not granted—that which the words of the grant could not comprehend. If, then, there are in the Constitution plain exceptions from the power over navigation, plain inhibitions to the exercise of that power in a particular way, it is a proof that those who made these exceptions, and prescribed these inhibitions, understood the power to which they applied as being granted. The 9th section of the 1st article declares that "no preference shall be given, by any regulation of commerce or revenue, to the ports of one State over those of another." This clause cannot be understood as applicable to those laws only which are passed for the purpose of revenue, because it is expressly applied to commercial regulations; and the most obvious preference which can be given to one port over another, in regulating commerce, relates to navigation. But the subsequent part of the sentence is still more explicit. It is, "nor shall vessels bound to or from one State,

be obliged to enter, clear, or pay duties, in another." These words have a direct reference to navigation.

22 U.S. at 191.

80. 22 U.S. at 190. Concerning the meaning of "commercial intercourse between . . . parts of nations, and in all its branches," Marshall went on to declare: "The subject . . . is commerce 'among the several States.' The word 'among' means intermingled with. A thing which is among others, is intermingled with them. Commerce among the States, cannot stop at the external boundary line of each States, but may be introduced into the interior." 22 U.S. at 194.

81. 22 U.S. at 190.

82. 22 U.S. at 190.

83. 22 U.S. at 214-15. Since "the power of Congress has been universally understood in America to comprehend navigation," Marshall dismissed Ogden's distinction "between the power to regulate vessels employed in transporting men for hire, and property for hire."

84. "The appropriate application of that part of the [Supremacy] Clause which confers the same supremacy on laws and treaties, is to such acts of the State Legislatures as do not transcend their powers, but, though enacted in the execution of acknowledged State powers, interfere with, or are contrary to the laws of Congress, made in pursuance of the Constitution, or some treaty made under the authority of the United States. In every such case, the act of Congress, or the treaty, is supreme, and the law of the State, though enacted in the exercise of powers not controverted, must yield to it." 22 U.S. at 211.

85. 22 U.S. at 209.

86. 22 U.S. at 209.

87. 22 U.S. at 198.

88. 22 U.S. at 232.

89. 22 U.S. at 226.

90. 22 U.S. at 231-32.

91. 22 U.S. at 199.

92. 22 U.S. at 199-200. In *Willson* v. *Black Bird Creek Marsh Company*, 27 U.S. 245 (1829), Marshall upheld a Delaware statute that authorized the Black Bird Creek Marsh Company to build a dam across Black Bird Creek, thereby obstructing the creek and preventing vessels possessing a federal coasting license, similar to the one held by Gibbons, from navigating it. Marshall, however, was not departing from his argument in *Gibbons* that states lacked a concurrent power to regulate commerce. He simply held that damming what was described by counsel as an unhealthy waterway was a justifiable exercise of the state's police powers, especially in the absence of congressional legislation regulating small navigable creeks.

93. 22 U.S. at 207.

94. 22 U.S. at 190.

95. 22 U.S. at 194.

96. 22 U.S. at 194.

97. 22 U.S. at 189.

98. 22 U.S. at 197.

99. M. St. Clair Clarke and D. A. Hall (eds.), *Legislative and Documentary History of the Bank of the United States* (Washington, D.C.: Gales and Seaton, 1832), 78.

Chapter 6

Altering the Original Federal Design: The Adoption and Ratification of the Seventeenth Amendment

The framers' original understanding of how federalism would be protected succeeded admirably for the first century.[1] The measures that Congress passed were understood, even by the Senate, to be consistent with the original federal design and as serving those interests that prompted the adoption and ratification of the Constitution in the first place.[2] With *Dred Scott*[3] as the principal exception, they were similarly understood by the Supreme Court as well.[4] Over time, however, the public became increasingly dissatisfied with the indirect election of the Senate and unappreciative of the protection it rendered to federalism. The public embraced the Progressives' belief that the solution to all the ills of democracy was more democracy.[5] Tocqueville offers an important insight as to why: "Men living in democratic ages do not readily comprehend the utility of forms"— Tocqueville's word for constitutional structure; in fact, quite the contrary, "they feel an instinctive contempt for them."[6]

Progressivism's Contempt for Constitutional Structure

Forms, Tocqueville argues, excite the contempt and hatred of men living in democratic ages. Since they "commonly aspire to none but easy and present gratifications" and since the "slightest delay exasperates them," they are "hostile to forms, which perpetually retard or arrest them in some of their projects." As Tocqueville goes on to argue, however, "this objection which the men of democracies make to forms is the very thing which renders forms so useful to freedom." "Their chief merit is to serve as a barrier between the strong and the weak"—in the case of federalism, between the national government and the states. And the stronger the national government becomes, the more important forms or structure—in this particular case, the mode of electing the Senate—become in the protection of the interests of states as states. As Tocqueville writes, "Forms become more necessary in proportion as the government becomes more active and more powerful, while private persons [and, one might add, the states] are becoming more indolent and more feeble." From this, Tocqueville draws the following conclusion: "[D]emocratic nations naturally stand more in need of forms than other nations, and they naturally respect them less. This deserves most serious attention."[7]

Over time, the public came to have less respect for constitutional forms. Forms—separation of powers, checks and balances, and federalism—were all associated by the Progressives with a mechanistic "Newtonian Theory" of politics that, as Woodrow Wilson insisted, had been superseded by a modern Darwinian Theory.[8] "The Constitution," Wilson argued, "was founded on the law of gravitation. The government was to exist to move by virtue of the efficacy of 'checks and balances.'" However, according to Wilson, "The trouble with th[is] theory is that government is not a machine, but a living thing. It falls, not under the theory of the universe, but under the theory of organic life. It is accountable to Darwin, not to Newton."[9] Moreover, constitutional forms were regarded by the Progressives as evidence of the framers' lack of confidence in the people. As Wilson argued in a chapter in *The New Freedom* entitled "The People Need No Guardians," the framers were "willing to act for the people, but . . . not willing to act *through* the people. Now we propose to act for ourselves."[10] Alexander Hamilton came under particularly heavy fire; because he relied on constitutional forms and not simply on the people, Wilson branded him a "great man, but, in my judgment, not a great American."[11]

Under the Progressives' tutelage, the people lost respect for constitutional forms and, hence, for the structural protection afforded federalism. They came to associate the election of the Senate by state legislatures with an outmoded, plutocratic constitution. Senators were no longer described in the grandiloquent terms of a Tocqueville: "[T]he Senate . . . contains within a small space a large proportion of the celebrated men of America. Scarcely an individual is to be seen in it who has not had an active and illustrious career: the Senate is composed of eloquent advocates, distinguished generals, wise magistrates, and statesmen of note, whose arguments would do honor to the most remarkable parliamentary debates of Europe."[12] Rather they were subjected to Beardian obloquy: "Some of them were political leaders of genuine talents but a majority possessed no conspicuous merits except the ownership of strong boxes well filled with securities."[13] By contrast, the people came to identify direct election of the Senate with reform, faith in the people, and progress. The people demanded change, and they eventually prevailed. On May 12, 1912, the Seventeenth Amendment, providing for direct election of the Senate, was approved by the Congress; it was ratified by the requisite three-fourths of the state legislatures in less than eleven months and declared to be a part of the Constitution in a proclamation by the secretary of state on May 31, 1913.

While state ratification of the Seventeenth Amendment came quickly and easily, adoption by the Congress did not. The first resolution calling for direct election of the Senate was introduced in the House of Representatives on February 14, 1826. From that date until the adoption of the Seventeenth Amendment eighty-six years later, 187 subsequent resolutions of a similar nature were also introduced before Congress, 167 of them after 1880.[14] The House approved six of these proposals before the Senate reluctantly gave its consent.[15] The factors that led to the Seventeenth Amendment's adoption and ratification need explanation.

Political and Social Factors that Led to the Adoption and Ratification of the Seventeenth Amendment

Legislative Deadlock

One factor was legislative deadlock over the election of senators brought about when one party controlled the state assembly or house and another the state senate.[16] It should be noted, however, that the real problem was not so much divided party government as a law passed by Congress in 1866, under its Article I, Section 4 power to prescribe the time and manner of electing senators.[17] Some background on this law is necessary.

Article I, Section 3 of the Constitution provides that senators shall be chosen by state legislatures. However, it does not provide, in the words of Joseph Story, "for the manner, in which the choice shall be made by the state legislatures, whether by a joint, or by a concurrent vote; the latter is, where both branches form one assembly, and give a united vote numerically; the former is, where each branch gives a separate and independent vote."[18] As a consequence, states adopted different practices to suit themselves.

Chancellor James Kent notes that, in New York State, the legislature initially chose senators by concurrent vote (as initially did most states) but subsequently moved to joint vote (along with about half the states). The reason was clear; in Kent's words, "As the legislature may prescribe the manner, it has been considered and settled in this state, that the legislature may prescribe that they shall be chosen by joint vote or ballot of the two houses," because otherwise, if the two houses could not separately concur in a choice, the "weight" of the state in the United States Senate would be "dissipated."[19] Kent personally took exception to electing senators by a joint vote; while he conceded that this practice "has been too long settled . . . to be now disturbed," he insisted that, "if the question was a new one, that when the Constitution directed that the senators should be chosen by the legislature, it meant not the members of the legislature per capita, but the legislature in the true technical sense, being the two houses acting in their separate and organized capacities, with the ordinary constitutional right of negative on each other's proceedings."[20] Story, however, challenged Kent's logic. Story argued that, if the election of a senator was a legislative act, then it would be subject to the veto of the governor, but universal practice had been against recognizing any such executive participation in the choice of senators. "The executive," Story wrote, "constitutes a part of the legislature for such a purpose, in cases where the state constitution gives him a qualified negative upon the laws. But this has been silently and universally settled against the executive participation in the appointment."[21]

Varied and changing state practices regarding the election of senators posed a variety of "annoying" problems for the Senate.[22] Article I, Section 4 of the Constitution specifies that "each House shall be the Judge of the Elections, Returns, and Qualifications of its own Members"; it thereby imposed on the Senate the onerous burden of determining whether a state's senators had, in fact, been properly elected. The Senate was forced, for example, to deal with the unusual election of two Indiana senators in 1857.[23] Throughout the 35th Congress, Indiana had been represented by only one senator. With less than a month to go before that Congress was to adjourn sine die, a minority of the Indiana Senate, which had been in deadlock with the House, met with a majority (but not a legal quorum) of the House members and proceeded to elect one senator to fill the existing vacancy and another to succeed the senator whose term was about to expire. The individuals elected as a result of this questionable joint vote presented themselves to the United States Senate, which accepted their credentials. Formal protests were made by a majority of the Indiana Senate, who contended that the joint session was not legally summoned and was therefore not competent to elect senators. These protests were unavailing, and the United States Senate refused to reverse its decision. In its next session, the Indiana legislature, which in the interim had come under Republican control in both houses, treated both seats as vacant and proceeded by concurrent vote to elect two senators to fill the alleged vacancies. The Senate, however, excluded these newly elected senators on the ground that the legislature of a state had no authority to revise the decision of the Senate under its constitutional authority to judge the qualifications of its own members.

While the Indiana case was before the Senate, Simon Cameron's election in Pennsylvania in 1857 was also contested on the ground that there had not been a concurrent majority of each house in his favor. The Senate in this instance rejected the challenge as untenable under both Pennsylvania law and "the uniform practical construction of the Federal Constitution for the last half-century."

Legislation was introduced in the Senate that would have allowed it to avoid such questions in the future by prescribing the time and manner of electing senators, but, with the onset of the Civil War, the Congress was occupied with weightier matters. Upon the war's conclusion, however, troubling questions concerning senatorial elections again embroiled the Senate when John Stockton's election as senator in New Jersey in 1866 was challenged. It was contended that the joint assembly that elected him had exceeded its powers by declaring that Stockton was elected when he had received only a plurality of the votes cast (forty votes out of eighty-one). Initially, by a vote of twenty-two to twenty-one, with Stockton himself voting, the Senate accepted a committee report that held that the joint assembly was, for purposes of electing senators, the legislature and that it was entitled to lay down the plurality rule. But three days later, it reconsidered, held that Stockton should not have voted on the question of his own seat, and voted to unseat him. Not only had the Senate exhausted its patience addressing such issues, but Stockton was a Democrat and the Senate Republicans saw his expulsion as increasing the likelihood that they would be able to overturn President Andrew Johnson's veto of the Civil Rights Act of 1866.[24] The Senate then proceeded to approve legislation (which was subsequently agreed to by the House) regulating the time and manner of holding senatorial elections. This 1866 law provided, in brief, that, on the second Tuesday after the meeting and organization of a legislature, when a senator is to be elected, the two houses shall meet separately and openly and, by a voice vote, "name one person for senator." On the following day "at twelve o'clock meridian," the members of the two houses shall meet in joint assembly and the results of the previous day's vote shall be canvassed. If each house has given a majority vote to the same person, that person is elected senator. If not, "the joint assembly shall then proceed to choose, by a viva voce vote of each member present a person for the purpose aforesaid, and the person having a majority of all the votes of the said joint assembly, a majority of all the members elected to both houses being present and voting, shall be declared duly elected." If no person received a majority vote on that first day, "the joint assembly shall meet at twelve o'clock, meridian, of each succeeding day during the session of the legislature, and take at least one vote until a senator shall be elected."[25]

This legislation interestingly included provisions for both concurrent and joint voting. As George H. Haynes had written, "In order to lessen the changes of a failure to elect . . . , it was felt that some provision must be made for a joint vote; yet, out of deference to the predilections for a concurrent vote—a concession, it is said, to the practice in New York and in New England—the law was made to provide that the first vote should be taken by the two houses separately, with a resort to a joint convention, in case the concurrent vote failed to elect."[26] But what protection the legislation offered against deadlock by its provision for joint voting, it took away through its requirement for an open voice vote during the first day of voting when the two houses met separately. The legislation provided for the disclosure of the preference of each member and the difference between the two houses; it thereby revealed at the outset what a small minority would need to know to prevent, if it could not control, the election.

This legislation also revealed an astonishing willingness on Congress's part to dictate to the states. According to James G. Blaine, this "was the natural result of the situation in which the nation was placed by the war." Prior to the Civil War, Blaine noted that "every power was withheld from the national government which could by any possibility be exercised by the state government." After the Civil War, "[a]nother theory and another practice were to prevail; for it had been demonstrated to the thoughtful statesmen who then controlled the government that everything which may be done by either nation or state may be better and more securely done by the nation." This change, Blaine observed, "was important, and led to far-reaching consequences."[27] One of these consequences was that an increasingly confident Congress felt little compunction about placing an enormous burden on the states. To spare itself relatively infrequent if annoying problems regarding senatorial elections, it imposed procedures on the states that not only dramatically increased the prospects for deadlock, but also ensured that these deadlocks would consume an enormous amount of valuable state legislative time by requiring that a majority (as opposed to a plurality) of the state legislators must agree to the election of a senator and that they must do so by meeting daily in joint assembly.

Thanks in no small part to Congress's passage of the 1866 act, the number of legislative deadlocks began to soar. In 1885, the Oregon legislature failed, after sixty-eight ballots, to elect a senator and eventually did so only in a special session. Two years later, West Virginia failed to elect anyone. In 1892, Louisiana failed to elect a senator. In 1893, the legislatures in Montana, Washington, and Wyoming deadlocked and failed to elect senators, and when the governors of these states filled the vacancies by appointment, the Senate denied them their seats on the grounds that only the state legislatures could elect senators. Kentucky failed to elect a senator in 1896; Oregon in 1897; California, Utah, and Pennsylvania in 1899; Rhode Island in 1907; and Colorado in 1911. Deadlock was perhaps most evident and embarrassing in Delaware; it was represented by only one senator in three Congresses and was without any representation at all from 1901 to 1903.[28] From 1885 to 1912, there were seventy-one such legislative deadlocks, resulting in seventeen Senate seats going unfilled for an entire legislative session or more. (The following table provides information on each of these seventy-one deadlocks.) These protracted deadlocks often led to the election of "the darkest of the dark horse" candidates,[29] occasionally deprived the affected states of representation in the Senate, always consumed a great deal of state legislative time that was therefore not spent on other important state matters, and powerfully served to rally the proponents of direct election.[30]

Legislative Deadlocks over the Election of Senators

Date	State	Ballots Cast[a]	Senator Elected
1885	Oregon	68 in regular session, special session necessary to elect	John H. Marshall
1887	West Virginia	Failed to elect a man due to recalcitrant minority in Dem. ranks. Senator appointed by governor	
1887	Indiana	16	Daniel Turpie
1891	Florida[b]	75 in 35 days	Wilkinson Call
1891	North Dakota	17 in 3 days	H. C. Hansbrough
1891	South Dakota	40 in 27 days	J. H. Kyle
1892	Louisiana	44	No election

a. Number of ballots taken before an election was made.
b. The number of days intervening from the time of the first ballot to the last.

Legislative Deadlocks over the Election of Senators (continued)

Date	State	Ballots Cast	Senator Elected
1893	Montana	44 in 50 days	No election. Governor's appointee rejected by Senate
1893	Nebraska	17 in 21 days	W. V. Allen
1893	North Dakota	61 in 33 days	W. N. Roach: Democrat elected when 14 Republicans refused to support caucus nominee.
1893	Washington	101 in 51 days	No election. Republicans divided among themselves. Senate rejected Governor's appointee.
1893	Wyoming	No election.	Governor's appointee resigned upon learning of Senate's attitude on such appointments.
1895	Delaware	217 in 114 days	No election. Governor's appointee rejected by Senate.
1895	Idaho	52 in 51 days	G. L. Shoup
1895	Oregon	60 in 32 days	G. W. McBride
1895	Washington	28 in 9 days	J. L. Wilson
1896	Kentucky	54 in 58 days	No election
1896	Louisiana	6 in 9 days	S. D. McHenry
1896	Maryland	9 in 8 days	G. L. Wellington
1897	Florida	Estimated 45 in 24 days	S. R. Mallory
1897	Idaho	Balloting for 15 days	Henry Heitfelt
1897	Kentucky	112 in 36 days	W. J. DeBoe
1897	Oregon	57 days in session.	No ballot possible No election
1897	South Dakota	27 in 29 days	J. H. Kile
1897	Utah	53 in 17 days	J. L. Rawlins
1897	Washington	25 in 7 days	George Turner
1898	Maryland	10 in 7 days	L. E. McComas
1898	Tennessee	7 in 7 days	T. B. Turley
1899	California	103 in 67 days	No election
1899	Delaware	113 in 64 days	No election

Legislative Deadlocks over the Election of Senators (continued)

Date	State	Ballots Cast	Senator Elected
1899	Montana	17 in 17 days	W. A. Clark
1899	Nebraska	43 in 50 days	M. L. Hayward
1899	Utah	161-165 in 52 days	No election
1899	Pennsylvania	79 in 92 days	No election
1899	Wisconsin	6 in 8 days	J. V. Quarles
1901	Delaware	46 in 52 days	No election
1901	Delaware	46 in 52 days	No election
1901	Montana	66 in 51 days	Paris Gibson
1901	Nebraska	54 in 72 days	C. H. Dietrich
1901	Nebraska	54 in 72 days	J. H. Millard
1901	Oregon	53 in 22 days	J. H. Mitchell
1903	Delaware	36 in 41 days	J. F. Allee
1903	Delaware	36 in 41 days	L. H. Ball
1903	North Carolina	9 in 10 days	L. S. Overman
1903	Washington	13 in 9 days	Levi Ankey
1903	Oregon	42 in 32 days	C. W. Fulton
1903	Colorado	4 days Republicans absented themselves from joint ballot so Democrats could not muster a quorum.	H. M. Teller
1904	Maryland	12 in 16 days	Isidor Rayner
1905	Delaware	51 in 80 days	No election
1905	Missouri	67 in 60 days	William Warner
1905	Montana	7 in 6 days	T. H. Carter
1905	Washington	14 in 10 days	S. H. Piles
1907	New Jersey	14 days	Frank O. Briggs
1907	Rhode Island	81 in 98 days	No election
1907	Wisconsin	80 in 31 days	Isaac Stephenson
1908	Kentucky	35 in 45 days	William O. Bradley
1909	Illinois	95 in 59 days	William Lorimer
1909	Wisconsin	24 in 36 days	Isaac Stephenson
1910	Mississippi	58 in caucus	Leroy Percy
1911	Colorado	102 days	No election
1911	Iowa	67 in 85 days	Wm. S. Kenyon
1911	Montana	79 in 51 days	H. L. Meyers, but not until just before legislature adjourned.
1911	New York	64 in 73 days	J. A. O. Gorman
1911	Tennessee	12 or 13 in 13 days	Luke Lea

Legislative Deadlocks over the Election of Senators (continued)

Date	State	Ballots Cast	Senator Elected
1912	New Mexico	8	Thomas B. Catron, Albert B. Fall
1913	Delaware	11 in 8 days	Willard Saulsbery
1913	Idaho	12 days	James H. Brady
1913	New Hampshire	42 in 42 days	Henry F. Hollis
1913	Tennessee	8 in 9 days	John K. Shields
1913	Tennessee	8 in 9 days	W. R. Webb
1913	West Virginia	12 in 15 days	Republican caucus took several votes before Goff was nominated. Nathan R. Goff

Source: Wallace Worthy Hall, "The History and Effect of the Seventeenth Amendment," Ph.D. diss., Department of Political Science, University of California, Berkeley (1936), Appendix E, 506-11.

Bribery and Corruption

A second factor undermining support for the election of senators by state legislatures often followed on the heels of the first: Scandal resulted when deadlocks were occasionally loosened by the lubricant of bribe money. Prior to the passage of the 1866 act, the Senate had investigated only one case of alleged bribery in the election of a senator.[31] However, between 1866 and 1900, the Senate was called on nine times to investigate alleged bribery in Senate election cases;[32] by 1912, that number had increased by another five.[33] In the 59th Congress alone, 10 percent of the Senate's entire membership was put on trial or subjected to legislative investigation.[34] Two of the most infamous cases involved the elections of Montana Senator William A. Clark in 1899 and Illinois Senator William Lorimer a decade later. Clark confessed to a "personal disbursement" of more than $140,000 to the legislators of Montana and resigned his seat during floor deliberations regarding a unanimous Senate committee report recommending his expulsion on the grounds that he was not "legally elected" since the support of more than half of his majority in the state Senate (eight of fifteen) had been obtained through bribery.[35] Lorimer, a dark-horse candidate acceptable to both parties, was elected in 1909 by a bipartisan coalition in the Illinois legislature, thereby breaking a protracted stalemate; however, a year later, the *Chicago Tribune* broke the story of how four state legislators were bribed to change their vote on his behalf, and, in 1912, nearly half-way through the completion of his term, Lorimer was expelled by the Senate.[36]

Instances of bribery and corruption were, in truth, few in number. As Todd Zwicki has pointed out, "Of the 1,180 senators elected from 1789 to 1909, only fifteen were contested due to allegations of corruption, and only seven were actually denied their seats."[37] Corruption was proved to be present in only .013 percent of the elections during that period. Nonetheless, these instances were much publicized and proved crucial in undermining support for the original mode of electing senators.

Populism and Progressivism

A third factor, closely related to the second, was the growing strength of the Populist movement and its deep-seated suspicion of wealth and influence. It presented the Senate as "an unrepresentative, unresponsive 'millionaires club,' high on partisanship but low in integrity."[38] In the House, proponents of direct election proclaimed a need to "awaken . . . in the Senators . . . a more acute sense of responsibility to the people."[39] And in the Senate, they proclaimed the Senate to be "a sort of aristocratic body— too far removed from the people, beyond their reach, and with no especial interest in their welfare."[40]

While Populism waned, Progressivism waxed in its place, providing still a fourth factor: Progressivism's belief in "the redemptive powers of direct democracy,"[41] i.e., its conviction that the solution to all the problems of democracy was more democracy.[42] The people could be trusted to act for themselves; government was to be not only "of, by, and for" the people, but "through the people."[43] Thus, Senator William Jennings Bryan, a Democrat from Nebraska, argued on the floor that, "if the people of the United States have enough intelligence to choose their representatives in the State legislature . . . , they have enough intelligence to choose the men who shall represent them in the United States Senate."[44] Senator David Turpie, a Democrat from Indiana, agreed: However valid the reasons might have been for the framers' original mode of electing senators, the people at the end of the nineteenth century were "a new people living and acting under an old system."[45]

Political Forces at Work at the State Level

Over time, election of senators by state legislatures came to be associated with stalemate, corruption, plutocracy, and reaction; by contrast, direct election of senators was associated with reform, integrity, democracy, and progress. The public demanded change and repeatedly carried this message to the Congress itself through direct petitions. Beginning with a petition from the citizens of Kendall and LaSalle, Illinois, dated January 18, 1886, and continuing through the day the Seventeenth Amendment received congressional approval, the Congress received 238 petitions from farmers' associations, labor groups, and other citizens' groups calling for direct election of the Senate.[46]

Politicians also demanded change. Beginning with the platform of the Nebraska Republican Party in 1872 and continuing until the ratification of the Seventeenth Amendment, 239 party platforms called for direct election of the Senate, including 220 state party platforms and 19 national party platforms.[47]

Even the states themselves demanded change. Beginning with a memorial from the California State Legislature on February 18, 1874, and continuing through congressional adoption of the Seventeenth Amendment in 1912, the Congress received 175 memorials from state legislatures urging adoption of direct election of the Senate.[48] State legislatures did more, however, than merely demand change by sending memorials to the Congress; they took other steps as well to bring it about. Thus, by 1912, thirty-three states had introduced the use of direct primaries,[49] and twelve states had adopted some form of what was known as the "Oregon System."[50]

South Carolina was the first state to introduce the direct primary in 1888.[51] The direct primary democratized the election of senators in the same way that the election of the president had been democratized. As Alan Grimes explains, "[I]n the same fashion in which state members of the Electoral College cast their votes for the presidential candidate who had received the greatest popular vote in the state, so the state legislatures were asked to elect that candidate for senate who had received the greatest popular vote in a preferential primary."[52]

The direct primary, however, shared the same problem as the democratized Electoral College: the faithless elector. State legislators were not legally bound to abide by the results of the primary and could ignore the wishes of the voters. In an attempt to solve this problem, the State of Oregon passed by initiative in 1904 the "Oregon System." Under this system, a general election runoff was held between the primary nominees for the Senate of the major parties, and candidates for the state legislature were "permitted" to include in their platform one of two statements regarding their views on the election of senators. "Statement No. 1" pledged the candidate to abide by the results of the general election and, regardless of party affiliation, to vote "for that candidate for United States Senator in Congress who has received the highest number of the people's vote for that position at the general election." "Statement No. 2" declared that the candidate would treat the results of the general election "as nothing more than a recommendation" and would vote according to his personal discretion.[53]

Eleven other states (Idaho, Nebraska, Nevada, Colorado, California, Kansas, Minnesota, New Jersey, Ohio, Montana, and Arizona) quickly imitated the "Oregon System," with many going even further. Nebraska, for example, required that, after each candidate's name on the primary ballot for the state legislature the following words would appear: "Promises to vote for people's choice for United States Senator" or "Will not promise to vote for people's choice for United States Senator."[54]

The states took another decisive step as well to bring about direct election of the Senate; they exercised their power under Section V of the Constitution and called for a convention to consider amending the Constitution to provide for direct election of the Senate. Calling for a constitutional convention was a high-risk strategy. Article V of the Constitution makes no provision for the manner of selecting and apportioning the delegates to such a constitutional convention, for the place of holding such a convention, for the rules of its proceedings, or for the scope of its authority. As a consequence, many argue that once a convention is called, there is no way to confine its deliberations; such a convention might consider itself authorized to propose other amendments to the Constitution as well—or even to propose an entirely new Constitution organized on completely different principles.[55] Nevertheless, the states seemed willing "to risk opening Pandora's Box for the sake of securing the popular election of senators."[56] In 1893, California became the first state to apply to Congress for such a convention; it was followed six years later by Texas. In 1900, the Pennsylvania legislature took the decisive step of suggesting to the states a coordinated effort to demand a convention; believing that the Senate would not act until two-thirds of the states forced it to do so, it sent to all the states a copy of its convention petition and encouraged them to submit one as well.[57] Momentum was gained, for (in addition to Pennsylvania) Michigan, Colorado, Oregon, and Tennessee all made application to Congress for a convention in 1901. Kentucky applied in 1902, and Arkansas, Washington, and Illinois followed suit in 1903. Nebraska applied in 1907, as did Indiana, Iowa, Kansas, Louisiana, Missouri, Montana, Nevada, New Jersey, North Carolina, Idaho, Oklahoma, South Dakota, Utah, and Wisconsin in 1908. By 1910, when Maryland applied to Congress for a convention, twenty-seven of the thirty-one state legislatures then required to call a convention had formally petitioned the Congress. Because of its call in 1908 for a convention for another reason (to abolish polygamy), Delaware was widely regarded by the proponents of direct election as constituting a twenty-eighth state; as they pointed out, all that it took to determine that a state's application for a convention was legitimate was a simple majority in both houses of Congress. Arizona and New Mexico were about to become states and were expected to increase the ranks of those supporting such a amendment to thirty. While their admission to the Union would also increase the necessary two-thirds of the states to thirty-two, proponents of direct election noted that Alabama and Wyoming had already submitted resolutions supporting the idea of a convention, although without formally calling for one, and that the language of their resolutions could be easily rectified.[58] The fear of a "runaway" constitutional convention, along with the fact that most senators represented states whose legislatures were on record as favoring direct election of the Senate, proved decisive.[59] Thus, on May 12, 1912, the 62nd Congress finally approved the Seventeenth Amendment by a vote in the Senate of 64 to 24 (with 3 not voting) and by a vote in the House of 238 to 39 (with 110 not voting).

Congressional Adoption of the Seventeenth Amendment

All of the social and political factors and state agitation discussed above played themselves out in the Congress of the United States, and so a brief history of the legislative efforts to secure direct election of the Senate is therefore appropriate.[60] Initially, calls for a change in the mode of electing senators came in at a trickle, but, over time, they became a torrent. Resolutions in the House calling for direct election that opponents could at one time confidently assign to committee, secure in the knowledge that they would never be heard of again, began finally to receive favorable committee action and, eventually, approval by the full chamber. Over time, that same process was repeated in the Senate. Like water on rock, legislative barriers to reform were eventually worn away over an eighty-six-year period by the continued flow of resolutions and arguments on their behalf.

On February 14, 1826, Representative Henry Randolph Storrs, a Federalist from New York, offered the first resolution providing for direct election of senators. He proposed that it be resolved that "[i]t is expedient that the Constitution of the United States be amended that the Senators from the several States shall not be appointed by the legislatures of the States but shall be chosen by the electors in each State having the qualifications requisite for the electors of the most numerous branch of the State Legislature."[61] His resolution was tabled and died. Three years later, Representative John Crafts Wright from

Ohio offered an elaborate resolution that provided in part that each state should have four senators chosen for four-year terms in any manner that the legislature of each state might prescribe.[62] It, too, was tabled on the day of its introduction. Six years later in the 23rd Congress, the second attempt to provide for direct election by the people was made by Representative Edward Allen Hannegan, a Democrat from Indiana. The first resolution in the Senate proposing that its members be directly elected by the people was made by Jeremiah Clemens, a Democrat from Alabama, on January 14, 1850.[63] His bill was read twice, sent to the Committee on the Judiciary, and never heard of again.

Future president Andrew Johnson took up the issue as a personal cause, first as a member of the House of Representatives when he served as a Democrat from Tennessee. He submitted a joint resolution on direct election in the House on February 21, 1851,[64] which was referred to the Committee of the Whole on the State of the Union, from which it never emerged. He offered it again the following year,[65] again without success, and eight years later, on December 13, 1860, as a senator.[66] Later, as president, he would issue a special message to Congress in 1868 calling for direct election.[67]

Representative Daniel T. Mace, a Democrat from Indiana, was another early proponent of direct election. In both the 33rd and 34th Congresses, he introduced resolutions to that effect that died in committee.[68]

The Civil War and its aftermath effectively halted efforts to bring about the popular election of senators. All of Congress's attention was focused on the colossal tasks of preserving the Union and of Reconstruction.[69] However, with the end of the Reconstruction era, calls for reform began again, and with increased frequency and vigor. In the 42nd Congress (1871-73), two joint resolutions were introduced in the House and one in the Senate, and, in the next Congress, the number increased to four: three in the House and one in the Senate. The 43rd Congress also marked the first time that a committee reported on a resolution referred to it: On May 27, 1874, the Judiciary Committee of the House adversely reported on H. J. Res. 86, introduced six weeks earlier by Representative Thomas James Creamer, a Democrat from New York. It was also the first Congress to receive a memorial on the subject by a state legislature. On February 18, 1874, Senator John S. Hager, a Democrat from California, introduced in the Senate the following resolution from the state legislature:

> That our Representatives in Congress be requested and our Senators be instructed to use their best efforts to secure the passage of a law in Congress submitting to the legislatures of the several States of the Union for their ratification, an amendment to the Constitution of the United

States, providing for the election of United States Senators by a direct
vote of the people; and that the legislature of the State of California send
greetings to her sister States of the Union and request their cooperation
in calling the attention of their Representatives and Senators in Congress
to the importance of this subject and securing their action upon the same.[70]

On January 6, 1876, in the 44th Congress, Representative Samuel
Addison Oliver, a Republican from Iowa, introduced H. J. Res. 28, calling
for an amendment that would have not only provided for direct election of
the Senate but also given Congress power over the conduct of such elections,
thereby expanding the power originally granted to Congress in Article I,
Section 4.[71] While Oliver's resolution died in committee, his proposal that
Congress have power to regulate senatorial elections did not, for it touched
on the sensitive question whether the states, under an amendment providing
for direct election of Senators, would be as subject in Senate elections as
they were in House elections to laws passed by Congress regulating the
time, manner, and place of such elections.

Two resolutions calling for an amendment providing for direct election
of the Senate were introduced in each Congress during the 44th, 45th, 46th,
and 47th Congresses; three were introduced in the 48th Congress and six in
the 49th Congress. All died in committee.

The 49th Congress stands out in particular for two reasons: The first
was S. Res. 89, introduced on December 16, 1886, by Senator Charles
Henry Van Wyck of Nebraska. A month earlier, General Van Wyck had
received an overwhelming majority of the votes cast in Nebraska's
preferential primary (46,100 of the 50,448 votes cast). However, when the
Nebraska legislature met the following January, General Van Wyck was
not elected. While he received a plurality of the votes cast on the first two
ballots, he was subsequently defeated when the Republicans in caucus voted
to support Algernon Sidney Paddock.[72]

The second reason was the House Judiciary Committee's reaction to
H. J. Res. 239. It declared that "Your committee believe that the potent
reasons which made the framers of our Constitution declare that there shall
be 'two senators from each state, chosen by the legislature thereof' . . .
have lost none of their force, nor been affected by any countervailing
considerations. We therefore recommend that the resolution be laid upon
the table."[73] However, the resolution was not tabled; upon the request of
Representative James Baird Weaver, a Populist from Iowa, it was placed
on the House Calendar, where it died. This, however, marked the furthest
advance to date toward congressional consideration of any proposal for
direct election of the Senate.

Of the five resolutions submitted in the 50th Congress calling for direct election of senators, H. J. Res. 141 deserves comment, as it appeared in the form of a majority report from the chairman of the Committee on the Revisions of Laws, Representative William Calvin Oates, a Democrat from Alabama. The committee report stated that the resolution was a response to popular demand in many sections of the country, a way of making the Senate more responsive to the people's wishes, and an antidote to the allegations of corruption: "Whether this suspicion be just or not, an election by the legal voters of the State would be free from any such taint because no man can corrupt the popular voice."[74] A vigorous minority report was filed by Representative Henry Gray Turner, a Democrat from Georgia, who expressed grave doubts that the committee had the jurisdiction to proceed with such a resolution and who argued that, "however well-intentioned" such a resolution might be, it betrayed a "distrust of the States as States." "We think that there is at this day too great a tendency to degrade the States and reduce their importance. In our opinion, there is an urgent necessity to restore their just weight and authority in our complex system of government."[75]

During the 51st Congress, twelve resolutions calling for direct election of senators were proposed—nine in the House and three in the Senate. On April 22, 1890, Senator John H. Mitchell, a Republican of Oregon, set forth his reasons for proposing S. Res. 6. He argued, first of all, that indirect election was undemocratic in that it "circumscribed" the individual right of the voter and "mangled his will." "The system is unrepublican, not democratic, and vicious in all respects. It carries with it the implication that the people, the qualified voters of the State, are for some reason unfit for full exercise of the elective franchise in the choice of high government officials, except in a qualified and highly restricted sense." He then argued that the popular mind was of the view that the Senate was not giving "proper deference" to "the demands and interests of the people, largely because of the fact that they were not responsible to the people but rather to state legislatures which were transient bodies." He asserted that it was "quite immaterial" whether this belief in the public mind was "well-founded or otherwise"; the only means of removing it was "a change in the mode of electing Senators."[76] His proposal died in committee.

Momentum, however, was building, and, in the 52nd Congress, a total of twenty-five resolutions were introduced—twenty-one in the House and four in the Senate. There were several reasons for this marked increase. To begin, a Democratic landslide in the congressional elections of 1890 swept away a 17-seat Republican majority in the 51st Congress and replaced it with a 140-member majority for the Democrats (who generally favored direct election more than did the Republicans). This huge shift was attributed principally to the fact that the Republican-backed McKinley tariff that increased duties in general and added a number of household articles to the dutiable list went into effect just one month prior to the November election.[77] A second factor was a sharp increase in legislative deadlocks over the election of senators; from 1891 to 1893, there were nine deadlocks in the states, with four of them resulting in the failure to elect a senator. A third factor was the increased public attention given to the issue by party platforms; during this same two-year period, twenty-nine state party platforms and one national party platform were drafted that contained planks calling for direct election of senators.

In the 52nd Congress, William Jennings Bryan, a Democrat from Nebraska serving his first term in the House, began his long quest for direct election of the Senate. He proposed H. Res. 13, which contained what came to be known as the Optional Plan. It left Article I, Section 3 unaltered but added the following: "Provided that such senators may be elected by a direct vote of all the electors of any State qualified to vote for members of the most numerous branch of the state legislature, whenever such State shall, by law, so provide."[78] However, of far greater importance, on February 16, 1892, H. J. Res. 90, providing for direct election of senators, was presented in a majority report of the Committee on the Election of the President, Vice President, and Representatives in Congress. Representative Henry St. George Tucker, a Democrat of Virginia, issued the report which recommended changing Article I, Section 3, Clause 1 to read: "The Senate of the United States shall be composed of two senators from each state elected by the people thereof, and each senator shall have one vote." Audaciously, it also gave the state legislatures complete control over the time, place, and manner of regulating elections.[79] (A minority report was issued by Representative Allen Ralph Bushnell, a Democrat from Wisconsin, who proposed instead that the Bryan plan, with the optional state-choice method, be adopted.) Five months later, on July 12, the House brought H. J. Res. 90 to the floor, where Representative Eugene F. Loud, a Republican from California, unsuccessfully proposed an amendment that would have given Congress the power to control the elections of senators within each state.[80] When the House failed to reach a vote on the resolution before the end of the first session, it was carried over to the second session, when, on January 16, 1893, it passed by the requisite two-thirds majority on a voice vote and became the first proposed amendment on direct election of the Senate to be approved by the House.

H. J. Res. 90 was then referred to the Senate, where it remained in the Committee on Privileges and Elections until the 52nd Congress adjourned on March 4, 1893. Unavailing were memorials from eight states asking Congress to submit a constitutional amendment on direct election, notification by California's Governor H. H. Markham that the people of his state had given their approval (by a vote of 187,987 to 13,342) to direct election of senators on a referendum during the general election in November of 1892, and the resulting request (the first of its kind) of the California Legislature to the Congress to call a convention to consider adoption of such an amendment.[81]

During the 52nd Congress, however, the Senate did debate S. Res. 6, introduced by Senator David Turpie, a Democrat from Indiana. He defended his measure from the charge that the national-state relationship would be affected by direct election. During that debate on December 17, 1891, he asserted that the states would not lose their representation as states and that direct election would "cause the character of the people to be transposed more perfectly into the modes of government." This, he insisted, "would cause the needs, wants, aims, and aspirations of the masses of men in our free communities to be more faithfully reflected, more clearly imaged forth in the laws of the country and their administration."[82] The measure was sent to the Committee on Privileges and Elections, from which, on June 8, 1882, it was reported out negatively. In the majority report, Senator William E. Chandler, a Republican from New Hampshire, made several arguments against the proposal. He objected on the grounds that direct election would inevitably usher in the popular election of the president and vice president and that it would require the "adoption of complete, supreme, and uniform Federal election laws which would need to be administered by national election officials." He refused to conclude that wealthy men bought their seats or, if they did, that they would be prevented from doing so simply because of a popular electoral system. In addition, he argued, improper influence was just as likely to be utilized in party conventions as it was in state legislatures. He did not feel that there was sufficient need to make such a significant alteration in the Constitution and the administration of government, especially because there was no evidence that indirect election was "wrong or unjust." He also considered it more important to ensure that Blacks were permitted their right to vote under the Fifteenth Amendment than it was to make further constitutional revisions.[83]

The 53rd Congress was convened in special session by President Grover Cleveland on the same day the 52nd Congress adjourned. On April 3, 1893, during that special session, the Senate Committee of Privileges and Elections, led by Senator George Hoar, a Republican from Massachusetts, reviewed negatively H. J. Res. 90, passed by the House in the previous Congress. Hoar listed ten reasons for rejecting the proposed constitutional amendment. He argued that (1) senators were as dignified a group of men as were the popularly elected governors; (2) a time of discontent and popular clamor provided a sufficient reason not to rush into imprudent action; (3) party conventions were as likely to be corrupted as were state legislatures, and the trust the people had in parties would soon evaporate; (4) just as freedom to debate had been restricted in the House, it would also come to be curtailed in the Senate; (5) popular election had been shown (in the case of House members, for example) to be highly susceptible to various forms of fraudulent voting, including "false counts, fraudulent naturalization, personations of voters, fraudulent residences, forged returns, intimidation and mob violence"; (6) partisanship, not the best interest of the states, would be the determining factor in all popular elections and would thus ruin popular faith in the Senate ("The method of election is indispensable to secure the peculiar quality of the body to be elected."); (7) the electoral advantage, instead of being evenly distributed among the parts of the states, would reside heavily in the cities; (8) contrary to the assertion that the Senate was ill-equipped and not disposed to respond to the will of the people, the Senate had initiated many of the most important legislative acts, beneficial to the people at large, in the history of the country; (9) if the direct election of senators were to be effected, the direct election of the president, vice president, and judges would soon follow "by the mere brutal force of numbers," which would be not only against the will of the people but also contrary to the ends of the Constitution; and (10) direct election of senators would permit the larger states to be free of "the constitutional obligation which secures the equal representation of all States in the Senate by providing that no State shall be deprived of that equality without its own consent."[84] Hoar's arguments proved decisive, and the Senate took no further action on H. J. Res. 90.

Apart from the Senate's rejection of H. J. Res. 90, the 53rd Congress also considered fifteen other resolutions on direct election (twelve in the House and three in the Senate). One was H. J. Res. 20; it was identical in language to H. J. Res. 90 that had passed in the previous Congress—it even had appended to it the previous committee report for H. J. Res. 90. H. J. Res. 20 was reported affirmatively from the Committee on the Election of the President, Vice President, and Representatives in Congress by Representative Tucker on May 22, 1894. When debate on the resolution finally began in the House on July 19, it became clear that the overriding objection to H. J. Res. 20 was that it took away all regulatory control of senatorial elections from the Congress. On July 20, Senator Stephen A. Northway, a Republican from Ohio, challenged his colleagues: "Is there any reason for allowing the general government to control the election of members of Congress when through the same ballot box the people would be permitted to vote for United States Senators, and Congress have no control in that matter? Is there any sense in making this distinction? . . . Mr. Speaker, I am opposed, diametrically opposed to taking from the Federal Government any power it may now have relative to the election of officials of the Federal Government."[85] With that, he proposed what became known as the Northway Amendment to the resolution, which would have struck all language permitting the states to control the "times, the places, and the manner of holding the elections."

Representative Robert E. DeForest, a Democrat from Connecticut, attacked the Northway Amendment on the grounds that it tended toward centralization and that "every safeguard which the Constitution affords against the tendency of strengthening the Federal Government at the expense of the States should be strengthened."[86] He, in turn, was rebutted by Representative Franklin Bartlett, a Democrat from New York, who argued eloquently that if the goal was to protect the interests of the states as states, the senators should remain representatives of their state governments and should continue to be elected by state legislatures. Bartlett quoted statements made by George Mason and John Dickinson during the Constitutional Convention and by James Madison in *Federalist* No. 62 in support of his conclusion: "It follows, therefore, that the Framers of the Constitution, were they present in this House today, would inevitably regard this resolution as a most direct blow at the doctrine of State's rights and at the integrity of the State sovereignties; for if you once deprive a State as a collective organism of all share in the General Government, you annihilate its federative importance."[87]

In hopes of forging a compromise between the proponents of the Northway Amendment to H. J. Res. 20 and the advocates of the Resolution itself, Representative Bryan reintroduced his Optional Plan, which left it to states to decide for themselves between direct election or election by the state legislature. The House, however, voted down both the Northway Amendment (by a vote of 137 to 67, with 4 answering present and 143 not voting) and the Bryan Optional Plan (by a vote of 108 to 87).[88] On the next day, July 21, the House approved H. J. Res. 20 by a vote of 141 to 50 (with 2 answering present and 158 not voting), thus giving it the necessary two-thirds majority. Republicans strongly opposed the resolution, accounting for 45 of the 50 negative votes.[89]

Once it passed the House, H. J. Res. 20 was referred by the Senate to its Committee on Privileges and Elections on July 24. *The Nation* accurately predicted the outcome: "The passage by the House of the resolution for a Constitutional amendment providing that Senators shall be elected by the people was generally expected but it is universally admitted that the matter will be shelved in the other branch. There will be little protest against such action by the Senate for public sentiment has not yet become pronounced in favor of the change."[90] True to the prediction, the resolution was not reported out of committee until the very end of the third session of the 53rd Congress (and when it was, on February 12, 1895, it was reported out unfavorably). In a harbinger of things to come, a minority report, filed by Senators Turpie, Mitchell, and John M. Palmer, a Democrat of Illinois, strongly defended direct election of senators but included as well language similar to the House's Northway Amendment.[91]

In the 54th Congress, ten new resolutions on direct election of senators were introduced (seven in the House and three in the Senate). One of these, H. J. Res. 106, was amended and favorably reported by the House Committee on the Election of the President, Vice President, and Representatives in Congress on March 30, 1896, thereby marking the first time that a committee report on the subject had endorsed the Optional Plan.[92] It received, however, no further action in the House.

Another resolution, S. Res. 6, was favorably reported by the Senate Committee on Privileges and Elections on March 20, 1896. In its report, the committee scolded the opponents of direct election, especially those who argued that it would affect the relationship between the national government and the states. Responding directly to Representative Bartlett's comments in the 53rd Congress, the majority report revealed just how little the members of the committee comprehended how and why the framers relied on the mode of electing the Senate to protect federalism.

> The share of representation to be accorded to each state in the Senate is one thing, and the mode or manner of selecting that representation, whatever it may be, is quite another and a different thing. The one—the former—relates to the question that senators are more particularly the representatives of the states in their political capacity; while the other relates only to what perhaps may be considered by some to be the more unimportant matter, as to how and by whom the state shall choose this representation, whether by their legislatures or by direct vote of the people. ... It is therefore made apparent to your committee that the question as to whether the Senate of the United States should be regarded as the representative of the people of the states, was determined so far as that question has ever been determined, not by the mode or manner in which the Senators should be chosen ... but rather in the consideration and determination of the question as to the fixed ratio of representation that each State should have in respect to its sister States in the Senate of the United States.[93]

S. Res. 6, however, died without a vote with the adjournment of the 54th Congress on March 4, 1897.

In the 55th Congress, eight resolutions on direct election were introduced (six in the House and two in the Senate). H. J. Res. 5, which would have made the election of senators optional with the states, was favorably reported by the Committee on the Election of President, Vice President, and Representatives in Congress on January 12, 1898. The committee report made much of the legislative deadlocks that had occurred in fourteen states during the previous Congress; three of these deadlocks—in Delaware, Kentucky, and Oregon—had resulted in the failure of these states to elect a senator and therefore to their being without full senatorial representation during the 55th Congress.

On May 5, H. J. Res. 5 was called up for consideration by the House, at which time Representative Oscar W. Underwood, a Democrat from Alabama, immediately moved to strike the Optional Plan in favor of an amendment that made the direct election of senators mandatory on all the states.[94] Representative John Blaisdell Corliss, a Republican from Michigan and the sponsor of the joint resolution, opposed this amendment on the grounds that only a constitutional amendment incorporating the Optional Plan had any possibility of being adopted by the Senate or ratified by the states. On May 11, 1898, after extensive debate, the Underwood amendment passed on a nonrecord vote, and, later that day, H. J. Res. 5 passed by a vote of 185 to 11 (with 10 answering present and 149 not voting). For the third time in four Congresses, the House had passed an amendment on the direct election of senators. On the following day, it was read in the Senate and sent to the Committee of Privileges and Elections, from which it never emerged.

The 56th Congress was convened on December 4, 1899, and, on that day, Representative Corliss introduced H. J. Res. 28, which again included the Optional Plan. (It was one of eleven resolutions introduced in that Congress—six in the House and five in the Senate.) H. J. Res. 28 was referred to the House Committee on the Election of the President, Vice President, and Representatives in Congress, of which Corliss was the chairman, and it was favorably reported on January 22, 1900. The majority report differed from previous reports in that it included a list of gubernatorial appointees who had been refused admittance to the Senate because of that body's decision that a governor of a state could not appoint an individual to a vacancy created by the failure of the legislature to elect a senator.[95] A minority report, omitting the Optional Plan and giving states control over the regulation of elections, was submitted on February 7, 1900.[96]

Debate on H. J. Res. 28 was held on April 12 against the backdrop that Congress might be compelled by the state legislatures to call a constitutional convention to consider direct election. The House again rejected the Optional Plan and, by a vote of 135 to 30, approved the minority report as an amendment to the resolution but only after its provision giving the control over the regulation of elections to the states was removed. The actual joint resolution was then passed by the requisite two-thirds majority by a vote of 242 to 15 (with 4 answering present and 89 not voting).[97]

Amended H. J. Res. 28 came to the Senate on April 16, 1900, and, at the request of Chairman Chandler and to the horror of Senator Marion Butler, it was referred to the Committee on Privileges and Elections. Butler, a Populist from North Carolina, had watched the rapid death of all such resolutions in that committee, and he attempted to have it calendared immediately.[98] He failed, however, when Senator Hoar contended that the gravity of the matter necessitated review in committee. H. J. Res. 28 was not taken up for consideration before the 56th Congress adjourned on March 4, 1901, and so, for the fourth time, a proposed amendment on direct election that had been passed in the House died in the Senate.

When the 57th Congress convened in December of 1901, Delaware became, because of a protracted deadlock in its state legislature, the first state in the history of the Senate to be without any representation whatsoever in that branch. (This embarrassment arose after legislative deadlocks in California, Utah, Pennsylvania, and Delaware had reduced the senatorial representation of those states to one each in the 56th Congress.) Alarmed at this situation and anxious to remedy it, Senator Julius Caesar Burrows, a Republican from Michigan and chairman of the Committee on Privileges and Elections, introduced, on December 4, S. Res. 7, which provided that, when no election of a senator was possible, because of a deadlock in the state legislature, the people should then be permitted to elect their senator. Even Senator Hoar found the amendment unobjectionable. As he wrote to Burrows, "I do not think that there would be any serious objection to the constitutional amendment proposed by you." Hoar, however, questioned the strategy. "I am very much afraid that if it were proposed by the Committee, it might get amended in the Senate so as to substitute for it the naked proposition of the election of Senators by the people, which, as you are well aware, I think would be very bad indeed."[99] The proposal, sent to the Committee of Privileges and Elections, was never brought up again.

S. Res. 7 was one of ten resolutions introduced in the 57th Congress—five each in the House and Senate. On December 2, 1901, Representative Corliss introduced H. J. Res. 41, calling for the direct election of senators without either the Optional Plan or Burrows's Default Plan. It was referred to the Committee on the Election of President, Vice President, and Representatives in Congress and reported favorably by a unanimous committee vote on January 21, 1902. On February 13, it was debated and passed by a two-thirds voice vote. On February 14, it was introduced in the Senate and referred to the Committee on Privileges and Elections.

On April 10, Senator Chauncey M. Depew, a Republican from New York, presented an amendment to H. J. Res. 41 that was then referred to committee. It sought to establish throughout the United States uniform voting qualifications for those electing both Senators and members of the House of Representatives. In his proposal, Congress was also to be empowered "to provide for the registration of citizens entitled to vote, the conduct of such elections, and the certification of the result."[100] Depew's amendment stirred up intense opposition from the Southern states, who resisted any proposal that provided for federal control of elections. Depew responded, however, noting that many Southern states, through their use of literacy tests and poll taxes (from which many White votes were spared the consequences through "grandfather clauses"), were preventing their Black citizens (one-third to one-half of their citizens) from voting. He continued:

> If in the election of the United States Senators a small oligarchy can send here a representative equal to that of the great states like New York which have manhood suffrage; if states in which half of the voters are disfranchised are to have an equal voice in this body with states like Pennsylvania, of five and ten times their population and with manhood suffrage; if New York which casts, because of its manhood suffrage, 1,547,912 votes, is to be neutralized in legislation affecting her vast interests by Mississippi casting 55,000 votes because the majority of her citizens are disfranchised—then the situation becomes intolerable.[101]

Senator Hernando DeSoto Money, a Democrat from Mississippi, rose to defend his state's honor. The literacy tests and poll taxes, he insisted, imposed no hardship on voters. Concerning literacy tests, he declared that "there is not a man with intelligence to entitle him to vote who cannot in three months time acquire the qualifications necessary to vote, at the public schools scattered all over the State of Mississippi." And, concerning poll taxes, he announced that "the provision that hurts in Mississippi and keeps in the rear ground a vast number of voters is the tax. You cannot get certain improvident people, who refuse to look beyond the needs of today in their physical wants, to pay $2.00 in February that they may vote next November. They will not do it. . . . There is not a man in the

State who cannot pay $2.00 to vote if he wants to vote."[102] He also alleged that "it was not the States of the South that have been asking for [direct election]. The State of Mississippi has not asked for this change, and there are a great many others in her category. . . . [T]he demand is from the States where there is no Negro population. They are the people who ask for an election of senators by the people. They are the Republican States."[103]

Depew countered powerfully:

> Notwithstanding the exceedingly ingenious and exceedingly able explanation given by the Senator from Mississippi, everybody knows that there is no fairness to the tests which are provided by the Constitution of the State for the registration of voters. The canvassing board are all of one party. The canvassing board are selected for one purpose—to prevent the Negro from voting, no matter what his intelligence may be; to prevent the Negro from being registered, no matter what his intelligence may be.[104]

This exchange is most illuminating, for its sheds light on what, in fact, prompted many Southern senators and representatives to oppose federal control of senate elections. Quite apart from their respectable argument that state legislatures should be given the power to control the time, manner, and place by which the people would directly elect senators to offset the fact that state legislatures would be relinquishing the power to elect senators themselves, they also made other arguments of a baser nature that suggested their true motives. These arguments occasionally surfaced, as they did during the Depew-Money exchange, and, when they did, they helped to paint with a racist brush all who resisted direct election of the Senate—even those who argued on the grounds that it weakened the structural walls of federalism. The racist motivations of many of those who opposed direct election of senators unless it was coupled with complete state control over the time, place, and manner of their election either embarrassed into silence or estranged many who might otherwise have opposed direct election because of the serious harm it would cause constitutional structure and the original federal design.

After several efforts to discharge H. J. Res. 41 from committee, on May 27, the Committee on Privileges and Elections made its report on the resolution. The report was inconclusive; it revealed that (1) a majority of the committee opposed the resolution; (2) a majority of one favored the Depew amendment; and (3) a majority opposed the resolution as amended.[105]

Parliamentary questions regarding the status of the report followed, with some senators considering it tantamount to an adverse report. To resolve the matter, Senator George L. Wellington, a Republican from Maryland, moved that the committee be discharged from further deliberation on H. J. Res. 41 and that it be placed on the calendar.[106] Senator Hoar then succeeded in amending Wellington's motion, adding a provision similar to what Senator Depew had previously proposed.[107] The Wellington motion as amended by Hoar was debated on June 11, at which time it failed by a vote of twenty-one to thirty-five (with thirty-two not voting, including Wellington).[108] The committee thus retained the report for the rest of the 57th Congress, making this the third consecutive Congress in which the House had approved an amendment providing for direct election of the Senate that the Senate subsequently buried.

During the 58th Congress, only six resolutions were introduced concerning direct election of senators (four in the House and two in the Senate), and none emerged from committee. In the 59th Congress, eleven resolutions were introduced—all in the House. On March 14, 1906, late in the first session, Representative George Norris, a Republican from Nebraska, introduced H. J. Res. 120; it not only provided for the direct election of senators but also called for increasing the terms of members of the House of Representatives from two to four years.[109] This proposal was favorably reported on April 11 from the Committee on the Election of the President, Vice President, and Representatives in Congress, of which Norris was the chair. There was little discussion of the issue of direct election of senators, as the committee members considered direct election so popular in the House, and among the public, that further arguments were unnecessary. Debate focused instead on the length of House terms, with many members arguing that longer terms were both undemocratic and opposed by the people. The linkage of the two propositions inevitably led to the resolution's defeat and, with it, the prospects for direct election of the Senate in that Congress.

The 60th Congress did little more: Only thirteen resolutions on direct election of the Senate were introduced (eleven in the House and two in the Senate). The only action occurred in the Senate, where Senator Robert Owen, a Democrat from Oklahoma, introduced S. Res. 91 on May 21, 1908. It was tabled on that day, and then called up on May 23 by Senator Owen, who wished to dispense with what he felt was unnecessary debate, due to the large number of states (twenty-seven) that had called for a convention to consider an amendment for direct election. Despite his complaints, the resolution was referred to the Committee on Privileges and Elections.[110] An amendment proposed by Senator Depew was also sent to committee; essentially the same as his previously introduced amendment, it died in committee, as did S. Res. 91.

The 61st Congress was different. Unlike several preceding Congresses that had been characterized by little activity concerning direct election of senators, it was marked by the introduction of thirteen resolutions on the subject (nine in the House and four in the Senate). In addition, on July 5, 1909, Senator Joseph Bristow, a Republican from Kansas, unsuccessfully sought to amend the income tax amendment to include a provision for the direct election of senators.[111]

The real action occurred during the 61st Congress's third session. On January 11, 1911, Senator William Borah, chairman of the Senate Judiciary Committee and a Republican from Idaho, favorably reported S. Res. 134 out of his committee. The committee report stressed several reasons for favoring direct election: (1) the method of senatorial election had no bearing on the equality of representation in the Senate; (2) the method of senatorial election would not affect the federal-state relationship; (3) the fact that the American public had spent more than seventy-five years considering whether to embrace direct election was an ample reply to those who counseled more deliberation before attempting to amend the Constitution; and (4) it would enable the state legislatures to devote their undivided time and attention to state matters without the worry of legislative deadlocks or charges of corruption.[112] Two days later, Senator George Sutherland, a Republican from Utah, presented an amendment giving Congress the same power to regulate the time, place, and manner of Senate elections as it had over the election of members of the House of Representatives (the Judiciary Committee report having assigned this power to the states), and Senator Depew again proposed his amendment that would have established uniform voter qualifications throughout the nation for those voting in Senate and House races.[113]

When debate began on S. Res. 134 on January 19, Senator Sutherland defended his amendment on the grounds that some state legislatures otherwise in favor of direct election might refuse to ratify if the supervisory power of Congress over the election of senators were withdrawn.[114] On January 24, Senator Depew also spoke on behalf of his amendment. He contended that, if S. Res. 134 were to be adopted by Congress and ratified by the states, it would effectively repeal the Fourteenth and Fifteenth Amendment: "The proposed amendment . . . seems to me to be an effort under the guise of popularizing the election of United States Senators to permit under the Constitution the States to disfranchise large classes of their electors. Instead of providing that Senators shall be elected by the people of the several states, it virtually denies the people the right to elect senators by impairing the Fourteenth and Fifteenth amendments, which were intended to secure the elective franchise to all citizens of the United States."[115]

Senator Henry Cabot Lodge, a Republican of Massachusetts, joined the debate on February 3. He spoke powerfully against granting the states the power to regulate the time, place, and manner of senatorial elections:

> It is proposed to take from the United States any power to protect its own citizens in the exercise of their rights, no matter how great the need might be for such protection. If this amendment should become a law, twenty-three states, including perhaps a minority of the population could at any moment arrest the movement of the government and stop all of its operations [simply by refusing to elect senators]. . . . To call such a scheme as this progressive is mockery; it is retrogression and reaction of the worst kind. . . . Self-preservation is the first law of governments as it is of nature and it seems to me that no matter how we should decide the question of the methods by which senators should be elected, the preservation of the power of the United States to control those elections, if need be, is essential to the Government's safe and continued existence.[116]

A week later, on February 10, Senator Elihu Root, a Republican from New York, gave perhaps the most eloquent and thoughtful defense of the election of senators by state legislatures that has ever been delivered in the Senate. He began by expressing his belief that the American people should avoid the temptation of seeking frequent changes to the Constitution, for stability in government "was a matter of vital concern."[117] He also noted that legislative deadlocks could be eliminated without the need for a constitutional amendment by the simple expedient of changing the law of July 25, 1866, which provided the procedure the state legislatures had been following in the election of senators.[118] He also argued that direct election of senators would ultimately destroy state sovereignty: "Let me tell the gentlemen who are solicitous for the preservation of the sovereignty of their States that there is but one way in which they can preserve that sovereignty, and that is by repudiating absolutely and forever the fundamental doctrine on which this resolution proceeds." He stressed that depriving state legislatures of the opportunity to elect senators would rob them "of power, of dignity, of consequence" and would lead them to grow "less and less competent, less and less worthy of trust, and less and less efficient in the performance of their duties. You can never develop competent and trusted bodies of public servants by expressing distrust of them, by taking power away from them." He worried aloud that, if the state legislatures were perceived as untrustworthy in the exercise of their power to elect senators, the result would be an expansion of the federal government. "If the State government is abandoned, if we recognize the fact that we cannot have honest legislatures, sir, the tide that now sets toward the Federal Government will swell in volume and power." With state legislatures removed from the process, he predicted that "[t]he time will come when the Government of the United States will be driven to the exercise of more arbitrary and unconsidered power, will be driven to greater concentration, will be driven to extend its functions into the internal affairs of the States." "We shall go," he warned, "through the cycle of concentration of power at the center while the States dwindle into insignificance." [119]

Debate on the Sutherland Amendment to S. Res. 134 continued until the waning days of the 61st Congress. Senator Borah defended his resolution and charged that the Sutherland Amendment was proposed for no other reasons than to cause any direct-election provision to fail. He also asserted that the purported objectives of the Sutherland Amendment could be realized under Article I, Section 5 of the Constitution, which empowered each house to be "the judge of the Elections, Returns, and Qualifications of its own Members." [120] On February 24, the Senate passed the Sutherland Amendment by a vote of fifty to thirty-four (with four not voting). Only three southern senators (from Arkansas, Kentucky, and West Virginia) supported it, while the other twenty-five voted "no." Only four western senators and no eastern senators opposed the resolution. [121] Four days later (and for the first time in its history), the Senate voted on a constitutional amendment providing for direct election of the Senate. The amended resolution was defeated when it fell four votes short of the requisite two-thirds majority; the vote was fifty-four in favor of the amendment, thirty-three opposed, and (critically) four not voting. [122]

In the 62nd Congress, the Senate finally yielded. On April 4, 1911, a special session of Congress was called by President William Howard Taft to review the reciprocal trade agreement with Canada. At this time, Democrats were a minority in the Senate but had made significant gains in the 1910 elections with the defeat of ten Republicans opposed to direct election; they also continued to have a large majority in the House. The Democrats met three days prior to the beginning of the special session and, determining that adopting a resolution providing for direct election would consume less than a week of House time, agreed among themselves that it should therefore be taken up immediately. [123] Accordingly, Representative William Waller Rucker, a Democrat from Missouri, presented H. J. 39 on April 5. [124] Substantially the same as the joint resolutions reported by Senator Borah in the 61st Congress, H. J. 39 provided for direct election and stipulated state control of elections. One week later, the Committee on the Election of the President, Vice President, and Representatives in Congress, of which Rucker was the chairman, favorably reported the joint resolution to the floor.[125] On April 13, Representative Horace Olin Young, a Republican from Michigan, proposed an amendment to H. J. Res. 39 that was essentially the Sutherland Amendment of the preceding Congress.[126] After a six-hour debate, Young's amendment was defeated along party lines by a vote of 123 to 189—all Republicans voted for it, and all but two Democrats opposed it.[127] Later that same day, the House proceeded to adopt H. J. Res. 39 by the requisite two-thirds majority. The final ballot was 296 to 16 and revealed widespread bipartisan support for direct election as 107 Republicans, 188 Democrats, and 1 Socialist all voted in favor of the resolution.

H. J. Res. 39 was introduced in the Senate on April 17, 1911, at which time it was referred first to the Committee on Privileges and Elections and subsequently to the Judiciary Committee. It emerged from the Judiciary Committee with a favorable report on May 1.[128] On May 15, Senator Bristow offered a substitute for the joint resolution that provided for direct election of senators but that omitted the provision relating to exclusive state control over the time, places, and manner of holding senatorial elections.[129] Debate on the Bristow Amendment began on May 23. This measure won the vocal support of Senators Root and Sutherland, who contended that, had the framers of the Constitution determined that senators were to have been directly elected by the people, they certainly would have given Congress supervisory power over such elections.[130]

On June 12, when the time came to vote on the Bristow Amendment, Senator Leroy Percy, a Democrat from Mississippi, expressed the view of many Southern Democrats concerning federal control of senatorial elections:

> While it may be true that immigration to some of the Southern States has reduced the gravity of the Negro problem, yet it cannot be true that this change has made senators from those states deaf to the appeals of their brethren from less fortunate states, and it is only by a Democratic vote that this substitute can be adopted. *Even admitting that the substitute is needed to make the Fourteenth and Fifteenth amendments more effective, does that furnish a reason for the Democrats voting for the substitute?*[131]

The vote on the Bristow Amendment was tied—forty-four to forty-four, with three not voting. The Republican Vice President, James Sherman, was therefore called on to break the tie. This he did by voting for the substitute, thus securing its adoption. (Five Republicans voted against the measure, with just one lone Democrat voting for the substitute.) On that same day (June 12), the resolution itself passed with a final vote of sixty-four to fourteen, giving it the necessary two-thirds majority and marking the first time in the eighty-five year campaign to secure direct election that the Senate had given its approval to such an amendment.

On June 21, the House began to review the Senate amendment to its joint resolution. When Representative Marlin Edgar Olmstead, a Republican from Pennsylvania, moved to concur in the Senate amendment, a three-and-one-half-hour debate ensued.[132] Representative Martin Barnaby Madsen, a Republican from Illinois, voiced the fears of many members of his party that the Democrats favored state control over senatorial elections in order to

> destroy the franchise of the Negro. They want him, while ostensibly free, to remain the chattel of designing politicians of the South. . . . They want the States to have unrestricted control. They want to be able to pass laws through the State legislatures which cannot be laid aside by Congress. They will not admit it but if they are given the unlimited and unrestricted power to do so they will forever prevent a black man from exercising the right to vote. . . . The Democrats are in control in this body—they have the votes to pass the amendment in any form they choose—the responsibility is yours, gentlemen; exercise it or you will give this additional evidence of your hatred of the Negro.[133]

Southern Democrats, however, saw it differently. Representative Samuel Andrew Witherspoon, a Democrat from Mississippi, contended that the Republicans were attempting to

> overthrow white supremacy and to reinstate Negro domination in the Southern States. . . . The Republican position . . . boldly warns us that the object and aim of the amendment is Negro rule in the South, is federal interference with southern elections, is Federal compulsion of what is denominated honest and fair elections in the South, but avows its purpose under the Bristow amendment, to usurp control of southern elections whenever necessary to preserve the progressive civilization of the day.[134]

By a vote of 111 to 171, the House refused to concur in the Senate's Bristow Amendment to H. J. Res. 39. The vote was cast along party and regional lines—only one Republican voted against the amendment, and Southern Congressmen cast more than half the opposing votes. On June 27, the House action was officially reported to the Senate. Senator Clarence D. Clark, a Republican from Wyoming, moved that the Senate insist upon its amendment and ask for a conference. The motion was agreed to, and the Vice President appointed as Senate conferees Senators Clark, Augustus Octavius Bacon, a Democrat from Georgia, and Knute Nelson, a Republican from Minnesota.[135] On July 5, the House agreed to a conference and appointed as its conferees Representatives Rucker, Olmstead, and Michael F. Conry, a Democrat from New York.[136] Over the next nine months, the conference committee met sixteen times but was unable to reach agreement, prompting Senator Clark on April 23, 1912, to move that the Senate persist in its Bristow Amendment to H. J. Res. 39. His motion passed by a vote of forty-two to thirty-six.[137] (Again, party lines were sharply drawn, with forty-one Republicans and one Democrat supporting the motion and only one Republican opposing it.) On May 13, Clark's resolution, insisting on acceptance of the Senate's amendment, was read in the House. At this time, Representative Rucker, the author of H. J. Res. 39, moved that the House "recede from its disagreement to the Senate amendment known as the Bristow Amendment and concur in the same."[138]

Many Southern Democrats strenuously objected to Rucker's motion to concur in the Bristow Amendment, insisting that it would bring ruin to the South. They rallied around an amendment proposed by Representative Charles Lafayette Bartlett, a Democrat from Georgia, that declared:

> Congress shall not have the power to provide for the qualifications of electors of the United States senators within the various states of the United States, nor to authorize the appointment of supervisors of election, judges of election, or returning boards to certify the results of any such election, nor to authorize use of the United States marshals or the military forces of the United States or the troops of the United States at the polls during the said election.[139]

Most members of Congress, however, regarded these fears as exaggerated and groundless and insisted that, unless they yielded, direct election of senators would again die in Congress. While many did not particularly agree with the Bristow Amendment, they nonetheless felt its passage was critical in the fight for direct election; were this battle to be lost, they worried that the subject might not be taken up again in the foreseeable future. Representative Underwood clearly articulated this view: "Now, if I could select, I would enact the bill that we voted for in the House originally. I prefer that form of the bill, but I realize as every other man within the sound of my voice realizes that if you do not pass this bill as it is proposed by the Chairman of the Committee, the gentleman from Missouri [Mr. Rucker], you defeat the proposition, and it will not be submitted to the people of the United States for them to pass upon."[140]

At the conclusion of the debate, the Bartlett Amendment failed by a vote of 89 to 189 (only 2 of the supporting votes came from Republicans, and only 9 opposing votes came from the South).[141] The House then proceeded on that same day, May 13, to accept Rucker's motion to concur in the Bristow Amendment. By so doing, the Seventeenth Amendment was adopted by the Congress. The requisite two-thirds majority was easily secured; the vote was 238 to 39 (with 110 not voting and 5 answering "present").[142] The joint resolution was signed by the presiding officers of both houses on May 14 and was formally submitted to the State Department the next day. Secretary of State Philander C. Knox officially distributed the proposed constitutional amendment to the states for their consideration on May 17, 1912.

State Ratification of the Seventeenth Amendment

The Seventeenth Amendment was quickly ratified by the states in less than eleven months. (At the time, the only amendment to have been ratified more quickly was the Twelfth Amendment.[143]) Connecticut was the requisite thirty-sixth state to ratify on April 8, 1913. Not only was it ratified quickly, but it was ratified by overwhelming numbers. Two statistics show how overwhelming: In fifty-two of the seventy-two state legislative chambers that voted to ratify the Seventeenth Amendment, the vote was unanimous, and in all thirty-six of the ratifying states, the total number of votes cast in opposition to ratification was only 191, with 152 of these votes coming from just two legislative chambers: 77 from the Connecticut House and 75 from the Vermont House.

Massachusetts was the first state to ratify the Seventeenth Amendment, doing so on May 22, 1912. So anxious was the state to ratify that, two days before the amendment was actually sent to the states, a resolution proposing ratification was introduced in the lower house. Action was withheld until May 17, when the Assembly adopted the resolution by acclamation. The Senate, by a vote of 30 to 0, then passed the measure just five days after the proposed amendment had been officially communicated to the states.[144]

Arizona followed suit when, on May 21, 1912, Governor George W. P. Hunt called Arizona's first legislature after its admission into statehood into a special session. Among the matters for legislative action was Hunt's request for a speedy ratification of the Seventeenth Amendment. On May 31, the Arizona House passed a joint resolution providing for ratification by a vote of 33 to 0; the Senate concurred on June 3, also by the unanimous vote of 18 to 0.

The last state to approve the proposed amendment in 1912 was Minnesota. On June 12 both houses of the legislature unanimously adopted it (the House by a vote of 90 to 0 and the Senate by a vote of 51 to 0).

New York was the first state to adopt the Seventeenth Amendment in 1913. The Governor, William Sulzer,[145] wasted no time in advocating ratification, asking the legislature to do so on New Year's Day. The Assembly agreed to ratify on January 14 by a vote of 128 to 4, and the Senate concurred on January 15 by a vote of 45 to 4. The Kansas legislature was considering the amendment at the same time. On January 16, the Senate adopted a concurrent resolution by a vote of 40 to 0, and, the next day, the House approved it by a vote of 113 to 1. Governor George Hodges, a strong proponent of direct election, signed the concurrent resolution on January 21, 1913. On January 13, in his biennial message to the state legislature, Governor Oswald West of Oregon urged the legislature to approve the proposed amendment. The Senate did so unanimously, 30 to 0, on January 22, and the House, under a suspension of the rules, concurred in the action of the Senate the next day. North Carolina was the next to ratify, with both of its houses unanimously approving the measure on voice votes—the Senate on January 14 and the House on January 25.

In California, the proposed amendment was referred to the legislature by Governor Hiram Johnson on January 17; the Assembly approved a joint resolution providing for ratification on January 21 by a vote of 73 to 0, and, seven days later, the Senate concurred unanimously by a vote of 67 to 0. On January 2, Governor Woodbridge N. Ferris urged speedy ratification of the Seventeenth Amendment in his inaugural address before the Michigan legislature, and, on January 22, the Senate agreed to ratification unanimously (32 to 0); six days later, the Assembly likewise approved the proposed amendment unanimously (89 to 0).

While the new governor of Iowa, George W. Clark, made no mention of the proposed amendment in his inaugural address on January 16, he did transmit it to the legislature six days later. On January 29, under a suspension of the rules, the House adopted the proposal 105 to 0, and, the next day, the Senate followed suit, adopting the amendment, 44 to 0. The Montana legislature also ratified the proposed amendment on January 30 (the vote in the House was 79 to 0, and in the Senate, 29 to 0). However, the resolution itself was without effect until February 8, when it was signed by Governor S. V. Stewart. Idaho ratified on January 31, with a House vote of 52 to 0 and a Senate vote of 22 to 1.

West Virginia was the first state to take action in February. Governor W. E. Glasscock urged adoption of the proposed amendment in his message to a special session of the state legislature in January 24, and, on February 1, the House passed the measure unanimously (75 to 0). After a vote, some minor amendments, and a second vote, the Senate unanimously approved the measure on February 4 by a vote of 28 to 0. Nevada ratified next; the vote in the House on January 30 was 45 to 0, and the vote in the Senate on February 6 was 19 to 0. Texas followed on Nevada's heels; its House approved the proposed amendment on January 31 by a vote of 106 to 1, and, on February 7, its Senate likewise approved, 24 to 1.

In the state of Washington, both the outgoing and incoming governors appealed to the legislature to adopt the Seventeenth Amendment. The House unanimously approved a joint resolution proposing ratification on February 6 by a vote of 82 to 0, and the Senate followed suit the next day, approving it unanimously by a vote of 31 to 0. Wyoming was the next state to ratify; on February 11, the House voted to approve, 52 to 0, and the Senate, 25 to 2. Colorado ratified next, with the House voting 63 to 0 on February 5, and the Senate voting 31 to 0 on February 13.

As in Washington, both the retiring and incoming governors of Illinois urged quick adoption of the proposed amendment. The Senate responded on February 12 with a unanimous vote in favor of ratification, 50 to 0; the next day, the House voted to ratify, 146 to 1. North Dakota ratified on February 18 when the Senate unanimously approved the amendment, 47 to 0, the House having already given its endorsement on January 24 by a vote of 102 to 0.

The New England states took more time to consider the matter. The governor of Vermont presented the proposed amendment to the legislature on October 15, 1912. The House and Senate sent the measure to a joint committee with members of both houses, charging it to make any suggestions the members felt necessary. On February 18, 1913, the committee reported its opinion that the amendment should be ratified, and, on that same day, the Senate voted its approval, 15 to 9. On the next day, the House did likewise, 125 to 75. On February 19, the Maine House voted to ratify by a vote of 129 to 0; the Senate concurred unanimously, 28 to 0, one day later. Governor S. D. Felker of New Hampshire encouraged the state legislature to adopt the proposed amendment in his January 3, 1913, inaugural address. On a voice vote, the House passed a joint resolution calling for ratification on February 18, and the Senate voted approval the next day by a vote of 20 to 2.

On February 13, the Wisconsin Senate unanimously approved ratification by a vote of 28 to 0, and five days later, the Assembly concurred by a vote of 89 to 1.[146] On January 9, 1913, the Indiana legislature was urged by Governor Thomas R. Marshall (then vice president-elect) to ratify the Seventeenth Amendment. The Senate did so on February 5, voting 38 to 0, and the House followed suit two weeks later on February 19 with a vote of 94 to 0. The South Dakota Senate unanimously ratified the proposed amendment on January 21 by a vote of 44 to 0, and the House followed on February 19, voting 92 to 0.

Ohio was the next state to ratify, with Governor James M. Cox strongly advocating the issue in his first address to the state legislature on January 14, 1913. The House was quick to act, voting unanimously to ratify the next day, 114 to 0. The Senate was somewhat slower and did not agree to ratify until February 20 when it did so by a vote of 30 to 1. The Oklahoma House affirmed by a vote of 83 to 0 a joint resolution in favor of ratification on January 21, 1913; the Senate agreed on February 24, voting 30 to 2. On February 11, the Arkansas House agreed to ratify the Seventeenth Amendment by a vote of 87 to 1; its Senate unanimously took similar action on February 28 by a vote of 34 to 0.

On January 9, 1913, Governor Herbert Hadley of Missouri requested in a letter that the state legislature ratify the proposed amendment. The House did so on January 28, voting 128 to 1; the Senate did likewise by a vote of 22 to 0 on March 7. The Nebraska governor, John H. Morehead, also urged the passage of the Seventeenth Amendment, calling for it during his inaugural address on January 13. On February 14, the House passed a joint resolution calling for ratification, by a vote of 94 to 0; the Senate agreed to ratify on March 14 by a vote of 25 to 0.

At the first meeting of the legislature of the new state of New Mexico in 1912, Governor W. C. McDonald urged ratification of what would become both the Sixteenth and Seventeenth Amendments. However, it was not until the next session in 1913 that the legislature acted, voting in favor of ratification of direct election on March 15 by a vote of 42 to 0 in the House and 23 to 0 in the Senate. New Jersey was next; Governor Woodrow Wilson (then president-elect) urged the legislature on January 14 to ratify both the Sixteenth and Seventeenth Amendments. On February 13, the House unanimously adopted a resolution to ratify the Seventeenth Amendment by a vote of 42 to 0; on March 17, the Senate likewise approved by a vote of 18 to 1.

Tennessee voted in favor of ratification on April 1; its House approved by a vote of 81 to 0 and its Senate by a vote of 27 to 3. In Pennsylvania, Governor John K. Tener mentioned the proposed amendment in his biennial address to the legislature on January 5 but made no recommendation to guide the legislature. The House approved ratification on February 3 by a vote of 193 to 3, and, after extensive debate, the Senate concurred on April 2 by a vote of 40 to 0.

Connecticut had the distinction of being the requisite thirty-sixth state to ratify the Seventeenth Amendment, thereby making it a part of the Constitution. The governor, Simeon K. Baldwin, noted in his inaugural address on January 8, 1913, the importance of ratifying the proposed amendment. Although the original resolution calling for ratification was adversely reported from the House committee on federal relations on March 27, the House was able to adopt a substitute resolution on April 8 by a vote of 151 to 77, and, five minutes later, the Senate concurred by a voice vote.[149] While Connecticut was the last requisite state to vote ratification and did so on April 8, the Seventeenth Amendment did not become a part of the fundamental law of the land until May 31, 1913, because of the failure of the proper officials in a number of the states promptly to notify the State Department of the favorable action of their state legislatures.[148]

Other states also played a role in this drama. Although the Louisiana legislature was in session when Congress adopted the proposed amendment, it did not give its approval until June 11, 1914, more than a year after the Seventeenth Amendment had gone into effect. Georgia was the only state that simply refused to vote on the ratification of the Seventeenth Amendment. On July 2, 1912, Governor Joseph M. Brown raised the question of whether Congress had properly adopted the proposed amendment when the House of Representatives approved the amended H. J. Res. 39 by two-thirds of those present and voting rather than by two-thirds of the entire membership. A committee was appointed to answer this question. Its answer: two-thirds meant two-thirds of the entire membership and, therefore, the amendment had not been properly adopted. On August 12, the House, by a vote of 108 to 35, accepted the committee report, and, on August 14, the Senate concurred.

Kentucky, on the other hand, did not ratify the proposed amendment, because the Kentucky legislature had adjourned for the session before Congress had adopted the amendment, and, being a biennial legislature and not called into a special session, it did not convene again until 1914, after the requisite number of states had ratified the Seventeenth Amendment. Mississippi, Alabama, Maryland, Virginia, and Florida likewise did not vote to ratify for the same reason.

By contrast, Utah, Rhode Island, and Delaware actually voted to reject the Seventeenth Amendment. In Utah, the House voted, 35 to 3, to approve a joint resolution approving ratification on February 17, 1913, but the Senate, after what was recorded as ten minutes of consideration, rejected the amendment by a vote of 3 to 10. The Rhode Island House passed a resolution in favor of direct election of senators, but the same resolution died in the Senate's Judiciary Committee on April 8. Delaware's House passed a resolution supporting the adoption of the amendment by a vote of 30 to 0, but the Senate defeated the same resolution by a vote of 6 to 10.

Progressivism and the "Silent Artillery of Time"

What is particularly noteworthy of the lengthy debate over the adoption and ratification of the Seventeenth Amendment was the absence of any serious or systematic consideration of its potential impact on federalism.[149] The consequences of the Seventeenth Amendment on federalism went almost completely unexplored. The popular press, the party platforms, the state memorials, the House and Senate debates, and the state legislative debates during ratification focused almost exclusively on expanding democracy, eliminating political corruption, defeating elitism, ensuring either congressional or state control over senatorial elections, and freeing the states from what they had come to regard as an onerous and difficult responsibility. Almost no one (not even among the opposition) paused to weigh the consequences of the amendment on federalism.[150]

Only three exceptions are apparent in the voluminous record. One was Representative Franklin Bartlett, the Democrat from New York, who argued powerfully and eloquently during the 53rd Congress that the interests of the states as states could only be preserved by keeping the senators as representatives of state governments. He fully appreciated that "the Framers of the Constitution, were they present in this House today, would inevitably regard this resolution as a most direct blow at the doctrine of State's rights and at the integrity of the State sovereignties; for if you once deprive a State as a collective organism of all share in the General Government, you annihilate its federative importance."[151]

The other two exceptions were in the Senate: George F. Hoar, the Republican from Massachusetts, and Elihu Root, the Republican from New York. On the Senate floor during the 53rd Congress, Senator Hoar defended indirect election of the Senate, declaring that the "state legislatures are the bodies of men most interested of all others to preserve State jurisdiction. . . It is well that the members of one branch of the Legislature should look to them for their reelection, and it a great security for the rights of the States."[152] After quoting approvingly from Joseph Story's *Commentaries* that election of the Senate by the state legislatures "would increase the public confidence by securing the national government from any encroachments on the powers of the states,"[153] Hoar continued: "The State legislature will be made up of men whose duty will be the administration of the State authority of their several State interests and the framing of laws for the government of the State which they represent. The popular conventions, gathered for the political purpose of nominating Senators, may be quite otherwise composed and guided. Here, in the State legislature, is to be found the great security against the encroachment upon the rights of the States."[154] In the 61st Congress, Senator Root argued against direct election of the Senate on the very same grounds—if the sovereignty of the states was to be preserved, the original mode of electing the Senate had to be preserved.[155]

Most political leaders during this lengthy campaign to secure the adoption and ratification of the Seventeenth Amendment clearly did not appreciate the framers' understanding that the principal means of protecting federalism and preventing the transfer of the "residuary and inviolable sovereignty of the states"[156] to the national government was the mode of electing the Senate. They did not worry about altering constitutional structure, because they embraced the Progressive dogma that the Constitution is a living organism that must constantly adapt to an ever-changing environment. They did not worry that their alterations would break a Newtonian, clock-like mechanism; rather, they celebrated the Darwinian adaptability of the Constitution and the evolution of its principles. To invoke Lincoln's imagery from his Lyceum Address, in the glare of the Progressives' white-hot confidence in the justice and superiority of simple majoritarian democracy, the framers' arguments for relying instead on a more complex, mitigated democracy "faded" from their view. Over their eighty-six-year campaign to make the Senate more democratic, their memories of the framers' understanding that federalism could only be rendered secure by the mode of electing the Senate "gr[e]w more and more dim by the lapse of time." They no longer appreciated the importance of constitutional walls for directing and channeling self-interest toward the public good, and so, aided in their assault by the "silent artillery of time,"[157] they leveled the walls of federalism. The consequences of their assault is the subject of the next chapter.

Notes

1. See Todd J. Zywicki, "Beyond the Shell and Husk of History: The History of the Seventeenth Amendment and Its Implications for Current Reform Proposals," *Cleveland State Law Review* 45 (1997): 174: "[S]tatistical and anecdotal evidence suggests that the Senate played an active role in preserving the sovereignty and independent sphere of action of state governments. Rather than delegating lawmaking authority to Washington, state legislators insisted on keeping authority close to home. . . . As a result, the long-term size of the federal government remained fairly stable and relatively small during the pre-Seventeenth Amendment era. Although the federal government grew substantially in size in response to particular crises, most notably wars, it returned to its long-term stable pattern following the abatement of the crisis. The 'rachet effect' of federal intervention persisting after the dissipation of the crisis which purportedly spawned it, was absent from American history until 1913."

2. Included among these measures is the passage of the Fourteenth Amendment. While that amendment nationalized citizenship and provided Congress with enormous power under Section 5, so long as the Senate that had to concur in the actual employment of that enormous power was elected by state legislatures, federalism and the interests of the states as states remained secure. Also included are the passage of the Interstate Commerce Act of 1887, 24 Stat. 379, the Sherman Anti-Trust Act of 1890, 26 Stat. 209, and the Pure Food and Drug Act of 1906, 34 Stat. 768. Passage of the Interstate Commerce Act was prompted by *Wabash, St. L. & P. R.* v. *Illinois*, 118 U.S. 551 (1886), in which the Supreme Court made railroads an interstate issue by declaring that states could not regulate interstate railroad traffic within their own borders, even in the absence of congressional legislation. The Sherman Anti-Trust Act and the Pure Food and Drug Act were appropriate measures for dealing with an emerging national economy, and all three regulatory measures were, as Theodore J. Lowi has pointed out, "traditional," "rule-bound," and "proscriptive." *The End of Liberalism: Ideology, Policy, and the Crisis of Public Authority* (New York: W. W. Norton, 1969), 134.

3. 60 U.S. 393 (1857). The Court in *Dred Scott* v. *Sandford* declared unconstitutional the Missouri Compromise of 1820 and Congress's attempt to regulate the spread of slavery in the territories.

4. During the entire period prior to the ratification of the Seventeenth Amendment, the Supreme Court's invalidations of congressional measures on federalism grounds were few in number and, with the exception of *Dred Scott*, of little consequence. It invalidated only seven congressional measures in the following cases: *Dred Scott* v. *Sandford*, 60 U.S. 393 (1857); *United States* v. *DeWitt*, 76 U.S. 41 (1870); *United States* v. *Fox*, 95 U.S. 670 (1878); the *Trademark Cases*, 100 U.S. 82 (1879); the *Employers' Liability Cases*, 207 U.S. 463 (1908); *Keller* v. *United States*, 213 U.S. 138 (1909), and *Coyle* v. *Smith*, 221 U.S. 559 (1911). An eighth statute considered in *Matter of Heff*, 197 U.S. 488 (1905), could possibly be added here. However, since the Court explicitly overturned *Matter of Heff* in *United States* v. *Nice*, 241 U.S. 591 (1916), it is not included in these totals.

5. Christopher H. Hoebeke, *The Road to Mass Democracy: Original Intent and the Seventeenth Amendment* (New Brunswick, N.J.: Transaction, 1995), 18-24.

6. Alexis de Tocqueville, *Democracy in America*, trans. Henry Reeve, ed. Phillips Bradley, 2 vols. (New York: Random House, 1945), 2: 344.

7. Tocqueville, *Democracy in America*, 2: 344.

8. Woodrow Wilson, *The New Freedom: A Call for the Emancipation of the Generous Energies of a People* (New York: Doubleday, Page, 1913), 47.

9. We have here as well the origin of the unfortunate notion of a "living Constitution" that continues to pollute our constitutional law. See Justice Oliver Wendell Holmes' famous language in *Missouri* v. *Holland*, 252 U.S. 416, 433 (1920): "[W]hen we are dealing with words that also are a constituent act, like the Constitution of the United States, we must realize that they have called into life a being the development of which could not have been foreseen completely by the most gifted of its begetters. It was enough for them to realize or to hope that they had created an organism; it has taken a century and has cost their successors much sweat and blood to prove that they created a nation. The case before us must be considered in the light of our whole experience and not merely in that of what was said a hundred years ago."

10. Wilson, *The New Freedom*, 69. Emphasis in the original.

11. Wilson, *The New Freedom*, 55.

12. Tocqueville, *Democracy in America*, 1: 211-12.

13. Charles A. Beard and Mary R. Beard, *The Rise of American Civilization*, 2 vols. (New York: Macmillan, 1933), 2: 559.

14. For a table providing the date, author, title, disposition, and citation for each of these 188 joint resolutions, see Wallace Worthy Hall, "The History and Effect of the Seventeenth Amendment," Ph.D. diss., Department of Political Science, University of California, Berkeley (1936), Appendix A, 443-56.

15. The House approved these proposals by a two-thirds voice vote on January 16, 1893; by a vote of 141 to 50 on July 21, 1894; by a vote of 185 to 11 on May 11, 1898; by a vote of 242 to 15 on April 12, 1900; by a two-thirds voice vote on February 13, 1902; and by a vote of 296 to 16 on April 13, 1911. See David E. Kyvig, *Explicit and Authentic Acts: Amending the U.S. Constitution, 1776-1995* (Lawrence: University Press of Kansas, 1996), 209, and Hall, "The History and Effect of the Seventeenth Amendment," 163-64.

16. Although, see California, where this pattern was not the case. The two legislative deadlocks that each time left the state with only one senator for an entire Congress were caused by other factors. In 1855, the deadlock resulted from a split between the northern (or "Tammany") and southern (or "Chivalry") factions of the Democratic Party. The two terms come from Zoeth Skinner Eldredge, *History of California*, 5 vols. (New York: Century History, 1915), 4: 136. In 1899, the deadlock came about when the Republicans divided in "a contest between Los Angeles and San Francisco." See A. A. Gray, *History of California: From 1542*

(New York: D. C. Heath, 1934), 526. When the term of Senator Stephan M. White, a Democrat from Los Angeles, expired in 1899, a falling-out between Governor Henry T. Gage, a Republican from Los Angeles, and Michael H. de Young, Republican publisher of the *San Francisco Chronicle*, led to deadlock in the Republican-controlled legislature. After 104 ballots, and with the depletion of the legislators' expense allowance for the session, the legislature adjourned on March 19 without electing a senator. The seat remained vacant until Thomas R. Bard, a Republican from Ventura, filled it in 1901. See Ralph J. Roske, *Everyman's Eden: A History of California* (New York: Macmillan, 1968), 447-48; Rockwell D. Hunt, *California and Californians.* 5 vols. (Chicago: Lewis, 1926), 2: 414; and Royce D. Delmatier, Clarence F. McIntosh, and Earl G. Waters, *The Rumble of California Politics: 1848-1970* (New York: John Wiley & Sons, 1970), 133-37.

17. 14 Stat. 245 (1866). As Zywicki writes of this 1866 law requiring that senators be elected by a majority of the state legislators, "Majority votes were difficult to come by in states with evenly balanced party competition and third-parties who could prevent either of the dominant parties from receiving a majority in the state legislatures. Amending this 1866 statute to permit election by plurality or requiring run-offs would have solved the deadlock problem without the need for a constitutional amendment." Zywicki, "Beyond the Shell and Husk of History," 199.

18. Joseph Story, *Commentaries on the Constitution of the United States*, 3 vols. (New York: Hilliard & Gray, 1833), § 703, 2: 183.

19. James Kent, *Commentaries on American Law,* 4 vols. (New York: O. Halsted, 1826), 1: 211.

20. Kent, *Commentaries on American Law*, 1: 211; see also 225-26.

21. Story, *Commentaries on the Constitution of the United States*, 2: 183.

22. George H. Haynes, *The Election of Senators* (New York: Henry Holt, 1906), 20.

23. The following discussion relies heavily on Haynes, *The Election of Senators*, 21-24.

24. Jay S. Bybee, "Ulysses at the Mast: Democracy, Federalism, and the Sirens' Song of the Seventeenth Amendment," *Northwestern University Law Review* 91 (1997): 547.

25. 14 Stat. 245.

26. Haynes, *The Election of Senators*, 27.

27. James G. Blaine, *Twenty Years of Congress,* 2 vols. (Norwich, Conn.: Henry Bill, 1884-86), 2: 160.

28. Kyvig, *Explicit and Authentic Acts*, 209. See also George H. Haynes, *The Senate of the United States: Its History and Practice*, 2 vols. (New York: Houghton Mifflin, 1938), 2: 92, and Hall, "The History and Effect of the Seventeenth Amendment," 287-301. As Zywicki, "Beyond the Shell and Husk of History," 199, points out, however, despite these problems, Delaware affirmatively voted to reject the Seventeenth Amendment.

29. For example, George Haynes reports that, in Oregon in 1895, the individual (G. W. McBride) elected senator on the sixtieth ballot "by a majority of one had not even been nominated until just fifteen minutes before the hour when the legislature's term must expire." Haynes, *The Senate of the United States*, 1: 88.

30. "Each ballot took a considerable amount of time, and when sessions were limited to forty or sixty days, incessant balloting could not fail to curtail very materially the time available for the legislator's normal work in the service of the state. ... [I]t must [also] be recognized that, as the session wore on, the animosities engendered in the deadlock projected themselves into the ordinary work of the legislature, giving a party color to the most nonpartisan measures, and distorting the legislator's views upon many state issues." Haynes, *The Senate of the United States*, 1: 93.

31. Zywicki, "Beyond the Shell and Husk of History," 196.

32. Haynes, *The Senate of the United States*, 1: 91.

33. Hoebeke, *The Road to Mass Democracy*, 91.

34. Haynes, *The Election of Senators*, 165.

35. Interestingly, however, Montana returned Senator Clark the following year. Hoebeke, *The Road to Mass Democracy*, 92.

36. See Hoebeke, *The Road to Mass Democracy*, 96, who argues, contrary to the view that the Senate was aloof and unresponsive to the people, that "the final settlement of the Lorimer case illustrates just how amenable the Senate could be to popular opinion." See also Hall, "The History and Effect of the Seventeenth Amendment," 252-74.

37. Zywicki, "Beyond the Shell and Husk of History,"197.

38. Kyvig, *Explicit and Authentic Acts*, 209. See also Hoebeke, *The Road to Mass Democracy*, 101.

39. "Election of Senators," *House Reports*, 50th Cong., 1st Sess., No. 1456, 2. See Bybee, "Ulysses at the Mast," 544.

40. *Senate Reports*, 54th Cong., 1st Sess., No. 530, 10.

41. Zywicki, "Beyond the Shell and Husk of History," 185.

42. See Hoebeke, *The Road to Mass Democracy*, 18-24.

43. Wilson, *The New Freedom*, 55.

44. *Congressional Record*, 53rd Cong., 2nd Sess., 7775.

45. *Congressional Record*, 54th Cong., 1st Sess., 1519. John D. Buenker, "The Urban Political Machine and the Seventeenth Amendment," *Journal of American History* 56 (September 1969): 305, has written: "With the possible exception of the giant corporation, no institution was so severely castigated by the middle-class progressive as the urban political machine." Yet, with regard to direct election of senators, the urban political machine appears to have worked hand-in-glove with the progressives. Urban machines often represented a different party from the one that dominated the state legislature (e.g., Democratic machines in Republican northeastern states) or a different faction of the Democratic Party (as in many southern states). The leaders of these machines reasoned that if they could give the selection of U.S. senators directly to the people, taking it away from legislatures

that were typically malapportioned to the detriment of urban interests, they could mobilize a sufficient number of their constituents to dominate statewide senatorial elections. I want to thank John Kincaid of Lafayette College for this important insight.

46. Forty-four of the petitions came from various local and state Grange associations; twelve from chapters of the Farmers Mutual Benevolent Association, and thirteen from various labor unions. For a table providing the date and sponsoring group for each of these 238 petitions, see Hall, "The History and Effect of the Seventeenth Amendment," Appendix B, 457-81.

47. The National Democratic Party Platform of 1900 was the first platform of a major party to contain a plank calling for direct election of the Senate. For a table providing the particulars of these 239 party platforms, see Hall, "The History and Effect of the Seventeenth Amendment," Appendix D, 490-505.

48. For a table providing the dates of, and state legislatures responsible for, these 175 state memorials, see Hall, "The History and Effect of the Seventeenth Amendment," Appendix F, 512-27.

49. Hall, "The History and Effect of the Seventeenth Amendment," 319. State direct primary laws fell into three classes:

(1) Laws giving the party state committee the discretion of holding a primary either under state control or party auspices for the purpose of selecting the party senatorial nominee were passed in Georgia (1890-91), Florida (1901), South Carolina (1902), Alabama (1903), Idaho (1903), Virginia (1904), Arkansas (1905), and Kentucky (1907).

(2) Laws making it mandatory upon the parties to select their candidates for senator by means of the direct primary were passed in Mississippi (1902), Oregon (1904), Wisconsin (1904), Louisiana (1906), Iowa (1907), Michigan (1907), Missouri (1907), Nebraska (1907), North Dakota (1907), South Dakota (1907), Texas (1907), Washington (1907), Oklahoma (1907-08), Kansas (1908), Maryland (1908), New Jersey (1908), Nevada (1909), Tennessee (1909), Colorado (1910), Maine (1911), Minnesota (1911), and Montana (1913).

(3) Laws providing that senatorial candidates might submit their names in primary elections but that the vote cast was to be considered by the legislature as an advisory vote only were passed in Illinois (1906), Ohio (1908), and California (1909).

These laws prompted Zywicki, "Beyond the Shell and Husk of History," 190, to argue that, "by the time the Seventeenth Amendment was adopted, direct election of Senators was already a *fait accomplis.*"

50. Hall, "The History and Effect of the Seventeenth Amendment," 335. The twelve states were Oregon (1904), Idaho (1909), Nebraska (1909), Nevada (1909), Colorado (1910), California (1911), Kansas (1911), Minnesota (1911), New Jersey (1911), Ohio (1911), Montana (1912), and Arizona (1912).

51. Sara Brandes Crook, "The Consequences of the Seventeenth Amendment: The Twentieth Century Senate," Ph.D. diss., Department of Political Science,

University of Nebraska, Lincoln (1992), 27. The direct primary was, of course, preceded by the public canvass, in which senatorial candidates would barnstorm the state seeking support for their parties in the state legislature in hopes of securing a governing majority there, which would determine who would be sent to Washington as senator. William Riker, "The Senate and American Federalism," *American Political Science Review* 49 (1955): 453, 463, contends that the first public canvass occurred in Mississippi in 1834; it did not become widespread, however, until the Lincoln-Douglas debates of 1858. Roger G. Brooks, "*Garcia, the Seventeenth Amendment, and the Role of the Supreme Court in Defending Federalism*," *Harvard Journal of Law and Public Policy* 10 (1987): 207.

52. Alan P. Grimes, *Democracy and Amendments to the Constitution* (Lexington, Mass.: Lexington Books, 1978), 76.

53. See Allen H. Eaton, *The Oregon System: The Story of Direct Legislation in Oregon* (Chicago: A. C. McClurg, 1912), 92-98. "By 1909, when Oregon's Republican legislature elected a Democratic senator who had won the popular contest, the system's effectiveness was demonstrated." Kyvig, *Explicit and Authentic Acts*, 210.

54. As a consequence, when George Norris, the Republican Party primary nominee for the Senate, defeated his Democratic Party opponent in the 1912 general election, the Democratically controlled Nebraska Legislature duly elected Norris and sent him to the Senate. Crook, "The Consequences of the Seventeenth Amendment," 30.

55. There are substantial arguments to the contrary. See Grover Rees III, "The Amendment Process & Limited Constitutional Conventions," *Benchmark* 2 (March -April 1986): 66-108. See also American Bar Association Special Constitutional Convention Study Committee, *Amendment of the Constitution: By the Convention Method under Article V* (Chicago: American Bar Association, 1974).

56. Hoebeke, *The Road to Mass Democracy*, 149.

57. Kyvig, *Explicit and Authentic Acts*, 210.

58. Hoebeke, *The Road to Mass Democracy*, 149-50.

59. "The wake-up call to the Senate was apparently the defeat in 1910 of ten Republican senators who had opposed the proposed amendment." Bybee, "Ulysses at the Mast," 537-38.

60. The following discussion relies heavily on Hall, "The History and Effect of the Seventeenth Amendment."

61. *Congressional Debates*, 19th Cong., 1st Sess., 1348.

62. *Congressional Debates*, 20th Cong., 2nd Sess., 362.

63. *Congressional Globe*, 31st Cong., 1st Sess., 88.

64. *Congressional Globe*, 31st Cong., 2nd Sess., 627.

65. *Congressional Globe*, 32nd Cong., 1st Sess., 443.

66. *Congressional Globe*, 36th Cong., 2nd Sess., 72.

67. James D. Richardson, *Compilation of Messages and Papers of the Presidents* (New York: Bureau of National Literature), 6: 643.

68. *Congressional Globe*, 32nd Cong., 1st Sess., 284; 33rd Cong., 1st Sess., 36.

69. Hall, "The History and Effect of the Seventeenth Amendment," 16.

70. *Senate Miscellaneous Documents*, 43rd Cong., 1st Sess., No. 66.

71. *Congressional Record*, 44th Cong., 1st Sess., 229.

72. Haynes, *The Election of Senators*, 142, and Hall, "The History and Effect of the Seventeenth Amendment," 323.

73. *House Reports*, 49th Cong., 2nd Sess., No. 3796.

74. *House Reports*, 50th Cong., 1st Sess., No. 1456: 2.

75. *House Reports*, 50th Cong., 1st Sess., No. 1456: 4.

76. *Congressional Record*, 51st Cong., 1st Sess., 3658.

77. Thomas B. Reed, Republican Speaker of the House, declared: "I am inclined to think that the most important factor in the result of this election was the women of the country. It is the women who do the shopping, and who keep the run of prices, who have the keenest scent for increased cost. They heard in every store the clerks behind the counters explain how this article or that could not be sold hereafter for the former price because of the McKinley Bill. They went home and told their husbands and fathers and their stories had a tremendous effect at the ballot box." *The Nation* 51 (November 20, 1890): 393.

78. Haynes, *The Election of Senators*, 117. Bryan was not the first to propose some form of the Optional Plan. Representative J. C. Wright was the first to do so in 1829. See text accompanying note 59.

79. *House Reports*, 52nd Cong., 1st Sess., No. 368: 2.

80. *Congressional Record*, 52nd Cong., 1st Sess., 6070. Henry Cabot Lodge would advocate the same amendment on January 16, 1893, during the second session. *Congressional Record*, 52nd Cong., 2nd Sess., 618.

81. Hall, "The History and Effect of the Seventeenth Amendment," 60-61.

82. *Congressional Record*, 52nd Cong., 1st Sess., 79.

83. *Senate Reports*, 52nd Cong., 1st Sess., No. 794, Part 1: 3. On April 12, 1892, Senator Chandler had previously defied the advocates of direct election to prove that it would provide "any greater men, better men, or nobler men" than those who had the opportunity to serve in the Senate under legislative election. He especially demeaned the common assertion that too many Senators were millionaires, noting that there were many millionaire governors who had been elected directly, and thus the same likelihood that millionaires would be elected to the Senate would exist under popular election. *Congressional Record*, 52nd Cong., 1st Sess., 3193.

84. *Congressional Record*, 53rd Cong., Special Session of the Senate, 102-10.

85. *Congressional Record*, 53rd Cong., 2nd Sess., 7726.

86. *Congressional Record*, 53rd Cong., 2nd Sess., 7770-71.

87. *Congressional Record*, 53rd Cong., 2nd Sess., 7774.

88. Both votes were largely along party lines: Republicans cast sixty-two of the sixty-seven votes for the Northway Amendment and no votes against it, and

they also cast fifty-two of the eighty-seven votes for the Bryan Optional Plan and only two votes against it.

89. *Congressional Record*, 53rd Cong., 2nd Sess., 7782.

90. *The Nation* 56 (July 26, 1894): 57.

91. *Congressional Record*, 53rd Cong., 3rd Sess., 2062.

92. *House Reports*, 54th Cong., 1st Sess., No. 994.

93. *Senate Reports*, 54th Cong., 1st Sess, No. 530: 2, 4.

94. *Congressional Record*, 55th Cong., 2nd Sess., 4811.

95. *House Reports*, 56th Cong., 1st Sess., No. 88: 5-6.

96. *House Reports*, 56th Cong., 1st Sess., No. 88, Part 2: 2.

97. *Congressional Record*, 56th Cong., 1st Sess., 4128.

98. Senator Butler noted, "There has grown up a custom here, that I think is unwarranted, of committees holding matters they do not themselves approve, and smothering them, if the term is not offensive, at least letting them die and not reporting them. Whether that is ever justifiable or not, it surely is not in the case of a proposition of this nature, when thirty-four states through their legislatures have passed resolutions, petitioning Congress to submit to them such a proposition. When the House has repeatedly passed the measure and there is so much public sentiment for it, it deserves the consideration of a committee." *Congressional Record*, 56th Cong., 1st Sess., 4207.

99. Quoted in Hall, "The History and Effect of the Seventeenth Amendment," 108-9.

100. *Congressional Record*, 57th Cong., 1st Sess., 3925.

101. *Congressional Record*, 57th Cong., 1st Sess., 3925.

102. *Congressional Record*, 57th Cong., 1st Sess., 3978.

103. *Congressional Record*, 57th Cong., 1st Sess., 3979.

104. *Congressional Record*, 57th Cong., 1st Sess., 3980.

105. *Congressional Record*, 57th Cong., 1st Sess., 5953.

106. *Congressional Record*, 57th Cong., 1st Sess., 5954.

107. *Congressional Record*, 57th Cong., 1st Sess., 6024.

108. *Congressional Record*, 57th Cong., 1st Sess., 7280.

109. *House Reports*, 59th Cong., 1st Sess., No. 3165: 1.

110. *Congressional Record*, 60th Cong., 1st Sess., 6806.

111. *Congressional Record*, 61st Cong., 1st Sess., 4105-06.

112. *Senate Reports*, 61st Cong., 3rd Sess., No. 961.

113. *Congressional Record*, 61st Cong., 3rd Sess., 847.

114. *Congressional Record*, 61st Cong., 3rd Sess., 1166.

115. *Congressional Record*, 61st Cong., 3rd Sess., 1335.

116. *Congressional Record*, 61st Cong., 3rd Sess., 1976.

117. *Congressional Record*, 61st Cong., 3rd Sess., 2241.

118. In fact, early in the 62nd Congress (on April 6, 1911), Senator Root introduced a bill to amend the law of 1866 so that, after a legislature had cast

ballots for twenty days in an unsuccessful attempt to elect a senator by majority vote, a mere plurality vote would be sufficient. On June 6, the Committee on Privileges and Elections reported the bill favorably, but the Senate took no action on the matter. See *Senate Reports,* 62nd Cong., 2nd Sess., No. 58.

119. *Congressional Record,* 61st Cong., 3rd Sess., 2243.

120. *Congressional Record,* 61st Cong., 3rd Sess., 2645.

121. *Congressional Record,* 61st Cong., 3rd Sess., 3307.

122. *Congressional Record,* 61st Cong., 3rd Sess., 3696.

123. Hall, "The History and Effect of the Seventeenth Amendment," 161.

124. H. J. Res. 39 was one of seventeen resolutions introduced in the 62nd Congress—thirteen in the House and four in the Senate. Of these seventeen, fourteen were introduced during the first week of the first session.

125. *House Reports,* 62nd Cong., 1st Sess., No. 2.

126. *Congressional Record,* 62nd Cong., 1st Sess., 207.

127. *Congressional Record,* 62nd Cong., 1st Sess., 241.

128. *Congressional Record,* 62nd Cong., 1st Sess., 787.

129. *Congressional Record,* 62nd Cong., 1st Sess., 1205.

130. *Congressional Record,* 62nd Cong., 1st Sess., 1486-90.

131. *Congressional Record,* 62nd Cong., 1st Sess., 1917. Emphasis added.

132. *Congressional Record,* 62nd Cong., 1st Sess., 2404.

133. *Congressional Record,* 62nd Cong., 1st Sess., 2425-26.

134. *Congressional Record,* 62nd Cong., 1st Sess., 2415.

135. *Congressional Record,* 62nd Cong., 1st Sess., 2548-49.

136. *Congressional Record,* 62nd Cong., 1st Sess., 2650.

137. *Congressional Record,* 62nd Cong., 2nd Sess., 5172.

138. *Congressional Record,* 62nd Cong., 2nd Sess., 6346.

139. *Congressional Record,* 62nd Cong., 2nd Sess., 6346.

140. *Congressional Record,* 62nd Cong., 2nd Sess., 6362.

141. *Congressional Record,* 62nd Cong., 2nd Sess., 6367.

142. *Congressional Record,* 62nd Cong., 2nd Sess., 6367.

143. The Twenty-Sixth Amendment holds the record today for quickest ratification. It was approved by the Congress on March 10, 1971, and ratified by the requisite thirty-eighth state on July 1 of the same year.

144. The following discussion relies heavily on the research of Hall, "The History and Effect of the Seventeenth Amendment," 337-72.

145. When a member of Congress, Sulzer held the distinction of being the author of more joint resolutions proposing direct election of senators than anyone else in congressional history.

146. It was subsequently discovered that Wisconsin had ratified the original H. J. Res. 39, which gave the states full control of senatorial elections, rather than the final joint resolution with the Bristow Amendment. As a consequence, the Wisconsin legislature voted again on May 7, approving ratification in the House by a vote of 76 to 0 and in the Senate by a vote of 32 to 0.

147. The state that had the distinction of making the Seventeenth Amendment part of the Constitution also had the distinction of being the state that cast the most votes against it.

148. Interestingly, the secretary of state who was able to announce that the Seventeenth Amendment had been formally ratified and was therefore part of the Constitution was the long-time advocate of direct election of senators, William Jennings Bryan.

149. "It may seem incredible that what seemed to the Framers the obvious and crucial anticentralizing function of indirect election should pass almost unnoticed in 1911." Brooks, "*Garcia*, the Seventeenth Amendment, and the Role of the Supreme Court in Defending Federalism," 206. See also Bybee, "Ulysses at the Mast," 505, 538.

150. The same can be said of those who have studied the history and consequences of the Seventeenth Amendment. Hall, for example, reports the beneficial effects of the amendment to be (1) the elimination of legislative deadlocks, (2) the separation of state and national issues in state political campaigns, and (3) the prevention of certain scandalous legislative elections. He finds the baneful effects to be (1) increased costs to secure election to the Senate, (2) an accentuation of the time-consuming, nonlegislative functions of senators, and (3) the encouragement of demagogy. He also reports little or no change in such matters as the age, length of service, or previous occupations of senators and notes that popularly elected senators had less previous governmental service (although more were former governors) than their predecessors prior to 1913. He offers, however, no commentary whatsoever on the impact of the Seventeenth Amendment on federalism. Hall, "The History and Effect of the Seventeenth Amendment," 438-42.

Crook reports on the demographic, behavioral, and institutional consequences of the Seventeenth Amendment but likewise without ever mentioning federalism. She finds, demographically, that popularly elected senators have fewer family ties to Congress, are more likely to be born in the states they represent, are more likely to have an Ivy League education, and are likely to have had a higher level of prior governmental service. She finds, behaviorally, that House members are now more likely to seek a seat in the Senate and to do so with less tenure in the House. And she finds, institutionally, that the states are now more likely to have a split Senate delegation, and that the Senate now more closely matches the partisan composition of the House. Crook, "The Consequences of the Seventeenth Amendment," 183-95. In neither her conclusions nor her section on "Future Research" (195-97) does she even hint at the consequences of the amendment on the federal-state balance. See also Crook and John R. Hibbing, "A Not-So-Distant Mirror: The Seventeenth Amendment and Congressional Change," *American Political Science Review* 91 (December 1997): 845.

Hoebeke also ignores the federalism question in *The Road to Mass Democracy*. While the subtitle to his book is "Original Intent and the Seventeenth Amendment," he sees the original intent of those who provided for the election of the senate by state legislatures to be to check the excesses of popular government, not to protect the federal-state balance and the interest of the states as states.

Kyvig likewise presents the consequences of the Seventeenth Amendment in wholly democratic terms: It "altered political decision making both substantially and symbolically as it replaced the Founders' system of vesting power in an elite insulated from the masses with one that rendered the Senate more directly responsive to the public. " *Explicit and Authentic Acts,* 214; see also, 478.

The only genuine exceptions to this characterization of the scholarship on the Seventeenth Amendment are various contributions to the law journals. See Vikram David Amar, "Indirect Effects of Direct Election: A Structural Examination of the Seventeenth Amendment," *Vanderbilt Law Review* 49 (1996): 1347; Brooks, "*Garcia*, the Seventeenth Amendment, and the Role of the Supreme Court in Defending Federalism"; Bybee, "Ulysses at the Mast"; Laura E. Little, "An Excursion into the Uncharted Waters of the Seventeenth Amendment," *Temple Law Review* 64 (1991): 629; Virginia M. McInerney, "Federalism and the Seventeenth Amendment," *Journal of Christian Jurisprudence* 7 (1988): 153; Todd J. Zywicki, "Senators and Special Interests: A Public Choice Analysis of the Seventeenth Amendment," *Oregon Law Review* 73 (1994): 1007; and Zywicki, "Beyond the Shell and Husk of History."

151. *Congressional Record,* 53rd Cong., 2nd Sess., Vol. 26, 7774.

152. Senator Hoar's speech was printed as a Senate Document in 1906: "Speech by Senator George F. Hoar," April 6-7, 1893, *Senate Documents,* 59th Cong., 1st Sess., No. 232: 22.

153. "Speech by Senator George F. Hoar," 21. Hoar was quoting from Story, *Commentaries on the Constitution of the United States,* 2: 183.

154. "Speech by Senator George F. Hoar," 22.

155. *Congressional Record,* 61st Cong., 3rd Sess., 2243.

156. Alexander Hamilton, James Madison, and John Jay, *The Federalist,* ed. Jacob E. Cooke (New York: World Publishing Company, 1961), No. 39, 256

157. Abraham Lincoln, "The Perpetuation of Our Political Institutions," Address before the Springfield Young Men's Lyceum in 1838, in Richard N. Current (ed.), *The Political Thought of Abraham Lincoln* (New York: Bobbs-Merrill, 1967), 20.

Chapter 7

The Supreme Court's Attempts to Protect
the Original Federal Design

By ratifying the Seventeenth Amendment, the people in their pursuit of more democracy inattentively abandoned what the framers regarded as the primary constitutional means for the protection of the federal-state balance and the interests of the states as states.[1] Senator Elihu Root accurately predicted what followed: a rapid expansion by Congress of the reach and power of the national government at the expense of the states.[2] Since 1913, there has been a profound increase in the number and intrusiveness of congressional measures invading the "residuary sovereignty" of the states.[3]

Examples abound: The Federal Child Labor Act of 1916[4] and the Federal Child Labor Tax Act of 1919[5] were early examples; they trenched on the police power of the states to regulate the health, safety, and morals of the community by banning or by taxing the sale of goods in interstate commerce that, while themselves harmless, had been produced by child labor. The Adamson Act of 1916,[6] imposing maximum hours and minimum wages on the railroads, was another.[7]

They were followed in due course by the New Deal[8] and the passage of the Agricultural Adjustment Acts of 1933[9] and 1938,[10] regulating something as local as the amount of wheat farmers could grow for consumption on their own farms; the Railroad Retirement Act of 1934,[11] establishing a compulsory retirement and pension system for all carriers subject to the Interstate Commerce Act; the National Industrial Recovery Act of 1933[12] and the Fair Labor Standards Act of 1938,[13] regulating wages and hours for those engaged in interstate commerce; the Bituminous Coal Conservation Act of 1935,[14] regulating production and labor in the coal industry; the National Labor Relations Act of 1935,[15] protecting the rights of workers to form unions and to bargain collectively; the Social Security Act of 1935,[16] establishing a retirement plan for persons over the age of sixty-five; and the National Housing Act of 1937,[17] providing authority to lend money to local agencies for public housing.

There is no lack of more recent examples as well. They include the 1974 amendments to the Fair Labor Standards Act,[18] extending minimum wage/maximum hours requirements to the employees of states and their political subdivisions; the National Minimum Drinking Age Amendment Act of 1984,[19] conditioning a state's receipt of a portion of federal highway funding on whether it had raised the drinking age to twenty-one; the Low-Level Radioactive Waste Policy Amendments Act of 1985,[20] mandating that the states themselves must take title to radioactive waste within their borders if they fail otherwise to provide for its disposal; the Brady Handgun Violence Prevention Act of 1993,[21] mandating that state law-enforcement officers must conduct background checks for all individuals wishing to buy handguns; the Religious Freedom Restoration Act of 1993,[22] barring all governments (federal, state, or local) from burdening the free exercise of religion without a compelling state interest; the Motor-Voter Act of 1993,[23] requiring state departments of motor vehicles to distribute voter registration forms to those applying for driver's licenses or automobile registration; the Violence against Women Act of 1994,[24] providing a civil remedy in federal courts for victims of gender-motivated violence on the ground that state courts are unable or unwilling to provide appropriate relief; and, of course, scores of other equally intrusive but lower-profile federal mandates on the states and their political subdivisions.[25]

Not only have these post-Seventeenth Amendment congressional measures increased in number and intrusiveness, they have also become, in Theodore J. Lowi's terms, more abstract, general, novel, discretionary, and prescriptive (in contrast to earlier pre-Seventeenth Amendment legislation that was more concrete, specific, traditional, rule-bound, and proscriptive).[26] This development has led to what Lowi calls "policy without law"[27] and has weakened not only the states but the Congress itself—after all, with the Senate no longer answerable to state legislatures, it has felt increasingly free to join the House in legislating on every social, economic, or political problem that it perceives as confronting the nation, even if the resulting measures are little more than blank checks of authority to the executive branch and the federal bureaucracy.[28]

The Supreme Court's initial reaction to this congressional expansion of national power at the expense of the states was to attempt to fill the gap created by the ratification of the Seventeenth Amendment and to protect federalism by invalidating congressional measures either on dual-federalism grounds or through its narrow construction of the Commerce Clause. Using its power of judicial review in a manner never anticipated by the founding generation and never practiced or endorsed by the Marshall Court, it attempted to draw strict lines between federal and state power. These, however, were lines that the framers denied could be drawn; saw no need to try to draw, given the mode of electing the Senate; and neither intended nor authorized the Court to draw, identify, or enforce. Nonetheless, the Court came to regard its own analytical judgments concerning the limits of the powers of the federal government as an appropriate (and necessary) substitute for the now-dismantled structural solution of the framers. Perceiving the popularly elected Senate as no longer able to protect federalism, the Court undertook to perform that task itself, and during the period from the ratification of the Seventeenth Amendment in 1913 to its jurisprudential turnabout in the *Jones & Laughlin* case in 1937, it did exactly that, invalidating more federal statutes on federalism grounds during that quarter of a century[29] than it had during the entire period prior to the ratification of the Seventeenth Amendment.[30]

The Supreme Court became a passionate defender of the original federal design. It seemed completely unaware, however, that the Seventeenth Amendment had fundamentally altered that original design by making the Constitution both much more democratic and much less federal. It made the Constitution much more democratic because the people would thereafter directly elect the Senate, and it made the Constitution much less federal because those senators would no longer represent the interests of the states as such, but rather of the people who elected them.[31] By altering who the Senate represents and how federalism is protected, the Seventeenth Amendment altered the very meaning of federalism itself. The Supreme Court, however, refused to acknowledge this fact. While fond of quoting Chief Justice Marshall's words in *Marbury* v. *Madison*[32] that it is duty of the courts to interpret the Constitution and to say what the law is, it curiously but steadfastly refused to allow the Seventeenth Amendment and its structural and democratic consequences to enter its interpretation of the Constitution. It refused to recognize that, in the post-Seventeenth Amendment era, the original federal design is no longer controlling; it is no more a part of the Constitution the Supreme Court is called upon to interpret than, after the ratification of the post-Civil War amendments, the Constitution's original accommodation of slavery.

The Court's "Dual-Federalism" Jurisprudence

The Court's post-Seventeenth Amendment defense of the original federal design began with *Hammer* v. *Dagenhart*,[33] in which it invalidated on dual-federalism grounds the Federal Child Labor Act of 1916. In that act, Congress had prohibited the shipment in interstate commerce of goods produced in factories that employed children under the age of fourteen or that permitted children under the age of sixteen to work at night or for more than eight hours a day. The Court asserted that the states were coequal sovereigns with the federal government, that each level of government was supreme within its own sphere, and that the federal government could not therefore undertake any action, even in the exercise of its enumerated powers, that touched upon those functions the Constitution had reserved to the states. According to Justice William Day in his opinion for a five-member majority, the regulation of child labor was a "matter purely local in its character and over which no authority has been delegated to Congress in conferring the power to regulate commerce among the states."[34] Therefore, he concluded, because control over child labor was vested in the states under their traditional police power, Congress could not employ its delegated power to regulate commerce among the several states to interfere in this matter. "The grant of authority over a purely federal matter was not intended to destroy the local power always existing and carefully reserved to the states in the Tenth Amendment to the Constitution."[35]

This conclusion was, of course, in striking contrast to the Court's pre-Seventeenth Amendment opinions in *Champion* v. *Ames*,[36] *Hipolite Egg Company* v. *United States*,[37] and *Hoke* v. *United States*.[38] In each of these cases decided during the decade prior to the Amendment's ratification, the Court acknowledged that Congress could employ its powers under the Commerce Clause to regulate matters also subject to regulation under the states' traditional police powers.

In 1903, in *Champion*, the Court upheld the constitutionality of an 1894 federal statute prohibiting the interstate transportation of lottery tickets, even though the law served police-power ends. The first Justice John Marshall Harlan began by summarizing the Supreme Court's understanding of the Commerce Clause from *Gibbons* v. *Ogden* forward. He declared that the power to regulate commerce among the several states "is vested in Congress as absolutely as it would be in a single government," that this power "is plenary, complete in itself, and may be exerted by Congress to its utmost extent, subject only to such limitations as the Constitution imposes upon the exercise of powers granted by it," and that "in determining the character of regulations to be adopted Congress has a large discretion which is not to be controlled by the courts, simply because, in their opinion, such regulations may not be the best or most effective that could be employed."[39] Applying these principles, he declared that Congress clearly had the power "to provide that such commerce shall not be polluted by the carrying of lottery tickets from one state to another." Chief Justice Melville Fuller objected in his dissent on the grounds that the Congress could never legitimately employ the Commerce Clause as a means for reaching ends not delegated by the Constitution to it. "To hold that Congress has general police power [under the Commerce Clause] would be to hold that it may accomplish objects not entrusted to the general government, and to defeat the operation of the Tenth Amendment."[40] To this, Harlan replied that "if it be said that the 1894 act is inconsistent with the Tenth Amendment . . . the answer is that the power to regulate commerce among the states has been expressly delegated to Congress."[41]

Champion was a five-to-four decision, but eight years later, the Court unanimously applied Justice Harlan's logic in the *Hipolite Egg* case. Justice Joseph McKenna upheld Congress's power to pass the Pure Food and Drug Act of 1906,[42] arguing that "the power to regulate interstate commerce . . . is complete in itself, subject to no limitations except those found in the Constitution,"[43] and that Congress's power to ban adulterated goods from interstate commerce includes, as "an appropriate means to that end," the power to pass laws "seizing and condemning those goods at their point of destination." "The selection of such means is certainly within that breadth of discretion which we have said Congress possesses in the execution of the powers conferred upon it by the Constitution."[44]

And, in *Hoke*, handed down just months before the ratification of the Seventeenth Amendment, Justice McKenna again wrote for a unanimous Court when he upheld the White Slave Act.[45] The law, which forbade "the persuasion, inducement, and enticement of any women or girl to go from one place to another in interstate or foreign commerce, whether with or without her consent," for the "purpose of prostitution," was challenged on the grounds that "the right to regulate and control prostitution or any other immoralities of citizens, comes within the reserved police power of the several states and, under the Constitution, Congress cannot interfere therewith, either directly or indirectly, under the grant of power 'to regulate commerce between the states.'"[46] McKenna observed that "there is unquestionably a control in the states over the morals of their citizens, and, it may be admitted, it extends to making prostitution a crime. It is a control, however, which can be exercised only within the jurisdiction of the states." But, he continued, "there is a domain which the states cannot reach and over which Congress alone has power; and if such power be exerted to control what the states cannot, it is an argument for—not against—its legality." McKenna acknowledged that "our dual form of government has its perplexities, state and nation having different spheres of jurisdiction." Yet he stressed that "it must be kept in mind that we are one people, and the powers reserved to the states and those conferred on the nation are adapted to be exercised, whether independently or concurrently, to promote the general welfare, material and moral."[47] And, reviewing "the principle established" by the Court's past cases, he declared that "Congress's power ... over transportation 'among the several States' ... is complete in itself" and that rules by Congress adopted under the Commerce Clause "may have the quality of police regulations."[48] The only conclusion, therefore, was that, "[i]f the facility of interstate transportation can be taken away from the demoralization of lotteries, the debasement of obscene literature, the contagion of diseased cattle or persons, the impurity of food and drugs, the like facility can be taken away from the systematic enticement to and enslavement in prostitution and debauchery of women and, more insistently, of girls."[49]

Congress responded to *Hammer* by passing the Federal Child Labor Tax Law of 1919, which banned the use of child labor by imposing a 10 percent tax on the profits of all businesses engaged in interstate commerce that employed children. However, in *Bailey* v. *Drexel Furniture Company*,[50] the Court once again used dual-federalism arguments to invalidate this measure as well. Chief Justice William Howard Taft reiterated Justice Day's point in *Hammer* that the regulation of child labor was "a purely state authority"[51] and argued that, just as the first child labor act "was not, in fact, regulation of interstate commerce, but rather that of state concerns," so, too, the second child labor act was not really a tax but a penalty to reach and regulate what the Constitution had reserved exclusively for state control.

These cases are well-known; less well-known is *Hill* v. *Wallace*,[52] in which the Court declared that *Bailey* "completely covers this case" and held unconstitutional a provision of the Future Trading Act of 1921 that imposed a "tax of 20 cents a bushel on every bushel involved therein, upon each contract of sale of grain for future delivery, except ... where such contracts are made by or through a member of a board of trade which has been designated by the Secretary of Agriculture as a 'contract market.'" Chief Justice Taft condemned the provision as "a complete regulation of [state] boards of trade" and therefore not "a valid exercise of the taxing power."[53]

The Court's use of dual federalism in *Hammer, Bailey,* and *Hill* was unfortunate. To begin with, it was imprudent. Prior to these cases, its most notorious use of dual federalism was in Chief Justice Roger Taney's infamous majority opinion in *Dred Scott*, wherein he argued that Congress's attempt through the Missouri Compromise of 1820 to limit the spread of slavery in the territory of the United States unconstitutionally infringed on the states' reserved power to legislate on slavery.[54] Taney made the bizarre argument that Congress's power under Article IV, section 3 of the Constitution to regulate the territory of the United States was, in fact, limited simply to that territory which at the time the Constitution was ratified "belonged to, or was claimed by, the United States . . . and can have no influence upon a territory afterwards acquired from a foreign Government."[55] The Congress, Taney insisted, could acquire and regulate new territory only as a "trustee" or "agent" of "the people of the several states"[56] and could exercise no power under the Constitution over the slave property of the people "beyond what that instrument confers, nor lawfully deny any right which it has reserved."[57] Taney, therefore, held that Congress acted unconstitutionally when it passed the Missouri Compromise and prohibited the spread of slavery into that portion of the Louisiana Purchase north of thirty-six degrees thirty minutes north latitude.[58]

Taney's opinion in *Dred Scott* stands in stark contrast to Marshall's opinion in *McCulloch*. Marshall began his opinion by acknowledging that the question of the limits of Congress's delegated powers had to be "decided peacefully" or it would "remain a source of hostile legislation, perhaps of hostility of a still more serious nature."[59] His answer to that question was to declare that, since the Congress was as "equally" representative of the people and the states as the state legislatures themselves, it was up to the "Congress alone . . . [to] make the election" of where "the respective powers" of the federal government ended and those of the states began.[60] He adopted Madison's and Hamilton's "means-ends" approach to constitutional interpretation, emphasizing as well the importance of taking into consideration long-standing practice when considering the limits of congressional power. Taney, by contrast, employed the principle of dual federalism and flatly refused to allow Congress to "elect" what it considered to be appropriate means to the ends of the Constitution. He also totally ignored Congress's long-standing practice of "regulating" the Louisiana Purchase. By denying to Congress what Marshall fully granted, Taney and his dual-federalism premises helped bring about that very "hostility of a still more serious nature" that Marshall feared (i.e., the Civil War).[61]

Prudentially, it was not wise for Day or Taft to ground their findings of unconstitutionality on the logic of *Dred Scott*. Their failing, however, goes beyond a mere lack of prudence. Dual federalism, even prior to the ratification of the Seventeenth Amendment and its fundamental alteration of federalism, was vulnerable to one devastating objection, cogently expressed by Justice Oliver Wendell Holmes in his dissent in *Hammer*: "[I]f an act is within the powers specifically conferred upon Congress, it seems to me that it is not made any less constitutional because of the indirect effects that it may have, however obvious it may be that it will have those effects, and that we are not at liberty upon such grounds to hold it void."[62] In their efforts to overcome this objection, both Day and Taft were forced implicitly to rewrite the Commerce and Tax Clauses so that they would read: Congress shall have power to regulate commerce among the several states or to lay and collect taxes, unless these powers interfere with the domestic policies of a state. Justice Day felt compelled to go even further and explicitly rewrite the Tenth Amendment as well, declaring that "the Nation is made up of States to which are entrusted the powers of local government. And to them and to the people the powers not *expressly* delegated to the National Government are reserved."[63] In so doing, he denied the historical record; when the First Congress considered what would become the Tenth Amendment, it flatly rejected a proposal by Elbridge Gerry to insert into it the word "expressly."[64] He also ignored judicial precedent; in *McCulloch*, Marshall held that, since the word "expressly" had been intentionally omitted from the amendment, the question whether the Congress could exercise a particular power was to be answered by "a fair construction of the whole instrument."[65]

Day appears to have been driven to these lengths because of his belief that the Court was the sole defender of federalism. "This court," he declared, "has no more important function than that which devolves upon it the obligation to preserve inviolate the constitutional limitations upon the exercise of authority federal and state to the end that each may continue to discharge, harmoniously with the other, the duties entrusted to it by the Constitution."[66] Day never identifies the source of the Court's obligation to "preserve inviolate" the original federal design, nor does he address the fact that the framers expected that federalism would be protected structurally—by the mode of electing the Senate—rather than judicially. For Day, federalism was at risk, some body needed to act, and that body was the Court: "The far-reaching result of upholding the act cannot be more plainly indicated than by pointing out that, if Congress can thus regulate matters entrusted to local authority by prohibition of the movement of commodities in interstate commerce, all freedom of commerce will be at an end, and the power of the States over local matters may be eliminated, and, thus, our system of government be practically destroyed."[67] Day utterly failed to appreciate that the original federal design (which, of course, is what he means when he speaks of "our system of government") was, if not "destroyed," then surely profoundly altered by the Seventeenth Amendment.

Moreover, he seems wholly unaware that there is simply no historical evidence to suggest that the people who, in the name of democracy, ratified the Seventeenth Amendment, intended to transfer the power to protect that original federal design from the indirectly elected Senate to an appointed Court so that it might invalidate the very measures now passed by their democratically elected Senate.[68]

The Court's Narrow Construction of the Commerce Clause

The many deficiencies of dual federalism became so painfully apparent that the Court no longer employed it to invalidate a congressional enactment after *Trusler* v. *Crooks*[69] in 1926.[70] Rather, the Court shifted its ground and found offensive federal legislation unconstitutional based on its narrow reading of the Commerce Clause and its use of the "direct effects/indirect effects" test. To do so, it had to abandon Marshall's expansive understanding of the Commerce Clause as he had articulated it in *Gibbons*. "The word 'commerce,'" the Court now insisted, "is the equivalent of the phrase 'intercourse for the purposes of trade.'"[71] On that basis, it denied that the Congress had plenary power under the Commerce Clause to regulate agriculture in *United States* v. *Butler*[72] and mining in *Carter* v. *Carter Coal Company.*[73]

These, of course, were not the first cases in which the Court had narrowed Marshall's expansive definition of commerce in *Gibbons*. In *United States* v. *E. C. Knight Company* in 1895, the Court asserted that "commerce succeeds to manufacture, and is not a part of it"[74] and, on that basis, held that the Sherman Anti-Trust Act of 1890 could not be used against the American Sugar Refining Company and its monopoly control of the nation's sugar refining business. It was not, however, until the post-Seventeenth Amendment era that the Court began to declare federal statutes unconstitutional based on its narrow definition of commerce.[75]

Unlike Marshall in *Gibbons*, the Court, in the initial post-Seventeenth Amendment era, was simply unwilling to trust "the wisdom and discretion of Congress" as "the sole restraint" to "secure" the people from "abuse" of the Commerce Clause.[76] It saw the very principle of federalism itself as hanging in the balance. As Justice George Sutherland noted in his majority opinion in *Carter Coal Company*:

> Every journey to a forbidden end begins with the first step, and the danger of such a step by the federal government in the direction of taking over the powers of the states is that the end of the journey may find the states so despoiled of their powers, or—what may amount to the same thing—

so relieved of the responsibilities which possession of the powers
necessarily enjoins, as to reduce them to little more than geographical
subdivisions of the national domain. It is safe to say that, if, when the
Constitution was under consideration, it had been thought that any such
danger lurked behind its plain words, it would never have been ratified.[77]

Sutherland seemed unaware that the people who ratified the Constitution
feared no such danger, for they were secure in the knowledge that the mode
of electing the Senate would ensure that the states would not be reduced to
"geographical subdivisions." The ratification of the Seventeenth Amendment
removed that democratic and structural protection of federalism and
apparently warranted, in the minds of the members of the Court majority in
these cases, the Court's activist intervention. Since this judicial protection
was neither democratically nor structurally based, it was destined to fail.

In *E. C. Knight*, the Court acknowledged that, while sugar manufacturing
was not commerce, it nevertheless could affect interstate commerce. It
insisted, however, that the American Sugar Refining Company was not
covered by the Sherman Anti-Trust Act, because its monopoly control of
sugar refining affected commerce "only incidentally and indirectly."[78] The
Court thereby introduced a crucial distinction between intrastate activities
having a "direct effect" on commerce (and therefore subject to congressional
regulation) and intrastate activities having only an "indirect effect" on
commerce (and therefore beyond Congress's reach). Again, however, it
was not until after the Seventeenth Amendment was ratified that the Court
began to use this "direct effects/indirect effects" test to invalidate, as opposed
to merely limit the reach of, a federal statute. It did this for the first time in
1935 when it held in *A. L. A. Schechter Poultry Corporation* v. *United
States*[79] that the National Industrial Recovery Act of 1933 was
unconstitutional because, inter alia, Congress was attempting to regulate
intrastate acts that only indirectly affected interstate commerce. The next
year, in *Carter* v. *Carter Coal Company*, it again employed this test to find
Congress's efforts to regulate coal production unconstitutional.

In *Schechter*, Chief Justice Charles Evans Hughes confidently asserted
that the distinction between a direct and an indirect effect was "clear in
principle";[80] however, just one year later in *Carter Coal*, Justice Sutherland
confessed that, "[w]hether the effect of a given activity or condition is direct or
indirect is not always easy to determine." Struggling to articulate a distinction,
he declared that "[t]he word 'direct' implies that the activity or condition invoked
or blamed shall operate proximately—not mediately, remotely, or collaterally—
to produce the effect. It connotes the absence of an efficient intervening agency
or condition." And, he continued, "the extent of the effect bears no logical

relation to its character. The distinction between a direct and an indirect effect turns not upon the magnitude of either the cause or the effect, but entirely upon the manner in which the effect has been brought about." He acknowledged that "[i]t is quite true that rules of law are sometimes qualified by considerations of degree," but he insisted that "the matter of degree has no bearing upon the question here, since that question is not what is the extent of the local activity or condition, or the extent of the effect produced upon interstate commerce, but what is the relation between the activity or condition and the effect?"[81] Sutherland's clarification was, of course, completely unhelpful, and it came as no surprise that, in *Jones & Laughlin*, decided during its next term, the Court totally abandoned the "direct effect/indirect effect" test and held that, if intrastate activities "have such a close and substantial relation to interstate commerce that their control is essential or appropriate to protect that commerce from burdens and obstructions, Congress cannot be denied the power to exercise that control."[82]

With its decision in *Jones & Laughlin*, the Court abandoned its defense of federalism; no longer would it attempt to draw lines that the framers denied could be drawn and that they never intended the Court to try to draw;[83] no longer would it attempt to define narrowly a congressional power that was, in fact, plenary. David P. Currie argues that, with *Jones & Laughlin*, "constitutional federalism died."[84] A better formulation still would have been to declare that federalism died in 1913 with the ratification of the Seventeenth Amendment,[85] but it took until 1937 for the Supreme Court to learn this lesson.

What it took the Court a quarter of a century to learn, it took it another thirty-nine years to forget. In 1976, in *National League of Cities* v. *Usery*,[86] the Court attempted once again to breathe life into the corpse of federalism when it held that Congress could not exercise its power under the Commerce Clause "in a fashion that impairs the States' integrity or their ability to function effectively in a federal system."[87] Announcing for a bare majority that Congress lacked the power "to directly displace the States' freedom to structure integral operations in areas of traditional governmental functions,"[88] Justice William Rehnquist declared unconstitutional the 1974 amendments to the Fair Labor Standards Act that extended maximum hours and minimum wage requirements to employees of states and their political subdivisions. "One undoubted attribute of state sovereignty is the States' power to determine the wages which shall be paid to those whom they employ in order to carry out their governmental functions, what hours those persons will work, and what compensation will be provided where these employees maybe called upon to work overtime."[89]

The federal design created by the framers obliged the Court to rule as it did, or so Justice Rehnquist asserted: "If Congress may withdraw from the

States the authority to make those fundamental employment decisions upon which their systems for the performance of these functions must rest, we think there would be little left of the States' 'separate and independent existence.'"[90] The implication of Rehnquist's opinion was clear. In the absence of the structural protection of federalism provided by the original mode of electing the Senate, the Court could no longer consider Marshall's arguments in *Gibbons* valid and Congress's power under the Commerce Clause "plenary";[91] rather, it would treat Congress's Commerce Clause power as limited by the Court's judgment concerning what "would impair the States' ability to function effectively in the federal system."[92] It needs to be underscored, however, that Rehnquist was speaking about the federal system as originally designed, not as fundamentally altered by the adoption and ratification of the Seventeenth Amendment.

Eight years later, the Court again abandoned its efforts to defend federalism in *Garcia* v. *San Antonio Metropolitan Transit Authority*;[93] it explicitly overturned *Usery* and held that government-owned mass-transit systems were indeed subject to the obligations of the Fair Labor Standards Act. It confessed that it was simply unable to draw the line, on which the logic of *Usery* fundamentally depended, between "traditional" governmental functions that the Court was to protect from congressional interference and "nontraditional" or "proprietary" functions performed by state and local governments that the Congress was allowed to regulate.[94] "We doubt that courts ultimately can identify principled constitutional limitations on the scope of the Congress's Commerce Clause powers over the States merely by relying on a priori definitions of state sovereignty."[95]

Justice Harry Blackmun held for the majority (but, as in *Usery* itself, only for a five-member majority) that the protection of federalism must come from the political process, not the courts. "[T]he principal means chosen by the Framers to ensure the role of the States in the federal system lies in the structure of the Federal Government itself." He elaborated:

> It is no novelty to observe that the composition of the Federal Government was designed in large part to protect the States from overreaching by Congress. The Framers thus gave the States a role in the selection both of the Executive and the Legislative Branches of the Federal Government. The States were vested with indirect influence over the House of Representatives and the Presidency by their control of electoral qualifications and their role in Presidential elections. They were given more direct influence in the Senate, where each State received equal representation and each Senator was to be selected by the legislature of his State. The significance attached to the States' equal representation in

the Senate is underscored by the prohibition of any constitutional amendment divesting a State of equal representation without the State's consent.[96]

Blackmun's language, while an accurate-enough description of how federalism was originally protected,[97] was nonetheless misleading in a crucial respect: He maintained the fiction that federalism continues to be protected structurally.[98] With this assertion, Blackmun showed that he, no less than Rehnquist in *Usery*, had forgotten the fundamental lesson of the Seventeenth Amendment, viz., that federalism was dead. While Blackmun did acknowledge "that changes in the structure of the Federal Government have taken place since 1789,"[99] and specifically mentioned the adoption and ratification of the Seventeenth Amendment in that regard, he nevertheless insisted that the structural limitation "that the constitutional scheme imposes on the Commerce Clause to protect the 'States as States'" remained sufficiently in place and that federalism retained its vitality.[100]

As proof that federalism was alive and well, Blackmun noted that, while the Congress had subjected state mass-transit systems to federal wage-and-hours obligations, it had simultaneously provided extensive funding (over $22 billion) for state and local mass transit. He reported that "Congress has not simply placed a financial burden on the shoulders of states and localities that operate mass transit systems, but has provided substantial countervailing financial assistance as well, assistance that may leave individual mass transit systems better off than they would have been had Congress never intervened at all in the area." Blackmun therefore drew what he considered to be the only conclusion: "Congress' treatment of public mass transit reinforces our conviction that the national political process systematically protects States from the risk of having their functions in that area handicapped by Commerce Clause regulation."[101] Blackmun's evidence, however, utterly fails to support his contention that the current constitutional structure actually protects the interests of "States as States" or that constitutional federalism retains any vitality whatsoever. Quite the contrary; it shows only that, in the post-Seventeenth Amendment era, members of Congress will look after the interests of those subordinate to them and that the states have now been reduced to that subordinate status. Whereas, for the framers, senators could be trusted to look after the interests of the states because the state legislatures were their masters, for Blackmun and his colleagues, the members of Congress can be trusted to look after the interests of the states because the states are now their supplicants whose well-being depends on their grace.

What Justice Antonin Scalia said of the *Lemon* test[102] in *Lamb's Chapel v. Center Moriches Union Free School District*[103] can also be said of the corpse of federalism: It is "[l]ike some ghoul in a late night horror movie that repeatedly sits up in its grave and shuffles abroad, after being repeatedly killed and buried." It is therefore not surprising that, eleven years after *Garcia*, the Court's desire to exhume the original federal design and to draw lines between the Congress's permissible and impermissible use of its Commerce Clause power once again became irresistible. In *United States* v. *Lopez*,[104] it declared unconstitutional the Gun Free School Zones Act of 1990, not because it trenched on "state integrity" or the "attributes of state sovereignty" but simply because it exceeded the scope of the Commerce Clause. Reviewing case law, Chief Justice Rehnquist held for what was again a bare majority that the Congress can regulate intrastate activity only when it "substantially affects interstate commerce."[105] Did possession of a handgun within 1000 feet of a school substantially affect interstate commerce? The federal government in its defense of the statute and the four dissenting justices said "yes," claiming that possession of a firearm in a school zone may result in violent crime and that violent crime can be expected to affect the functioning of the national economy because the costs of violent crime are substantial and because violent crime reduces the willingness of individuals to travel to areas within the country that are perceived to be unsafe. They also claimed that the presence of guns in schools poses a substantial threat to the educational process by threatening the learning environment and that a handicapped educational process, in turn, results in a less-productive citizenry, thereby adversely affecting the nation's economic well-being. However, Rehnquist and his colleagues in the majority said "no," insisting that, if they were to accept the federal government's argument, it would be "difficult to perceive any limitation on federal power, even in areas such as criminal law enforcement or education where States historically have been sovereign. Thus, if we were to accept the Government's arguments, we [would be] . . . hard pressed to posit any activity by an individual that Congress is without power to regulate."[106]

Rehnquist admitted "legal uncertainty" concerning whether "an intrastate activity is commercial or noncommercial,"[107] and he acknowledged that there were no "precise formulations"[108] for what the Congress could or could not regulate. He even conceded that "some of our prior cases have taken long steps" down the road to "convert[ing] congressional authority under the Commerce Clause to a general police power of the sort retained by the States" and that "[t]he broad language in these opinions has suggested the possibility of additional expansion."[109] Nonetheless, Rehnquist "declined" to take that next step. Rather, he put his foot down and said "no," even though he never provided a compelling explanation for why he drew where he did the line between Congress's permissible and impermissible use of the Commerce Clause.

Justice Clarence Thomas concurred in *Lopez* even as he rejected the majority's use of the substantial-effects test. He declared that much of Congress's enumerated powers in Article I, Section 8 (including the Foreign and Indian Commerce Clauses themselves) "would be surplusage" if Congress has authority over all matters that substantially affect interstate commerce. An interpretation of the Commerce Clause that renders "the rest of Section 8 superfluous simply cannot be correct. Yet," Thomas continued, "this Court's Commerce Clause jurisprudence has endorsed just such an interpretation: the power we have accorded Congress has swallowed Article I, Section 8."[110] He attributed the growth of federal power to the Court's failure to interpret the Commerce Clause correctly, but a more likely culprit was the Seventeenth Amendment's elimination of the structural protection that the election of the Senate by state legislatures had provided to federalism.[111]

Thomas said that he awaited "a future case" in which the Court could reconsider the substantial-effects test and construct a new "standard" that better "reflects the text and history of the Commerce Clause."[112] There is, however, little reason to expect that a future Court will be more successful than past ones in drawing a clear line between the powers of the federal and state governments. As Lino A. Graglia has noted, judicial second-guessing of Congress's use of its Commerce Clause power can never effectively protect federalism, for "principled limits cannot be defined. Because the power to regulate interstate commerce would seem necessarily to include the power to regulate things that affect it, and all things affect it, the question is unavoidably one of degree. The question presented in each case is not whether a particular activity affects interstate commerce, but whether it affects it significantly enough to justify federal regulation, considering the loss of local autonomy involved." Graglia states the inevitable conclusion: Since that question "is one of magnitude (an empirical question), the Court is in no position to contradict a (presumed) congressional determination of the substantiality of the effect. It is difficult for the Court to contradict Congress's definition of substantiality when it has no alternative definition of its own."[113]

A better approach in that "future case" would be for the Court forthrightly to announce that federalism died with the ratification of the Seventeenth Amendment, that the Court therefore is withdrawing explicitly from reviewing congressional power under the Commerce Clause, and that it will hereafter treat Commerce Clause questions as political questions, acknowledging in the language of *Baker* v. *Carr*[114] that there are no "judicially discoverable and manageable standards for resolving" them and that the resolution of these questions was "constitutionally commit[ted]"

by the framers to "a coordinate political department,"[115] i.e., to the Congress
consisting of the House (elected by the people) and the Senate (whether
elected indirectly by state legislatures or directly by the people).

The Court's Commandeering Jurisprudence

While the Court has attempted, for the most part, to protect the original
federal design primarily through its use of dual-federalism principles or its
narrow construction of the Commerce Clause, as of late, it has also begun
to protect it by declaring that Congress lacks the power to "commandeer"
state officials into carrying out federal programs. In *New York* v. *United
States*,[116] the Court held unconstitutional a key provision of the Low-Level
Radioactive Waste Policy Amendments Act of 1985 that required a state
that had failed to provide for the disposal of all of its internally generated
waste by a particular date to take title to and possession of that waste and
become liable for all damages suffered by the generator or owner of that
waste as a result of the state's failure to take prompt possession. Justice
Sandra Day O'Connor, a former state legislator and state court judge,
asserted for a six-member majority that, "[n]o matter how powerful the
federal interest involved, the Constitution simply does not give Congress
the authority to require the States to regulate. The Constitution instead gives
Congress the authority to regulate matters directly and to preempt contrary
state regulation. Where a federal interest is sufficiently strong to cause
Congress to legislate, it must do so directly; it may not conscript state
governments as its agents."[117]

Why does the Congress have the authority to regulate either directly or
through preemption but not through conscription or commandeering?
O'Connor's provisional answer is that commandeering diminishing the
"accountability of both state and federal officials."[118] If Congress pre-empts
state law-making and regulates directly, "it is the Federal Government that
makes the decision in full view of the public, and it will be federal officials
that suffer the consequences if the decisions turn out to be detrimental or
unpopular." If, on the other hand, Congress commandeers the states to
regulate, "it may be state officials who will bear the brunt of public
disapproval, while the federal officials who devised the regulatory program
may remain insulated from the electoral ramifications of their decision."[119]
Accountability is, of course, an important consideration, and interestingly,
it was fostered by the original mode of electing the Senate—if a state's
senators were to agree to federal legislation that conscripted their state's
officials to carry out onerous and unpopular programs, their state legislature

would be certain not to reelect them. The ratification of the Seventeenth Amendment, however, removed that mechanism for promoting accountability and apparently, for O'Connor, made it necessary for the Court to step in and fill the gap. But clearly O'Connor felt uneasy about declaring commandeering unconstitutional because of its tendency to undermine accountability, and so she was obliged to move on to her final answer which is that coercing the states into enacting or enforcing a federal regulatory program "infringe[s] upon the core of state sovereignty reserved by the Tenth Amendment" and "is inconsistent with the federal structure of our Government established by the Constitution."[120]

O'Connor acknowledged that the Tenth Amendment declares but "a truism that all is retained which has not been surrendered." Nonetheless, she insisted that the Tenth Amendment is as enforceable and contains limitations as identifiable as the First Amendment itself.

> Congress exercises its conferred powers subject to the limitations contained in the Constitution. Thus, for example, under the Commerce Clause Congress may regulate publishers engaged in interstate commerce, but Congress is constrained in the exercise of that power by the First Amendment. The Tenth Amendment likewise restrains the power of Congress, but this limit is not derived from the text of the Tenth Amendment itself, which, as we have discussed, is essentially a tautology. Instead, the Tenth Amendment confirms that the power of the Federal Government is subject to limits that may, in a given instance, reserve power to the States.[121]

How are these limits to be determined if they are not "derived from the text"? O'Connor's exposition is unclear on this matter, but the answer apparently is that they come from the Court's own sense of its responsibility to protect the original federal design and the "core of state sovereignty." As she asserts, "[t]he Tenth Amendment thus directs *us* to determine, as in this case, whether an incident of state sovereignty is protected by a limitation on an Article I power."[122] How does a truism, a tautology, help the Court to "determine" whether that core has been penetrated by the federal government, whether the line separating constitutionality from unconstitutionality has been crossed? It is a question O'Connor sidesteps.

O'Connor's answers to the questions of what are the limits that the Tenth Amendment imposes on the federal government and where is the line to be drawn separating permissible from impermissible federal legislation contrast strikingly with the answers of the founding generation. Their entire understanding of the Tenth Amendment was intimately connected to their understanding of federalism and their sense of how it was protected by the mode they had provided for electing the Senate. Senators could be trusted to scrutinize whether proposed federal legislation would violate the "core of state sovereignty" and to refuse to assent to it if it did. The Tenth Amendment was appropriately a truism, for the mode of electing the Senate ensured that the reserved power of the states would remain inviolable. Once the Seventeenth Amendment was ratified, however, the framers' structural answer to these questions was no longer available, leaving O'Connor and her colleagues to choose between only two other possible answers: trusting the line drawn by the popular branches or trusting the line they would draw. Not surprisingly, O'Connor and her colleagues chose the answer most flattering to the Court.

The issue of "commandeering" state officials surfaced again in *Printz* v. *United States*,[123] as the Court considered the constitutionality of that provision of the Brady Handgun Violence Prevention Act of 1993 that temporarily commanded state and local law-enforcement officers to conduct background checks on prospective handgun purchasers. In a five-to-four decision, Justice Scalia found this congressional command to be "fundamentally incompatible with our constitutional system of dual sovereignty" and therefore unconstitutional.[124] A close look at his opinion, however, reveals just how problematic Justice Scalia considered the Court's commandeering jurisprudence to be, for he ultimately held the law to be unconstitutional, not because it violated the principle of federalism but because it violated the principle of separation of powers.

Unlike O'Connor in *New York*, Scalia conceded that there is "no constitutional text," not even the Tenth Amendment, that would justify Court invalidation of a commandeering statute so long as it was enacted by Congress pursuant to an express delegation of power enumerated in Article I, Section 8.[125] On what bases, then, could Scalia find such a statute to be unconstitutional? He identified three: historical understanding and practice, the structure of the Constitution, and the Court's past decisions.

Concerning the first basis, historical understanding and practice, Scalia reviewed the historical records of the early Congresses, observed that they had studiously "avoided use of this highly attractive power," and concluded that, since "the power was thought not to exist" in the early Republic, it therefore does not exist now.[126] His conclusion, however, cannot withstand scrutiny. Scalia equated the failure of the early congresses to use its power to commandeer state officials with a conviction on their part that they did not possess such a power in the first place. As Justice John Paul Stevens noted in his dissent, "we have never suggested that the failure of the early Congresses to address the scope of federal power in a particular area or to exercise a particular authority was an argument against its existence."[127] Scalia did not consider the possibility that the power to commandeer may indeed have been understood by the early Congresses to exist but that the pre-Seventeenth Amendment Senate, representing the interests of the states as states, simply refused to accede to its use. Contemporaneous use of a power that Congress has always had, but that it has not previously exercised because the mode of electing the Senate practically prevented it use, is not rendered constitutionally suspect simply because the structural impediment against its use has been removed by constitutional amendment.

Scalia then turned to his second basis for finding the statute unconstitutional: the structure of the Constitution. Here, however, Scalia completely ignored federalism and focused instead only on separation of powers. He noted that "[t]he Constitution does not leave to speculation who is to administer the laws enacted by Congress; the President, it says, 'shall take Care that the Laws be faithfully executed,' personally and through officers whom he appoints." The Brady Act, however, effectively transferred this responsibility to thousands of state and local law-enforcement officers in the fifty states who were commanded to implement the program "without meaningful Presidential control." Scalia pointed out that the framers insisted on "unity in the Federal Executive—to insure both vigor and accountability." That unity," he concluded, "would be shattered, and the power of the President would be subject to reduction, if Congress could act as effectively without the President as with him, by simply requiring state officers to execute its laws."[128] This is a powerful argument, and it is, in fact, one that Scalia had made before in his dissent in *Morrison* v. *Olson.*[129] It is not, however, a federalism argument; it is not an argument justifying invalidation of federal law on the grounds of preserving "our constitutional system of dual sovereignty."

The fact that Scalia felt obliged to wrap the kernels of his separation-of-powers argument in the husk of federalism shows his mastery of the persuasive arts—when Scalia made this same separation-of-powers argument explicitly in *Morrison*, he spoke for himself alone; when he hid it in a defense of federalism, he spoke for a five-member majority. The fact that Scalia found it necessary to shift the ground on which the Court's commandeering jurisprudence was based from the shifting sands of federalism to the rock-solid principles of separation of powers shows also how problematic the Court's reasoning in *New York* was, and it shows what little faith Scalia put in the Court's past decisions—the third basis he identified for finding the commandeering provisions of the Brady Bill unconstitutional. While he insisted that "the prior jurisprudence of this

Court" was "conclusive,"[130] and while he paid painstaking obeisance to "our constitutional system of dual sovereignty," it was clear that his intention was to rely on, and his goal was to vindicate, his view of separation of powers in *Morrison*, not O'Connor's view of federalism in *New York*.

City of Boerne and Section 5 of the Fourteenth Amendment

City of Boerne v. *Flores* is perhaps the most brazen effort by the recent Supreme Court to protect a pre-Seventeenth Amendment understanding of federalism at the expense of the people's post-Seventeenth Amendment commitment to democracy. In *City of Boerne*, the Supreme Court, in the name of protecting the "federal balance," struck down the Religious Freedom Restoration Act of 1993, passed unanimously by the United States House of Representatives and by a vote of ninety-seven to three in the Senate and enthusiastically signed into law by President William Clinton. The Court asserted that the Congress unconstitutionally exceeded the powers conferred on it by Section 5 of the Fourteenth Amendment and thereby upset federalism. However, if ever there was an amendment intended to enhance the power of Congress at the expense of the Court, it was the Fourteenth Amendment. After all, it begins in Section 1 by explicitly repudiating the Supreme Court's outrageous assertion in *Dred Scott* that Blacks could not be citizens of the United States, and it concludes in Section 5 by giving to the Congress, and not to the Court, the power to enforce its provisions. Additionally, if ever there was an amendment consciously intended to strengthen the power of Congress at the expense of the states, it was also the Fourteenth Amendment.[131] The Civil War established on the fields of battle that we were indeed a nation, not a confederacy, and the Fourteenth Amendment ratified that fact both in how it limited the states and in how it empowered the Congress—the mode of electing the Senate ensuring that Congress's vast new powers under Section 5 would, nevertheless, not be used to the detriment of the states. Yet, in *City of Boerne*, the Court, in the name of federalism[132] and in the face of a virtually unanimous Congress, arrogantly exercised its power of judicial review. Its obsession with protecting the original federal design, weakened by the Fourteenth Amendment and left without structural support and thereby fundamentally altered by the Seventeenth Amendment, was matched by its complete disregard for the democratic principle embodied in the Seventeenth Amendment.

To rule as it did, the Court majority had to (1) ignore the original understanding of those who drafted the Fourteenth Amendment; (2) reject the seminal construction of Section 5 of the Fourteenth Amendment given by the Court in *Ex Parte Virginia*;[133] (3) repudiate an entire series of recent cases based on *Ex Parte Virginia*, on which both its modern voting rights and civil rights jurisprudence is built; (4) construe Congress's power to "enforce" the provisions of the Fourteenth Amendment so narrowly that it becomes merely remedial; and (5) curtail even that power to remedying only those problems that the Court itself considers serious enough to justify federal intervention.

Concerning the original understanding of those who drafted the Fourteenth Amendment, Justice Anthony Kennedy argued that "[t]he Fourteenth Amendment's history confirms the remedial, rather than substantive, nature of the Enforcement Clause."[134] His historical analysis was so infirm, however, that, as Michael W. McConnell notes, "the Court's most outspoken proponent of originalist interpretation, Justice Scalia, declined to join this section of the opinion."[135] Kennedy was forced to ignore, for example, the statement from Senator Jacob Howard of Michigan, who, in introducing the Fourteenth Amendment in the Senate, described Section 5 as a "direct affirmative delegation of power to Congress." Senator Howard continued:

> It casts upon Congress the responsibility of seeing to it, for the future, that all the sections of the amendment are carried out in good faith, and that no State infringes the rights of persons or property. I look upon this clause as indispensable for the reason that it thus imposes upon Congress this power and this duty. It enables Congress, in case the States shall enact laws in conflict with the principles of the amendment to correct that legislation by a formal congressional enactment.[136]

In fact, in complete contradiction of Kennedy's conclusion, the historical record can actually sustain the contentions that Section 5 grants exclusively to Congress the power to enforce the Fourteenth Amendment and that judicial enforcement constitutes an encroachment upon legislative prerogatives. This clearly was the understanding of Judge Learned Hand,[137] and there is considerable evidence to support it. Thus, Representative James F. Wilson of Iowa, Chairman of the House Judiciary Committee and floor manager of the Civil Rights Acts of 1866, argued as follows concerning the meaning of Section 2 of the Thirteenth Amendment, which provides in language identical to Section 5 of the Fourteenth Amendment that "Congress shall have power to enforce this article by appropriate legislation":

> Here, certainly, is an express delegation of power: How shall it be exercised? Who shall select the means through which the office of this

power shall effect the end designed by the people when they placed the provision in the Constitution?

> Who will say that the means provided by this second section (of the Civil Rights Act of 1866) are not appropriate for the enforcement of . . . the amendment abolishing slavery . . . ? The end is legitimate, because it is defined by the Constitution itself. The end is the maintenance of freedom to the citizen. . . . A man who enjoys the civil rights mentioned in this bill cannot be reduced to slavery. Anything which protects him in the possession of these rights insures him against reduction to slavery. This settles its constitutionality. . . . Of the necessity of the measure Congress is the sole judge. . . . If this bill shall pass both Houses and become a law, that fact of itself determines the question of necessity, *and from this decision there is no appeal except to another Congress.*[138]

Wilson's argument was that Congress has broad authority under Section 2 to determine the meaning of slavery and involuntary servitude and that the only appeal to Congress's determination is not to the courts but to a subsequent Congress. This same view of Congress's broad power to define the substance of Section 1 of the Fourteenth Amendment was shared by Senator Howard, who in his introduction of the amendment, also observed:

> As I have already remarked, section one is a restriction upon the States, and does not, of itself, confer any power upon Congress. The power which Congress has, under this amendment, is derived, not from that section, but from the fifth section, which gives it authority to pass laws which are appropriate to the attainment of the great object of the amendment. I look upon the first section, taken in connection with the fifth, as very important. It will, if adopted by the States, forever disable every one of them from passing laws trenching upon those fundamental rights and privileges which pertain to citizens of the United States, and to all persons who may happen to be within their jurisdiction.[139]

This preference for Congress over the judiciary exhibited in the enforcement sections of the Thirteenth, Fourteenth, and Fifteenth Amendments is readily understandable. As Jacobus TenBroek has so succinctly declared: "Slavery was deeply entrenched in the courts."[140] After establishing judicial review in *Marbury* v. *Madison* in 1803, the Court had not exercised it again to invalidate a federal statute until the notorious *Dred Scott* case fifty-four years later, and, as Robert J. Harris stated, Congress "had not forgiven the Court for this decision."[141] *Dred Scott* exacerbated the ill will generated by such fugitive slave cases as *Prigg* v. *Pennsylvania*[142] and *Ableman* v. *Booth*,[143] and prompted Senator Charles Sumner of Massachusetts to seek to bar the customary, memorial placement of Chief Justice Roger Taney's bust in the Supreme Court Chamber and to insist that his name be "hooted down in the pages of history."[144] Given this deep-seated mistrust of the Court, there was, as Joseph B. James has written, "little inclination to bestow new powers on the judiciary."[145] Rather, those who drafted the Fourteenth Amendment were eager to augment the powers of Congress and to make it "the primary organ for the implementation of the guarantees of privileges and immunities, due process, and equal protection."[146]

This understanding of the meaning of Section 5 was also reflected in the Supreme Court's decision in *Ex Parte Virginia*. In this seminal interpretation of Congress's enforcement powers, the Court upheld a provision of the Civil Rights Act of 1875 that made it a crime for state officials to exclude any citizen from serving as a juror on account of the citizen's race, color, or previous condition of servitude. The Act "created a sword for persons discriminatorily excluded from juries," thereby going beyond the Constitution, which had only provided "a shield for defendants against prosecution in a court with a discriminatorily chosen jury."[147] Justice William Strong wrote for a seven-member majority when he declared that Section 5 provided Congress with full power to legislate on this matter. Proclaiming that the post-Civil War amendments "derive[d] much of their force" from their enforcement sections, he narrowed his focus to the Fourteenth Amendment and continued: "It is not said [in Section 5] the judicial power of the general government shall extend to enforcing the prohibitions and to protecting the rights and immunities guaranteed. It is not said that this branch of the government [i.e., the judiciary] shall be authorized to declare void any action of a State in violation of the prohibitions." Rather, he noted, "[i]t is the power of Congress which has been enlarged. Congress is authorized to enforce the prohibitions by appropriate legislation."[148] Strong's words left little doubt concerning the meaning of Section 5: The Court has no role in enforcing the protections of the Fourteenth Amendment (or, for that matter, the other post-Civil War amendments). That responsibility was assigned solely to the Congress. And, what doubt might remain, Strong removed later in the same opinion when he argued that, "[w]ere it not for the fifth section of the amendment, there might be room for argument that the first section is only declaratory of the moral duty of the States."[149]

Strong emphasized that the post-Civil War amendments were not self-executing and that "[s]ome legislation is contemplated to make the[m] . . . fully effective." And that legislation, he insisted, is to be treated most deferentially by the Court: "Whatever legislation is appropriate, that is, adopted to carry out the objects the amendments have in view, whatever tends to enforce submission to the prohibitions they contain, and to secure to all persons the enjoyment of perfect equality of civil rights and the equal protection of the laws against State denial or invasion, if not prohibited, is brought within the domain of congressional power."[150] But, was the Act, in fact, prohibited by the Constitution? That was the contention of Judge J. D. Coles, a Virginia county court judge and the defendant in this criminal case; he had argued that, whether or not the legislation was appropriate, it was clearly prohibited because it trenched on state sovereignty. Justice Strong's response applies no less forcefully to RFRA than it did to the Civil Rights Act of 1875:

> The prohibitions of the Fourteenth Amendment are directed to the States, and they are to a degree restrictions on State power. It is these which Congress is empowered to enforce, and to enforce against State action, however put forth, whether that action be executive, legislative, or judicial. Such enforcement is no invasion of State sovereignty. No law can be, which the people of the States have, by the Constitution of the United States, empowered Congress to enact. This extent of the powers of the general government is overlooked, when it is said, as it has been in this case, that the act of March 1, 1875, interferes with States rights. It is said the selection of jurors for her courts and the administration of her laws belong to each State, that they are her rights. This is true in general. But in exercising her rights, a State cannot disregard the limitations which the Federal Constitution has applied to her power. Her rights do not reach to that extent. Nor can she deny to the general government the right to exercise all its granted powers, though they may interfere with the full enjoyment of rights she would have if those powers had not been thus granted. Indeed, every addition of power to the general government involves a corresponding diminution of the governmental powers of the States. It is carved out of them.[151]

In *City of Boerne*, the Supreme Court not only rejected its seminal interpretation of Section 5 in *Ex Parte Virginia* but also repudiated an entire series on recent cases based on *Ex Parte Virginia* and on which both its modern voting rights and civil rights jurisprudence is built. These cases include *Katzenbach* v. *Morgan*,[152] *Jones* v. *Alfred H. Mayer Company*,[153] *Oregon* v. *Mitchell*,[154] *Fitzpatrick* v. *Bitzer*,[155] and *City of Rome* v. *United States*.[156] Together, the Court in these five cases held that, under the enforcement sections of the post-Civil War amendments, Congress may independently interpret the Constitution and, when it does so, the Court will defer to these congressional judgments, even if the Court is not persuaded that, acting independently, it would have reached the same conclusion.[157]

Katzenbach v. *Morgan* was a declaratory action brought by New York voters and joined by the state attorney general, challenging the constitutionality of Section 4(e) of the Voting Rights Act of 1965,[158] which provided that no state could bar any person from voting solely on grounds of English literacy if that person could demonstrate that he had been educated in an American-flag school "in which the predominant classroom language was other than English." Practically, the only beneficiaries of Section 4(e) were Puerto Ricans living in New York State who had been barred from voting by that state's literacy requirement, enacted in its constitution of 1922, decades before any significant number of Puerto Ricans moved to the state.[159] A three-judge United States District Court declared Section 4(e) unconstitutional;[160] its purpose, after all, was to overturn in part the Supreme Court's decision in *Lassiter* v. *Northampton Election Board*,[161] in which it had upheld the constitutionality of an English language literary requirement for voting.

However, in a seven-to-two opinion written by Justice William Brennan, the Supreme Court sustained Section 4(e); moreover, it did so without reaching the separate question whether, in the Court's independent judgment, New York's literacy requirement violated equal protection.[162] New York's attorney general argued that, unless the Court were to make an independent determination that the English-literacy requirement was a violation of equal protection, Section 4(e) exceeded Congress's power under Section 5 of the Fourteenth Amendment.[163] Justice Brennan flatly rejected this contention and advanced two independent grounds to sustain Congress's actions. First, Congress might have found that the state had discriminated against Puerto Ricans in the delivery of governmental services, such as public schools, public housing, and law enforcement, and that "eliminating the state restriction on the right to vote" was a remedial measure designed to cure that discrimination.[164] Second, Congress itself might have determined that application of the English-literacy requirement was a violation of the Equal Protection Clause. As long as the Court could "perceive a basis" upon which Congress might have predicated such a judgment, it would sustain Section 4(e).[165]

The first ground advanced by Justice Brennan merely affirmed the Court's reasoning earlier that term in *South Carolina* v. *Katzenbach*,[166] in which it had sustained the provisions of the Voting Rights Act primarily designed to suspend literacy tests in southern states. While the legislative record was much more substantial and persuasive in *South Carolina* than it was in *Morgan*, the logic of both cases was the same and uncontroverted: under Section 2 of the Fifteenth Amendment no less than under Section 5 of the Fourteenth Amendment, Congress is given broad remedial discretion to extirpate the effects of past discriminations and to prevent future ones. Justice Brennan's second ground in *Morgan*, however, was "much more significant because it accorded Congress the authority to define the meaning of the Fourteenth Amendment."[167] He quoted from *Ex Parte Virginia* that "[i]t is the power of Congress which has been enlarged. Congress is authorized to enforce the prohibitions by appropriate legislation. Some legislation is contemplated to make the amendments fully effective." And he continued, "A construction of Section 5 that would require a judicial determination that the enforcement of the state law precluded by Congress violated the Amendment, as a condition of sustaining the congressional enactment, would depreciate both congressional resourcefulness and congressional responsibility for implementing the Amendment. It would confine the legislative power in this context to the insignificant role of abrogating only those state laws that the judicial branch was prepared to adjudge unconstitutional, or of merely informing the judgment of the judiciary by particularizing the 'majestic generalities' of Section 1 of the Amendment."[168] He concluded by explaining that, "by including Section 5, the draftsmen sought to grant to Congress, by a specific provision applicable to the Fourteenth Amendment, the same broad powers expressed in the Necessary and Proper Clause."[169]

In *Jones* v. *Alfred H. Mayer Company*, the Supreme Court held that Congress had the power to regulate purely private property transactions in which racial discrimination is present. In his opinion for a seven-member majority, Justice Potter Stewart exhumed the Civil Rights Act of 1866[170] and held that it "bars all racial discrimination, private as well as public, in the sale or rental of property, and that the statute, thus construed, is a valid exercise of the power of Congress to enforce the Thirteenth Amendment."[171] In the *Civil Rights Cases* of 1883, on which Justice Kennedy heavily relies in *City of Boerne*,[172] the Court held that the Thirteenth Amendment "merely abolishes slavery"[173] and that "[i]t would be running the slavery argument into the ground to make it apply"[174] to "badges of slavery."[175] In *Jones*, however, Justice Stewart made many of the same arguments found in the first Justice John Marshall Harlan's dissent in the *Civil Rights Cases*, insisting that the Thirteenth Amendment authorized Congress not only to dissolve the legal bonds by which slaves had been held to their masters but also to determine rationally what "the badges and incidents of slavery"[176] are and to translate that determination into effective legislation. The Court in *Jones* therefore acknowledged that Congress had the power to construe the Thirteenth Amendment expansively, even as the Court itself continued to interpret it narrowly and to hold that it did nothing "more than abolish slavery."[177] For example, in the contemporaneous case of *Palmer* v. *Thompson*,[178] the Court rejected a Thirteenth Amendment challenge to a city's decision to close its public swimming pools rather than comply with a desegregation order. It did, however, expressly refer the problem to Congress to address under its enforcement power. "[A]lthough the Thirteenth Amendment is a skimpy collection of words to allow this Court to legislate new laws to control the operation of swimming pools throughout the length and breadth of this Nation, the amendment does contain other words that we held in *Jones* v. *Alfred H. Mayer Company* could empower Congress to outlaw badges of slavery."[179] Matt Pawa has drawn from all of this the only appropriate conclusion: "[I]n Thirteenth Amendment jurisprudence, the Court readily accepts congressional power to prohibit conduct that does not itself violate the Constitution."[180]

In *Oregon* v. *Mitchell,* the Court held, among other things,[181] that Congress had power under Section 2 of the Fifteenth Amendment to include language in the Voting Rights Act of 1970 that suspended the use of literacy tests throughout the United States, for both federal and state and local elections. The Court was badly divided on other questions addressed in *Mitchell,* but it was unanimous on this matter, and so, even though the Court continued to adhere to its belief, which it expressed in *Lassiter,* that the use by the states of literacy tests did not violate the Fifteenth Amendment, it held that Congress was fully empowered by its Section 2 to bar their use. Justice Brennan observed that, when it came to enforcing the Fifteenth Amendment, "Congress may paint with a much broader brush than may this Court."[182] Justice Black agreed: Congress was free to bar the use of literacy tests based on "evidence that literacy tests reduce voter participation in a discriminatory matter not only in the South but throughout the Nation." It was free to conclude, based on the substantial testimony it received during its extensive legislative hearings, "that a nationwide ban on literacy tests was appropriate to enforce the Civil War amendments."[183] Even Justice Harlan, who had vigorously dissented in *Morgan,* concurred: "Although the issue is not free from difficulty, I am of the opinion that this provision can be sustained as a valid means of enforcing the Fifteenth Amendment. Despite the lack of specific instances of discriminatory application or effect, *Congress could have determined* that racial prejudice is prevalent throughout the Nation, and that literacy tests unduly lend themselves to discriminatory application, either conscious or unconscious. This danger of violation of Section 1 of the Fifteenth Amendment was sufficient to authorize the exercise of congressional power under Section 2."[184]

The Court in *Fitzpatrick* v. *Bitzer* held that there are no federalism limitations on the enforcement powers of the post-Civil War amendments in cases involving forms of discrimination other than race or rights other than voting. *Fitzpatrick* was a gender-discrimination case; it was a class-action suit against the state of Connecticut brought on behalf of all of its current and retired male employees claiming discrimination in its state retirement benefit plan in violation of the 1972 amendments of Title VII of the Civil Rights Act of 1964. These amendments extended Title VII's coverage to the states and were enacted by a Congress that explicitly cited Section 5 of the Fourteenth Amendment for its authority to do so. While the District Court granted the employees injunctive relief, it denied them either retroactive retirement benefits or attorneys' fees on the ground that monetary relief against the state was barred by the Eleventh Amendment. Speaking for a seven-member majority, then Justice Rehnquist held that, under Section 5 of the Fourteenth Amendment, Congress was authorized to make states liable for damages and attorneys' fees for unlawful employment discrimination.[185] He declared: "[W]e think that the Eleventh Amendment, and the principles of state sovereign immunity which it embodies, are necessarily limited by the enforcement provisions of Section 5 of the Fourteenth Amendment. In that section Congress is expressly granted authority to enforce 'by appropriate legislation' the substantive provisions of the Fourteenth Amendment, which themselves embody significant limitations on state authority." He continued: "When Congress acts pursuant to Section 5, not only is it exercising legislative authority that is plenary within the terms of the constitutional grant, it is exercising that authority under one section of a constitutional Amendment whose other sections by their own terms embody limitations on state authority."[186] *Fitzpatrick* was decided prior to *Craig* v. *Boren,*[187] in which the Court for the first time held that gender was a protected class in equal protection cases, and so *Fitzpatrick* is yet another case in which the Court held that Congress could use its enforcement powers under the post-Civil War amendments to bar conduct that the Court, based on its own interpretation of the relevant provision, could not have prohibited on its own.

Finally, in *City of Rome* v. *United States*, the Supreme Court once again illuminated Congress's broad enforcement powers under the post-Civil War amendments. In it, the Court held that Congress, under Section 2 of the Fifteenth Amendment, could prohibit electoral schemes with discriminatory effects, even though, on the same day in *City of Mobile* v. *Bolden,*[188] it held that such schemes do not of themselves violate the Fifteenth Amendment. Section 5 of the Voting Rights Act of 1965[189] prohibits electoral changes that "have the effect of denying or abridging the right to vote on account of race or color" in all "covered jurisdictions" and requires preclearance by the Attorney General of the United States of any change in a "standard, practice, or procedure with respect to voting" in those jurisdictions. Rome, Georgia, had argued that Section 5 was unconstitutional, because it exceeded Congress's power to enforce the Fifteenth Amendment. It contended that Section 1 of the Amendment prohibits only purposeful racial discrimination in voting and that, in enforcing that provision pursuant to Section 2, Congress may not prohibit voting practices lacking discriminatory intent even if they are discriminatory in effect. Justice Thurgood Marshall wrote for a six-member majority when he declared that "under Section 2 of the Fifteenth Amendment Congress may prohibit practices that in and of themselves do not violate Section 1 of the Amendment, so long as the prohibitions attacking racial discrimination in voting are 'appropriate,' as that term is defined in *McCulloch* v. *Maryland* and *Ex Parte Virginia.*"[190] Turning to the specific question before him, he held that "the Act's ban on electoral changes that are discriminatory in effect is an appropriate method of promoting the purposes of the Fifteenth Amendment, even if it is assumed that Section 1 of the Amendment prohibits only intentional discrimination in voting." And he continued: "Congress could rationally have concluded that, because electoral changes by jurisdictions with a demonstrable history of intentional racial discrimination in voting create the risk of purposeful discrimination, it was proper to prohibit changes that have a discriminatory impact. We find no reason, then, to disturb Congress' considered judgment . . . banning electoral changes that have a discriminatory impact."[191] For the Court to rule as it did in *City of Boerne*, it had to repudiate this entire series of cases, often decided by substantial majorities, and, by so doing, it had to be willing to call into question most of its voting rights jurisprudence and key elements of its modern civil rights jurisprudence.

The Court also had to construe Congress's power under Section 5 to "enforce" the provisions of the Fourteenth Amendment so narrowly that Congress can use it only to remedy violations of judicially defined rights.[192] But, as David Cole points out, "the word 'enforce' cannot bear the weight of that claim."[193] Section 5 simply does not say that Congress has power only to "provide remedies for constitutional violations identified by the courts"; rather it says in much more expansive terms that Congress has power to enforce, by "appropriate" means, the provisions of Section 1. Cole continues: "Had the Framers [of the Fourteenth Amendment] sought to restrict Congress's power to remedial measures, they could have done so expressly."[194]

A much more reasonable construction, and one faithful to the original understanding of its framers, is that Section 5 allows Congress to "implement" the preceding provisions of the Fourteenth Amendment.[195] That clearly was the construction Congress gave to Section 5 when it passed RFRA. For example, the Senate Report on RFRA observed that "the Fourteenth Amendment's 'fundamental concept of liberty . . . encompasses the liberties guaranteed by the First Amendment,' which, of course, include a right to practice one's faith free of laws prohibiting the free exercise of religion."[196] It proclaimed that "Section 5 gives Congress 'the same broad powers expressed in the necessary and proper clause' with respect to State governments and their subdivisions," and it concluded: "[C]ongressional power under Section 5 to enforce the 14th Amendment includes congressional power to enforce the free exercise clause. Because the Religious Freedom Restoration Act is clearly designed *to implement* the free exercise clause—to protect religious liberty and eliminate laws 'prohibiting the free exercise' of religion—it falls squarely within Congress's Section 5 enforcement powers."[197] The House Report agreed, arguing that, pursuant to Section 5 of the Fourteenth Amendment and the Necessary and Proper Clause, Congress "has been given the authority to provide statutory protection for a constitutional value when the Supreme Court has been unwilling to assert its authority" and that "the Supreme Court has repeatedly upheld such congressional action after declining to find a constitutional protection itself."[198]

That construction is also the one most in keeping with the Court's language in *Ex Parte Virginia* that, "[w]ere it not for the fifth section of the amendment, there might be room for argument that the first section is only declaratory of the moral duty of the States."[199] It is also the construction most in keeping with the principle that acts of Congress are entitled to a presumption of constitutionality.[200] This principle of deference to the political branches has been with us from the beginning. Chief Justice John Marshall stated it well in *Fletcher* v. *Peck*: In order for the Court to declare an act of Congress unconstitutional, "the opposition between the constitution and the law should be such that the judge feels a clear and strong conviction of their incompatibility with each other."[201] He stated it even more powerfully in *Dartmouth College* v. *Woodward*: "[I]n no doubtful case would [the Court] pronounce a legislative act to be contrary to the Constitution."[202] This principle is also with us today. As Justice Souter declared in his concurrence in *Washington* v. *Glucksberg*, the Court "has no warrant to substitute one reasonable resolution of the contending positions for another, but authority to supplant the balance already struck between the contenders only when it falls outside the realm of the reasonable."[203] And, finally, that construction is the one most in keeping with what Michael McConnell calls the "institutional dimensions of Section Five."[204]

> [W]hen Congress interprets the provisions of the Bill of Rights for purposes of carrying out its enforcement authority under Section Five, it is not bound by the institutional constraints that in many cases lead the courts to adopt a less intrusive interpretation from among the textually and historically plausible meanings of the clause in question. Because these institutional constraints are predicated on the need to protect the discretionary judgments of representative institutions from uncabined

judicial interference, there is no reason for Congress—the representatives of the people—to abide by them. Congress need not be concerned that its interpretations of the Bill of Rights will trench upon democratic prerogatives, because its actions are the expression of the democratic will of the people. Indeed, the same institutional constraints that lead the courts, in many cases, to adopt a reading of the Constitution that produces a more modest judicial role should have led the Court to be more respectful of the congressional decision represented by RFRA.[205]

Finally, to rule as it did in *City of Boerne*, the Court had to restrict even Congress's remedial powers under Section 5 to remedying problems that the Court itself considers serious enough to justify federal intervention. The Court held that Congress could employ its Section 5 powers only in those instances in which there was "a congruence and proportionality between the injury to be prevented or remedied and the means adopted to that end."[206] Violating once again the principle of judicial deference to the popular branches, the Court asserted that it was the sole judge of what was congruent and proportional. Congress's claim for the need for RFRA, based on extensive legislative hearings, was dismissed by the majority as "anecdotal evidence."[207] The Court simply asserted that there was no wide-spread religious discrimination in the United States that Congress needed to remedy and therefore concluded that RFRA was "so out of proportion to a supposed remedial or preventive object that it cannot be understood as responsive to, or designed to prevent, unconstitutional behavior."[208] Justice Kennedy and the majority in *City of Boerne* can be said to have accepted the invitation that Chief Justice Marshall declined in *McCulloch* when Joseph Hopkinson, one of the attorneys for the State of Maryland, asked the Court to declare that, while creating the Bank of the United States may have been necessary (and therefore proper) in 1791, it was unnecessary (and therefore unconstitutional) in 1816. In *McCulloch*, in response to this invitation, Chief Justice Marshall declared that it was only for Congress to "inquire into the degree of its necessity" and that if the Court were to follow Hopkinson's suggestion and do so, it "would pass the line which circumscribes the judicial department."[209] In *City of Boerne*, Kennedy and his activist colleagues felt perfectly free to embrace the "pretensions to such a power"[210] that Marshall had "disclaim[ed]"in *McCulloch* and demonstrated the lengths to which the Court would go to protect a federalism that died with the adoption and ratification of the Seventeenth Amendment.

The Court's State Sovereign Immunity Jurisprudence

City of Boerne, despite its many failings, has quickly become an extremely influential precedent, especially in the Court's recent attempts to protect the original federal design by still another means, namely, by invalidating congressional measures on the grounds that they trench upon the states' sovereign immunity. Thus, the Court has subsequently relied on *City of Boerne* to declare unconstitutional federal laws abrogating state sovereign immunity in cases in which the states are charged with violating trademark or patent laws or are sued by their own employees for discrimination on the basis of age or disability or for refusing to pay the minimum wage, and it has employed it to strike down the Violence Against Women Act. In each of these cases, the Court has construed Congress's powers under Section 5 so narrowly that Congress is prohibited from passing remedial legislation if, in the Court's mind, the remedy chosen by Congress is out of proportion to the injury individuals are suffering at the hands of the states. In each of these cases, therefore, the Court has perversely transformed Section 5 of the Fourteenth Amendment, intended by its drafters to be a sword by which Congress could protect individuals from constitutional violations of their rights by the states, into a shield by which state governments are protected from the consequences of their constitutional violations. The Court has done all of this in the name of protecting federalism, but, with friends like this, federalism needs no enemies. The Court may have protected states' rights, but, by linking federalism in the public's mind with the right of state governments to violate individual rights, it has further undermined the states' moral and political standing. As Charles R. Kesler has noted, the Court in these cases has done little to "relieve the taint of slavery and segregation—the suspicion that states' rights too often come at the expense of individual rights—that has besmirched American federalism for so long."[211] This, of course, represents still another irony of the Court's efforts to protect federalism.

The Court's opinions in the area of state sovereign immunity have done more than damage federalism; they have also damaged the Court's own reputation. To begin with, in these opinions, the Court has had to assert—contrary to its repeated concessions elsewhere that the Congress has a capacity for fact finding that is superior to its own[212]—that the problems that Congress has concluded (typically on the basis of extensive legislative hearings) were serious enough to be addressed through the use of its Section 5 powers were of too little consequence for Congress to remedy. Determining whether a remedy is "congruent" and "proportionate" is a factual question, and hence one for Congress to determine.[213] By refusing to allow Congress to make the determination of what problems justify use of its plenary powers under Section 5, the Court becomes an arrogant and cloistered opponent of the protection of individual rights, blind to the injustices that a concerned Congress, closer to the people and therefore better able to appreciate their problems, is attempting to address.

The Court's sovereign immunity jurisprudence has damaged its reputation in a second way as well: It has compelled the Court to ignore the very words of the Constitution it claims it is its duty to interpret.[214] The Eleventh Amendment simply does not bar the kinds of suits against states that the Court has barred in *Seminole Tribe,* the two *Florida Prepaid* cases, *Kimel* and *Garrett.* It bars only suits arising under the federal courts' diversity jurisdiction, not under their federal question jurisdiction. The Court has therefore been obliged to argue against a "blind reliance upon the text" of the Eleventh Amendment and has been forced to contend that what is important is "not so much" what the Eleventh Amendment says as "the presupposition . . . which it confirms."[215] For the Court to invalidate a congressional measure abrogating state sovereign immunity, not because it violates the text of the Eleventh Amendment but because it violates what the Court thinks the framers of the Eleventh Amendment should have written, is the height of judicial activism—and arrogance. The Court's handling of the state sovereign immunity issue in *Alden* was even more egregious. In it, the Court held that state employees could not file suit in state court against a state government for its failure to abide by the overtime pay provisions of the Fair Labor Standards Act. In so doing, the Court not only treated the Eleventh Amendment, which is a limitation on the kinds of suits against the states that Congress can authorize to be brought in the federal courts, as a limitation as well on Congress's power to authorize suits in state courts, but it also completely ignored the Supremacy Clause—the extension by Congress of the Fair Labor Standards Act to state governments had previously been held by the Court in *Garcia* to be "made in pursuance of the Constitution," and it was therefore a part of the "supreme law of the land" that every state judge is constitutionally obligated to enforce.

The Court's sovereign immunity cases damaged the Court's integrity and reputation in still another way. The Court's rigid and doctrinaire extension of the principles of *Seminole Tribe* and *City of Boerne* led the Court to lose sight of what the Court itself said was the "fundamental purpose" of federalism. In these cases, the Court ignored Justice O'Connor's words in *New York v. United States*: "The Constitution does not protect the sovereignty of States for the benefit of the States or state governments as abstract political entities. . . . To the contrary, the Constitution divides authority between federal and state governments for the protection of individuals. State sovereignty is not just an end in itself."[216]

Notes

1. Bybee speculates that the people "preferred democracy to representation and were willing to shoulder the loss to constitutional federalism." Jay S. Bybee, "Ulysses at the Mast: Democracy, Federalism, and the Sirens' Song of the Seventeenth Amendment," *Northwestern University Law Review* 91 (1997): 536.

2. *Congressional Record*, 61st Cong., 3rd Sess., 2243.

3. To repeat what was said in the introduction, it must be understood that this is not a "cause and effect" argument, for there are many factors that account for the rapid expansion of the national government. Among them are World Wars I and II, the subsequent Cold War, continued industrial growth, and breakthroughs in electronic communications. Moreover, as Bybee has written, it is "a maddeningly difficult proposition to prove" the exact effects of direct election of senators. Bybee, "Ulysses at the Mast," 547. Nevertheless, it is clear that the ratification of the Seventeenth Amendment removed a previously existing constitutional impediment to these centralizing tendencies, and, as a result, federalism has been reduced to "a pale imitation of its pre-Seventeenth Amendment vigor." Todd J. Zywicki, "Beyond the Shell and Husk of History: The History of the Seventeenth Amendment and Its Implications for Current Reform Proposals," *Cleveland State Law Review* 45 (1997): 212.

4. 39 Stat. 675 (1916).

5. 40 Stat. 1057 (1919).

6. 39 Stat. 721 (1916).

7. "Conventional wisdom states that the New Deal commenced a radical shift in the scope of the federal government. In fact, the growth in the federal government began almost immediately after the passage of the Progressive Era amendments. . . . The New Deal simply confirmed the constitutional revolution which had already transpired." Zywicki, "Beyond the Shell and Husk of History," 174-75.

8. "Roosevelt's New Deal would not have been possible without the institutional changes caused by the Progressive Era amendments. The Sixteenth Amendment allowed for the federal government to raise revenues on an unprecedented scale. At the same time, the Seventeenth Amendment destroyed the systems of federalism and bicameralism which had previously checked expansionist federal activity." Zywicki, "Beyond the Shell and Husk of History," 233.

9. 48 Stat. 31 (1933).

10. 52 Stat. 31 (1938).

11. 48 Stat. 1283 (1934).

12. 48 Stat. 195 (1933).

13. 52 Stat. 1060 (1938).

14. 49 Stat. 991 (1935).

15. 49 Stat. 449 (1935).

16. 49 Stat. 620 (1935).

17. 50 Stat. 888 (1937).

18. 88 Stat. 55 (1974).

19. 98 Stat. 437 (1984).

20. 99 Stat. 1842 (1985).

21. 107 Stat. 1536 (1993).

22. 107 Stat. 1488 (1993).

23. 107 Stat. 77 (1993).

24. 108 Stat. 1941 (1994).

25. The Civil Rights Act of 1964, 78 Stat. 241, barring private discrimination in public accommodations, the Civil Rights Act of 1968, 82 Stat. 81 (1968), prohibiting discrimination in housing, and the Voting Rights Acts of 1965, 79 Stat. 439, and of 1982, 96 Stat. 134, are not included as examples, because Congress (including the pre-Seventeenth Amendment Senate) had demonstrated throughout the post-Civil War era a repeated willingness to use its enforcement powers under the Thirteenth, Fourteenth, and Fifteenth Amendments to enact legislation regulating what was once thought to be exclusively within the province of the states.

26. Theodore J. Lowi, *The End of Liberalism: Ideology, Policy, and the Crisis of Public Authority* (New York: W. W. Norton, 1969), 134-35.

27. Lowi, *The End of Liberalism*, 126.

28. See the lengthy discussion of the effect of the Seventeenth Amendment on the delegation of lawmaking authority in Vikram David Amar, "Indirect Effects of Direct Election: A Structural Examination of the Seventeenth Amendment," *Vanderbilt Law Review* 49 (1996): 1360-89.

29. During that period, it invalidated ten congressional measures in the following cases: *Hammer* v. *Dagenhart,* 247 U.S. 251 (1918); *Bailey* v. *Drexel Furniture Co.,* 259 U.S. 20 (1922); *Hill* v. *Wallace,* 259 U.S. 44 (1922); *Trusler* v. *Crooks,* 269 U.S. 475 (1926); *Railroad Retirement Board* v. *Alton Railway,* 295 U.S. 330 (1935); *Schechter Poultry Corp.* v. *United States,* 295 U.S. 495 (1935); *Hopkins Savings Association* v. *Cleary,* 296 U.S. 315 (1935); *United States* v. *Butler,* 297 U.S. 1 (1936); *Rickert Rice Mills* v. *Fontenot,* 297 U.S. 110 (1936); *Carter* v. *Carter Coal Co.,* 298 U.S. 238 (1936); and *Ashton* v. *Cameron County District,* 298 U.S. 513 (1936).

30. During the entire period prior to the ratification of the Seventeenth Amendment, it invalidated seven congressional measures in the following cases: *Dred Scott* v. *Sandford,* 60 U.S. 393 (1857); *United States* v. *DeWitt,* 76 U.S. 41 (1870); *United States* v. *Fox,* 95 U.S. 670 (1878); the *Trademark Cases,* 100 U.S. 82 (1879); the *Employers' Liability Cases,* 207 U.S. 463 (1908); *Keller* v. *United States,* 213 U.S. 138 (1909); and *Coyle* v. *Smith,* 221 U.S. 559 (1911). An eighth statute considered in *Matter of Heff,* 197 U.S. 488 (1905), could possibly be added here. However, the Court explicitly overturned *Matter of Heff* in *United States* v. *Nice,* 241 U.S. 591 (1916), and consequently, it is not included in the totals.

31. See James Wilson's comments in the Constitutional Convention. Max Farrand (ed.), *The Records of the Federal Convention of 1787, Rev. ed.,* 4 vols. (New Haven: Yale University Press, 1937), 1: 344. In that connection, consider

also the Sixteenth Amendment which was ratified, as George Anastaplo has noted, "primarily in order to expand the power of the General Government." Also ratified in 1913, "The Sixteenth Amendment is still another indication that citizens can be dealt with directly by the General Government, without any mediation by the States in any way." George Anastaplo, *The Amendments to the Constitution: A Commentary* (Baltimore: Johns Hopkins University Press, 1995), 187.

32. 5 U.S. 137 (1803).

33. 247 U.S. 251 (1918).

34. 247 U.S. at 276.

35. 247 U.S. at 274.

36. 188 U.S. 321 (1903).

37. 220 U.S. 45 (1911).

38. 227 U.S. 308 (1913).

39. 188 U.S. at 353.

40. 188 U.S. at 365.

41. 188 U.S. at 357.

42. 34 Stat. 768 (1906).

43. 220 U.S. at 57.

44. 220 U.S. at 58.

45. 36 Stat. 825 (1910). Its official name was "An Act to Further Regulate Interstate and Foreign Commerce by Prohibiting the Transportation Therein for Immoral Purposes of Women and Girls, and for Other Purposes."

46. 227 U.S. at 320.

47. 227 U.S. at 322.

48. 227 U.S. at 321, 323.

49. 227 U.S. at 322.

50. 259 U.S. 20 (1922)

51. 259 U.S. at 39.

52. 259 U.S. 44 (1922).

53. 259 U.S. at 66-67. It also held that Congress was attempting to regulate commerce that was wholly between persons contracting within the State of Illinois respecting the purchase or sale of grain which formed a part of the common property of that state and that it was therefore intrastate and not interstate. Finally, it held that Congress violated the Tenth Amendment by interfering with the right of Illinois to provide for and regulate the maintenance of grain exchanges within its borders upon which were conducted the making of contracts that were merely intrastate transactions.

54. *Dred Scott* was the first and most notorious use of dual federalism, but there were four other cases prior to *Hammer* in which the Court also used dual-federalism premises to invalidate congressional measures. In *United States v. DeWitt*, 76 U.S. 41, 44 (1870), the Court held that Congress's general prohibition under the Commerce Clause of the sale of naphtha for illuminating purposes if it were inflammable at a temperature of fewer than 110 degrees F. was unconstitutional

because, "[s]tanding by itself, it is plainly a regulation of police." In *United States* v. *Fox*, 95 U.S. 670 (1878), it held that a provision of the Bankruptcy Act of 1867 that penalized individuals who defrauded creditors by obtaining credit with the intention of thereafter commencing bankruptcy proceedings was a police regulation not within the bankruptcy power of the Congress and was therefore unconstitutional. In *Matter of Heff*, 197 U.S. 488 (1905), it held that a federal statute regulating the sale of intoxicating liquor to reservation Indians violated the principles of dual federalism as "[t]he regulation of the sale of intoxicating liquors is within the power of the State." However, it expressly overturned *Matter of Heff* in *United States* v. *Nice*, 241 U.S. 591, 601 (1916): "As, therefore, these allottees remain tribal Indians and under national guardianship, the power of Congress to regulate or prohibit the sale of intoxicating liquor to them . . . is not debatable." Finally, in *Keller* v. *United States*, 213 U.S. 138 (1909), the Court held that a provision in the Immigration Act of 1907 that penalized "whoever . . . shall keep, maintain, control, support, or harbor in any house or other place, for the purpose of prostitution . . . any alien woman or girl, within 3 years after she shall have entered the United States" was an exercise of the state's reserved police power and not within the control of Congress over immigration.

55. 60 U.S. at 432. See David P. Currie, *The Constitution in the Supreme Court: The First Hundred Years, 1789-1888* (Chicago: University of Chicago Press, 1985), 269: "Taney's construction seems singularly unpersuasive; he might as convincingly have argued that the *ex post facto* clause applied only to the thirteen original states."

56. 60 U.S. at 448.

57. 60 U.S. at 450.

58. Taney also invoked the Fifth Amendment and found the Missouri Compromise unconstitutional on substantive due process grounds: "[A]n act of Congress which deprives a citizen of the United States of his liberty or property, merely because he came himself or brought his property into a particular Territory of the United States, and who had committed no offence against the laws, could hardly be dignified with the name of due process of law." Nothing in the Constitution, Taney added, "gives Congress a greater power over slave property, or . . . entitles property of that kind to less protection than property of any other description." 60 U.S. at 452.

59. 17 U.S. at 400-401.

60. 17 U.S. at 421, 401.

61. "From a lawyer's viewpoint, *Scott* was a disreputable performance. The variety of feeble, poorly developed, and unnecessary constitutional arguments suggests, if nothing else, a determination to reach a predetermined conclusion at any price." Currie, *The Constitution in the Supreme Court: The First Hundred Years*, 273.

62. 247 U.S. at 277.

63. 247 U.S. at 275. Emphasis added.

64. Helen E. Veit, Kenneth R. Bowling, and Charlene Bang Bickford (eds.), *Creating the Bill of Rights: The Documentary Record of the First Federal Congress* (Baltimore: Johns Hopkins University Press, 1991), 51, 199.

65. 17 U.S. at 406.

66. 247 U.S. at 276.

67. 247 U.S. at 276.

68. See Bybee, "Ulysses at the Mast," 568: "It is unclear that the Supreme Court should be responsible for guaranteeing the role of the states and protecting the people from themselves. The Seventeenth Amendment took the power to elect senators from state legislatures (which, after all, represent people) and gave it to the people (who would now represent themselves). It seems to me that states as political entities in a federal system were more aggressively represented in Congress through their legislatures, but since the Constitution now provides otherwise, the people cannot complain about the Court when the people demanded control of the Senate and then failed to exercise it with the same vigilance as their legislatures." For a different understanding of the relationship between the Seventeenth Amendment and the Supreme Court, see Roger G. Brooks, "*Garcia,* The Seventeenth Amendment, and the Role of the Supreme Court in Defending Federalism," *Harvard Journal of Law and Public Policy* 10 (1987): 208-9: "Because the Seventeenth Amendment was not intended to reduce that zone of state sovereignty, it did not lessen the pre-existing constitutional right of States to exercise their reserved sovereignty unhindered. . . . As a result, the Supreme Court cannot properly excuse itself from judging whether a challenged federal law does violate that state sovereignty."

69. 269 U.S. 475 (1926). In *Trusler,* the Court invalidated Section 3 of the Future Trading Act of 1921, which imposed a tax of 20 cents per bushel on all options trading. The Court held that its purpose was not to raise revenue but rather was simply to ban, by penalty, the use of options altogether.

70. The Court continued to make dual-federalism arguments in *United States v. Butler,* 297 U.S. 1 (1935), and *Carter v. Carter Coal Co.,* 298 U.S. 238 (1936), but it did not base its conclusion that the underlying statutes at issue in these cases were unconstitutional on that basis. In fact, it did not officially repudiate the use of the principle of dual federalism in interpreting the Commerce Clause until *United States v. Darby Lumber Co.,* 312 U.S. 100 (1941), when it explicitly overturned *Hammer v. Dagenhart.* It should be noted, moreover, that several members of the Court continued to employ dual-federalism principles in matters of taxation. See *United States v. Kahriger,* 345 U.S. 22 (1953), for example, in which both the majority opinion by Justice Stanley Reed and the dissent by Justice Felix Frankfurter employed dual-federalism reasoning: Justice Frankfurter was quite emphatic in defending this form of reasoning. "[W]hen oblique use is made of the taxing power as to matters which substantively are not within the powers delegated to Congress, the Court cannot shut its eyes to what is obviously, because designedly, an attempt to control conduct which the Constitution left to the responsibility of the States, merely because Congress wrapped the legislation in the verbal cellophane of a revenue measure." 345 U.S. at 38. See also C. Herman Pritchett, *The American Constitution* (New York: McGraw-Hill, 1968), 239-40.

71. *Carter v. Carter Coal Co.,* 298 U.S. at 303.

72. 297 U.S. 1 (1935).

73. 298 U.S. at 303-4: "[T]he word 'commerce' is the equivalent of the phrase 'intercourse for the purposes of trade.' Plainly, the incidents leading up to and culminating in the mining of coal do not constitute such intercourse. The employment of men, the fixing of their wages, hours of labor and working conditions, the bargaining in respect of these things—whether carried on separately or collectively—each and all constitute intercourse for the purposes of production, not of trade. The latter is a thing apart from the relation of employer and employee, which, in all producing occupations, is purely local in character. Extraction of coal from the mine is the aim and the completed result of local activities. Commerce in the coal mined is not brought into being by force of these activities, but by negotiations, agreements, and circumstances entirely apart from production. Mining brings the subject matter of commerce into existence. Commerce disposes of it." See also *Railroad Retirement Board* v. *Alton Railroad Company*, 295 U.S. 330 (1935), in which the Court held that Congress's power to regulate interstate commerce did not extend to regulations related to the social welfare of the worker. These regulations were based on the theory that, by engendering contentment and a sense of personal security, they would induce more efficient service. 295 U.S. at 367.

74. 156 U.S. 1, 13 (1895).

75. See also *Rickert Rice Mills, Inc.* v. *Fontenot*, 297 U.S. 110 (1936), in which the Court held that the infirmities of the Agricultural Adjustment Act of 1933, which were the bases for holding it unconstitutional in *Butler*, had not been cured by the Amendatory Act of August 24, 1935, as that act likewise was a means for effectuating the regulation of agricultural production and was not, therefore, a matter within the powers of Congress.

76. 22 U.S. at 197.

77. 298 U.S. at 295-96. See also *Hopkins Savings Association* v. *Cleary*, 296 U.S. 315 (1935), and *Ashton* v. *Cameron County District*, 298 U.S. 513 (1936). In *Hopkins Savings Association*, the Court held that the provision of the Federal Home Owners' Loan Act of 1933 permitting a state building and loan association to convert itself into a federal savings and loan association without the consent of the state that created it was an unconstitutional encroachment upon the reserved powers of the states. In *Ashton*, it held that a 1934 amendment to the Bankruptcy Act permitting municipal corporations and other political subdivisions of the states, unable to pay their debts as they mature, to resort to the federal bankruptcy courts to effect readjustment of obligations was likewise unconstitutional, for it trenched on the reserved powers of the states. "If obligations of States or their political subdivisions may be subjected to the interference here attempted, they are no longer free to manage their own affairs; the will of Congress prevails over them." 298 U.S. at 531.

78. 156 U.S. at 12. "Doubtless the power to control the manufacture of a thing involves a certain sense of control of its disposition, but it is a secondary, and not the primary, sense."

79. 295 U.S. 495 (1935).

80. 295 U.S. at 546.

81. 298 U.S. at 307-8.

82. *National Labor Relations Board* v. *Jones & Laughlin Steel Corp.*, 301 U.S. at 37.

83. See, however, Brooks, *"Garcia,* the Seventeenth Amendment, and the Role of the Supreme Court in Defending Federalism," 210. Brooks argues that "[t]he Court certainly recognizes that a constitutional line between state and federal authority exists; it regularly strikes down state laws as encroaching on federal prerogatives." (See also Zywicki, "Beyond the Shell and Husk of History," 228.) Brooks, however, refuses to recognize that, from the founding onward, it is the Congress and not the Court that is to draw the line between state and federal authority. He also fails to understand that, when the Court strikes down state laws that encroach on federal power, it is not drawing the line itself but merely enforcing the line that Congress has drawn, consistent with the Supremacy Clause of Article VI.

84. David P. Currie, *The Constitution in the Supreme Court: The Second Century, 1888-1986* (Chicago: University of Chicago Press, 1990), 238.

85. It is the hope of resuscitating federalism that led Bybee to propose that the Seventeenth Amendment be repealed. Bybee, "Ulysses at the Mast," 568. Zywicki agrees that this is a "good idea" but quickly concedes that "[t]he tide of democracy is generally difficult to contain, much less reverse." Zywicki, "Beyond the Shell and Husk of History," 226.

86. 426 U.S. 833 (1976).

87. 426 U.S. at 844.

88. 426 U.S. at 852.

89. 426 U.S. at 845.

90. 426 U.S. 851.

91. 22 U.S. at 197.

92. 426 U.S. at 851. See, however, Currie's defense of Rehnquist's opinion in *The Constitution in the Supreme Court: The Second Century,* 564-65.

93. 469 U.S. 528 (1984).

94. 469 U.S. at 539, 545.

95. 469 U.S. at 548.

96. 469 U.S. at 550-51.

97. Blackmun mentions the mode of electing the Senate only in passing and places most of his emphasis on equal representation of the states in the Senate. His argument is reminiscent of the Senate Committee Report in 1986 responding to Congressman Bartlett. See *Senate Reports,* 54th Cong., 1st Sess., No. 530: 2, 4.

98. See also *South Carolina* v. *Baker,* 485 U.S. 505, 512 (1988), in which Justice William Brennan declared that the "limits on Congress' authority to regulate state activities" set out in *Garcia* "are structural, not substantive, i.e., States must find their protection from congressional regulation through the national political process, not through judicially defined spheres of unregulable state activity."

99. 469 U.S. at 554.

100. Amar, "Indirect Effects of Direct Election," 1380. Amar argues that the Court removed itself from the business of protecting state entities from the

application of federal law "largely on the theory that the federal structure enables state governmental entities to protect themselves through the political process. I think it fair to say that Justice Blackmun's opinion did not really grapple with the fundamental change in that structure reflected by direct election."

101. 469 U.S. at 555.

102. The three-part test introduced by Chief Justice Warren Burger in *Lemon* v. *Kurtzman*, 403 U.S. 602 (1971), helps the Court to determine whether a statute violates the First Amendment's Establishment Clause.

103. 508 U.S. 384, 398 (1993).

104. 514 U.S. 549 (1995).

105. 514 U.S. at 559.

106. 514 U.S. at 564.

107. 514 U.S. at 566.

108. 514 U.S. at 567.

109. 514 U.S. at 567.

110. 514 U.S. at 589.

111. Interestingly, it was that very "absence of structural mechanisms" that ultimately persuaded Justice Anthony Kennedy to join the majority opinion in *Lopez*. His vote was quite surprising in light of statements he had made earlier in his concurring opinion. He acknowledged, for example, that, unlike the "workable standards to assist in preserving separation of powers and checks and balances" that the Court had developed, "[o]ur role in preserving the federal balance seems more tenuous." 514 U.S. at 574. He also admitted that the conclusion "could be drawn from *The Federalist Papers* . . . that the balance between national and state power is entrusted in its entirety to the political process. Madison's observation that 'the people ought not surely to be precluded from giving most of their confidence where they may discover it to be most due,' *The Federalist* No. 46, can be interpreted to say that the essence of responsibility for a shift in power from the State to the Federal Government rests upon a political judgment." 514 U.S. at 577.

112. 514 U.S. at 585.

113. Lino A. Graglia, "*United States* v. *Lopez*: Judicial Review under the Commerce Clause," *Texas Law Review* 74 (March 1996): 721. See also 722: "Although the Constitution contemplates a federal system of divided powers rather than a national system of totally centralized power, it is doubtful that such a system can be made a matter of a judicially enforceable legal or constitutional guarantee. Discussions of federalism that speak, as most do, of the need to maintain separate 'spheres' or 'areas' of federal and state authority and to maintain the 'boundaries' between them tend more to mislead than to aid understanding of the problem. Political power is not a physical or spatial entity subject to such a division." For a contrary view, see John C. Yoo, "The Judicial Safeguards of Federalism," *Southern California Law Review* 70 (1997): 1311, 1312, who argues that, "although the Court has and will continue to debate where the line is to be drawn between federal enumerated powers and state sovereignty, there seems to be little dispute on the Court [or in Yoo's mind] over its institutional obligation to draw that line."

114. 369 U.S. 186 (1962).

115. 369 U.S. at 217. See Graglia, *"United States* v. *Lopez,"* 767-71.

116. 505 U.S. 144 (1992).

117. 505 U.S. at 178.

118. 505 U.S. at 168.

119. 505 U.S. at 168-69.

120. 505 U.S. at 177.

121. 505 U.S. at 156-57.

122. 505 U.S. at 157. Emphasis added.

123. 521 U.S. 898 (1997).

124. 521 U.S. at 935.

125. 521 U.S. at 905. This is a rather remarkable concession from a textualist like Scalia. See Antonin Scalia, *A Matter of Interpretation: Federal Courts and the Law,* ed. Amy Gutmann (Princeton: Princeton University Press, 1997). See also Ralph A. Rossum, "The Textualist Jurisprudence of Justice Scalia," *Perspectives on Political Science* 28 (Winter 1999): 5.

126. 521 U.S. at 905.

127. 521 U.S. at 949.

128. 521 U.S. at 922.

129. 487 U.S. 654 (1988).

130. 521 U.S. at 925.

131. See generally Thomas W. Beimers, "Searching for the Structural Vision of *City of Boerne* v. *Flores*: Vertical and Horizontal Tensions in the New Constitutional Architecture," *Hastings Constitutional Law Quarterly* 26 (Summer 1999): 789-852.

132. 521 U.S. at 536.

133. 100 U.S. 339 (1880).

134. 521 U.S. at 520.

135. Michael W. McConnell, "The Supreme Court, 1996 Term: Comment: Institutions and Interpretation: A Critique of *Boerne* v. *Flores,"* *Harvard Law Review* 111 (November 1997): 153, 164.

136. *Congressional Globe,* 39th Cong., 1st Sess., 2766, 2768. See also Raoul Berger's reliance on, and use of, the passage from Senator Howard in *Government by Judiciary: The Transformation of the Fourteenth Amendment* (Cambridge, Mass.: Harvard University Press, 1977), 227-29. It contributes to his conclusion that "[a] reasoned argument for a judicial power of enforcement of the Fourteenth Amendment . . . has yet to be made."

137. See Learned Hand, *The Bill of Rights* (New York: Athenaeum, 1965), 55. See also Kathryn Griffith, *Judge Learned Hand and the Role of the Federal Judiciary* (Lincoln: University Press of Nebraska, 1973), 138.

138. *Congressional Globe,* 39th Cong., 1st Sess., 1118. Emphasis added.

139. *Congressional Globe,* 39th Cong., 1st Sess., 2766.

140. Jacobus TenBroek, *Equal under Law* (London: Collier Books, 1965), 149.

141. Robert J. Harris, *The Quest for Equality* (Baton Rouge: Louisiana State University Press, 1960), 54.

142. 41 U.S. 539 (1842).

143. 62 U.S. 506 (1858).

144. Berger, *Government by Judiciary,* 222.

145. Joseph B. James, *The Framing of the Fourteenth Amendment* (Urbana: University of Illinois Press, 1965), 184.

146. Harris, *The Quest for Equality,* 53-54.

147. Matt Pawa, "When the Supreme Court Restricts Constitutional Rights, Can Congress Save Us: An Examination of Section 5 of the Fourteenth Amendment," *University of Pennsylvania Law Review,* 141 (January 1993): 1029, 1057. The "shield" aspect of the Fourteenth Amendment was upheld in *Strauder* v. *West Virginia,* 100 U.S. 303 (1879).

148. 100 U.S. at 345-46.

149. 100 U.S. at 347.

150. 100 U.S. at 346.

151. 100 U.S. at 347.

152. 384 U.S. 641 (1966).

153. 392 U.S. 409 (1968).

154. 400 U.S. 112 (1970).

155. 427 U.S. 445 (1976).

156. 446 U.S. 156 (1980).

157. See Erwin Chemerinsky, "Reflections on *City of Boerne* v. *Flores*: The Religious Freedom Restoration Act Is a Constitutional Expansion of Rights," *William and Mary Law Review* 39 (February 1998): 601, 610. See also Frank B. Cross, "Institutions and Enforcement of the Bill of Rights," *Cornell Law Review* 85 (September 2000): 1529.

158. 79 Stat. 439 (1965).

159. 384 U.S. at 645, n. 3.

160. 247 F. Supp. 196 (D.D.C 1965).

161. 360 U.S. 45 (1959).

162. Two members of the *Morgan* majority, Justices William O. Douglas and Abe Fortas, indicated in a companion case, *Cardona* v. *Power,* 384 U.S. 672, 675 (1966), that they were prepared to reach this result independently, but the other five members of the majority appear to have affirmed a contrary proposition, i.e., that the Court, acting independently, was reluctant to reach this result under the Equal Protection Clause but was eager to defer to a contrary congressional judgment construing the Clause.

163. 384 U.S. at 648.

164. 384 U.S. at 652-53.

165. 384 U.S. at 655-56.

166. 383 U.S. 301 (1966).

167. Chemerinsky, "Reflections on *City of Boerne* v. *Flores*," 611.

168. 384 U.S. at 648-49. Brennan rejected the argument, stated by Justice John Marshall Harlan in his dissent, that, if the Congress had power to expand the substantive meaning of the post-Civil War amendments beyond what the Court said they meant, it could also restrict their meaning to less than what the Court said they meant. "Contrary to the suggestion of the dissent . . . , Section 5 does not grant Congress power to exercise discretion in the other direction. . . . We emphasize that Congress's power under Section 5 is limited to adopting measures to enforce the guarantees of the Amendment; Section 5 grants Congress no power to restrict, abrogate, or dilute these guarantees." 384 U.S. 651, n. 10.

169. 384 U.S. at 650. While the Court in *Morgan* held that Congress has the power to define the meaning of the Fourteenth Amendment, a question could be raised whether Congress has the power to define the meaning of the various Bill of Rights provisions—in the case of *City of Boerne*, the Free Exercise Clause—that the Court has held the Fourteenth Amendment has incorporated to apply to the states. That question was answered in the affirmative in *Hutto* v. *Finney*, 437 U.S. 678 (1978), in which the Court upheld an award of attorney's fees in an Eighth Amendment civil rights suit. The Court held that Congress could authorize an award of attorney's fees even though the Eighth Amendment, standing alone, would not provide for such an award. Justice John Paul Stevens spoke for an eight-member majority when he invoked *Fitzpatrick* v. *Bitzer* and declared: "Congress has plenary power to set aside the States' immunity from retroactive relief in order to enforce the Fourteenth Amendment." 437 U.S. at 693. As Pawa notes, "This holding recognized that under Section 5 of the Fourteenth Amendment, Congress can enforce incorporated rights. In fact, the Eleventh Amendment would have prohibited monetary awards but for the federal statute." Pawa, "When the Supreme Court Restricts Constitutional Rights," 1069.

170. 14 Stat. 27 (1866).

171. 392 U.S. at 413.

172. See, for example, 525 U.S. at 524.

173. 109 U.S. at 25.

174. 109 U.S. at 24.

175. 109 U.S. at 25.

176. 392 U.S. at 440.

177. *Memphis* v. *Greene*, 451 U.S. 100, 125-26 (1980).

178. 403 U.S. 217 (1970).

179. 403 U.S. at 227.

180. Pawa, "When the Supreme Court Restricts Constitutional Rights," 1059.

181. *Oregon* v. *Mitchell* addressed various provisions of the Voting Rights Act of 1970, 84 Stat. 314. The case is perhaps best known for that portion of the decision in which the Supreme Court upheld, by a five-to-four vote, Congress's power to lower the voting age to eighteen in federal elections but rejected, by a vote of five-to-four, Congress's power to lower the voting age to eighteen in state elections.

182. 400 U.S. at 284. Justice Brennan's argument with respect to Section 5 of the Fourteenth Amendment was the same as his argument with respect to Section 2 of the Fifteenth Amendment:

> The nature of the judicial process makes it an inappropriate forum for the determination of complex factual questions of the kind so often involved in constitutional adjudication. . . . Limitations stemming from the nature of the judicial process, however, have no application to Congress. Section 5 of the Fourteenth Amendment provides that "the Congress shall have power to enforce, by appropriate legislation, the provisions of this article." Should Congress, pursuant to that power, undertake an investigation in order to determine whether the factual basis necessary to support a state legislative discrimination exists, it need not stop once it determines that some reasonable men could believe the factual basis exists. Section 5 empowers Congress to make its own determination of the matter. It should hardly be necessary to add that if the asserted factual basis necessary to support a given state discrimination does not exist, Section 5 of the Fourteenth Amendment vests Congress with power to remove the discrimination by appropriate means.

400 U.S. at 247-48.

183. 400 U.S. at 133.

184. 400 U.S. at 216. Emphasis added.

185. Justices Brennan and Stevens separately concurred in the judgment.

186. 427 U.S. at 456.

187. 429 U.S. 190 (1976).

188. 446 U.S. 156 (1980). See Bonnie I. Robin-Vergeer's important commentary on *Bolden*:

> Despite this constitutional ruling [i.e., that the Fourteenth and Fifteenth Amendments require proof of a discriminatory purpose in order to establish a constitutional violation], Congress rejected an intent standard for the Voting Rights Act and instead amended Section 2 of the statute in 1982 to reinstate the 'results test' that the Court had announced in *White* v. *Regester* [340 U.S. 755 (1973)] and applied prior to *Bolden*. The Court later acknowledged [in *Thornburg* v. *Gingles*, 478 U.S. 30, 43 (1986)] that in amending the statute Congress 'dispositively reject[ed] the position of the Court in *Mobile* v. *Bolden*,' and yet the Court proceeded to interpret and enforce the amendment without any suggestion that Congress had intruded into the judicial domain or violated the separation of powers doctrine. The parallels between RFRA and the 1982 Voting Rights Act amendments are particularly striking, for in both instances, Congress rejected Supreme Court standards requiring intentional interference with constitutional rights (*Bolden* and *Smith*) in favor of earlier judicially enunciated standards that were concerned with effects as well as intent (*Regester* and *Sherbert/Verner*).

Robin-Vergeer, "Disposing of Red Herrings: A Defense of the Religious Freedom Restoration Act," *Southern California Law Review* 69 (January 1996): 589, 673.

189. 79 Stat. 437 (1965).

190. 446 U.S. at 177.

191. 446 U.S. at 177; see also at 173: "We hold that, even if Section 1 of the Amendment prohibits only purposeful discrimination, the prior decisions of this Court foreclose any argument that Congress may not, pursuant to Section 2, outlaw voting practices that are discriminatory in effect."

192. See Chemerinsky, "Reflections on *City of Boerne* v. *Flores*," 609.

193. David Cole, "The Value of Seeing Things Differently: *Boerne* v. *Flores* and the Congressional Enforcement of the Bill of Rights," in Dennis J. Hutchinson, David A. Strauss, and Geoffrey R. Stone (eds.), *1997 Supreme Court Review* (Chicago: University of Chicago Press, 1998), 49.

194. Cole, "The Value of Seeing Things Differently," 49. Cole's words are reminiscent of Chief Justice John Marshall's words in *Barron* v. *Baltimore*, 32 U.S. 243 (1833), in which he denied that the Bill of Rights applied to the states. He did so in part by remarking that "[h]ad Congress engaged in the extraordinary occupation of improving the Constitutions of the several States by affording the people additional protection from the exercise of power by their own governments in matters which concerned themselves alone, they would have declared this purpose in plain and intelligible language." 32 U.S. at 250.

195. Chemerinsky, "Reflections on *City of Boerne* v. *Flores*," 607-8.

196. *Senate Reports*, 103rd Cong., 1st Sess., No. 111, 13-14.

197. *Senate Reports*, No. 111, 14. Emphasis added.

198. *House Reports,* 103rd Cong., 1st Sess., No. 88, 52.

199. 100 U.S. at 347.

200. As Michael McConnell notes, this principle "goes by different names: the presumption of constitutionality, deference to the political branches, judicial minimalism and—most commonly—judicial restraint." McConnell, "Institutions and Interpretation: A Critique of *Boerne* v. *Flores*," 185. See also Stephen L. Carter, "The *Morgan* 'Power' and the Forced Reconsideration of Constitutional Decisions," *University of Chicago Law Review* 53 (Summer 1986): 819.

201. 10 U.S. 87, 128 (1810).

202. 17 U.S. 518, 625 (1819).

203. 521 U.S. 702, 764 (1997).

204. McConnell, "Institutions and Interpretation: A Critique of *Boerne* v. *Flores*," 184.

205. McConnell, "Institutions and Interpretation: A Critique of *Boerne* v. *Flores*," 156. Justice Breyer subsequently made much the same argument concerning Congress's passage of ADA in *Trustees of the University of Alabama* v. *Garrett*, 121 S.Ct. 955, 972 (2001): "The problem with the Court's approach is that neither the 'burden of proof' that favors States nor any other rule of restraint

applicable to *judges* applies to *Congress* when it exercises its Section 5 power. . . . [T]he Congress of the United States is not a lower court."

    206. 521 U.S. at 520.

    207. 521 U.S. at 531.

    208. 521 U.S. at 532.

    209. 17 U.S. 316, 423 (1819).

    210. 17 U.S. at 423.

    211. Charles R. Kesler, "The Return of States' Rights?" *IntellectualCapital.com*, January 27, 2000.

    212. See, for example, *Katzenbach* v. *Morgan*, 384 U.S. at 656, in which the Court acknowledged Congress's "specially informed legislative competence" to determine whether particular state practices discriminate against individuals, and in which it asserted that if it were to reject Congress's conclusions on these matters, it "would require us to be blind to the realities familiar to the legislators." 384 U.S. at 653. See also *Oregon* v. *Mitchell*, 400 U.S. at 247: "The nature of the judicial process makes it an inappropriate forum for the determination of complex factual questions of the kind so often involved in constitutional adjudication. . . . Limitations stemming from the nature of the judicial process, however, have no application to Congress."

    213. Chemerinsky, "Reflections on *City of Boerne* v. *Flores*," 634.

    214. In these cases, the Court has repeatedly quoted *Marbury* v. *Madison* that "it is emphatically the province and duty of the judicial department to say what the law is." See *City of Boerne* v. *Flores*, 521 U.S. at 516; *College Savings Bank* v. *Florida Prepaid Postsecondary Education Expense Board*, 527 U.S. at 688; *Alden* v. *Maine*, 527 U.S. at 812; *United States* v. *Morrison*, 529 U.S. at 669, 675, and 676.

    215. *Seminole Tribe* v. *Florida*, 517 U.S. at 69, 54, and *Alden* v. *Maine*, 527 U.S. 729.

    216. 505 U.S. at 181.

Conclusion

In his January 27, 1838, speech to the Springfield Young Men's Lyceum, entitled "The Perpetuation of Our Political Institutions," Abraham Lincoln worried that the founding principles of the republic were "fading" from view. He said that he did not fear that they would ever be entirely forgotten, but "that like every thing else, they must fade upon the memory of the world and grow more and more dim by the lapse of time."[1] Nevertheless, Lincoln warned that the consequences were profound. Those founding principles, he proclaimed, "were a fortress of strength; but what invading foemen could never do, the silent artillery of time has done; the leveling of its walls."

Lincoln's words perfectly describe the fate that has befallen the Constitution. The framers regarded the walls of constitutional structure as the "remedy for the diseases most incident to Republican Government."[2] They knew that republican government was inherently problematic, and they devoted their efforts to designing constitutional structures that would rescue it from the "opprobrium" under which it had previously labored and make it worthy of "the esteem and adoption of mankind."[3] They succeeded so admirably that, with the "lapse of time," the problematic nature of republican government faded from the people's memory, leaving them unaware of the peril of altering or abandoning the very constitutional structures that rendered our particular republican institutions nonproblematic in practice. The Seventeenth Amendment was one such alteration. With its ratification, federalism, one of the structural walls of the Constitution, was leveled by the "silent artillery of time"—by faded memories lulled into believing that republican government is inherently nonproblematic and now too dim to appreciate the structural features of the Constitution that once succeeded in making it so.

The framers understood, in the words of *Federalist* No. 51, that the "great difficulty" they faced in drafting a new constitution to govern America's extended republic was to give the new federal government power enough "to controul the governed" while, at the same time, obliging it "to controul itself."[4] The new government needed to have enough power to avoid the "imbecility,"[5] "infirmities,"[6] and "weakness"[7] of the Articles of Confederation that had rendered precarious the "security of private rights"[8] and "the steady dispensation of justice."[9] It had to be granted all those powers necessary for the security of the nation and the preservation of the union, and, in addition, it had to be granted those powers necessary to ensure domestic peace and tranquility. Moreover, it had to be granted these powers, as Alexander Hamilton noted in *Federalist* No. 23, "without limitation." Since it was impossible to foresee "the extent and variety of national exigencies," either foreign or domestic, that the new nation might confront, Hamilton argued that it was therefore impossible to define "the correspondent extent and variety of the means which may be necessary to satisfy them. The circumstances that endanger the safety of nations are infinite; and for this reason no constitutional shackles can wisely be imposed on the power to which the care of it is committed. This power ought to be coextensive with all the possible combinations of such circumstances."[10] The framers agreed and refused to shackle the new government with restrictions that they knew could not be observed. They knew "that every breach of the fundamental laws, though dictated by necessity, impairs that sacred reverence, which ought to be maintained in the breast of rulers towards the constitution of a country, and forms a precedent for other breaches, where the same plea of necessity does not exist at all, or is less urgent and palpable."[11] They therefore gave the new federal government all the power it needed to deal with the various purposes for which it was being established.

But they also sought to oblige it to "controul itself," employing the lessons they had learned from their "new discoveries" and "great improvements" in the "science of politics."[12] To begin with, they labored diligently and diplomatically to bring all of the states into an "extended republic," containing such a "multiplicity of interests" that "a coalition of a majority of the whole society could seldom take place on any other principles than those of justice and the general good."[13] They understood that the larger and more extensive was the republic, the greater would be the variety of parties, interests, and sects within it, the more moderate and diffuse would be its political conflicts, and the more it could be trusted to exercise its great powers without raising the spectre of democratic tyranny.

In addition, they sought to oblige the new federal government to "controul itself" by the new form of separation of powers they created. They established a balance of constitutional powers among three coordinate branches, with each of them performing a blend of constitutionally differentiated functions. They placed great faith in their new form of separation of powers, for, as Herbert J. Storing has noted, it required only "the private interests and ambitions of citizens and representatives to keep it in motion."[14] The framers trusted in the inclination of men to pursue their interests and designed constitutional structures to direct and channel them through the process of mutual checking so that the new federal government could simultaneously "controul" the governed while being obliged to "controul itself."

Finally, they devised a new form of federalism in which power was, in some cases, divided between, and in other cases, shared by the states and the new government they were creating, and in which various federal elements were blended into the structure and procedures of the new government itself. They gave the new government only certain enumerated powers and reserved the rest to the states or the people. They gave the new government power to act upon both the states and the people, and, to ensure that it "controul[led]" itself when it so acted, they saw to it that both were represented in it. Thus, they mixed in varying proportions both federal and national elements to create a new federalism that was "neither wholly federal nor wholly national" but "a composition of both."[15] This blend of federal elements in the government they created was apparent in the mode by which the Constitution was ratified, in the amendment process, in the Electoral College, and especially in the Senate, whose members were elected by state legislatures, in which the states were equally represented, and to which it alone was assigned such traditional federal functions as the approval of treaties.

The framers placed great faith in their new federalism. Because of it, they were willing to entrust the new federal structure with far more power than they would have been willing to grant to either the states or the federal government alone; they thereby assured that the new federal structure had sufficient power to avoid the near-anarchy that had existed under the Articles of Confederation. Because of it, they believed they would be able to oblige both the federal and state governments to "controul" themselves. By creating two levels of government and dividing power between them, they made each level less threatening to liberty. By interjecting federal elements into the new government itself, they checked the threat of tyranny from regionally concentrated factious majorities. By expressly limiting state power in Article I, Section 10 of the Constitution and by making the Constitution and federal law passed pursuant to it the supreme law of the land, they mitigated the threat of tyranny at the state level. And, by placing the two levels of government in competition with each other to win the confidence of the people, they assured that neither would have an interest in abusing and oppressing the very people whose support they required.

The framers placed great faith in their new form of federalism, as they, in turn, placed great faith in the mode of electing the Senate to protect this federalism. The election of the Senate by state legislatures was the structural protection that ensured that the interests of the states as states would be taken into account when any law was passed by the Congress. It was the structural protection that ensured that "the proper line of partition, between the authority of the general, and that of the State Governments,"[16] would be drawn, not by reliance on "parchment barriers"[17] or "the cloudy medium of words"[18] and not by the interventions of an activist Supreme Court but, rather, by the self-interest of senators in whose interest it would be to protect the states from actions by the federal government that trenched on their "residuary and inviolable sovereignty."[19] It was this structural protection that ensured that the vast powers the framers provided to the federal government would not be abused and that the federal design they had created would be preserved. That structural protection has also been a casualty of the "silent artillery of time."

Over time, the public's understanding of the reasons for that structural protection faded; the walls of federalism were leveled by the ratification of the Seventeenth Amendment and the public's desire to make the Constitution more democratic. To mix metaphors, the Seventeenth Amendment effectively killed federalism, something that the public did not anticipate and that the Supreme Court has repeatedly failed to appreciate. Occasionally convincing itself that federalism is still alive and that it is the proper province of the Court to try to resuscitate it, the Court has—sporadically since 1913 and with depressing regularity since 1992—invalidated congressional measures that trench on state sovereignty, doing so on the grounds that they, inter alia, violate the principles of dual sovereignty, go beyond a proper construction of the Commerce Clause, commandeer state officials, exceed

Congress's enforcement powers under Section 5 of the Fourteenth Amendment or offend the Eleventh Amendment and the principle of state sovereign immunity. These efforts have always failed for they are akin to attempting to breathe life into a corpse.

The Court, of course, would reject this comparison. It would describe its activist decisions as attempts to rebuild the wall of federalism or at least as attempts to keep federal government from trespassing on state ground once protected by the wall of federalism. But the Court has also failed in this more modest endeavor, for, as it has candidly confessed on numerous occasions, it cannot determine exactly where the wall of federalism should go, i.e., it cannot identify a principled line demarcating federal from state powers.

The Court's memory concerning federalism—less than the public's—has also faded. While it remembers that the framers valued federalism and wanted it to be protected, it has forgotten that they believed that it could be protected only by constitutional structure, not by an activist Court. (And, it remains oblivious of the harm to federalism it has wreaked through its incorporation of the Bill of Rights to apply to the states.) Its interventions, since inconsistent with the original design, have been unprincipled, unsuccessful, and damaging both to federalism and its own reputation. They have served "neither the purposes of federalism nor the ideals of democracy."[20] The Court should acknowledge that fact and allow the original federal design to rest in peace—the victim of the "silent artillery of time."

Notes

1. Richard N. Current (ed.), *The Political Thought of Abraham Lincoln* (New York: Bobbs-Merrill, 1967), 20.

2. Alexander Hamilton, James Madison, and John Jay, *The Federalist*, ed. Jacob E. Cooke (New York: World Publishing Company, 1961), No. 10, 65. See chapter 2.

3. *Federalist*, No. 10, 61.

4. *Federalist*, No. 51, 349.

5. *Federalist*, No. 9, 55; No. 15, 92; No. 18, 116; No. 22, 138.

6. *Federalist*, No. 22, 145; No. 43, 294.

7. *Federalist*, No. 5, 24; No. 18, 111; No. 19, 122; No. 25, 161.

8. *Federalist*, No. 26, 164.

9. Max Farrand (ed.), *The Records of the Federal Convention of 1787*, 4 vols. (New Haven: Yale University Press, 1937), 1: 134.

10. *Federalist*, No. 23, 147. Hamilton called this "one of those truths, which to a correct and unprejudiced mind, carries its own evidence along with it; and may be obscured but cannot be made plainer by argument or reasoning. It rests upon axioms as simple as they are universal. The *means* ought to be proportioned to the *end*; the persons; from whose agency the attainment of any *end* is expected, ought to possess the *means* by which it is to be attained." Emphasis in the original.

11. *Federalist* No. 25, 163. See also No. 41, 270: "The means of security can only be regulated by the means and the danger of attack. They will, in fact, be ever determined by these rules, and by no others. It is in vain to oppose constitutional barriers to the impulse of self-preservation. It is worse than in vain; because it plants in the Constitution itself necessary usurpations of power, every precedent of which is a germ of unnecessary and multiplied repetitions."

12. *Federalist* No. 9, 51.

13. *Federalist* No. 51, 353, 352. As Madison wrote in No. 51: "It is no less certain than it is important . . . that the larger the society, provided it lie within a practicable sphere, the more duly capable it will be of *self-government*. And happily for the republican cause, the practicable sphere may be carried to a very great extent, by the judicious modification and mixture of the federal principle." Emphasis added.

14. Herbert J. Storing, *What the Anti-Federalists Were For: The Political Thought of the Opponents of the Constitution* (Chicago: University of Chicago Press, 1981), 62.

15. *Federalist* No. 39, 257.

16. *Federalist* No. 37, 234.

17. *Federalist* No. 48, 333.

18. *Federalist* No. 37, 237.

19. *Federalist* No. 39, 256.

20. Jay S. Bybee, "Ulysses at the Mast: Democracy, Federalism, and the Sirens' Song of the Seventeenth Amendment," *Northwestern University Law Review* 91 (1997): 567.

Works Cited

Allen, W. B. (ed). *Works of Fisher Ames*. 2 vols. Indianapolis: Liberty Fund, 1983.

Amar, Vikram David. "Indirect Effects of Direct Election: A Structural Examination of the Seventeenth Amendment." *Vanderbilt Law Review* 49 (1996): 1347-405.

American Bar Association Special Constitutional Convention Study Committee. *Amendment of the Constitution: By the Convention Method under Article V.* Chicago: American Bar Association, 1974.

An American Citizen [Tench Coxe]. "An Examination of the Constitution of the United States." In *Friends of the Constitution: Writings of the "Other" Federalists: 1787-1788*, ed. Colleen A. Sheehan and Gary L. McDowell. Indianapolis: Liberty Fund, 1998.

Anastaplo, George. *The Amendments to the Constitution: A Commentary.* Baltimore: Johns Hopkins University Press, 1995.

———. *The Constitutionalist: Notes on the First Amendment.* Dallas: Southern Methodist University Press, 1971.

———. *The Constitution of 1787: A Commentary.* Baltimore: Johns Hopkins University Press, 1989.

Annals of Congress. 1789-1811.

Anonymous. "An Argument on the Right of the Constituent to Instruct His Representative in Congress." *The American Review of History and Politics* 6 (1812): 137-71.

Bator, Paul. "Judiciary Act of 1789." In *Encyclopedia of the American Constitution*, ed. Leonard W. Levy, Kenneth L. Karst, and Dennis J. Mahoney. 5 vols. New York: Macmillan, 1986.

Beard, Charles A., and Mary R. Beard. *The Rise of American Civilization*. 2 vols. New York: Macmillan, 1933.

Beccaria, Cesare. *On Crimes and Punishments*. Translated by Henry Paolucci. New York: Bobbs-Merrill, 1963.

Beimers, Thomas W. "Searching for the Structural Vision of *City of Boerne* v. *Flores*: Vertical and Horizontal Tensions in the New Constitutional Architecture." *Hastings Constitutional Law Quarterly* 26 (summer 1999): 789-852.

Berger, Raoul. *Government by Judiciary: The Transformation of the Fourteenth Amendment*. Cambridge, Mass.: Harvard University Press, 1977.

———. "A Lawyer Lectures a Judge." *Harvard Journal of Law and Public Policy* 18 (1995): 851-65.

Blackstone, Sir William. *Commentaries on the Laws of England*. 4 vols. Oxford: Clarendon, 1765.

Blaine, James G. *Twenty Years of Congress*. 2 vols. Norwich, Conn.: Henry Bill, 1884-86.

Bond, Julian (ed). *The Papers of Thomas Jefferson*. 18 vols. Princeton: Princeton University Press, 1955.

Bourguignon, Henry J. "The Federal Key to the Judiciary Act of 1789." *South Carolina Law Review* 46 (1995): 647-702.

Bowling, Kenneth R., and Veit, Helen E. (eds). *The Diary of William Maclay and Other Notes on Senate Debates: March 4, 1789-March 3, 1791*. Baltimore: Johns Hopkins University Press, 1988.

Brennan, William J. "The Constitution of the United States: Contemporary Ratifications." Presentation at the Text and Teaching Symposium, Georgetown University, Washington, D.C., October 12, 1985.

Brooks, Roger G. "*Garcia*, The Seventeenth Amendment, and the Role of the Supreme Court in Defending Federalism." *Harvard Journal of Law and Public Policy* 10 (1987): 189-211.

Buenker, John D. "The Urban Political Machine and the Seventeenth Amendment." *Journal of American History* 56 (September 1969): 305-22.

Bybee, Jay S. "Ulysses at the Mast: Democracy, Federalism, and the Sirens' Song of the Seventeenth Amendment." *Northwestern University Law Review* 91 (1997): 500-569.

Carey, George W. *In Defense of the Constitution*. Indianapolis: Liberty Fund, 1995.

Carter, Stephen L. "The *Morgan* 'Power' and the Forced Reconsideration of Constitutional Decisions." *University of Chicago Law Review* 53 (summer 1986): 819-63.

Chemerinsky, Erwin. "Reflections on *City of Boerne* v. *Flores*: The Religious Freedom Restoration Act Is a Constitutional Expansion of Rights." *William and Mary Law Review* 39 (February 1998): 601-36.

Choper, Jesse H. *Judicial Review and the National Political Process: A Functional Reconsideration of the Role of the Supreme Court.* Chicago: University of Chicago Press, 1980.

Clarke, M. St. Clair, and D. A. Hall (eds). *Legislative and Documentary History of the Bank of the United States.* Washington, D.C.: Gales and Seaton, 1832.

Cole, David. "The Value of Seeing Things Differently: *Boerne* v. *Flores* and the Congressional Enforcement of the Bill of Rights." *1997 Supreme Court Review,* ed. Dennis J. Hutchinson, David A. Strauss, and Geoffrey R. Stone. Chicago: University of Chicago Press, 1998.

Congressional Debates. 1826-1829.

Congressional Globe. 1850-1860.

Congressional Record. 1876-1912.

Crook, Sara Brandes. "The Consequences of the Seventeenth Amendment: The Twentieth Century Senate." Ph.D. dissertation, Department of Political Science, University of Nebraska, Lincoln, 1992.

Crook, Sara Brandes, and John R. Hibbing. "A Not-So-Distant Mirror: The Seventeenth Amendment and Congressional Change." *American Political Science Review* 91 (December 1997): 845-53.

Cross, Frank B. "Institutions and Enforcement of the Bill of Rights." *Cornell Law Review* 85 (September 2000): 1529-608.

Current, Richard N. (ed). *The Political Thought of Abraham Lincoln.* New York: Bobbs-Merrill, 1967.

Currie, David P. *The Constitution in Congress: The Federalist Period, 1789-1801.* Chicago: University of Chicago Press, 1997.

———. *The Constitution in the Supreme Court: The First Hundred Years, 1789-1888.* Chicago: University of Chicago Press, 1985.

———. *The Constitution in the Supreme Court: The Second Century, 1888-1986.* Chicago: University of Chicago Press, 1990.

Dellinger, Walter, and H. Jefferson Powell. "The Constitutionality of the Bank Bill: The Attorney General's First Constitutional Law Opinions." *Duke Law Journal* 44 (1994): 110-33.

De Pauw, Linda Grant, Charlene Bangs Bickford, and LaVonne Marlene Siegel (eds). *Senate Legislative Journal.* Vol. 1: *Documentary History of the First Federal Congress of the United States of America.* Baltimore: Johns Hopkins University Press, 1972.

Diamond, Martin. "The Ends of Federalism." *Publius* 3, no. 2 (fall 1973). Reprinted in William A. Schambra (ed), *As Far as Republican Principles Will Admit: Essays by Martin Diamond.* Washington, D.C.: AEI Press, 1992.

———. "*The Federalist* on Federalism: Neither a National nor a Federal Constitution, But a Composition of Both." *Yale Law Journal* 86, no. 6 (May 1977): 1273-85.

———. "What the Framers Meant by Federalism." In *A Nation of States,* ed. Robert A. Goldwin. 2d ed. Chicago: Rand McNally, 1974.

The Documentary History of the Ratification of the Constitution. Vol. 13: *Commentaries on the Constitution: Public and Private.* Vol. 1: *21 February to 7 November 1787.* Ed. John P. Kaminski and Gaspare J. Saladino. Madison: State Historical Society of Wisconsin, 1981.

The Documentary History of the Ratification of the Constitution. Vol. 2: *Ratification of the Constitution by the States: Pennsylvania.* Ed. Merrill Jensen. Madison: State Historical Society of Wisconsin, 1976.

Eaton, Allen H. *The Oregon System: The Story of Direct Legislation in Oregon.* Chicago: A. C. McClurg, 1912.

Eidelberg, Paul. A. *Discourse on Statesmanship: The Design and Transformation of the American Polity.* Urbana: University of Illinois Press, 1974.

Eisgruber, Christopher L., and Lawrence G. Sager. "Congressional Power and Religious Liberty after *City of Boerne* v. *Flores.*" *1997 Supreme Court Review,* ed. Dennis J. Hutchinson, David A. Strauss, and Geoffrey R. Stone. Chicago: University of Chicago Press, 1998.

Eldredge, Zoeth Skinner. *History of California.* 5 vols. New York: Century History Company, 1915.

Elliot, Jonathan (ed). *The Debates in the Several State Conventions on the Adoption of the Federal Constitution as Recommended by the General Convention in Philadelphia in 1787.* 5 vols. Philadelphia: Lippincott, 1863.

Farrand, Max (ed). *The Records of the Federal Convention of 1787.* 4 vols. New Haven: Yale University Press, 1937.

Flaumenhaft, Harvey. "Hamilton on the Foundation of Good Government." *Political Science Reviewer* 6 (fall 1976): 143-214.

Ford, Paul Leicester (ed). *Pamphlets on the Constitution of the United States.* Brooklyn, N.Y.: Historical Printing Club, 1888.

Frank, John. "Historical Bases of the Federal Judicial System." *Law and Contemporary Problems* 13 (1948): 3.

Fritz, Jean. *Cast for a Revolution: 1728-1814.* Boston: Houghton Mifflin, 1972.

Goebel, Julius Jr. *The Oliver Wendell Holmes Devise History of the Supreme Court of the United States.* Vol. 1: *Antecedents and Beginnings to 1801.* New York: Macmillan, 1971.

Goldwin, Robert A. *From Parchment to Power: How James Madison Used the Bill of Rights to Save the Constitution.* Washington, D.C.: AEI Press, 1997.

Graglia, Lino A. "*Church of Lukumi Babalu Aye:* Of Animal Sacrifice and Religious Persecution." *Georgetown Law Journal* 85 (November 1996): 719-71.

———. "*United States* v. *Lopez*: Judicial Review under the Commerce Clause." *Texas Law Review* 74 (March 1996): 1-69.

Gray, A. A. *History of California: From 1542.* New York: D. C. Heath, 1934.

Greve, Michael S. *Read Federalism: Why It Matters, How It Could Happen.* Washington, D.C.: AEI Press, 1999.

Griffith, Kathryn. *Judge Learned Hand and the Role of the Federal Judiciary.* Lincoln: University Press of Nebraska, 1973.

Grimes, Alan P. *Democracy and Amendments to the Constitution.* Lexington, Mass.: Lexington Books, 1978.

Gunther, Gerald (ed). *John Marshall's Defense of McCulloch v. Maryland.* Stanford: Stanford University Press, 1969.

Hall, Wallace Worthy. "The History and Effect of the Seventeenth Amendment." Ph.D. dissertation, Department of Political Science, University of California, Berkeley, 1936.

Hammond, Bray. *Banks and Politics in America: From the Revolution to the Civil War.* Princeton: Princeton University Press, 1957.

Hand, Learned. *The Bill of Rights.* New York: Athenaeum, 1965.

Harris, Robert J. *The Quest for Equality.* Baton Rouge: Louisiana State University Press, 1960.

Haskins, George Lee, and Herbert A. Johnson. *The Oliver Wendell Holmes Devise History of the Supreme Court of the United States.* Vol. 2: *Foundations of Power: John Marshall, 1801-15.* New York: Macmillan, 1981.

Haynes, George H. *The Election of Senators.* New York: Henry Holt, 1906.

———. *The Senate of the United States: Its History and Practice.* 2 vols. Boston: Houghton Mifflin, 1938.

Hobson, Charles, and Robert A. Rutland (eds). *The Papers of James Madison.* 17 vols. Charlottesville: University Press of Virginia, 1981.

Hoebeke, Christopher H. *The Road to Mass Democracy: Original Intent and the Seventeenth Amendment.* New Brunswick, N.J.: Transaction Publishers, 1995.

Holt, Wythe. "'To Establish Justice': Politics, the Judiciary Act of 1789, and the Invention of the Federal Courts." *Duke Law Journal* 1989 (1989): 1421-531.

Hunt, Gaillard (ed). *The Writings of James Madison.* 9 vols. New York: G. P. Putnam's Sons, 1910.

Hunt, Rockwell D. *California and Californians.* 5 vols. Chicago: Lewis Publishing, 1926.

Jacobs, Clyde E. *The Eleventh Amendment and Sovereign Immunity.* Westport, Conn.: Greenwood Press, 1972.

James, Joseph B. *The Framing of the Fourteenth Amendment.* Urbana: University of Illinois Press, 1965.

Jenson, Merrill. *The Articles of Confederation.* Madison: University of Wisconsin Press, 1962.

Kent, James. *Commentaries on American Law.* 4 vols. New York: O. Halsted, 1826.

Kesler, Charles R. (ed). *Saving the Revolution: The Federalist Papers and the American Founding.* New York: Free Press, 1987.

Kurland, Philip B., and Ralph Lerner (eds). *The Founders' Constitution.* 5 vols. Chicago: University of Chicago Press, 1987.

Kyvig, David E. *Explicit and Authentic Acts: Amending the U.S. Constitution, 1776-1995.* Lawrence: University Press of Kansas, 1996.

Little, Laura E. "An Excursion into the Uncharted Waters of the Seventeenth Amendment." *Temple Law Review* 64 (1991): 629.

Lowi, Theodore J. *The End of Liberalism: Ideology, Policy, and the Crisis of Public Authority.* New York: W. W. Norton, 1969.

Luce, Robert. *Legislative Principles: The History and Theory of Lawmaking by Representative Government.* Boston: Houghton Mifflin, 1930.

Madison, James, Alexander Hamilton, and John Jay. *The Federalist,* ed. Jacob E. Cooke. New York: World Publishing Company, 1961.

Main, Jackson Turner. *The Antifederalists: Critics of the Constitution, 1781-1788.* Chicago: Quadrangle Books, 1961.

Marcus, Maeva, et al. (eds). *Documentary History of the Supreme Court of the United States, 1789-1800: Organizing the Federal Judiciary: Legislation and Commentaries.* New York: Columbia University Press, 1992.

McConnell, Michael W. "The Supreme Court, 1996 Term: Comment: Institutions and Interpretation: A Critique of *Boerne* v. *Flores.*" *Harvard Law Review* 111 (November 1997): 153-95.

McCloskey, Robert Green (ed). *The Works of James Wilson.* Cambridge: Belknap Press of Harvard University Press, 1967.

McDowell, Gary L. *Equity and the Constitution: The Supreme Court, Equitable Relief, and Public Policy.* Chicago: University of Chicago Press, 1982.

―――. "Were the Anti-Federalists Right?" *Publius: The Journal of Federalism* 12 (1982): 99-108.

McInerney, Virginia M. "Federalism and the Seventeenth Amendment." *Journal of Christian Jurisprudence* 7 (1988): 153.

McMaster, John Bach, and Frederick D. Stone (eds). *Pennsylvania and the Federal Constitution.* Philadelphia: Historical Society of Pennsylvania, 1888.

Meese, Edwin. "Toward a Jurisprudence of Original Intention." *Benchmark* 2, no. 1 (January/February, 1986): 1-10.

Meltzer, Daniel J. "The *Seminole* Decision and State Sovereign Immunity." *1996 Supreme Court Review*, ed. Dennis J. Hutchinson, David A. Strauss, and Geoffrey R. Stone. Chicago: University of Chicago Press, 1997.

Meyers, Marvin (ed). *The Mind of the Founder: Sources of the Political Thought of James Madison.* Rev. ed. Hanover, N.H.: Brandeis University Press, 1981.

Moore, Wayne D. "Reconceiving Interpretive Authority: Insights from the Virginia and Kentucky Resolutions." *Constitutional Commentary* 11 (1994): 315.

Pawa, Matt. "When the Supreme Court Restricts Constitutional Rights, Can Congress Save Us: An Examination of Section 5 of the Fourteenth Amendment." *University of Pennsylvania Law Review* 141 (January 1993): 1029-101.

Powell, H. Jefferson. *Languages of Power: A Sourcebook of Early American Constitutional History.* Durham: Carolina Academic Press, 1991.

Pritchett, C. Herman. *The American Constitution.* New York: McGraw-Hill, 1968.

Rees, Grover. "The Amendment Process & Limited Constitutional Conventions." *Benchmark* 2 (March-April 1986): 66-108.

Richardson, James D. (ed). *A Compilation of the Messages and Papers of the Presidents, 1789-1897.* Washington, D.C.: Government Printing Office, 1896.

Riker, William H. "The Senate and American Federalism." *American Political Science Review* 49 (1955): 452-69.

Ritz, Wilfred J. *Rewriting the History of the Judiciary Act of 1789: Exposing Myths, Challenging Premises, and Using New Evidence.* Ed. Wythe Holt and L. H. LaRue. Norman: University of Oklahoma Press, 1990.

Robin-Vergeer, Bonnie I. "Disposing of the Red Herrings: A Defense of the Religious Freedom Restoration Act." *Southern California Law Review* 69 (January 1996): 589-679.

Roske, Ralph J. *Everyman's Eden: A History of California*. New York: Macmillan, 1968.

Rossum, Ralph A. *Congressional Control of the Judiciary: The Article III Option*. Washington, D.C.: Center for Judicial Studies, 1988.

————. "Congress, the Constitution, and the Appellate Jurisdiction of the Supreme Court: The Letter and Spirit of the Exceptions Clause." *William and Mary Law Review* 24 (1983): 385-428.

————. "The Courts and the Judicial Power." In *The Framing and Ratification of the Constitution*, ed. Leonard W. Levy and Dennis J. Mahoney. New York: Macmillan, 1987.

————. "The Irony of Constitutional Democracy: Federalism, the Supreme Court, and the Seventeenth Amendment." *San Diego Law Review* 36, no. 1 (August/ September 1999): 671-741.

————. "James Wilson and the 'Pyramid of Government': The Federal Republic." *Political Science Reviewer* 6 (1976): 113-42.

————. "The Least Dangerous Branch?" In *The American Experiment: Essays on the Theory and Practice of Liberty*, ed. Peter Augustine Lawler and Robert Martin Schaefer. Lanham, Md.: Rowman & Littlefield, 1994.

————. "The Textualist Jurisprudence of Justice Scalia." *Perspectives on Political Science* 28 (winter 1999): 5-10.

Rotunda, Ronald D., John E. Nowak, and J. Nelson Young. *Treatise on Constitutional Law: Substance and Procedure*. 3 vols. St. Paul: West Publishing, 1986.

Scalia, Antonin. "The Doctrine of Standing as an Essential Element of the Separation of Powers." *Suffolk University Law Review* 17 (1983): 881-99.

————. *A Matter of Interpretation: Federal Courts and the Law*. Princeton: Princeton University Press, 1997.

Storing, Herbert J. (ed). *The Complete Anti-Federalist*. 7 vols. Chicago: University of Chicago Press, 1981.

————. "The Constitution and the Bill of Rights." In *The American Founding: Politics, Statesmanship, and the Constitution*, ed. Ralph A. Rossum and Gary L. McDowell. Port Washington, N.Y.: Kennikat Press, 1981.

————. (ed). *What Country Have I? Political Writings of Black Americans*. New York: St. Martin's, 1970.

————. *What the Anti-Federalists Were For: The Political Thought of the Opponents of the Constitution*. Chicago: University of Chicago Press, 1981.

Story, Joseph. *Commentaries on the Constitution of the United States*. 3 vols. New York: Hilliard & Gray, 1833.

Swift, Elaine K. *The Making of the American Senate: Reconstitutive Change in Congress, 1787-1841*. Ann Arbor: University of Michigan Press, 1996.

Syrett, Harold C., and Jacob E. Cooke (eds). *The Papers of Alexander Hamilton*. 26 vols. New York: Columbia University Press, 1961.

TenBroek, Jacobus. *Equal under Law*. London: Collier Books, 1965.

Thayer, James Bradley. "The Origin and Scope of the American Doctrine of Constitutional Law." *Harvard Law Review* 7 (1893): 129-56.

Tocqueville, Alexis de. *Democracy in America.* 2 vols. Translated by Henry Reeve. Ed. Phillips Bradley. New York: Random House, 1945.

Tucker, St. George. *Blackstone's Commentaries: With Notes of Reference to the Constitution and Laws of the Federal Government of the United States and the Commonwealth of Virginia.* 5 vols. Philadelphia, 1803.

Veit, Helen E., Kenneth R. Bowling, and Charlene Bangs Bickford (eds). *Creating the Bill of Rights: The Documentary Record from the First Federal Congress.* Baltimore: Johns Hopkins University Press, 1991.

Warren, Mercy. *History of the Rise, Progress, and Termination of the American Revolution.* 3 vols. Boston: Manning and Loring, 1805.

Waters, Earl G. *The Rumble of California Politics: 1848-1970.* New York: John Wiley & Sons, 1970.

Wechsler, Herbert. "The Political Safeguards of Federalism: The Role of the States in the Composition and Selection of the National Government." *Columbia Law Review* 54 (1954): 543-60.

White, G. Edward. *The Oliver Wendell Holmes Devise History of the Supreme Court of the United States.* Vols. 3-4: *The Marshall Court and Cultural Change, 1815-35.* New York: Macmillan, 1988.

Wilson, Woodrow. *The New Freedom: A Call for the Emancipation of the Generous Energies of a People.* New York: Doubleday, Page, 1913.

Wright, Benjamin F. "*The Federalist* on the Nature of Political Man." *Ethics: An International Journal of Social, Political, and Legal Philosophy,* Vol. 59, no. 2 (January 1949): 1-31.

Yoo, John C. "The Judicial Safeguards of Federalism." *Southern California Law Review* 70 (1997): 1311-405.

Zywicki, Todd J. "Beyond the Shell and Husk of History: The History of the Seventeenth Amendment and Its Implications for Current Reform Proposals." *Cleveland State Law Review* 45 (1997): 165-234.

———. "Senators and Special Interests: A Public Choice Analysis of the Seventeenth Amendment." *Oregon Law Review* 73 (1994): 1007.

Cases Cited

Ableman v. *Booth*, 62 U.S. 506 (1858).

A. L. A. Schechter Poultry Corporation v. *United States*, 295 U.S. 495 (1935).

Alden v. *Maine*, 527 U.S. 706 (1999).

Ashton v. *Cameron County District*, 298 U.S. 513 (1936).

Bailey v. *Drexel Furniture Company*, 259 U.S. 20 (1922).

Baker v. *Carr*, 369 U.S. 186 (1962).

Barron v. *Baltimore*, 32 U.S. 243 (1833).

Board of Trade of City of Chicago v. *Olsen*, 262 U.S. 1 (1923).

Cantwell v. *Connecticut*, 310 U.S. 296 (1940).

Cardona v. *Power*, 384 U.S. 672 (1966).

Carter v. *Carter Coal Company*, 298 U.S. 238 (1936).

Champion v. *Ames*, 188 U.S. 321 (1903).

Chisholm v. *Georgia*, 2 U.S. 419 (1793).

City of Boerne v. *Flores*, 521 U.S. 507 (1997).

City of Mobile v. *Bolden*, 446 U.S. 156 (1980).

City of Rome v. *United States*, 446 U.S. 156 (1980).

Civil Rights Cases of 1883, 109 U.S. 3 (1883).

Cleburne v. *Cleburne Living Center*, 473 U.S. 432 (1985).

College Savings Bank v. *Florida Prepaid Postsecondary Education Expense Board*, 527 U.S. 666 (1999).

Coyle v. *Smith*, 221 U.S. 559 (1911).

Craig v. *Boren*, 429 U.S. 190 (1976).

Dartmouth College v. *Woodward*, 17 U.S. 518 (1819).

Dred Scott v. *Sandford*, 60 U.S. 393 (1857).

Employers' Liability Cases, 207 U.S. 463 (1908).

Employment Division, Department of Human Resources of Oregon v. *Smith*, 494 U.S. 872 (1990).

Equal Employment Opportunity Commission v. *Wyoming*, 460 U.S. 226 (1983).

Ex Parte Virginia, 100 U.S. 339 (1880).

Fitzpatrick v. *Bitzer*, 427 U.S. 445 (1976).

Fletcher v. *Peck*, 10 U.S. 87 (1810).

Florida Prepaid Postsecondary Education Expense Board v. *College Savings Bank*, 527 U.S. 627 (1999).

Garcia v. *San Antonio Metropolitan Transit Authority*, 469 U.S. 528 (1985).

Gibbon v. *Ogden*, 22 U.S. 1 (1824).

Gregory v. *Ashcroft*, 501 U.S. 452, 458 (1991).

Hammer v. *Dagenhart*, 247 U.S. 251 (1918).

Heart of Atlanta Motel v. *United States*, 379 U.S. 241 (1964).

Hill v. *Wallace*, 259 U.S. 44 (1922).

Hipolite Egg Company v. *United States*, 220 U.S. 45 (1911).

Hodel v. *Indiana*, 452 U.S. 314 (1981).

Hodel v. *Virginia Surface Mining & Reclamation Association*, 452 U.S. 264 (1981).

Hoke v. *United States*, 227 U.S. 308 (1913).

Hopkins Savings Association v. *Cleary*, 296 U.S. 315 (1935).

Hutto v. *Finney*, 437 U.S. 678 (1978).

Jones v. *Alfred H. Mayer Co.*, 392 U.S. 409 (1968).

Katzenbach v. *McClung*, 379 U.S. 294 (1964).

Katzenbach v. *Morgan*, 384 U.S. 641 (1966).

Keller v. *United States*, 213 U.S. 138 (1909).

Kimel v. *Florida Board of Regents*, 528 U.S. 62 (2000).

Lamb's Chapel v. *Center Moriches Union Free School District*, 508 U.S. 384 (1993).

Lassiter v. *Northampton Election Board*, 360 U.S. 45 (1959).

Lemon v. *Kurtzman*, 403 U.S. 602 (1971).

Lopez v. *United States*, 514 U.S. 549 (1995).

Marbury v. *Madison*, 5 U.S. 137 (1803).

Maryland v. *Wirtz*, 392 U.S. 183 (1968).

Matter of Heff, 197 U.S. 488 (1905).

McCulloch v. *Maryland*, 17 U.S. 316 (1819).

Memphis v. *Greene*, 451 U.S. 100 (1980).

Missouri v. *Holland*, 252 U.S. 416 (1920).

Morrison v. *Olson*, 487 U.S. 654 (1988).

Myers v. *United States*, 272 U.S. 52 (1926).

National Labor Relations Board v. *Jones & Laughlin Steel Corporation*, 301 U.S. 1 (1937).

National League of Cities v. *Usery*, 426 U.S. 833 (1976).

New State Ice Company v. *Liebmann*, 258 U.S. 262 (1932).

New York v. *United States*, 505 U.S. 144 (1992).

Oregon v. *Mitchell,* 400 U.S. 112 (1970).

Palmer v. *Thompson,* 403 U.S. 217 (1970).

Parden v. *Terminal Railroad Company,* 377 U.S. 184 (1964).

Pennsylvania v. *Union Gas Company,* 491 U.S. 1 (1989).

Perez v. *United States,* 402 U.S. 146 (1971).

Prigg v. *Pennsylvania,* 41 U.S. 539 (1842).

Printz v. *United States,* 521 U.S. 898 (1997).

Railroad Retirement Board v. *Alton Railway,* 295 U.S. 330 (1935).

Reno v. *Condon,* 528 U.S. 141 (2000).

Rickert Rice Mills v. *Fontenot,* 297 U.S. 110 (1936).

Roth v. *United States,* 354 U.S. 476 (1957).

Seminole Tribe of Florida v. *Florida,* 517 U.S. 44 (1996).

Sherbert v. *Verner,* 374 U.S. 398 (1963).

South Carolina v. *Katzenbach,* 383 U.S. 301 (1966).

South Dakota v. *Dole,* 483 U.S. 203 (1987).

Strauder v. *West Virginia,* 100 U.S. 303 (1879).

Thornburg v. *Gingles,* 478 U.S. 30, 43 (1986).

Trademark Cases, 100 U.S. 82 (1879).

Trusler v. *Crooks,* 269 U.S. 475 (1926).

Trustees of the University of Alabama v. *Garrett,* 531 U.S. 356 (2001).

United States v. *Butler,* 297 U.S. 1 (1935).

United States v. *Darby Lumber Company,* 312 U.S. 100 (1941).

United States v. *DeWitt,* 76 U.S. 41 (1870).

United States v. *E.C. Knight Company,* 156 U.S. 1 (1895).

United States v. *Fisher,* 6 U.S. 358 (1805).

United States v. *Fox,* 95 U.S. 670 (1878).

United States v. *Fry,* 421 U.S. 542 (1975).

United States v. *Kahriger,* 345 U.S. 22 (1953).

United States v. *Morrison,* 529 U.S. 598 (2000).

United States v. *Nice,* 241 U.S. 591 (1916).

Wabash, St. L. & P. R. v. *Illinois,* 118 U.S. 551 (1886).

Washington v. *Glucksberg,* 521 U.S. 702 (1997).

White v. *Regester,* 340 U.S. 755 (1973).

Wickard v. *Filburn,* 317 U.S. 111 (1942).

Willson v. *Black Bird Creek Marsh Company,* 27 U.S. 245 (1829).

Wisconsin v. *Yoder,* 406 U.S. 205 (1972).

Index

About the Author

Ralph A. Rossum is the director of the Rose Institute of State and Local Government and the Henry Salvatori Professor of American Constitutionalism at Claremont McKenna College; he is also a member of the faculty of Claremont Graduate University. He earned his M.A. and Ph.D. from the University of Chicago and has published seven books, including *American Constitutional Law* (with G. Alan Tarr), a two-volume work now in the fifth edition, *Reverse Discrimination: The Constitutional Debate, The Politics of the Criminal Justice System: An Organizational Analysis,* and *The American Founding: Politics, Statesmanship, and the Constitution* (with Gary L. McDowell), and over sixty book chapters or articles in law reviews and professional journals.

Mr. Rossum has served as associate dean of the Graduate School at Loyola University of Chicago, as vice president and dean of the faculty at Claremont McKenna College, as a member of the Board of Trustees of the Episcopal Theological Seminary of Claremont, and as president of Hampden-Sydney College. He is currently chairman of the Council of Scholars of the American Academy of Liberal Education.

Mr. Rossum has an extensive record of public service. He was a member of the Police Reserve in Memphis, Tennessee. He served as deputy director for data analysis of the Bureau of Justice Statistics in the U.S. Department of Justice. He has also served as a member of the Advisory Board of the National Institute of Corrections in the U.S. Department of Justice and as a member of the Board of the Robert Presley Institute of Corrections Research and Training for the State of California.

CPSIA information can be obtained at www.ICGtesting.com
Printed in the USA
LVOW131952190712

290639LV00002B/42/P